Aging and Rehabilitation

Stanley J. Brody, J.D., M.S.W., volume editor and the Director of the University of Pennsylvania Rehabilitation Research and Training Center in Aging, is Professor of Physical Medicine and Rehabilitation in Psychiatry of the Department of Physical Medicine and Rehabilitation. He is also Professor of Health Care Systems, Wharton School of Finance and Commerce; Professor, School of Social Work; Senior Research Fellow, Leonard Davis Institute of Health Economics; and Consultant, Center for the Study of Social Work Practice, School of Social Work, all of the University of Pennsylvania. The second edition of his latest book, *Hospitals and the Aged: The New Old Market* (co-edited with N. A. Persily), was published in 1985. He has written more than 100 articles, which have been published in national and international journals and magazines and as chapters in various books. His special interests are in the fields of gerontology, rehabilitation, and long- and short-term support/care systems planning.

George E. Ruff, M.D., volume co-editor and the Director of Research of the University of Pennsylvania Rehabilitation Research and Training Center in Aging, is Professor of Psychiatry in the Department of Psychiatry. Dr. Ruff is certified by the American Board of Psychiatry and Neurology and was Acting Chairman of the Department of Psychiatry during 1971–1972 and from 1980 through most of 1984.

AGING AND REHABILITATION
ADVANCES IN THE STATE OF THE ART

Stanley J. Brody, J.D., M.S.W.
George E. Ruff, M.D.

Editors

Springer Publishing Company
New York

Springer Publishing Company, Inc.
536 Broadway
New York, NY 10012

86 87 88 89 90 / 5 4 3 2 1

Printed in the United States of America

This conference was supported by the National Institute of Handicapped Research, U.S. Department of Education, and the National Institute of Mental Health, U.S. Department of Health and Human Services, in cooperation with the National Institute on Aging.

Aging and rehabilitation.

Proceedings of a conference held in Washington, D.C., in December 1984.
"This conference was supported by the National Institute of Handicapped Research . . . in cooperation with the National Institute on Aging"—T.p. verso.
Includes bibliographies and index.
1. Aged—Rehabilitation—Congresses. I. Brody, Stanley J. II. Ruff, George E. III. National Institute of Handicapped Research (U.S.) IV. National Institute on Aging. [DNLM: 1. Aging—congresses. 2. Geriatrics—congresses. 3. Rehabilitation—in old age—congresses. WN 320 A267 1984]

RC952.A2A35 1986   618.97   86-10166
ISBN 0-8261-5360-7

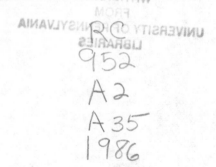

Contents

Contributors

Faye G. Abdellah, R.N., Ed.D., Sc.D., F.A.A.N., Deputy Surgeon General of the United States Public Health Service.

James C. Anderson, M.S., IBM Corporation.

Sheree J. Aston, O.D., Director of External Clinical Programs at the Pennsylvania College of Optometry, Philadelphia.

Neal J. Baumann, M.S., C.R.C., Assistant Vice-President (Employment, Education, and Research), Aging in America, Inc., Bronx, NY.

Robert Binstock, Ph.D., Henry R. Luce Professor for Aging, Health, and Public Policy, Case Western Reserve University, Cleveland, OH.

Hank L. Brammell, M.D., Director, Rehabilitation Research and Training Center in Cardiac Rehabilitation, and Associate Professor, Departments of Medicine and Physical Medicine and Rehabilitation, University of Colorado, Denver.

Elaine M. Brody, M.S.W., Director, Department of Human Services, and Senior Researcher, Philadelphia Geriatric Center, and Adjunct Associate Professor of Psychiatry, University of Pennsylvania Medical Center, Philadelphia.

Dudley S. Childress, Ph.D., Director, Rehabilitation Engineering Center, and Professor, Orthopaedic Surgery, Northwestern University Medical School, Chicago.

Paul David Cotten, M.N., Ph.D., Director, Boswell Retardation Center, Sanitorium, Mississippi, and Adjunct Professor of Psychology at the University of Southern Mississippi.

Anthony F. DiStefano, O.D., M.Ed., M.P.H., Project Director, NIHR Low Vision Research and Demonstration Center, and Assistant Dean of Academic Development, Pennsylvania College of Optometry, Philadelphia.

Carl Eisdorfer, Ph.D., M.D., Professor and Chairman, Department of Psychiatry and Behavior Science, University of Miami, Florida.

Douglas A. Fenderson, Ph.D., Director of the National Institute of Handicapped Research, Office of Special Education and Rehabilitative Services, U.S. Department of Education, from December 1982 through December 1984; currently Professor of Public Health and Research Coordinator, Department of Family Practice and Community Health, University of Minnesota Medical School, Minneapolis.

Shervert H. Frazier, M.D., Director Designate, National Institute of Mental Health, Rockville, MD.

John W. Frymoyer, M.D., Professor and Chairman, Department of Orthopaedics and Rehabilitation, University of Vermont, Burlington.

John P. Fulton, Ph.D., Research Sociologist, Department of Community Medicine, Rhode Island Hospital, and Assistant Professor of Community Health Research, Brown University, Providence, RI.

Howard Garber, Ph.D., Director of Research, Rehabilitation Research and Training Center, University of Wisconsin, Madison.

Laurel E. Glass, Ph.D., M.D., Director, Center on Deafness, University of California, and Adjunct Professor, Department of Psychiatry, University of California Medical School, San Francisco.

Carl V. Granger, M.D., Professor of Rehabilitation Medicine at the State University of New York (SUNY) at Buffalo, and Head of Rehabilitation Medicine at the Buffalo General Hospital.

Alan Jette, P.T., Ph.D., MGH Institute of Health Professions, Massachusetts General Hospital, Boston.

Paul E. Kaplan, M.D., Professor, Department of Rehabilitation and Physical Medicine and Department of Internal Medicine, Northwestern University Medical School; Vice-President of the Association of Academic Physiatrists and past President of the Illinois Society of Physical Medicine and Rehabilitation.

Sidney Katz, M.D., Associate Dean of Medicine, Professor of Community Health and Medicine, and Director, Southeastern New England Long Term Care Gerontology Center at Brown University, Providence, RI.

Bryan J. Kemp, Ph.D., Director of the Rehabilitation Research and Training Center in Aging and Co-director, Clinical Gerontology Service, Rancho Los Amigos Hospital, Downey, California; Associate Clinical Professor of Psychiatry and Behavioral Science, School of Medicine, University of Southern California, Los Angeles.

Barry Lebowitz, Ph.D., Chief, Center for Studies of the Mental Health of the Aging, National Institute of Mental Health, Rockville, MD.

Malcolm H. Morrison, Ph.D., Project Director, University of Pennsylvania Rehabilitation Research and Training Center in Aging; Director, Office of Vocational Rehabilitation Demonstration Programs, Social Security Administration, Baltimore.

Don A. Olson, Ph.D., Director of Academic Development, Rehabilitation Institute of Chicago, and Associate Professor, Department of Physical Medicine and Rehabilitation and Department of Neurology, Northwestern University Medical School, Chicago.

James J. Pattee, M.D., Coordinator, Geriatric Program, Department of Family Practice, University of Minnesota Medical School, and Medical Director, North Ridge Care Center, Minneapolis.

Burton V. Reifler, M.D., M.P.H., Associate Professor, Department of Psychiatry and Behavioral Sciences, University of Washington, Seattle.

Phyllis Rubenfeld, Ed.D., Assistant Professor, Department of Academic Skills, Hunter College, New York, and President, American Coalition of Citizens with Disabilities, Inc. (ACCD).

T. Franklin Williams, M.D., Director of the National Institute on Aging; member of the Committee on an Aging Society, National Academy of Sciences; and Clinical Professor of Internal Medicine, University of Virginia.

Preface

"The widely prevailing practice of medical care for the disabled older person is paradoxical in that it combines the finest technics of medical science for the preservation of life with negative and antiquated concepts about functional living."
[Rusk, H. (1977). *Rehabilitation medicine* (4th ed.) (p. 647). St. Louis: C. V. Mosby.]

RATIONALE

Major demographic changes have occurred in the last 40 years, a period of time that is parallel to both the development of the medical specialty of physical medicine and the maturation of the field of rehabilitation. During this period, rehabilitation has responded to changing target populations; those changed populations reflect, in turn, medical, public health, and environmental advances.

In the decade of the 1940s, rehabilitation was very much concerned with childhood diseases, poliomyelitis in particular. At the same time, rehabilitation skills were called for to modify the disabilities that arose from the casualties of World War II. A third major concern was for spinal injuries resulting from traumata.

This early stage was followed in the 1950s and 1960s by a new and expanded emphasis on vocational outcomes as measured by resettlement in the labor force. This goal, too, was a reflection of social concerns—in this instance, those relating to industrial trauma and the social cost of dependency.

The third period of rehabilitation took place during the 1960s and 1970s. Another discrete target group, the developmentally disabled, was recognized as not inevitably handicapped. The rehabilitation intervention was many-faceted. Physical medicine and the rehabilitation therapies advanced the expectation of independent living for this group. In addition, vocational training was available for the most seriously disabled. Society began to acknowledge its responsibility to provide barrier-free environments, transportation, and, to some extent, housing.

Throughout this period of evolution, the assessment methodology, which is rehabilitation's major diagnostic, treatment, and evaluation tool, responded to these target populations by focusing on maximizing the level of functioning. This rehabilitation objective, which considered the basic levels of Maslow's hierarchy of goals as the fundamental aim for rehabilitation, was focused on helping patients achieve skill in the essential bodily functions—mobility, eating, and toileting.

It is suggested that, as a fourth stage, rehabilitation has come of and to age. The language of recent rehabilitation legislation has dropped the word *vocational* from its title, and within the context of the act has added to the concern for independent living the term *geriatric*. Although we are familiar with the fact that 11% of our population is over 65 years of age, we are less aware that this population is aging so rapidly that the number of people in the 85 or over age group increased by 67% in the 9 years following 1970. Life expectancy at 65, which was relatively constant prior to 1970, has now increased by 2 years, a gain of about 20%. While survival to age 65 was the result of health and social programs, it is probable that the recent advances in longevity beyond age 65 are the result of medical/surgical interventions. The introduction of cardiac surgery, dialysis, and hypertensive drugs has enabled the elderly to live longer but with impairments and, more often, with disabilities. Furthermore, changes in life-style bring the promise not only of life extension but also of what Katz has identified as "active life expectancy" (see Katz, this volume).

Although not a disease process in itself, aging increases the time during which the individual is exposed to the possibilities of disease, at a stage of life when the physiological and social time processes have made the aged individual most vulnerable to the stresses caused by disease. The elderly are subject to a clustering of insults, of which disability or loss of function is one among many losses. From a rehabilitation perspective, the attendant reactive depression often compounds the treatment problems. Medical knowledge has established that the normal excess capacities of the various organ systems decrease over time; however, there is general consensus that the reduction of those reserve capacities, for whatever reason, still leaves the aged individual with adequate resources to function effectively in a reasonably sympathetic environment.

There are three subgroups of disabled elderly who are increasingly utilizing rehabilitation medicine. Many developmentally disabled people are now surviving past middle age for the first time. The introduction of antibiotics and the control of respiratory infection have enabled a large cohort of the mentally retarded to face the problems of aging. Second, adults who have suffered trauma at an earlier time are also aging in large numbers because of improved medical care. The third and largest group are those aged who have become disabled because of traumata (such as falls and other accidents) or diseases, which become more prevalent or intense in the eighth stage of life (i.e., aging), and for whom medical/surgical intervention has been effective but with a residual impairment.

This tripartite group of elderly is the new population that challenges rehabilitation and tests the therapeutic optimism that characterizes the field. How do we mobilize our knowledge and skills to respond to this growing new population? What are our goals for the disabled elderly? Maximum functioning at the basic levels may be one goal, but it is modified by the physiological realities of decreased muscle strength and reaction time and by decrease of maximal oxygen consumption, which are but two qualifying considerations. What should be the admission criteria for inpatient and outpatient services for this new patient group?

Clearly, vocational goals may not be appropriate, but homemaker skills are appropriate for the many elderly living alone. Even that objective may not be realistic and independent living not a relevant or even desirable goal. For many elderly, some level of dependency must be accepted as a legitimate condition, and the goals of rehabilitation should be organized in terms of restoring the level of functioning of the family or caregiving unit that existed premorbidly. In many instances, the objectives of treatment may be minimal but significant to the quality of life.

Similarly, criteria for admission to rehabilitation services must be reexamined in light of these reconsidered rehabilitation goals. From the restatement of the mission of rehabilitation flows reevaluation of such well-established criteria as "medically stable" and "cognitively alert." Treatment modalities may also be altered to respond to this new population and to the revised mission.

The first step is yet to be taken. We have to come to grips with the issue of appropriate rehabilitation goals for this new target population, the disabled elderly.

With those ideas in mind, the Rehabilitation Research and Training Center in Aging at the University of Pennsylvania (RT-27), supported by the National Institute of Handicapped Research (NIHR) and National Institute of Mental Health (NIMH), proposed, in 1982, that a national conference be convened to identify the data base of this new changing rehabilitation target population and to develop responsive treatment goals. This proposal was approved by NIHR and NIMH, and the Interagency Committee on Handicapped Research (ICHR)—chaired by Dr. Douglas Fenderson and staffed by Dr. Joseph Fenton—was designated as the planning group.

The ICHR, made up of more than 20 federal agencies, adopted the following rationale for supporting the conference:

Background

The elderly population, particularly the disabled elderly, represent one of the biggest challenges to health and social services facing the United States today. The number of persons over age 65 is currently about 26.5 million or about 12% of the total population.

The elderly population is more at risk of incurring illnesses, multiple disabilities, and resulting functional limitations than are younger persons. This results in a large proportion of the handicapped and chronically impaired elderly who have major physical, mental, social and independent living deficits. The following data illustrates the status of the elderly in America:

— Eighty-six percent of all elderly persons suffer from one or more chronic conditions of varying degrees of severity.
— Fifty-six percent of those over age 75 are limited in activities of daily living due to chronic conditions.
— In 1977 the elderly had health expenditures that were 28% of the total for all Americans.
— Approximately 50% of the physically handicapped elderly also have psychiatric disabilities severe enough to warrant assistance.
— The majority of persons over age 65 living alone are eventually institutionalized.

Attitudinal barriers are as overwhelming and perhaps depressing as the demographic information stated above. Stereotyping has occurred with limited recognition that wide ranges of individual differences exist. The outcome results in the majority of effort and funds being used to sustain a debilitated group of geriatric patients while the elderly with rehabilitation potential drift or acquire more serious and complex problems.

Rehabilitation services, if provided to elderly persons with handicapped conditions, can often reduce the effects of impairment and enhance residual functional abilities to the extent that the need for nursing home care is avoided or substantially reduced. Yet, rehabilitation is not an integral part of the services delivery system for the elderly. A public health policy incorporating rehabilitation principles is needed which will encompass the coordinated efforts of many health related disciplines and agencies.

The Issue

The National Institute of Handicapped Research and the Center for the Studies of the Mental Health of Aging of the National Institute on Mental Health jointly fund the University of Pennsylvania Research and Training Center on the Rehabilitation of Aged Handicapped Individuals. Plans contained in the current grant include convening a *"state-of-the-art"* conference to focus on the physical, psychosocial, and vocational rehabilitation concepts relating to the following two groups of elderly persons:

a) those with *early-life onset* of handicapping conditions who have become elderly, and

b) those who have acquired handicapping conditions as a result of environmental circumstances, disease or trauma *after* they have become elderly.

A "state-of-the-art" conference of this nature should consider rehabilitation interventions to achieve maximum physical and mental restoration and/or maintenance of functional skills for independent living and the prevention of institutionalization. As appropriate, other concerns may include counseling, employment, leisure and recreation, housing, the application of technology, architectural barriers, nutrition, financial resources, discrimination, long term care and other areas related to the responsibilities of many Federal agencies.

Recommendation

There are numerous Federal agencies represented on the ICHR concerned with programs and research relating to the rehabilitation of aged handicapped individuals who have an interest in a "state-of-the-art" conference relating to that population. The outcomes of such a conference have the potentialities for identifying program needs, research priorities, reducing institutionalization, opportunities for collaborative efforts, and the development of a dynamic of which would enhance the physical, mental and social well being of the aged handicapped population and enable them to live productively in their own homes and communities for extended periods of time.

It is therefore recommended that the Interagency Committee on Handicapped Research join in the sponsorship of the conference. In so doing, it is further recommended that each ICHR member agency with programmatic or research interest in aging, designate a representative to participate on a planning committee for this conference. The planning committee will participate in identifying issues, developing and implementing the conference agenda, recommending participants, speakers, and other relevant activities.

Following this resolution, the planning committee helped identify issues and speakers, which in part reflected their own research programs, so that virtually all presenters, other than public officials, were supported by grants primarily from NIHR and NIMH. It was the expectation of the committee that perhaps as many as 150 participants would be attracted to the program. RT27 staff were somewhat more optimistic in planning for 250. The response was almost thrice the latter figure, with more than 600 applications received. Because of space limitations, participation was limited to 425 professionals from rehabilitation, aging, mental health, and related fields, representing direct services, advocacy, administration, policy and planning, research, and education. The limitation of the choice of speakers to those primarily involved in sponsored research to some extent narrowed the formal participation in terms of the multidisciplinary professions. To assure such representation, the conveners of the various sectional presentations were selected to assure that the major rehabilitation professions were involved. The Conference, which was held at the Washington-Plaza

Hotel in Washington, DC, was also representative of a national cross section, with attendants from 39 states as well as from Canada and Yugoslavia.

Douglas Fenderson, Director of the National Institute of Handicapped Research, T. Franklin Williams, Director of the National Institute on Aging, and Barry Lebowitz, representing the Director of the National Institute of Mental Health, made presentations during the opening plenary session. The session was designed to set a tone of therapeutic optimism for rehabilitation of the elderly and provide general information on the elderly and the disabled elderly, as well as on society's response to this population in terms of public policy and services, and the informal support system. Faye Abdellah, Deputy Surgeon General of the United States, the luncheon speaker for the first day, discussed public health aspects of rehabilitation of the aged. Eleven special topic groups covered, in detail, specific diseases and disorders common among the elderly. Congressman Ron Wyden (OR), as speaker at the banquet, discussed legislative concerns about health services for the elderly. The luncheon on the second day featured Phyllis Rubenfeld, President of the American Coalition of Citizens with Disabilities, Inc. The closing plenary session addressed employment issues. The exhibit area displayed materials from the three sponsoring federal agencies, the two Rehabilitation Research and Training Centers in Aging (Rancho Los Amigos and the University of Pennsylvania), and several of the agencies represented on the Interagency Committee on Handicapped Research.

The Conference summarizers, Robert Binstock, Carl Eisdorfer, and Don A. Olson, captured the climate of excitement that the meeting generated and agreed that what emerged was a recognition that we are already into an aging society and that, within such a society, there must be a different set of priorities for health care. Continuity of care is paramount, and rehabilitation is a key service in assuring such continuity.

The Conference registration fee was kept at a minimum to cover meals and Conference materials. All other items were funded as a part of Grant #G008006801 to the University of Pennsylvania for the Rehabilitation Research and Training Center in Aging funded by NIHR and NIMH.

Although much can be funded, the enthusiasm, efficiency, and grace displayed by Virginia Smith, Director of Training, and her staff, and commented on by the sponsors and the participants, can be repaid only with our appreciation and acknowledgment. That is also the nature of our gratitude for the contribution Delores Foster-Kennedy has made over the years to our efforts and specifically here for the editorial review and preparation of these materials.

Introduction

This collection of papers represents the *Proceedings* of the first national conference on disability, rehabilitation, and the aged. It brings together, for the first time, rehabilitation-oriented professionals with those whose backgrounds are in geriatrics or gerontology, although, as we have noted, the two fields have been parallel in content for three decades.

We use the words *collection* and *proceedings* since the presenters and their papers were selected primarily because of their research funding associated with the National Institute of Handicapped Research (NIHR) and the National Institute of Mental Health (NIMH). Thus, as in any proceedings, the style and content of each presentation varies. Some subjects are treated thoroughly, with a review of the literature, a state-of-the-knowledge report, and suggestions for further research; others take one aspect of the field and delve into it, reflecting a single approach. The depth and content vary substantially.

On the other hand, a wide variety of subjects has been addressed, and through it all, a single theme became evident. Dr. T. Franklin Williams, Director of the National Institute on Aging, enunciated that theme when he identified rehabilitation as a philosophy as much as a set of skills. "Rehabilitation," he wrote, "is a point of view." We at the University of Pennsylvania Rehabilitation Research and Training Center in Aging have interpreted this point of view as "therapeutic optimism." Dr. Douglas Fenderson, then Director of NIHR, in commenting on the effects of the conference, wrote: "Of greatest importance was the degree of involvement and 'resonance' of the audience in the substance of the meeting. Although each person came with individual expectations and needs, there was something important for everyone." We hope the proceedings have the same utility.

Dr. Barry Lebowitz, Director of the Center on Aging at NIMH, reminded us that former Department of Health, Education and Welfare Secretary Wilbur Cohen had spoken of a "bill of rights" for older people. Income, health care, and housing were the first three rights, and rehabilitation was the fourth. Sixteen years from that day has brought us to the reaffirmation of that fourth right of rehabilitation for the aged.

The three summarizers from the geriatric and rehabilitation fields captured the spirit and, indeed, the primary purpose of the conference. Dr. Don Olson, representing rehabilitation, reported that the conference was "a unique experience." He acknowledged the common background of groups interested in the aged and disabled, the considerable knowledge both enjoy, and the common value basis on which to build programs. It is no accident that the 1986 annual conference of the American Congress of Rehabilitation Medicine at which Dr. Olson will preside will be focused on "Rehabilitation and Aging."

Dr. Robert Binstock, Henry Luce Professor of Aging, Health, and Society at Case Western Reserve University, representing gerontology, identified the conference as "the birth of a social movement." He went on to declare: "Let this conference mark the start of an era in which any meeting dealing with aging and functional disabilities will be structured to include an emphasis on *both* long-term care and rehabilitation." In the ensuing year, in regional and national professional conferences, Dr. Binstock's prediction has been fulfilled.

Finally, Dr. Carl Eisdorfer, who has roots in both geriatrics and rehabilitation, summarized the conference as having "unleashed" a belief system that says people are worth an investment; in those 2 days of meeting there was the beginning of a synthesis between the common multiple disciplines and professions of gerontology and rehabilitation.

It was fitting that the University of Pennsylvania was privileged to have a role in a conference that gave new life to Professor George Morris Piersol's injunction, given almost 50 years ago when he established rehabilitation at that medical school: "We have added years to life. Let us now add life to years."

Part I

An Overview of Rehabilitation and the Elderly

1

Aging, Disability, and Therapeutic Optimism

Douglas A. Fenderson

Thomas Hardy once wrote a poetic epitaph for a pessimist. It said:

> I'm Smith of Stoke aged sixty-odd,
> I've lived without a dame, from youth-time on;
> And would to God my dad had done the same.

If, as this poetic license suggests, the pessimist turns his back on life and says no to the validity of his own existence, then I would like to define the optimism of which I speak as the opposite—as saying yes to life, embracing life in all of its phases and changing scenes.

A major purpose of this volume is to consider the ways in which research in rehabilitation, especially during the past 20 years, is being applied and can be applied to geriatric care. I will not belabor the well-publicized demographic data on the elderly population and their use of medical and related health care services. But I must point out that the problems of older persons as they live progressively closer to their limits are essentially the same as those who are disabled earlier in life. Performance and opportunity may be compromised, social stigma experienced, physical restoration required, coping and communication skills augmented, housing and transportation barriers overcome, and often the harsh economic realities of disability—and aging—confronted.

In addition, disabled people, who in another era might have died at birth, are now surviving, often with near-normal life expectancies. During World War I, only 2% of those with paraplegia or quadraplegia survived more than a year.[1] Today, thanks to high standards of acute trauma care and rehabilitation, most can expect a near-normal life span. Other examples of disabled persons who are also aging include those surviving severe head trauma, former polio patients, and those with developmental disabilities. A Report of the Committee on Aging and Developmental Disabilities (Puccio, Janicki, Otis, & Rettig, 1983) states: "Improved medical practices and rehabilitative services have prolonged the life and well-being of a significant portion of handicapped persons and created a dynamic new social phenomenon that demands our attention."

This conference is built around at least two basic concepts: rehabilitation and rehabilitation research. Each deserves comment. A pioneering pediatric orthopedist recently described his long experience in orthopedic rehabilitation. He said, "Diagnosis is of little importance. Function is what counts." He was not disparaging the importance of diagnostic acumen and precision. But after that and the appropriate treatments and procedures, what matters to the patient is function—or perhaps more accurately, performance. The message here is strong. In rehabilitation, the therapeutic goals and emphases shift from diagnosis and treatment to function and performance. The goals are not limited to physical performance alone. They encompass, as do those of the relatively new medical specialty of family medicine, an "extended boundary" concept of the person in his/her environment.

Rehabilitation research, then, applies the methods and materials of science and technology to the process of restoring, preserving, or enhancing function or performance. Howard Rusk (1977), one of the pioneers in this field, often referred to it as "the third phase of medicine." Although many would argue that medicine is too confining an identification, the point is well made. Think for a moment of the other two phases. The first, in large part within the province of public health, is primary prevention—that is, to take actions that will prevent the accident, disease, or problem from occurring. The second phase—secondary prevention—recognizes the injury, disease, or dysfunctional circumstance and seeks the earliest possible definitive resolution so that the sequelae—physical, social, and economic— can be prevented or limited. In the third phase—tertiary prevention, as public health experts like to call it—the injury, disease, or situation will result in significant and continuing consequences potentially affecting all spheres of the person's life. The process addresses optimum performance within the range of choices available to the person.

Rehabilitation research is, therefore, the scientific study of this process of restoring, preserving, and enhancing function. It seeks to improve each of the therapeutic modalities in each of the respective disciplines. It seeks to understand more clearly the necessary and sufficient conditions through which the process becomes a unified and efficient effort. It seeks to examine the next layer of scientific underpinnings of each mode of treatment, always challenging the all too common "conventional wisdom" residing within each discipline and the process itself. Finally, rehabilitation research seeks to understand the systems through which its benefits become available to all who need, want, and can benefit from them.

In 1964 I was studying rehabilitation medicine teaching programs in American medical colleges. Of the many memorable experiences, one left an especially indelible impression. I had spent a couple of hours with the head of a department of physical medicine and rehabilitation (PM&R) talking about finite details of the program. My next appointment was with the curriculum committee, chaired by the new and young dean—an internist. During this meeting, he recounted an experience early in his specialty training. He was assigned to one of the sprawling New York hospitals. His mentor was a well-known and distinguished clinician. The dean said he worked very hard to achieve diagnostic triumphs on particularly challenging patient problems. He said the professor listened with polite disinterest to his self-vaunting tales of medical sleuthing, and would often end the sessions by asking what he had been able to do for the old men in the back wards. At first, the dean said, he tried to ignore his mentor's question, but after several episodes he decided he had better take a look at "the old men." He discovered many things. He discovered and learned to work with nurses who provided continuity of care—often with, to him, surprising insight and sophistication. He also learned something about the clinical contributions he was able to make; and perhaps more important, he discovered his role in a process that transcended any individual effort.

I tell this story for two reasons. The first is to point out that no one medical specialty or health care discipline has an exclusive claim to this field. And the second is to introduce a summary of some of the highlights of rehabilitation research of the past 20 years that I believe are directly pertinent to your day-to-day professional activities.

Regarding the first reason, you should note that, for a number of economic, demographic, and social reasons, the medical community is discovering rehabilitation. In October 1984, the Neurorehabilitation Subcommittee of the American Academy of Neurology met in Baltimore (Neurorehabilitation, 1984). They pointed out that at least one-third of the reported rehabilitation problems are of neurologic origin and that, citing Freud, "You probably can't make a living in neurology unless you can do something to help the patient." Similarly, I participated in two events this year sponsored by orthopedic groups that were beginning to move beyond the more limited domains of that speciality. In the field of rheumatic diseases, and with the stimulation of the American Rheumatism Foundation, rheumatologists, internists, pediatricians, and physiatrists are coming together on common ground. And because institutional care for persons with mental illness and retardation has gone out of style, the mental health professions have increased their emphasis on function or performance, in contrast to amelioration of symptomatic behavior.

One of the newest medical specialities, family practice, shares with PM&R the "extended boundary" concept of clinical care. Increasingly, this field is extending its interests into long-term management of persons with chronic conditions, particularly the elderly. Several national curriculum workshops have been held for family practice faculty on this subject under the direction of Dr. James Pattee of the University of Minnesota.[2] Recently, two physiatrists, Carl V. Granger[3] and Gary Okomato,[4] have written books on rehabilitation for the family physician.

Let us now consider some of the highlights of rehabilitation research that have, and will continue to have, an impact on your professional activities. Federal support for comprehensive rehabilitation research and training centers was first available in 1962 under what was then the Research Division of the Rehabilitation Services Administration.

The first of these centers was Howard Rusk's Rehabilitation Institute of New York University; the second, the Department of PM&R at the University of Minnesota; the third, the Department of Rehabilitation Medicine at the University of Washington in Seattle; and the fourth was the Texas Institute for Rehabilitation Research at Baylor College of Medicine in Houston. Currently, the National Institute of Handicapped Research (NIHR) supports 33 research and training centers (RTC), two of them in geriatric rehabilitation, and one of those in collaboration with the National Institute of Mental Health.

The RTCs were to be located within model clinical programs or departments affiliated with institutions of higher education. They were to be centers of leadership in clinical care, applied clinical research, and basic science research, together with educational programs at all levels, for both clinical service and research personnel. The RTC program became more clearly defined in 1978 with the passage of the rehabilitation amendments that established NIHR as a separate federal agency. The centers, and others that followed, initiated hundreds of studies. Their work often borrowed heavily from other fields such as physiology, kinesiology, biochemistry, bioengineering, and the behavioral sciences, representing as it does a mix of elements from several disciplines.

Perhaps the most pervasive contribution of these centers was in applied physiology. As a young flight surgeon, Howard Rusk, an internist, had shown that bed rest was potentially dangerous to healthy young men. Within limits of physical tolerance, those ill with acute conditions such as penumonia were kept physically active. Treatment time was reduced, and relapse rates were cut in half.

World War II also spawned other natural experiments such as early ambulation, post-surgery and post-partum. Controlled studies soon followed, using conscientious objectors who were put to bed to determine the biochemical and physiological effects of bed rest. Applications of this work showed that bones were not static structures. Without stress, bones surrendered calcium, became weak, and were implicated in such complications as ectopic calcification and acute osteoporosis. This work has had pervasive effects on medical care in general. In rehabilitation and geriatrics, management of spinal cord injuries and approaches to prevention of hip fractures in the elderly are obvious examples (Office of the Surgeon General, 1984). Exercise and fitness programs and dietary guidance have emerged as standard practice in many geriatric programs.

NIHR has supported a network of 17 regional spinal cord injury systems over the past decade. Of necessity, studies of the neurogenic bladder were of major interest. Results of this work done, for example, at the University of Alabama, the Texas Institute for Rehabilitation Research, and Northwestern University, have contributed substantially to clinical practice in this area. Cord injury studies also contributed knowledge about disuse atrophy of muscles, bone demineralization, heterotropic ossification, and peripheral vascular and deep venous thrombosis. A related and interesting finding reported by Corcoran (1981), based on a National Aeronautics and Space Administration study, shows that 5 to 10 weeks of vigorous exercise may be required to overcome the increased heart rate at rest and exertion resulting from 3 weeks of bed rest.

On the psychological side, the RTCs were quick to pick up the implications of what was popularly known as "the pathology of boredom." You recall the well-publicized experience of turn-of-the-century foundling homes in which children, deprived of physical and affection stimulation, simply died. What about children with long-term illnesses or chronic diseases? And what about adults in stimulus-deprived environments? World War II bomber pilots and over-the-road truckers reported experiencing hallucinations while confined to sensory-constant environments. Also, the acute and often permanently disabling episodes of anxiety experienced by Hudson Bay Eskimo seal hunters (kayak angst) suggested a psychological counterpart to the physiology of bed rest—namely, severe and potentially harmful effects of stimulus-constant or stimulus-deprived environments. Carefully controlled studies have provided a scientific basis for many of the programs of stimulation and activity commonly observed in rehabilitation and geriatrics care programs.

RTCs contributed to our understanding of the problem of chronic pain management (Fordyce 1981; Fordyce & Steger, 1979). The University of Washington has pursued this theme for at least a decade. Researchers there distinguished between acute and chronic pain management, and found that care appropriate to the former may be disastrous in the latter. Their work with "learned pain behavior" and a data-based approach to chronic pain management, has provided tools now found in pain clinics and other sites throughout the United States.

Rehabilitation research has contributed to our understanding of the so-called helping relationship, a vital tool used by each of you who have direct patient care responsibilities. In the 1960's, Charles Truax, (Truax, undated; Truax et al., 1966) and Robert Carkhuff (Carkhuff & Truax, 1966), rehabilitation psychologists then at the University of Arkansas, attempted to operationalize Carl Roger's work on the characteristics of the helping relationship. They found that Roger's principles—empathic accuracy, non-possessive warmth, and genuiness—could be taught to caregivers who had little or no professional training. Their thesis was that the entire interpersonal environment—for example, a mental hospital ward—could be therapeutic and that all personnel in such environments, including service support personnel, could learn to apply the principles of the helping relationship appropriately and consistently.

That work not only supported the thesis but stimulated two decades of further research in extending, refining, and applying this approach to increasingly diverse settings and populations. It has been extended by Carkhuff (1983b) to corporate and bureaucratic environments to make them both more humane and productive. Carkhuff's (1983a) book, *The Art of Helping*, is a standard text in many nursing and allied health curricula and is used extensively in in-service training by health care providers, as well.

The centers have spurred the development of technologies for the disabled. We support a computer catalogue of such devices, known as ABLEDATA, part of NIHR's National Rehabilitation Information Center (NARIC). We also support some 17 rehabilitation engineering centers (RECs) working on a vast array of problems pertinent to geriatric care. This work includes wheelchair design, seating design to prevent pressure sores, development of sensory aids for low-vision and blind individuals, a new generation of hearing aids for hearing-impaired persons and advanced technical aids for deaf persons, computerized aids and devices for persons who are unable to speak, and functional electrical stimulation (FES), which has led to the development of what are now called neurological prostheses to stimulate or control muscle function in ambulation and upper-extremity manipulation. FES also has been used experimentally for several years to control urinary and fecal incontinence. This will be the subject of a clinical evaluation workshop, sponsored by the NIHR-supported RTC at Rancho Los Amigos Hospital, to introduce the technology for large-scale clinical trial in the United States. This workshop for rehabilitation and health professionals in geriatrics care will be co-sponsored by the Administration on Aging.

Over the past 20 years, our RTCs and RECs have worked on the problems of functional assessment in rehabilitation. This is, in fact, the title of a recent book that was edited by Andrew Halpern and Marcus Fuhrer (1983). The book presents the current status of various instruments and procedures that are beginning to bring a more rigorous and scientifically defensible approach to assessment, prediction of outcome, and improved effectiveness.

For example, a controversial, privately funded study of stroke rehabilitation was begun recently, in which those patients who are conscious when first seen, can swallow, and have no bleeding lesion on brain scan are managed by a rehabilitation team entirely at home. The hypothesis is that functional outcomes and personal support relationships will be at least as good as for those hospitalized, and the cost will be substantially less. Such studies require valid and reliable scales to assess the several dimensions of function or performance of concern in the rehabilitation process.

The centers also have extended and elaborated the concept of prosthesis and orthosis. You are all familiar with such devices—artificial limbs, orthopedic shoes, lumbar supports, glasses and low-vision aids, hearing aids, wheelchairs, and the like. The silicon chip revolution is pushing the potential of such devices to unimagined levels: myoelectric control of limbs, computer-assisted design and manufacture of orthopedic shoes and appliances (CAD/CAM), portable two-way communication devices for deaf/blind persons, hearing aids with individually matched frequency enhancement, and talking or otherwise "intelligent" wheelchairs with which to control one's domestic environment. The proliferation is endless. But how about prosthetic and orthotic environments (Skinner, 1983), i.e., environments built to aid and enhance human performance irrespective of or adaptable to any particular limitation of function? This is a field of serious study by architects and engineers.[5]

In 1973, the Rehabilitation Act was amended to require that the Architectural and Transportation Barriers Compliance Board (ATBCB) be established. In August 1982, the Board published "Minimum Guidelines for Accessible Design." In August 1984, in cooperation with the four federal agencies that set design standards for the government (General Services Administration, Department of Defense, Department of Housing and Urban Development, Post Office) and the American National Standards Institute, the Board published in the *Federal Register* the "Uniform Federal Accessibility Standards" that must be used in all new or remodeled federal facilities. But architects tend to follow such standards now for all new major construction. The ATBCB also commissioned a significant report, released in March 1983, "Multiple Disabilities through the Lifespan." Efforts such as these are pointing the way to building environments that encourage and enhance human performance.

Disabled persons themselves, dissatisfied with professionally directed programs, have, through their own efforts, helped to shape public policy. Some have banded together as an oppressed minority, waging an effective fight for what might be considered the civil rights of the elderly and disabled. In the senior citizens area, a strong parallel is seen with the Gray Panthers, the National Association of Retired Persons, and other such groups. (I am reminded of an overheard comment to the effect that "some service programs, developed for our benefit are, for us, as ornithology is for the birds.")

This political activism in the past 15 years has led to such important legislation (DeJong, 1983) as the following:

1968 Architectural Barriers Act, P.L. 90-480
1970 Urban Mass Transit Act, P.L. 91-453
1973 Federal Highway Act, P.L. 93-87
1973 Rehabilitation Act, Section 504 and the ATBCB, P.L. 93-112
1975 Department of Transportation Appropriations Regarding Accessible Equipment, P.L. 93-391
1975 National Housing Amendments, Housing Support and Independent Living Office, P.L. 94-173
1978 Rehabilitation, Comprehensive Services, Developmental Disabilities Amendments, P.L. 95-602 (establishing independent living as an important rehabilitation goal)
1980 Social Security Amendments, P.L. 96-265 (removing some disincentives for employment and allowing deduction of independent living expenses in computing income tax).

In summary, this paper has presented definitions for rehabilitation and rehabilitation research pertinent to geriatric rehabilitation; described selected areas of research that have, and will influence our professional and leadership responsibilities; and has identified several pieces of legislation that affirm our commitment as a nation to removing barriers to the full participation of *all* citizens in mainstream American life.

What of the future? John Naisbitt (1982), in his book *Megatrends*, states that effective social and economic actions are shifting from institutional and national control to local and personal control. He also notes that, as information becomes a utility (like the electric light) generally available to all who want and can use it, hierarchical structures are flattened; and new balances are struck between service provider and consumer and between professional worker and patient/client. Twenty years ago it was said that a professional was a person who owns a mystery. What is the meaning of professional in the information age?

The data network for rehabilitation protocols, clinical-outcome base rates, and rehabilitation technology may well be the U.S. mail—simply order a data disk for local use. One of the dangers will be the emergence of cookbook (computer disk) amateurs who lack contextual knowledge and commitment to the problems and who lack the "critical mass" of experience and responsibility to make mature judgments.

The introduction contrasts pessimism, as a denial of life, with optimism, an embracing of life, in each of its phases. Rehabilitation is sustained, in part, by a value orientation—characterized by one of the Greek words for love, agape, to love or care because of the intrinsic worth of the individual. Our task is often simply to help remove barriers that impede the normal human desire for engagement, connectedness, and reproductive activity. The late Frank Krusen, one of the early and most influential leaders in rehabilitation, would encourage his audiences with a quotation from one of his mentors, George Piersol: "We have added years to life. Let us now add life to years." For those who would apply rehabilitation research to geriatrics, this is our challenge as well.

NOTES

1. *Technical Bulletin 48*. VA 2324. SCI-WWI. Twenty percent returned to the United States, but only 46 (2% of the original total) survived more than 1 year.

2. James Pattee, Department of Family Practice and Community Health, University of Minnesota.

3. Dr. Granger is Head of Rehabilitation Medicine at the Buffalo General Hospital.

4. Dr. Gary Okomato, Medical Director, Pacific Basin Rehabilitation Research and Training Center, Seattle, Washington.

5. Robert Anderson Aldrich, Clinical Professor, Division of Congenital Defects, Department of Pediatrics, University of Washington, Seattle: personal communication. "My major work for the last ten years has been to learn more about how the man-built environment influences the rehabilitation of children with handicaps."

REFERENCES

Carkhuff, R. R. (1983a). *The art of helping*. Amherst, MA: Human Resource Development Press.

Carkhuff, R. R. (1983b). *Sources of human productivity*. Amherst, MA: Human Resource Development Press.

Carkhuff, R. R., & Truax, C. B. (1966). Toward explaining success and failure in interpersonal learning experiences. *Personnel and Guidance Journal, 414*, 723–728.

Corcoran, P. (1981). Disability consequences of bed rest. In W. C. Stolov & M. P. Clowers. (Eds.), *Handbook of severe disability* (pp. 55-63), Washington, DC: U.S. Department of Education, Rehabilitation Services Administration.

DeJong, G. (1983). Disability and public policy. *Scientific American, 248* (6): 40–49.

Fordyce, W. E. (1981). Chronic pain. In W. C. Stolov & M. P. Clowers, (Eds.), *Handbook of severe disability* (pp. 219–229). Washington, DC: U.S. Department of Education, Rehabilitation Services Administration.

Fordyce, W. E., & Steger, J. C. (1979). Behavioral management of chronic pain. In O. Pomerleau & J. Brady, *Behavioral medicine: Theory and practice* (pp. 150–156). New York: Williams and Wilkins.

Halpern, A. S., & M. J. Fuhrer (Eds.). (1983). *Functional assessment in rehabilitation.* Baltimore: Paul H. Brookes.

Naisbitt, J. (1982). *Megatrends.* New York: Warner Books.

Neurorehabilitation papers sought for next AAN annual meeting. (1984). *Neurology, 34* (9) (September), 20A.

Office of the Surgeon General. (1984) *Proceedings of the Conference on Hip Fracture Prevention.* U.S. Department of Health and Human Services. Washington, DC: U.S. Government Printing Office.

Puccio, P. S., Janicki, M. P., Otis, J. P. & Rettig, J. (1983). *Report of the Committee on Aging and Developmental Disabilities.* New York: New York State Office of Mental Retardation and Developmental Disabilities.

Rusk, H. (1977). *Rehabilitation medicine* (4th ed.). St. Louis: C. V. Mosby.

Skinner, B. F. (1983). Intellectual self management in old age. *American Psychologist, 38,* 239–244.

Truax, C. B. (undated). *Toward a tentative measurement of the central therapeutic ingredients.* (ARR and TC Report No. 190). Fayetteville, AR: University of Arkansas, Arkansas Rehabilitation Research and Training Center.

Truax, C. B., Fisher, G. H., Leslie, G. R., Smith, S. W., Mitchell, K. M., Shapiro, J. G., & McCormick, A. G. (1966). Empathy, warmth, genuineness. *Rehabilitation Record, 7* (5), 10–11.

2

The Aging Process: Biological and Psychosocial Considerations

T. Franklin Williams

Let me begin by agreeing with Dr. Fenderson that the overall aim of this volume is to bring together the understanding and skills of investigators and leaders in the fields of aging and rehabilitation. In order to pursue this goal effectively, it is essential to have a background of understanding of the aging process—the biological, behavioral, and social aspects of aging and the problems that commonly occur in older people—before applying rehabilitative approaches to the disabilities and handicaps of older people.

My purpose in this presentation is to give an overview of those features, with emphasis on where we most need further knowledge, where the research frontiers appear to be.

We must begin with the question "What do we mean by normal aging?" It is very important to distinguish between changes that are due to harmful life styles or to diseases—that is, changes that may be preventable or modified with treatment—and those that apparently may be due to aging per se. Many of the changes, declines in function attributed to aging in the past, are being found to result from potentially modifiable circumstances.

There are indeed a number of myths about aging, perhaps the most pervasive being that there is inevitable decline in physical and mental functioning with age. Across entire populations this is probably true, given the prevalence of harmful life-styles and diseases in older people. But when healthy older people are studied carefully—people who are free of identifiable diseases—it is now being found that various organ functions may be just as well maintained as in young adults. One example is the recent work of Lakatta and his colleagues with the Baltimore Longitudinal Study of the Aging Volunteers (Rodeheffer, et al., 1984). Careful screening of these generally healthy older people, up to age 80, using the latest techniques for detecting even subtle degrees of coronary heart disease, revealed that approximately one-half had some evidence of this type. In the remaining half, who were free of any such evidence, the studies showed that their maximum cardiac output, in a standard stress test, was as good on average as 25-year-olds'; there was considerable variability but the range of responses was the same as in the young subjects.

Another example has to do with mental functioning. Careful longitudinal studies of responses on intelligence tests, carried out by Schaie(1983) and colleagues, show maintenance of the same level of performance by most subjects—again up to age 80—as far as they have been followed. Whatever level of performance the individual had earlier, he/she tended to maintain it. Other supportive work for maintenance of mental functioning comes from the Laboratory of Neurosciences of the National Institute on Aging (NIA) in Bethesda where, through use of the positron emission tomography (PET) technique, the investigators under Rapoport have shown that brain energy metabolism is the same in healthy older subjects as in younger (Creasey & Rapoport, 1985).

A second myth is that there are inevitable changes in personality with aging. In contradiction to this view, recent studies by Costa and McRae (1980, 1984), again with the Baltimore Longitudinal Study population of the NIA, show remarkable stability in personality over the years. Similarly, the myth that there is inevitable loss of sexual functioning has been modified by findings that sexual function can continue (perhaps with some decline) in most older people, depending mainly on the social circumstance.

There is also the myth that older people lose contact with their families. In actuality, Shanas (1979) and others have documented in various countries of the world, including our own, that most older people are in contact with close relatives weekly or more often. In the United States, 80% of older people see a close relative at least that often. This favorable finding should not blind us to the fact that for the remaining 20%, which includes many of the very old members of our society (those 80 and older), there is considerable loneliness, usually when they have outlived close relatives, even including children.

Finally, there is the myth that most older people end up in institutions, particularly in nursing homes. In fact, only approximately 5% of older people are living in nursing homes at any one time, and only 20% to 30% ever enter a nursing home. Most of the lives of older people continue in dwellings of their and/or their children's choice.

At the same time that we need to set aside these myths, we also need to be aware of and to seek more knowledge about changes that, in fact, do go on with what appears to be "normal" aging. We are learning more about such changes at the cellular level, where there are demonstrable declines in the response of cellular receptors to a number of hormones such as insulin and norepinephrine. Such changes have implications for the changing effects of drugs in older people. In addition, there is evidence for changes in protein molecules within cells, such as certain enzymes, with age; changes in the structure of collagen with resulting stiffening of connective tissues; and changes in nuclear chromosomes with potential genetic consequences. We need to learn much more about "normal" aging at all levels in order to understand better what older people may be capable of.

The other major topic to be addressed in understanding aging and its implications for rehabilitation is full awareness of the commonness of acquiring chronic diseases as people age, with the resultant frequent disabilities and handicaps. Eighty percent or more of persons over the age of 65 have at least one identifiable chronic disease. The most common are arthritis of some kind (reported by more than 40% of older people), impaired hearing or vision or both (20%–30%), diabetes (10%–15%), chronic heart conditions (15%–20%), and some degree of mental failing (5% or more). These conditions in turn lead to barriers in carrying out the ordinary activities of daily living: 20% of persons over the age of 70 report disabilities that require the help of another person at least some part of every day; this figure rises to 40% for those over the age of 80. Overall, the extent of disabilities is such that, unless we in this country do better about preventing or correcting the conditions causing loss of independence and/or do better in helping disabled older people who still live at home with home support services, we will be faced with the need for up to 50% more nursing home beds by the year 2000, given the rapid increases in the numbers of very old persons.

Let us consider in more detail the common problems of old age. Those of most concern to older people, and also of most interest in this symposium in relation to rehabilitative efforts, are functional losses. In addition to impairments in hearing and vision already referred to, the three major functional losses that place heavy burdens of care on family members or institutions are dementia, loss of mobility, and urinary incontinence. We have had a truly explosive awareness of the facts about dementia in the past few years, in particular the awareness that it is a disease or group of diseases and not a result of aging per se. Increased research efforts are giving us better understanding of the nature and course of dementia, in particular that of the Alzheimer type, and much exciting work is going on aimed at identifying the possible cause or causes and trials of treatment. Nevertheless, as of now we do not have clear answers, and we must depend on supportive care for Alzheimer's disease victims. Here rehabilitative approaches are important in helping family members and other caregivers create and maintain familiar, consistent, supportive environments and in helping caregivers maintain themselves in the face of the wearing burdens.

In the area of losses of mobility, the largest contributing condition is osteoarthritis, a disease that until recently had been written off as being simply the wear and tear of old age. We are beginning to learn that there are genetic or familial factors that make some people more susceptible to osteoarthritis than others. New research is showing that the characteristics of the cartilage in joints of persons who have osteoarthritis are different from those who do not. It will be most important to learn more about osteoarthritis, its causes and possible preventive and therapeutic measures. Meanwhile, those persons who have mobility limited by it offer excellent challenges to rehabilitative efforts, including the modalties of physical and occupational therapy, medications, and, when indicated, surgical replacement of affected joints.

A part of the functional problem area of mobility is the frequency of falls, the single most common reason that older people come to emergency rooms of hospitals. Research is now in progress on what may be the risk factors leading to falls and their unfortunate sequellae of hip fractures and other injuries. Hip fractures alone are estimated to be costing this country about $2 billion per year in medical care. Here preventive efforts related to preventing falls, plus preventing osteoporosis, will be the most important steps—a part of rehabilitation in the broadest sense.

Other common problems in older persons, which have both preventive and rehabilitative potentials, include alcoholism, the late effects of smoking, dental diseases, and misuse of medications. The effects of drugs in older persons are highly variable, depending on individual variabilities in function of various organs and the disease conditions that may be present—plus the prevalent use of multiple drugs, with the likelihood of drug interactions.

We also must keep in mind the special psychosocial characteristics of aging and older people in our society. These include the virtually inevitable occurrences of bereavement, loneliness, and retirement, plus the dramatic increase in multigenerational families: four generations are common now, and five are not so rare. We need to learn much more about how intergenerational relations can best serve everyone involved including support in both directions. It is noteworthy, for example, that recent studies show that, at least up to about age 75, older people are actually supplying more support of various types for their children and grandchildren than they are receiving from them. Also, often it is the grandchildren who are supplying much of the support for their frail or disabled grandparents (Ingersoll & Antonucci, 1983).

We also need to learn more about how the institutional environment can become more of a *community* environment for those who must live indefinitely in long-term care institutions, and how the rehabilitative approach can be made primary and pervasive in such institutions.

Throughout the many types of settings in which care of older persons is going on, several key principles and goals should be emphasized, all of which are essentially rehabilitative in their thrust: (a) emphasis on preventive, modifiable aspects of problems; (b) the importance of small gains; (c) the necessity for a comprehensive medical–nursing–social assessment, emphasizing functional status, as the first step in care; and (d) constant awareness of respecting the dignity and sense of worth of each older person.

Let me close by commenting briefly on the research opportunities related to rehabilitation and aging through the NIA. Our charter specifies that we support research and training in the biomedical, behavioral, and social aspects of aging and the common problems of older people. Within this large framework, as noted already, we place a strong emphasis on *functional* aspects of normal aging and the common functional disabilities of older age. This emphasis is clearly relevant to rehabilitative research interests. We provide support through all the mechanisms available in the National Institutes of Health: research grants, contracts, and awards for training and career development (NIA, 1984). Examples of present research supported by NIA that has direct rehabilitative features include a study of disability and coping with arthritis in the elderly, home-based behavioral treatment of elderly patients, supportive methods for coping with bereavement, mechanical stimulation and estrogens in bone remodeling, and prognostic characteristics in stroke patients on rehabilitative services and their families.

We need to strengthen our efforts to bring together the closely related interests of the fields of aging and rehabilitation. "The aim of rehabilitation, to restore an individual to his/her former functional and environmental status or, alternatively, to maintain or maximize remaining function, should be at the heart of all care of aging persons in order to help them continue to live as full a life as possible" (Williams, 1984).

REFERENCES

Costa, P. T., & McCrae, R. R. (1984). Concurrent validation after 20 years: The implications of personality stability for its assessment. *Advances in Personality Assessment, 4.*

Costa, P. T., McCrae, R. R. & Arenberg, D. (1980). Enduring disposition in adult males. *Journal of Personality and Social Psychology, 38* (5), 706–800.

Creasey, H., & Rapoport, S. I. (1985). The aging brain. *Annals of Neurology.* Boston: Little, Brown.

Ingersol, G., & Antonucci, T. C. (1983, November). *Negative social support: Another side of intimate relations.* Paper presented at the 36th Annual Meeting of The Gerontological Society of America, San Francisco.

National Institute on Aging. (1984). *Report on education and training in geriatrics and gerontology.* Washington, DC: Author.

Rodeheffer, R. J., Gerstenblith, G., Becker, L., Fleg, J., Weisfeldt, M., & Lakatta, E. (1984). Exercise cardiac output is maintained with advancing age in healthy human subjects: Cardiac dilation and increased stroke volume compensate for a diminished heart rate. *Circulation, 69* (2).

Schaie, K. W. (Ed.). (1983). The Seattle longitudinal study: A 21-year exploration of psychometric intelligence in adulthood, In K. W. Schaie (Ed.), *Longitudinal studies of adult psychological development.* (pp. 65–135). New York: The Guilford Press.

Shanas, E. (1979). Social myth as hypothesis: The case of the family relations of old people. *Gerontologist, 19* (1), 1–9.

Williams, T. F. (Ed.). (1984). *Rehabilitation in the aging.* New York: Raven Press.

3

Aging, Mental Health, and Rehabilitation

Shervert H. Frazier, Barry D. Lebowitz, and Larry B. Silver

In October 1968, Secretary of Health, Education and Welfare Wilbur J. Cohen, speaking before the National Conference of State Executives on Aging, proposed a "bill of rights" for older people. Income, health care, and housing were identified as the first three of those rights; rehabilitative services was proposed as the fourth. In the 16 years that have passed, much progress has been made in aging, in mental health, and in rehabilitation. The challenge before us now, in this conference and in the future, is to integrate these three different streams of activity and create out of them an agenda to guide our work.

The background for our concerns in these areas is what Morton Kramer (1980) has pointed out as the worldwide pandemic of mental disorders and associated chronic conditions. It is worth quoting from his important 1980 paper:

> The prevalence of mental disorders . . . is rising at an alarming rate. In contrast to a pandemic of a communicable disease like influenza, which rises to a peak and then falls off, there is every indication that the prevalence of the chronic illnesses will continue to increase.
>
> Two mechanisms are operating simultaneously to produce this situation. One is the large relative increases that are occurring in the number of persons in age groups at high risk for developing mental disorders and chronic diseases. This mechanism increases crude prevalence rates. The other mechanism is the increase in the average duration of chronic diseases resulting from the

successful application of techniques for arresting their fatal complications and prolonging the lives of the affected individuals. This raises the age specific prevalence rates. In the absence of effective techniques for reducing incidence, the prevalence of chronic diseases will continue to increase (p. 382).

We are thus confronted with a situation that Ernest Gruenberg (1977) has provocatively referred to as the "failure of our success." Gruenberg points out that the real revolution in gerontology and geriatrics has been less in keeping healthy people healthy than in keeping sick people alive. The average duration of life for victims of a wide range of conditions has been extended substantially. We need only look at the quintupling of the life expectancy of infants born with Down's syndrome during our lifetimes to realize the validity of this claim.

Therefore, in trying to achieve a synthesis of developments in mental health, aging, and rehabilitation it is going to be necessary to reconcile issues of quite different populations: those with chronic psychiatric illness, principally schizophrenia and depression, whose disabilities had an onset in early adulthood and who have now grown old, and those whose illnesses—schizophrenia, depression, and especially the dementing disorders—had an onset in later life.

The development of effective research, education, practice, and policy toward rehabilitation in this extraordinarily heterogeneous population is an enormous challenge. Yet this is only one part of the picture. A basic tenet of geriatric care is, or at least should be, that all potentially disabling conditions have behavioral, emotional, and therefore mental health components. The fundamental understandings of consultation and liaison in the mental health disciplines of psychiatry, psychiatric nursing, social work, and psychology are built on the premise that mental health issues are central to the care of many, if not most, persons with medical illness; this relationship is intensified in the elderly. Several studies have shown the very high prevalance of symptoms of psychopathology in older persons hospitalized with a medical illness, and in a review of 34 controlled studies of psychological interventions with patients recovering from surgery and heart attacks, Mumford, Schlesinger and Glass (1982) documented the efficacy of psychological intervention on mortality and length of hospital stay. As the cost-control philosophy underlying the establishment of diagnosis-related groups (DRG) in the Medicare program becomes firmly established, it is highly likely that mental health interventions to reduce length of stay will be seen as essential components of hospital care for all older persons.

The overlapping concerns of physical health and mental health are issues in which a great deal more research must be carried out. A 1984 conference sponsored jointly by the National Institute of Mental Health (NIMH) and the Working Group on Health and Behavior of the National Institutes of Health examined the mental health aspects of diseases in the elderly. In a systematic exploration of disease issues from neurology and dentistry to podiatry and dermatology, researchers attempted to identify mental health risk factors, correlates, and consequences of major chronic and acute physical disorders. In addition, investigators discussed the impact of psychiatric, emotional, and behavioral factors on the course of disease and on the processes of rehabilitation, relapse, recovery, mortality, and institutionalization. It was obvious in this conference that the gaps in our knowledge are substantially greater than the substantive information available on these issues. This must, therefore, be a matter of the highest priority in the development of new research.

Accordingly, our concerns include three quite distinct populations: chronically mentally ill individuals, who have grown old; older persons who develop a mental illness in later life; and, finally, those with physical illness who have associated psychiatric conditions. As prototypes of these three populations, we will consider those older persons with schizophrenia, those with senile dementia, and those with hip fracture. In this introductory essay we present some general information about these populations to use as an overview for the more focused discussions to follow in this conference.

SCHIZOPHRENIA AND CHRONIC MENTAL ILLNESS

Estimates of the prevalence rates for schizophrenia and schizophreniform disorders are slightly more than 1% of the noninstitutionalized adult population of the United States (Robins et al., 1984). Severe affective disorder is estimated to afflict some 600,000 to 800,000 adults, and estimates of depressive symptoms have been estimated to affect 15% or so of the elderly. For the bulk of those suffering from schizophrenia, the age of onset is adolescence or young adulthood. The duration of schizophrenia and other chronic mental disorders can be lifelong, and life expectancy is generally thought to be unaffected by the presence of the mental disorder (Goldman, 1983). The locus of care, once predominantly institutional in large public mental hospitals, has now been mostly replaced by community and outpatient facilities. In the 20 years from 1955 to 1975 the distribution of patient care episodes changed from 3:1 in favor of inpatient institutional care to the same ratio in favor of outpatient care and day treatment (Witkin, 1980). The inpatient population of large hospitals has been substantially reduced from more than 600,000 to approximately 150,000; length of stay is very short, typically less than 30 days, but hospitalizations can be expected to reoccur over a lifetime.

For the elderly chronic patient, however, the picture is somewhat different. Although the elderly constitute approximately 27% of the inpatient population, admission rates for that group are very low (only 5.5% of the admissions are age 65 years or older). These patients, once hospitalized, rarely leave, for their behavioral problems—especially assaultive or self-destructive actions—are so serious as to restrict treatment placement alternatives.

For most older persons whose psychiatric problems are sufficiently severe to require institutional care, the setting of choice is typically the nursing home, not the hospital. The philosophy of deinstitutionalization of mental health care in the 1960s and beyond was, for many elderly, trans-institutionalization, with large numbers of disabled elderly transferred or diverted from the hospital to the nursing home. In a 1983 NIMH conference devoted to the issues of mental illness in nursing homes, we learned that nursing homes are the single largest place of care for the chronically mentally ill elderly. It is estimated that 56% to 80% of the 1.4 million residents of nursing homes in the United States have chronic mental conditions. In addition, nursing homes house a sizable population of individuals now having, or at risk of having, behavioral problems. Eight to ten percent of the nursing home residents are former residents of state mental hospitals or long-term care specialty hospitals. Some of the most common behaviors and/or diagnoses in the nursing home are Alzheimer's disease, confusion, depression, wandering, disorientation, agitation, withdrawal, lethargy, frustration, stress reactions, dependency, apathy, guilt, irritability, rise and fall of self-esteem, persistent talk of a wish to die, paranoid delusions, and many other things. We learned as well that in most nursing homes recognition and treatment of psychiatric conditions is unavailable or inadequate.

At the same time, those chronic patients institutionalized in the hospital or the nursing home can, at least potentially, receive appropriate care. This, tragically, contrasts with those many homeless and disordered who are living (and dying) on the streets and in the shelters across our nation. Although not all of the homeless are mentally ill, epidemiological guesses place the proportion at very high levels. The 23 November 1984 *New York Times* documented the issue: "a 48-year-old homeless man who suffered from an organic brain disorder was found dead early Wednesday a few hundred feet from the shelter on Wards Island where he had been staying . . . [his] brain disorder made him unable to take care of himself and that required that he be watched more closely than the shelter's staff was able to." On that Tuesday night before Thanksgiving there were 24 staff and 8 security guards in a shelter filled to capacity with 850 homeless men.

SENILE DEMENTIA

The discussion of dementing disorders, particularly Alzheimer's disease, has fortunately been moved to the highest levels of our nation's policy circles. In its first report, the Secretary's Task Force on Alzheimer's disease of the U.S. Department of Health and Human Services (1984) quotes President Reagan's proclamation that Alzheimer's disease is "the most common cause of severe intellectual impairment in older individuals. Presently there is no established treatment that can cure, reverse, or stop the progression of this disorder . . . in 1.5–2.5 million elderly persons in the United States." The President's proclamation emphasized that Alzheimer's disease "deprives its victims of the opportunity to enjoy life and takes a serious toll on its victims' families and friends. The emotional, financial and social consequences of Alzheimer's disease are so devastating that it requires special attention."

Though there is variability from community to community, nearly one-half of the long-term care beds in our nation are devoted to persons with Alzheimer's disease, and estimates are that there are at least as many (and probably closer to twice as many) victims of the disease being cared for in the community by families (S. J. Brody, Paulshock, & Masciocchi, 1978).

This family care issue is a particular hallmark of Alzheimer's disease and was a major focus of the Departmental Task Force. As Elaine Brody (1983) indicated in her paper at the 1983 NIMH conference on mental illness in nursing homes: "The role of the family is so central to long-term care of the aged that gerontologists have reached firm consensus that the family, rather than the impaired individual alone, should be the focus in planning services to noninstitutionalized older persons." Brody goes on to point out that "coping with an older person with senile dementia is extraordinarily difficult and stressful. The anxiety, fear, panic, and sense of loss of control on the part of the afflicted elderly person has its parallel in the anxiety, fear, and inability to cope on the part of the family."

The search for cause and the search for cure of Alzheimer's disease must proceed with all possible commitment. At the same time, we should keep in view the important gaps in our information about treatment and management. The most pressing of these needs are in the development of approaches to address the mental problems (e.g., disorientation), the emotional problems (e.g., depression and delusions), and the behavioral problems (e.g., agitation and wandering) characteristic of Alzheimer's disease. These are the central concerns of the mental health field, and it is professionals in this field who are most often called on to treat victims of Alzheimer's disease and to assist their families to provide the necessary care.

It is encouraging to see the new wave of scientific attention being devoted to Alzheimer's disease; surely improvements in practice will follow as will new approaches to policy issues. In a major development, the Departmental Task Force recommendation to remove reimbursement limitations on physicians' services provided outside the hospital was accepted and implemented. Medicare rules limited medically appropriate physician services provided outside the hospital setting for patients with Alzheimer's disease when coded as a mental disorder. The department has now clarified that, except for psychotherapy, physician treatment services for patients with Alzheimer's disease and related disorders are not subject to the $250 limitation on outpatient psychiatric care; that is, the deciding factor is the nature of the service and not the diagnostic code. This is an important change in the rules for Medicare reimbursement and could provide a substantial benefit to the victims of Alzheimer's disease and to the families that care for them.

HIP FRACTURE

Hip fracture is neither the best nor the worst example of how mental and physical factors interact in older persons. Yet we select hip fracture for a number of reasons, including the often documented lay opinion that hip fracture leads to death. In fact, in his review of 26 clinical studies, Nickens (1983) shows cumulative 1-year characteristics of the population, with 25% mortality generally regarded as typical. In the United States there are approximately 200,000 hip fractures per year with every indicator pointing to future years of increased incidence. Hip fracture is predominantly a problem of women, and though the relative contributions of osteoporosis and falling are unknown, it is clear that with the exception of extreme cases (e.g., auto accidents) osteoporosis is probably a necessary condition for fracture.

Treatment for hip fracture typically involves a long period of hospitalization, followed by 2 to 3 months of inpatient rehabilitative care in a specialized facility or nursing home. If they are able, patients often return home after a hip fracture; for many, however, long-stay institutional care is the only feasible arrangement. In a significant contribution, Levitan and Kornfeld (1981) demonstrated that traditional liaison psychiatry reduced the average length of hospital stay by 12 days in a group of women hospitalized in an orthopedic surgical unit. In addition, a final discharge home was significantly more frequent in the women seen by the psychiatrist than in the control group. This impressive documentation of the efficacy of liaison psychiatry has potentially important implication for both the quality and the cost of care.

The important interaction of physical condition and mental state was underscored in a 1978 paper by Baker et al. (cited in Nickens, 1983), who showed that hip fracture patients with dementia were significantly worse 6 months post-fracture and that mortality was three times higher in that group. Thus, in hip fracture, we have illustrated the special relationship of mental health factors to the outcome of treatment for a medical condition. An additional point of concern is illustrated in this example of patients where a medical problem is added to either chronic or acute mental health problems. That is, the demented woman who fractures her hip, the person with schizophrenia who has a heart attack, and countless numbers of this new dual-diagnosis group challenge many of the treatment strategies and systems for care that have been developed. More significantly, they represent difficult and potentially costly arrangements for care. Sensitivity to these issues, though variable, is largely absent from our concerns with health care planning and containment of cost.

REHABILITATION

S. J. Brody (1984) has maintained that rehabilitation represents the critical link between hospital-based care and the family. We have tried to show that this link must take into account the critical mental health issues in rehabilitation of the aged. Some of those issues deal directly with psychiatric illness alone, and others deal with the psychiatric and behavioral components of medical illness. Putting together the concepts of aging, mental health, and rehabilitation has been a substantial challenge. The heterogeneity of the population of concern, the absence of well-validated models, and the ambiguity of action strategies continue to make our task difficult.

It is important for us to realize that rehabilitation is not an end in itself. As David Symington (1984) stated in the Thirty-Third Coulter Lecture of the American Congress of Rehabilitation Medicine: "A *first* step toward reducing the burden of handicap in society must be the consistent application of comprehensive caring rehabilitation services which ensure that *all* disabled persons are helped to achieve their maximum level of independence."

The maintenance of function and the reduction of burden are the important goals toward which we must move. This conference will set us firmly in the direction we must pursue, and we at NIMH are eager to contribute to these important developments.

REFERENCES

Brody, E. M. (1983). *The role of the family in nursing homes: Implications for research and public policy.* Prepared for the Conference on Mental Illness in Nursing Homes. Rockville, MD: National Institute of Mental Health.

Brody, S. J. (1984). Goals of geriatric care. In S. J. Brody & N. A. Persily (Eds.), *Hospitals and the aged: The new old market*, Chap. 4. Rockville, MD: Aspen Systems.

Brody, S. J., Poulshock, S. W., & Masciocchi, C. F. (1978). The family caring unit: A major consideration in the long-term support system. *The Gerontologist*, 18(6), 556–561.

Cohen, W. J. (1968). *Action line for aging*. National Conference of State Executives on Aging, Washington, DC, unpublished.

Goldman, H. H. (1983). *Long-term care for the chronically mentally ill*. Washington, DC: Urban Institute.

Gruenberg, E. M. (1977). The failure of success. *Health and Society—The Milbank Memorial Fund Quarterly*, 55, 3–23.

Levitan, S. J., & Kornfeld, D. S. (1981). Clinical and cost benefits of liaison psychiatry. *American Journal of Psychiatry*, 138, 790–793.

Kramer, M. (1980). The rising pandemic of mental disorders and associated chronic diseases and disabilities. *Acta Psychiatrica Scandinavica*, 62(Suppl. 285), 382–397.

Mumford, E., Schlesinger, H. J., & Glass, G. V. (1982). The effects of psychological intervention on recovery from surgery and heart attacks: An analysis of the literature. *American Journal of Public Health*, 72, 141–151.

Nickens, H. W. (1983). A review of factors affecting the occurrence and outcome of hip fracture, with special reference to psychological issues. *Journal of the American Geriatrics Society*, 31, 166–170.

Robins, L. N., Helzer, J. E., Weissman, M. M., Orvaschel, H., Gruenberg, E., Burke, J. D., & Regier, D. A. (1984). Lifetime prevalence of specific psychiatric disorders in three sites. *Archives of General Psychiatry*, 41, 949–958.

Secretary's Task Force on Alzheimer's Disease. (1984). *Alzheimer's disease* (DHHS Publication No. ADM 84-1323). Rockville, MD: National Institute of Mental Health.

Symington, D. C. (1984). The goals of rehabilitation. *Archives of Physical Medicine and Rehabilitation*, 65, 427–430.

Witkin, M. J. (1980). *Trends in inpatient care episodes in mental health facilities, 1955–1977* (Mental Health Statistical Note No. 154. DHHS Publication No. ADM 84-1323). Rockville, MD: National Institute of Mental Health.

4

Goals of Rehabilitation of the Disabled Elderly: A Conceptual Approach[1]

Carl V. Granger

AGE-RELATED CHANGES

It has been demonstrated that many important physiological functions decline with age (Shock, 1960). In spite of these physiological measures of decline in organ function, aging cannot be considered a "disease." This decline erodes excess organ reserve that is beyond immediate functional needs, except under circumstances of unusual stress. Therefore, chronological age is, at best, a rough approximation of the significance of these changes. Further, there is a range of differences in performance on age-related functions for any single age cohort (Costa & McCrae, 1980).

In a significant review of the biologic changes attributed to the process of aging, Bortz (1980) has demonstrated the close similarity between most of these changes and those associated with inactivity. Parallels are drawn between bodily changes of astronauts during periods of weightlessness and changes due to inactivity, such as enforced bed rest. Further, he suggests that insofar as changes may be due to disuse, they are subject to correction. In particular, he states, "Certainly, one of the most fundamental measurements that we can apply to ourselves is the maximum oxygen consumption ($VO_{2\,max}$), which ultimately describes the ability of the organism to transport

---

[1] Editor's note: Dr. Granger's chapter introduces functional assessment as a tool for defining the goals of rehabilitation. The reader who wishes further detail on the use of this method is referred to Granger & Gresham (1984).

oxygen from the atmosphere through the intermediate conduits, finally to the enzymatic reaction for which it is the spark." Numerous workers have shown that the $VO_{2\,max}$ declines with age at about 1% per year (Lakatta, 1979). DeVries (1978), Dehn and Bruce (1972), and others, however, have shown that a program of physical activity markedly alters this decline. From the data of Hodgson (1971), one can calculate that a conditioning program for the inactive can recapture 40 years' worth of $VO_{2\,max}$ (Bortz, 1980). It seems extremely unlikely that any future drug or physician-directed techniques will approach such a benefit. Similarly, bed rest deconditioning leads to a major decrease in $VO_{2\,max}$ that can be largely offset by a program of in-bed exercises (Birkhead et al., 1964; Saltin, Blomquist, & Mitchell, 1968). Even chair rest has been reported to decrease $VO_{2\,max}$ (Robinson, 1938). Conversely, trained athletes have high levels of $VO_{2\,max}$.

Fries and Crapo (1981) point out that markers such as "graying of hair, the elasticity of skin, the rigidity of the arteries, the kidney function and the opacification of the lens of the eye cannot be changed." On the other hand, "exercise tolerance (Pollock et al., 1974), maximal breathing capacity (Dehn and Bruce, 1972; DeVries, 1978), cardiac reserve reaction time (Spirduso, 1975; Spirduso, 1980; Spirduso & Clifford, 1978), physical strength, short-term memory (Langer et al., 1979), intelligence as measured by intelligence tests (Nesselroade et al., 1972; Plemons, 1978), ambulatory activities, and social abilities (Langer & Rodin, 1976) can be maintained or even improved with advancing age." These latter functions are the specific targets of selective rehabilitation interventions. However, a "formula" program for rehabilitating the elderly is inappropriate, and rehabilitation interventions must be tailored to match the needs of each individual at any particular point in time. Therefore, a well-directed rehabilitation program is a feasible way to enhance functional ability and promote vitality in the aged individual with chronic disease.

DISABLEMENT MODEL

Traditionally, medical and allied health educators have focused on the curative aspects of the disease process—the diagnosis and treatment of an organic impairment—rather than the long-term management of its consequences. Although such an approach may be satisfactory for treating acute conditions, it is inadequate when caring for patients with chronic health impairments. Diagnoses are an inadequate index of health because the range of severity within a diagnosis is often greater than that among diagnoses (Kane & Kane, 1981). Using functional assessment in a timely, comprehensive and continuous fashion will result in enhancement of health status and psychosocial well-being, these representing the goals of rehabilitation.

The following descriptive terms, adapted from definitions of the World

Health Organization's Classification System on Impairment, Disability, and Handicap (World Health Organization, 1980), characterize the "disablement model" and should be part of the working terminology of all health care workers.

Impairment is defined as any loss or abnormality of anatomic structure or physiological or psychological function at the *organ* level. When the degree of functional limitation is sufficient, the difficulty or inability to perform daily living activities leads to disability.

Disability occurs at the *person* level and represents any restriction of lack of ability (resulting from an impairment) to perform an activity in the manner or within the range considered normal for a person of the same age, culture, and education.

Handicap occurs at the *societal* level when conditions are imposed upon the person in such a way, through disadvantageous social norms and policy, that limits the individual in fulfillment of expected social roles. As an example of handicap, there are negative attitudes felt against the elderly that constitute a major barrier to securing adequate physical and mental health care and appropriate rehabilitative care for many persons over the age of 65 years.

FUNCTIONAL ASSESSMENT

Functional assessment is a method for describing abilities and limitations that an individual experiences in order to measure performance of the activities that are necessary to daily living. By using this technique, both needs and outcomes can be measured with the same instrumentation. The ultimate purpose of analysis of functional performance is to discover the presence of unmet needs at all levels—medical, psychosocial, and environmental—in order to develop appropriate interventions. It is commonly believed that early rehabilitative intervention is more likely to result in successful rehabilitative management. However, early identification of disability is not common to medical practice.

An excellent compendium of functional assessment instruments and scales is presented in Kane and Kane (1981, pp. 4, 5, 31). For example, the Barthel Index includes self-care, sphincter control, and mobility factors, and is scored from 0 (total dependence) to 100 (independence). The acronym PULSES refers to *p*hysical condition; *u*pper limb functions; *l*ower limb functions; *s*ight, speech and hearing; *e*xcretory functions; and *s*ituational factors. The scoring for each component ranges from 1 for intact to 4 for fully dependent.

Figure 4-1 illustrates application of the functional approach to medical care with analysis of need for intervention based on the disablement model.

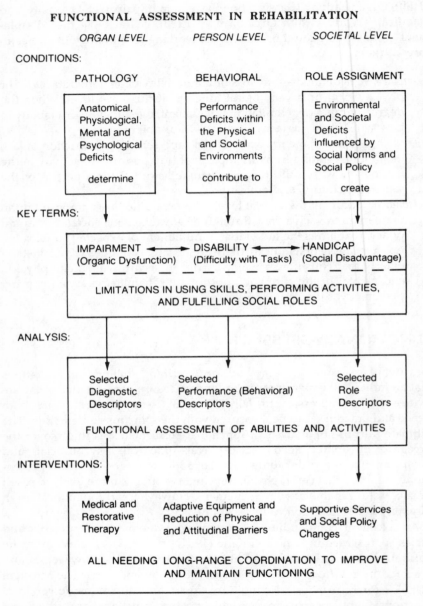

Figure 4-1   The functional approach to medical care and the disablement model.
(From C.V. Granger & G.E. Gresham, *Functional Assessment in Rehabilitation Medicine*, p. 20. Copyright © 1984 Williams and Wilkins, Baltimore. Used by permission.)

For persons less severely disabled, in terms of performance of personal care activities in particular, the Functional Assessment Screening Questionaire (FASQ) (Granger & Gresham 1984; Seltzer, Granger, & Wineberg, 1982) was developed to reflect the degrees of difficulty being experienced in a broad range of activities that include selected items of personal care, instrumental household activities, leisure time and socialization activities, occupationally related activities, and traveling. The FASQ was developed to identify and follow patients with early or minimal or moderate disability in an ambulatory care setting.

By assessing patients who are experiencing disability in the outpatient or office setting, the physician is able to identify areas of unmet need and then refer them to a resource for help. Resources may include supports from the formal service system, being either institutionally-based or home-based. Those services may include transportation, personal care, housekeeping, social activities, emergency assistance, food shopping, and food preparation.

By conducting a systematic inventory of what task items are performed and how they are performed, functional assessment collects information to represent the individual's experiences of living with disability. Analysis at this level may reveal reversible disability and indications for restorative therapy or for psychological adjustment and behavior modification. Analysis also may reveal disability that cannot be accounted for by the identified impairment, which indicates the need for additional evaluation in order to determine the presence of another impairment or social, environmental, or psychological factors that may be at work. With this comprehensive assessment, plans for further management may include: (a) investigation of unresolved issues, (b) amelioration of treatable impairment, (c) a rehabilitation medicine consultation if disability significantly impedes life roles, and/or (d) preparation of the patient and family members for any needed long-term personal adjustments and mobilization of appropriate community supports. The plan should recognize unrealistic expectations, problems in compliance, over- or underutilization of health care resources, and possible reasons for stress among family members.

A DEMONSTRATION PROJECT

A demonstration project was carried out in Wood River, Rhode Island (1982), with the objective to prevent or forestall admission to nursing homes through provision of health center and home-based services. The cohort studied consisted of 601 individuals, 204 (34%) men and 397 (66%) women; 7% were 60 years old, and more than half were over 70 years old. There were four major diagnostic impairment categories: neurological, 5%;

musculoskeletal, 14%; general medical (chiefly cardiac), 77%; psychiatric or neurosensory, 5%. The most frequently provided services were geriatric nurse practitioner, physician, home help worker, and transportation.

In order to examine a few hypotheses, a subset of patients (N = 163) who were active and receiving services during a 1-month period were chosen for analysis by Spence (1982). The hypotheses were as follows:

1. Service usage will increase as Barthel Index scores decrease.

    Increasing service needs were evident as scores on the Barthel declined. The correlation was significant enough to indicate that assessment is a useful tool and can be utilized as a meaningful predictor of service needs.

2. Persons 75 years and older will have higher service usage than persons under age 75.

    The data generated did not support this conclusion. Age, when correlated with service utilization, does not appear to be an indicator for service need. Age, as a predictor of service usage, is relevant only when combined with a Barthel score. Results illustrate that as age increases, Barthel scores tend to decrease, and with the lowering of Barthel scores, service usage will increase.

3. As decision-making declines, service usage will increase.

    Decision-making ability, for the purposes of this study, is defined as a cognitive ability enabling the person to maximize functional capacities in an independent manner. Fifty-three percent of the total population scored at the highest level on the decision-making scale and had a mean service rate of 138 min/month. In contrast, the 12 patients assessed as severely impaired had a mean service utilization rate of 445 min/month.

It appears that functional assessment is a useful tool and can be utilized as a meaningful predictor of service need, especially when variables including age and living arrangement also are included as part of the assessment. Functional assessment, as a means of determining service needs, can provide a suitable conceptual framework by providing a common understanding of functional capacity and overall well-being. The conceptualization of functional status and services into standardized components provides a basis for identifying, with some precision, the ways that clients present problems. Simply stated, it can be seen that in the Wood River Project, when functional abilities—both physical and cognitive—declined, service usage increased, and that this tendency was even more marked when the person was over 75 and lived alone. Although staff did not deliver service on the basis of assessment results, it appears that, in fact, service usage does have a predictable fit with certain patient characteristics.

These studies suggest that categorization of the elderly based on analysis of functional status can be useful for estimating prognosis in case management, program planning, and allocation of scarce and expensive resources. Resources should be allocated where the need is greatest and the results are likely to be most effective instead of assignment using a less discriminate approach.

Establishing a prognosis through functional assessment is not merely to confirm a self-fulfilling prophecy, but through appropriate intervention the outcome may be improved from what might have been otherwise expected. The functional assessment categorization allows the physician and members of the health care team to direct the patient toward rehabilitation treatment and social support systems in a more systematic and effective manner than is possible from knowing only the diagnosis and related treatments.

CONCLUSION

Although the treatment model of rehabilitation is important, the teaching model of rehabilitation is necessary for enduring benefit. Despite advanced years and fixed organic impairments, many eldery patients can benefit from an appropriately designed and applied medical rehabilitation program, provided that the patient is behaviorally flexible and that conditions are conducive to effecting and maintaining behavioral change.

Although rehabilitation is expensive, it is often the most cost-effective method for reducing the burden of care that results from disability. Rehabilitation is a necessary part of social policy if we are to maintain as many elderly as possible at home with family members or within appropriate community settings in preference to custodial institutional placement.

It is important to keep in mind that if a person experiencing disability does not use residual abilities and skills, these tend to become lost—in other words, "Use it or lose it."

REFERENCES

Birkhead, N. C., Haupt, G. J. Issekutz, B., et al. (1964). Circulatory and metabolic effects of different types of prolonged inactivity. *American Journal of Medical Science, 247,* 243.

Bortz, W. (1980). Effects of exercise on aging—effect of aging on exercise. *Journal of the American Geriatrics Society, 28,* 49–51.

Bortz, W. M. (1982). Disuse and aging. *Journal of the American Medical Association, 248,* 1203–1208.

Costa, P. T., & McCrae, R. R. (1980). Functional age: A conceptual and empirical critique. In S. G. Haynes & M. Feinleib, (Eds.), *Second Conference on the Epidemiology of Aging* (NIH Publication No. 80-969) (pp. 23–50). Washington, DC: U.S. Department of Health and Human Services.

Dehn, M. M., & Bruce, R. A. (1972). Longitudinal variations in maximal oxygen uptake with age and activity. *Journal of Applied Physiology, 33,* 805–807.

Department of Elderly Affairs, State of Rhode Island. (1982). *Family and community support systems (final report)* (AOA Grant No. 01-AM-00009).

DeVries, H. (1978). Physiologic effects of an exercise training regimen upon aged men aged 52–88. *Journal of Gerontology, 25,* 325–336.

Fries, J. F., & Crapo, L. M. (1981). *Vitality and aging.* San Francisco: W. H. Freeman.

Granger, C. V., & Gresham, G. E. (Eds.). (1984). *Functional assessment in rehabilitation medicine.* Baltimore: Williams and Wilkins.

Hodgson, J. (1971). *Age and aerobic capacity of urban midwestern males.* Unpublished master's thesis, University of Minnesota, Minneapolis.

Kane, R. A., & Kane, R. L. (1981). *Assessing the elderly: A practical guide to measurement.* Lexington, MA: D. C. Heath.

Lakatta, E. (1979). Alterations in the cardiovascular system that occur in advanced age. *Federation Proceedings, 38,* 163–167.

Langer, E. J. & Rodin, J. (1976). The effects of choice and enhanced personal responsibility for the aged: A field experiment in an institutional setting. *Journal of Personality and Social Psychology, 34,* 191–198.

Langer, E. J., et al. (1979). Environmental determinants of memory improvement in late adulthood. *Journal of Personality and Social Psychology, 37,* 2003–2013.

Nesselroade, J. F., Schaie, K. W., & Baltes, P. B. (1972). Ontogenetic and generational components of structural and quantitative change in adult behavior. *Journal of Gerontology, 27,* 222–228.

Plemons, J. K., Willis, S. L., & Baltes, P. B. (1978). Modifiability of fluid intelligence in aging: A short-term longitudinal training approach. *Journal of Gerontology, 33,* 224–231.

Pollock, M. L., Miller, H. S., & Wilmore, J. (1974). Physiological characteristics of champion American track athletes 40 to 75 years of age. *Journal of Gerontology, 29,* 645–649.

Robinson, S. (1938). Experimental studies of physical fitness in relation to age. *Arbeitsphysiologie, 4,* 251–323.

Saltin, B., Blomquist, G., Mitchell, J., et al. (1968). Response to exercise after bedrest and after training: A longitudinal study of adaptive changes in oxygen transport and composition. *Circulation, 38* (Suppl 7), 1–78.

Seltzer, G. B., Granger, C. V., & Wineberg, D. (1982). Functional assessment: Bridge between family and rehabilitation medicine within an ambulatory practice. *Archives of Physical Medicine and Rehabilitation, 63,* 453–457.

Shock, N. W. (1960). Discussion on mortality and measurement in aging. In B. L. Strehter, S. D. Ebert, H. R. Glass, & N. Shock, (Eds.), *The biology of aging: A symposium* (pp. 22–23). American Institute of Biological Sciences.

Spence, A. M. (1982). *An analysis of service usage by patient characteristics.* Unpublished master's thesis, University of Rhode Island, Kingston, RI.

Spirduso, W. W. (1975). Reaction and movement time as a function of age and physical activity level. *Journal of Gerontology, 30,* 435–440.

Spirduso, W. W. (1980). Physical fitness, aging and psychomotor speed: A review. *Journal of Gerontology, 35,* 850–865.

Spirduso, W. W., & Clifford, P. (1978). Replication of age and physical activity effects on reaction and movement time. *Journal of Gerontology, 33,* 26–30.

World Health Organization. (1980). *International classification of impairments, disabilities, and handicaps (ICIDH).* Geneva: World Health Organization.

5

Characteristics of the Disabled Elderly and Implications for Rehabilitation

John P. Fulton and Sidney Katz

Although the elderly have benefited from the growth of physical medicine and rehabilitation (PM&R) in this century, they have felt the benefits somewhat later and less strongly than younger people. It took a while for PM&R to move from military to civilian hospitals, where the elderly are found in greater numbers (Kottke, Stillwell, & Lehmann, 1982). Because rehabilitation is costly, it has tended to be concentrated on the young who are most likely to repay the cost to society through salvaged gainful employment. Certainly, this theme has been an important stimulus for the financial support of PM&R (Licht & Kamenetz, 1968; Rusk, 1977; Kottke et al., 1982). Furthermore, as Gullickson and Licht (1968) have asserted, traditional rehabilitation "is hard work for the patient and for the medical team." Thus, primary care physicians may have been disinclined to seek rehabilitation for all but their most robust elderly patients. However, attitudes toward the elderly are changing in this country. Medicine is paying more attention to the management of the chronically ill patient. Advances in the rehabilitation of cardiac and cancer patients in recent years (Rusk 1977), in addition to the revolution in the rehabilitation of hemiplegics since the 1950's, demonstrate an increasing emphasis on problems of the elderly, an emphasis that is likely to grow.

Although PM&R is admittedly difficult to define, Hirschberg has described its essence as "the restoration of the function of the individual in his environment in society" (cited in Gullickson & Licht, 1968). If PM&R is to take a more assertive role in the care of the disabled elderly, it must know about their potential for function, their current level of function, and the environment in which they function. We will address these issues by drawing heavily upon three sources, The Massachusetts Health Care Panel Study (Branch, Katz, Kniepmann, & Papsidero, 1984), the National Nursing Home Survey (NCHS, 1979), and the National Health Survey (NCHS, 1977). We will look at life expectancy of the disabled elderly to assess the limits of rehabilitation. We will estimate the proportions of elders who are independent in six activities of daily living and those who are not, and where they reside, in the community or a nursing home. We will look at the living arrangements of those who reside in the community with limitation of activity and those who reside in the community with no limitation of activity. We will assess the importance of prevalent chronic conditions as causes of activity limitation and potentially of institutionalization. Finally, we will discuss the implications of data for PM&R.

METHOD

Estimates of life expectancy and active life expectancy, by age, for Massachusetts, 1974, were taken from Katz et al. (1983) (Table 5-1). Dependent life expectancy by age was computed by subtracting active life expectancy from life expectancy. Although dependent life expectancy, by age, was not reported by these researchers, they used the concept in the interpretation of their results. For example, they estimated "the percentage of independent years in the total remaining years of life," and compared "the estimated duration of dependency" for the two sexes. Life expectancy for Massachusetts, 1974, was computed using standard techniques for the construction of abridged life tables. Active life expectancy was similarly computed, except that the life table cohort, 1_x, was diminished whenever one of its members died, lost independence in one of four activities of daily living (bathing, dressing, transferring, and eating), or was institutionalized in a nursing home.

Table 5-2, "Estimated proportions of the elderly who live in the community and nursing homes, by dependency status and age, United States, 1980" was constructed using four sources of data. The population of the United States by age in 1980 was taken from the 1980 United States Census of Population (Census Bureau, 1981). The population in each age group was split into those who live in the community and those who live in nursing homes, using age-specific data from the National Nursing Home Survey (NCHS, 1979). Then the population residing in the community was split into independent and dependent groups, by age, using age-specific data from the Massachusetts Health Care Panel Study (Branch et al., 1984).

Table 5-1 Life Expectancy in Years, Active Life Expectancy in Years, and Dependent Life Expectancy in Years, Massachusetts, 1974, by Age[a]

Age Group	Life Expectancy	Active Life Expectancy	Dependent Life Expectancy	Age Begin Dependency	Age End Dependency
65–69	16.5	10.0	6.5	75.0	81.5
70–74	14.1	8.1	6.0	78.1	84.1
75–79	11.6	6.8	4.8	81.8	86.6
80–84	8.9	4.7	4.2	84.7	88.9
85+	7.3	2.9	4.4	87.9	92.3

[a]From Katz et al. (1983).

"Independent" was defined as being independent in six activities of daily living, including bathing, dressing, transferring, eating, personal grooming, and walking across a small room. "Dependent" was defined as being dependent on the assistance of another person for at least one of these activities of daily living. Finally, the population residing in nursing homes was split into independent and dependent groups, by age, using age-specific data from the National Nursing Home Survey. For these data, "independent" was defined as being independent in six activities of daily living, including bathing, dressing, using the toilet, walking, continence, and eating. "Dependent" was defined as being dependent on special equipment or the assistance of another person for at least one of these activities of daily living.

Table 5-2 Estimated Proportions of the Elderly Who Live in the Community and Nursing Homes, by Dependency Status and Age, United States, 1980

Age Group	Live in Community		Live in Nursing Homes	
	Independent	Dependent	Independent	Dependent
65–74	0.878	0.108	0.002	0.012
75–84	0.746	0.186	0.005	0.063
85+	0.447	0.337	0.009	0.207
Total	0.800	0.151	0.004	0.045

Proportion of population by age, United States, 1980, from U.S. Bureau of the Census, 1981.

Proportion of population residing in nursing homes, United States, 1977, by age, from U.S. National Center for Health Statistics, 1979.

Of the population residing in the community, proportions independent and dependent, Massachusetts, 1974, by age, from Branch, Katz, Kneipmann, and Papsidero, 1984.

Of the population residing in nursing homes, proportions independent and dependent, United States, 1977, by age, from U.S. National Center for Health Statistics, 1979.

The data in Table 5-3 were taken from a report of the National Health Survey, United States, 1974 (NCHS, 1977). They refer to the non-institutionalized population of the United States, age 65 years and over. "Major activity refers to ability to work, keep house, or engage in school or preschool activities" (NCHS, 1977).

The data in Table 5-4 for the noninstitutionalized elderly were generated by the National Health Survey, United States, 1979 (Metropolitan Life Foundation, 1982). The figure for mental conditions, 0.034, was taken from a report of the National Health Survey, United States, 1974. The data in Table 5-4 for people living in nursing homes were taken from a report of the National Nursing Home Survey: 1977 Summary of the United States. "The primary diagnosis at last examination was the one condition reported by the nursing staff respondent as the major diagnosis noted at the resident's latest medical examination" (NCHS, 1979). Although these data were were not published by age, data from the same source indicate that those age 65 years and over represented 86.4% of the persons residing in nursing homes in the United States in 1977.

RESULTS

Life expectancy in Massachusetts, 1974 (Table 5-1), decreases 56%, from 16.5 years for elders age 65 to 69 to 7.3 years for elders age 85 and over. Active life expectancy decreases 71% from 10.0 years for elders age 65 to 69 to

Table 5-3 Proportions of the Noninstitutionalized Elderly (Ages 65+) Who Live in Different Community Settings, by Dependency Status, United States, 1974

Community Setting	Total Population	With No Limitation of Activity	Limited, But Not in Major Activity	Limited in Amount or Kind of Major Activity	Unable to Carry on Major Activity
W/Spouse[a]	0.532	0.554	0.448	0.463	0.584
Lives Alone	0.279	0.283	0.393	0.330	0.157
W/Oth Relat[b]	0.169	0.146	0.147	0.186	0.224
W/Non-Relat[c]	0.020	0.017	0.012	0.020	0.035
Total	1.000	1.000	1.000	1.000	1.000
All	1.000	0.542	0.066	0.221	0.171

From U.S. National Center for Health Statistics, 1977.
[a]Lives with spouse.
[b]Lives with relative(s) other than spouse.
[c]Lives with non-relative(s).

Table 5-4 Proportions of the Noninstitutionalized Elderly (Ages 65+) with Some Limitation of Activity, by Chronic Condition Causing Limitation and Degree of Limitation, United States, 1979 and Proportions of People Living in Nursing Homes by Primary Diagnosis at Last Examination, United States, 1977

| Chronic Condition or Primary Diagnosis | *Noninstitutionalized* | | Living in Nursing Homes |
	Any Limitation	Unable to Carry on Major Activity	
Arthritis, Rheumatism	0.253	0.077	0.043
Heart Conditions	0.239	0.102	0.058
Hypertension[a]	0.122	0.038	0.037
Diabetes	0.063	0.027	0.055
Mental Conditions[b]	0.034[c]	—	0.204

1979 data for the noninstitutionalized elderly from Metropolitan Life Foundation, 1982.
1977 data for people living in nursing homes from U.S. National Center for Health Statistics, 1979.
[a]Hypertension without heart involvement.
[b]"Mental and nervous conditions" for the noninstitutionalized elderly; "mental disorders and senility without psychosis" for people living in nursing homes.
[c]From U.S. National Center for Health Statistics, 1977.

2.9 years for elders age 85 and over. In contrast, dependent life expectancy is quite stable, decreasing 32% from 6.5 years for elders age 65 to 69 to 4.4 years for elders age 85 and over. Dependent life expectancy differs very little among the three age groups, 75 to 79, 80 to 84, and 85+—hovering between 4.2 and 4.8 years. This is more striking when one observes that the average age at which dependency begins is higher for each subsequent age group. For example, independent 75 to 79-year-olds have a dependent life expectancy of 4.8 years. For them, on average, dependency begins at approximately age 82. In contrast, independent 85+-year-olds have a not dissimilar dependent life expectancy of 4.4 years but on average become dependent at age 88.

It is estimated that 80% of all elders live independently in the community (Table 5-2). Although this percentage decreases with age, about 45% of those age 85 and over still live independently in the community. An estimated one-tenth of elders age 65 to 74 live in the community dependent upon others, whereas an estimated one-third of elders age 85 and older live in the community dependent upon others. The percentage of elders who live in nursing homes increases from 1.4% for those age 65 to 74 to 21.6% for those age 85 and over. Very few elders who are independent in six activities of daily living reside in nursing homes, but this percentage also increases with age, from 0.2% of all elders age 65 to 74 to 0.9% of all elders age 85 and over.

About one-half of the noninstitutionalized elderly live with spouses (Table 5-3). Slightly in excess of one-fourth live alone. About 17% live with relatives other than spouses. Only 2% live with nonrelatives. The proportions are roughly the same for those 54.2% of the noninstitutionalized elderly who have experienced no limitation of activity. However, for those elderly who have experienced at least some limitation of activity, living arrangements vary with the extent of limitation. As limitation increases, the percentage of elders who live alone decreases from 39.3% of those who are limited, but not in major activity, to 15.7% of those who are unable to carry on major activity. In contrast, the percentage of elders who live with others increases, regardless of type, as limitation increases: with spouses, from 44.8% to 58.4%; with relatives other than spouses, from 14.7% to 22.4%; even with nonrelatives, from 1.2% to 3.5%.

Among the noninstitutionalized elderly who have experienced some limitation of activity, approximately one-fourth have been limited in some way by rheumatic disorders and another one-fourth by heart conditions. (Table 5-4). Hypertension without heart involvement seems to limit approximately 12%; diabetes, approximately 6%; and mental conditions, approximately 3%. Approximately the same order of importance among causes exists for those noninstitutionalized elderly who are unable to carry on major activity.

Among all people living in nursing homes, of whom the elderly represented 86.4% in 1977, approximately one-fifth have primary diagnoses that are categorized as mental disorders or senility without psychosis. When mental retardation is excluded from this category, it still accounts for 17.2% of all primary diagnoses. The importance of each of the other four categories is considerably less, accounting for 3.7% to 5.8% of all primary diagnoses.

DISCUSSION

Potential for Function

Dependent life expectancy appears to be relatively stable across age groups. In the aggregate, loss of independence in bathing, dressing, transferring, or eating appears to be a better indicator of the extent of physiological aging than chronological age. Once independence is lost, the length of life may vary within considerably tighter bounds than before it is lost.

We do not know the extent to which the loss of function that occurs close to the end of life is reversible. Katz, et al. (1983) observed that the probability of restoring function diminishes with age in a sample of Massachusetts elders. We do not know the extent to which loss of function in this group is related to deconditioning or depression, both of which have been found to be reversible in some cases. The same is true about data from previous studies. Nonetheless, until it is demonstrated that rehabilitation is effective in restoring lost function to a meaningful proportion of the disabled elderly, we may conservatively infer from the Massachusetts data that rehabilitation of the disabled elderly should begin by emphasizing the maintenance of existing function and the compensation of lost function.

Current Level of Function

Clearly, a vast majority of the elderly are functionally independent. However, the proportion of elders who are functionally independent diminishes steadily with age. In the aggregate, function appears to be lost more rapidly after the age of 75 than before, although the available data are insufficiently precise to say much more. We need data that measure level of function more precisely within smaller age groupings of the elderly population. It would be especially interesting to observe whether function in elderly is lost as hierarchically as it is gained among recovering disabled patients (Katz & Akpom, 1976) and at what rate function is lost at particular levels of the hierarchy. Nonetheless, it is clear that if PM&R is to take a more assertive role in the care of the handicapped elderly, it must do so with elders of advanced age. Sixty-three percent of the disabled elderly are age 75 years and older.

The Environment in Which the Disabled Elderly Function

Most of the disabled elderly reside in the community, like elders who have not lost function. Shanas (1979a) reports very similar findings for a national sample of the noninstitutionalized elderly. Of disabled elders who live in the community, a substantial majority reside in their own homes, either with spouses or alone, across levels of disability. However, as disability increases, the proportion of disabled elders who live with others, either with spouses in their own homes or in the homes of relatives other than spouses, increases. Also, with advancing age the proportion of handicapped elders who reside in nursing homes increases. In short, one may infer from the data that while living in one's own home is desirable, even when disabled, the force of disability necessitates movement toward greater dependence, first on family, rarely on nonrelatives, and, last for some, on the formal care provided in nursing homes. These findings are supported by a large body of literature on the relationship between the handicapped elderly and their families.

Despite the passage of time, values concerning the care of the handicapped elderly by family members do not seem to have changed (E. Brody, Johnsen, Fulcomer, & Lang, 1983). Most handicapped elderly with family receive strong social support (Shanas, 1979a). Spouses are definitely the first line of support; in the absence of spouses, daughters provide the strongest social support to the disabled elderly (Stoller & Earl, 1983). Disabled elders with family are less likely to be institutionalized than disabled elders without family (Barney, 1977; Branch & Jette, 1982; Branch et al., 1984).

When sufficient family resources exist, there tends to be a progression of dependency, from independence in the elder's own home to dependence in the elder's own home, then to dependence in a relative's home, and finally, to dependence in a nursing home. Obviously, all elders do not necessarily experience this progression in full. Some have no family to care for them. Others have the resources to be cared for in their own homes, even if severely disabled. Furthermore, the elderly die in all of these settings and at all levels of ability to function. However, this progression of dependency appears to have substance in the aggregate, and between 25% and 50% of the elderly may spend some time in a nursing home before they die (Kastenbaum & Candy, 1973; Palmore, 1976; Vicente, Wiley, & Carrington, 1982).

Certain disabilities appear to exhaust family resources sooner than others. Mental conditions cause activity limitation in less than 5% of noninstitutionalized elders who have experienced at least some degree of activity limitation. At the same time, slightly in excess of 20% of people living in nursing homes (86.4% of whom are elderly) have a primary diagnosis that may be categorized as a mental disorder or senility without psychosis. *(However, it is likely that 20% grossly underrepresents the true proportion of elders who have been institutionalized in nursing homes because of mental disorders or senility without psychosis. Federal reimbursement rules encourage providers to list other diagnoses as primary.)*

Arthritic and heart conditions appear to cause substantial disability among noninstitutionalized elders but do not have a prominent place among the primary diagnoses of nursing home residents. This suggests that while family members may expend considerable energy on elders who have been disabled by arthritic or heart conditions, they may have substantially less tolerance for mental disabilities. The literature supports this inference (Branch & Jette, 1982; Deimling & Poulshock, 1984; Robinson, 1983; Smyer, 1982; Zarit, Reever, & Bach-Peterson, 1980; Zimmer, Watson, & Treat, 1984), and suggests an explanation for it, beyond the obvious need to supervise those with mental disabilities more than others.

Kivett and Learner (1980) state, "The ability to develop and maintain strong supports in the later years is positively related to the concept of reciprocal exchange." In short, even the most dedicated caregiver needs some reward for caregiving (Mindel & Wright, 1982). Perhaps the greatest reward a caregiver may receive is emotional support from the person to whom care is given. Shanas (1979b) quotes Talcott Parsons, "The family can be seen to have two primary functions, not one. On the one hand it is the primary agent of socialization for the child, while on the other it is the primary basis of security for the normal adult." This security is a two-way street between generations. Not only do elders derive security from their children; children may derive considerable security from their elderly parents. For example, Bankoff (1983) has demonstrated that recent widows derive considerable and irreplaceable support from aged parents. Robinson (1983) has demonstrated that caregiver strain is related inversely "with the understanding of their own problems by the expatient." In short, elders who are mentally disabled may be less able to reciprocate for care received with understanding and gratitude.

Unfortunately, even though the provision of care to elders may strain family resources, there is a tendency for the family to avoid formal support from outside agencies, such as homemaker services (McAuley & Arling, 1984). Some have suggested that such services are avoided because they symbolize a loss of societal status (Shanas, 1979a) or power (Stoller, 1984). Others have suggested that formal services are avoided because people do not perceive the need for them (Barney, 1977), or because people tend to persist in old behavioral patterns with regard to health care, despite increasing need (Coulton & Frost, 1982). Of course, in many cases the elderly and their families may be unable to pay for formal support in the home. Furthermore, formal home support tends to be fragmented, and therefore difficult to manage (consider S. Brody et al., 1978; McNally, 1983).

Institutionalization occurs when the family is no longer able or willing to care for the handicapped elder in the community (Mindel, 1979). However, because of the inherent strength of the American family (Shanas, 1979a), relatively few elders who reside in nursing homes have considerable physical and mental function. As Smyer (1982) put it, "the history of greater previous service use suggests that the institutionalized clients and their families had been coping with the problems of impairment for some time. The institution seems to be the option of last resort."

The challenge herein for PM&R is to help the elderly and their families manage an orderly progression of compensatory care, avoiding discontinuities and crises. Obviously, PM&R must consider ways of working smoothly with family caregivers. The family may need considerable training and counsel to meet their own objectives for care of elderly dependents. The PM&R provider must know when to suggest the use of formal services, including the nursing home. The provider may have to work hard to make formal home support more comprehensible and palatable to the family, if indeed it is affordable. Most importantly, PM&R providers must use the principle of reciprocity creatively. They must work to maintain that function in the handicapped elder that allows the elder to perform a useful role in the family. Mental function appears to be most important in this regard, but other functions are important as well. In short, the PM&R provider must care not only for the elderly client but for the client's family as well.

REFERENCES

Bankoff, E. A. (1983). Aged parents and their widowed daughters: A support relationship. *Journal of Gerontology, 38,* 226–230.

Barney, J. L. (1977). The prerogative of choice in long-term care. *Gerontologist, 17,* 309–314.

Branch, L. G., Katz, S., Kniepmann, K., & Papsidero, J. A. (1984). A prospective stitutionalization among the aged. *American Journal of Public Health, 72,* 1373–1379.

Branch, L. G., Katz, S., Kniepmann, K.,& Papsidero, J. A. (1984). A prospective study of functional status among community elders. *American Journal of Public Health, 74,* 266–268.

Brody, E. M., Johnsen, P. T., Fulcomer, M. C., & Lang, A. M. (1983). Women's changing roles and help to elderly parents: Attitudes of three generations of women. *Journal of Gerontology, 38,* 597–607.

Brody, S. J., Poulshock, S. W., & Masciocchi, C. F. (1978). The family caring unit: A major consideration in the long-term support system. *Gerontologist, 18,* 556–561.

Bureau of the Census. (1981). Age, sex, race, and Spanish origin of the population by regions, divisions, and states: 1980. *1980 Census of Population,* (Supplementary Reports, DOC PC 80-S1-1). Washington, DC: Government Printing Office.

Coulton, C., & Frost, A. K. (1982). Use of social and health services by the elderly. *Journal of Health and Social Behavior, 23* (12), 330–339.

Gullickson, G., Jr., & Licht, S. (1968). Definition and philosophy of rehabilitation medicine. In S. Licht & H. L. Kamenetz, (Eds.), *Rehabilitation and Medicine* (pp. 1–14). Baltimore: Waverly Press.

Kastenbaum, R., & Candy, S. (1973). The four percent fallacy. *Journal of Aging and Human Development, 4,* 15–21.

Katz, S., & Akpom, C. A. (1976). A measure of primary sociobiological functions. *Int. J. Health Ser, 6,* 493–507.

Katz, S., Branch, L. G., Branson, M. H., Papsidero, J. A., Beck, J. C., & Greer, D. S. (1983). Active life expectancy. *New England Journal of Medicine, 309,* 1218–1224.

Kivett, V. R., & Learner, R. M. (1980). Perspectives on the childless rural elderly: A comparative analysis. *Gerontologist, 20,* 708–716.

Kottke, F. J., Stillwell, G. K., & Lehmann, J. F. (1982). *Krusen's handbook of physical medicine and rehabilitation.* Philadelphia: W. B. Saunders.

Licht, S., & Kamenetz, H. L. (Eds.). (1968). *Rehabilitation and medicine*. Baltimore: Waverly Press.

McAuley, W. J., & Arling, G. (1984). Use of in-home care by very old people. *Journal of Health and Social Behavior, 25* (3), 54–64.

McNally, L. (1983, May–June). Long-term care services—the unfinished agenda. *Aging*, pp. 30–36.

Metropolitan Life Foundation. (1982). Health of the elderly. *Statistical Bulletin, 63*, 1–15.

Mindel, C. H. (1979). Multigenerational family households: Recent trends and implications for the future. *Gerontologist, 19*, 456–463.

Mindel, C. H., & Wright, R. Jr. (1982). Satisfaction in multigenerational households. *Journal of Gerontology, 37*, 483–489.

National Center for Health Statistics. (1977). National health survey: Limitation of activity due to chronic conditions, United States, 1974. *Vital and health statistics*, Series 10 No. 111. (DHEW Publication No. HRA 77-1537). Rockville, MD: Author.

National Center for Health Statistics. (1979). The national nursing home survey: 1977 summary for the United States. *Vital and health statistics*, Series 13, No. 43. (DHEW Publication No. PHS 79-1794). Hyattsville, MD: Author.

Palmore, E. (1976). Total chance of institutionalization among the aged. *Gerontologist, 16*, 504–507.

Poulshock, S. W., & Deimling, G. T. (1984). Families caring for elders in residence: Issues in the measurement of burden. *Journal of Gerontology, 39*, 230–239.

Robinson, B. C. (1983). Validation of a caregiver strain index. *Journal of Gerontology, 38*, 344–348.

Rusk, H. A. (1977). The philosophy and need of rehabilitation. In H. A. Rusk (Ed.), *Rehabilitation medicine* (pp. 1–3). St. Louis: C. V. Mosby.

Shanas, E. (1979a). The family as a social support system in old age. *Gerontologist, 19*, 169–174.

Shanas, E. (1979b). Social myth as hypothesis: The case of the family relations of old people. *Gerontologist, 19*, 3–9.

Smyer, M. A. (1982). The differential usage of services by the impaired elderly. In S. S. Tobin (Ed.), *Current gerontology: Long-term care* (pp. 13–19). Washington, DC: Gerontological Society of America.

Stoller, E. P., & Earl, L. L. (1983). Help with activities of everyday life: Sources of support for the noninstitutionalized elderly. *Gerontologist, 23*, 64–70.

Vincente, L., Wiley, J. A., & Carrington, R. A. (1982). The risk of institutionalization support for the noninstitutionalized elderly. *Gerontologist, 23*, 64–70.

Vincente, L., Wiley, J. A. & Carrington, R. A. (1982). The risk of institutionalization before death. In S. S. Tobin, (Ed.), *Current gerontology: Long-term care*, (pp. 5–11). Washington, DC: Gerontological Society of America.

Zarit, S. H., Reever, K. E., & Bach-Peterson, J. (1980). Relatives of the impaired elderly: Correlates of feelings of burden. *Gerontologist, 20*, 649–655.

Zimmer, J. G., Watson, N., & Treat, A. (1984). Behavioral problems among patients in skilled nursing facilities. *American Journal of Public Health, 74*, 1118–1121.

6

Public Health Aspects of Rehabilitation of the Aged

Faye G. Abdellah

The health status of elderly individuals has assumed a role of major importance for all health professions. Longer life expectancy and an increase in the proportion of older people in the population have brought their health problems to the forefront. Advances in the study of both medicine and aging have emphasized the fact that the elderly have special health needs. In addition, politicians and consumers alike agree that health is a basic human right.

The aging of our society is at once an indisputable triumph of medicine and public health and a demographic time bomb capable of severely altering the financing and delivery of health care. The numbers are well known and have been presented in other chapters.

The rapid growth of the elderly population in America has in some ways paralleled the growth of the rehabilitation field. Although they have been separate, both increases have occurred since the first of the century and both have been dramatic.

Chronological age in and of itself can be a factor that causes a person not to meet the criterion of eligibility for rehabilitation services. One need only review the literature on attitudes toward disabled persons to find that older people have been neglected by rehabilitation professionals. Certainly this raises several questions. Why have rehabilitation specialists, including health professionals, neglected older people in research, teaching, and practice? Has the rehabilitation profession widely internalized negative general stereotypes of older people? Does the preoccupation of the professional with vocational services and the cost–benefit orientation toward client selection conveniently eliminate older persons from the rehabilitation case load? Does the profession hold the view that older disabled persons cannot be helped? It is appropriate for all health professionals to examine their attitudes and values toward older people in general and those with disabilities in particular.

Dr. Williams (1984) has pointed out that "rehabilitation is an approach, a philosophy, and a point of view as much as it is a set of techniques"(viii). The aim of rehabilitation, "to restore an individual to his or her former functional and environmental status, or alternatively, to maintain or maximize remaining function, should be at the heart of all care of aging persons in order to help them continue to live as full a life as possible."

To identify mental and social well-being as contributory to the state of health was a significant and far-reaching concept 25 years ago, and a concept that society as a whole continues to have difficulty in justifying, especially from a cost–benefit point of view. The segment of society directly involved, those in the over-65 age group, have less difficulty in accepting this definition.

In the twentieth century, a number of social forces have worked in various ways to create the situation in which society in general, and the elderly in particular, now find themselves. It is interesting that the United States is not alone in facing this dilemma. Other highly industrialized nations have come to realize that they need to put forth a greater effort in solving the problems related to the elderly. There are driving factors and forces that we need to consider, such as the increasingly mobile population, the demise of multigeneration families living as a single unit, the economics of an industrial nation, the cost of health care, the cost of institutional care, and the general cost of living including food and property taxes, as well as the infirm family members. Concurrently, these same forces and the general worship of a youth culture have diverted society's attention from the elderly.

Today's older people are in far better health than commonly thought. Many assume, including health professionals, that a high percentage of the elderly are institutionalized. Actually only 5% are in institutions, and most of those are the very elderly. The median age of nursing home residents is 81.0 years. Seventy-three percent of the noninstitutionalized older population report that functional impairments do not interfere seriously with major activities of daily living. Older people with impairments confront multiple rejection. Their disabilities form the basis on which broader negative attitudes and social stereotypes toward older people are compounded. The fact that the majority of the elderly live independently has significant consequences in their health care and the prevention of disabilities.

It is recognized that during the aging process,whether or not it is accompanied by illness, there is an increasing movement away from the inter-

dependent state to the independent state, and possibly to one of dependence. This occurs because more physical and emotional effort is required
to maintain one's independence. Sustaining independence and interdependence among elderly people requires a high level of caring from others in
their environment, particularly from health professionals. They have a responsibility to assist those in their care to return to independence and inter-
dependence and to maintain as high a level of function as possible for as
long as possible.

MEDICAL ISSUES IN REHABILITATION OF OLDER PERSONS

The changes associated with aging are gradual in onset. Most older persons
either consciously or unconsciously adapt to them and have little or no
need for external assistance. However, many older individuals do need
some type of help. They fall into two categories. First are those persons who
live normal, healthy lives until the physical decrements of aging combine
to create disabilities. Second are those persons who become disabled prior
to middle or old age and whose existing disabilities are complicated by the
losses associated with age.

In general, older people get sick more often than younger persons. They
tend to have more chronic illnesses, and typically have a multiplicity of
chronic and incurable problems that must be treated simultaneously. The
5% of older persons who are institutionalized, plus approximately 15%
who are not, have mobility limitations that largely restrict them. A paper
prepared for the White House Conference on Handicapped Individuals estimated that 35% of aged individuals have physical handicaps.

The major impairments reported by older persons living in noninstitutional settings are as follows: arthritis (44.3%), hypertension
(38.5%), hearing impairments (28.2%), heart disease (27.4%), arterio-
sclerosis (12.0%), visual impairment (11.9%), and diabetes (8.0%).

Heart disease, stroke, and cancer account for three-fourths of all deaths
and are also major contributors to disability. Multiple pathology and
simultaneous multiple treatments are the norm in medical management of
older persons. Accurate assessment is essential.

MENTAL ILLNESS

Though only 12% of the population is elderly, mental health needs are dis-
proportionately large. Mental illness increases in incidence with age. Depression and organic mental disorders are widespread among older persons and available treatment is limited.

Between 25% and 65% of all older persons suffer from depression or some other potentially treatable mental disorder. Older persons comprise approximately 25% of those needing mental health care. They account for 16% of all suicides, with older white males with chronic illness having the highest rates. Only 2% to 4% of persons seen in outpatient mental health clinics are elderly. More than 60% of older persons admitted to mental hospitals received no psychiatric care prior to admission. More than 50% of elderly nursing home residents have a diagnosis of dementia or some other potentially treatable form of mental illness (RSA, 1980).

THE MEANING OF REHABILITATION

Maintaining a high level of function and at the same time fostering a dimension of caring are the crux of rehabilitation. Rehabilitation may be thought of as a process involving the concepts of prevention, maintenance, restoration, learning, and resettlement. Thus, the goal of rehabilitation is for the individual to achieve his/her maximum fulfillment, assuring the greatest personal, social, and economic usefulness, and the greatest independence.

Prevention in the rehabilitative process discourages the occurrence of complications that will interfere with the individual's maximum fulfillment. Complications are largely the result of disuse or disability due to inactivity, and misuse or disability caused by contraindicated activity.

Maintenance in rehabilitation is the maintenance of the functional abilities of the person—physical, emotional, and social—that are necessary for the individual to perform at his/her maximum potential. Health professionals often find it faster and easier for the staff to care for the patient; however, this only reinforces a pattern of dependence. It is the independent pattern that needs continuous reinforcement.

Restoration, another component of the rehabilitation process, is the return of the person to his/her former state of well-being or to an adequate adaptation within the life pattern. The loss of function may be isolated to one organ such as an eye, or ear, or may involve the whole organism. When related to the process of aging, similar losses of function usually occur gradually, are more permanent in nature, and follow an established course.

Learning to live with existing disabilities is an extremely important aspect of rehabilitation for both the individual and his/her family. It is important to minimize the handicapping aspects of the disabilities and to emphasize the abilities or assets. Because the emphasis should be a positive one, the term abilities is used, rather than disabilities. The task of the health professional is to help the individual understand the problem so that he/

she will be able to move towards solving problems in a more independent fashion.

Resettlement is the process of assisting the individual to adapt successfully to changes in his/her socioeconomic environment.

PHILOSOPHY OF REHABILITATION

The philosophy of rehabilitation can be applied to the older person who has no specific illness, to the individual who has a single illness, or to the one who has multiple disabilities. Most important, the rehabilitation process is each individual's rehabilitation—a personal task. Health professionals can only assist the individual and his/her family in solving their problems. It is the patient and his/her family who must make the adjustment.

Cardinal principles in the application of the philosophy of rehabilitation are as follows: (a) rehabilitation is constant adjustment to disabilities; (b) it is a slow process; (c) it requires a team approach; and (d) it requires use of available facilities and resources for promotion of maximum health and welfare of the individual and his family (Long, 1972, p. 6).

An underlying issue is whether by increasing life expectancy, we also improve health status and the quality of life (Brody, 1984, pp. 468–475). Data from the National Health Interview Survey, conducted annually since 1957 by the National Center for Health Statistics, found a disturbing general rise in recent years in morbidity and disability among persons of all age groups, but particularly those in middle life. Thus, it seems that while life expectancy increases, disabilities are also increasing.

MORBIDITY

Systematic data on morbidity and disability are limited, presenting a serious problem for formulation of health policy in relation to rehabilitation. Morbidity data are available from such efforts undertaken by the National Heart, Lung and Blood Institute's Framingham Heart Study; the National Cancer Institute's Surveillance, Epidemiology, and End Results (SEER) program; the morbidity reporting system of the Centers for Disease Control; and the National Institute on Aging's three established populations for epidemiologic studies of the elderly. These studies are recognized as being most valuable, but they do not provide the national coverage or the comprehensive scope of illness and disabilities necessary to admit the termination of relationship among disease, disabilities, health status, and age.

RECOMMENDATIONS FOR IMPROVED DATA[1]

1. It is a known fact that people are living longer. Morbidity and disability increase steadily with age, and there are no generally accepted data that show whether age-specific prevalence of these conditions is decreasing or increasing. Quality of life and health costs are largely a function of these parameters. It is suggested that the policymaker needs to have more accurate and useful information. Survey information and other health indicators do not indicate health status. It is possible that practical measurement tools already exist or could be developed. A costly but necessary study is the medical and social validation and interpretation of health survey and health indicator data. Particularly urgent and needed would be data regarding the health status of the population age 65 and older because it has been pointed out that during the next 50 years the size of this population will more than double.

2. Computer technology is making medical information concerning individual patients more available to health professionals. Brody (1984) also points out that the patient rarely knows what conditions he/she has had in the past or which tests were performed or their results. He states that "As a society we must weigh the issues of the right to privacy against the risks and cost to the patient, the doctor, and Medicare and other third party payors." Computerized data must be used for epidemiological research. Medical data should be merged with data from other sources such as the National Center for Health Statistics surveys, the Social Security Administration, Medicare and Medicaid, the National Death Index, the U.S. Bureau of the Census, and the Internal Revenue Service. It is proposed that with sophisticated analytical technology already available, we could make critical associations and develop new insights that would be beneficial to the individual and to society.

3. The value of health promotion among the elderly cannot be overestimated. As important as the area of prevention is, there is a danger of overstatement of knowledge in areas where scientific evidence is weak or lacking. It must be admitted that the scientific knowledge of the cause and prevention of most chronic disease is limited. It is apparent that only a fraction of the cancers, heart diseases, strokes, neurological diseases, and arthritis are understood. We know little about the causes and prevention of the senile dementias. Data on smoking and excessive drinking as being

[1]Provided by Dr. Jacob Brody of the National Institute on Aging.

harmful are evident. Data on lowering blood pressure are also strong, particularly in relation to the lowering of cholesterol levels. On the other hand, data are softer related to exercise, weight control, special diets, and salt restriction in the absence of hypertension. Another area of health promotion that requires rethinking is behavior modification through health education. It is recognized that benefits may accrue by altering life-styles. It is recognized that education does exert a powerful effect on life expectancy. Unfortunately, data suggest that persons with minimal education are not reached by the available means of health education. Eliminating smoking, moderation in alcohol consumption, diet control, and other attempts in modification of life-style have bypassed the less educated group. This suggests a new direction in behavior modification via health education, with the primary target being those with fewer years of education.

4. Health policy planners must include research and epidemiology as well as basic studies in the cause, prevention, and management of chronic disease. It is essential to improve the conditions of the ever increasing number of isolated elderly females and help to reduce premature mortality among males. Also needed is a better understanding of the causes of the decline in cardiovascular disease and the means to perpetuate this trend. Greater emphasis needs to be placed on the support of epidemiologic studies of precipitating events leading to hip fractures, and of accidents associated with medications with alcohol, which offer promise for reduction of morbidity and mortality.

Behavior modification strategies should be targeted to the high-risk, less educated population. Such studies should include social and medical validation of survey data and other health indicators. Certainly, we have an opportunity to utilize modern computer technology to exploit data already available or soon to become available (Brody, 1984, pp. 473–475).

Reorientation of rehabilitation professionals' behavior toward disabled elderly persons is suggested by the following four points:

1. *Promoting self care.* Rehabilitation professionals can determine sensory and bodily function changes and, through multidisciplinary team assessment and care planning, prescribe remedial care, and both develop and reinforce coping behavior that builds on self-care skills of disabled aged persons.
2. *Elimination of environmental barriers.* The rehabilitation professional can diagnose and adopt prescriptions for eliminating or reducing environmental barriers. These include architectural modifications within and outside the home that allow optimal use of existing sensory and ambulatory skills or reduce dependence on, or compensate for, lessened abilities.

3. *Economic support and social interaction.* Rehabilitation professionals need to be aware of social and economic needs of older impaired persons. These all infringe on and affect the quality of life.
4. *Assuring a meaningful purpose in life.* Aging is a composite of life history—growth, physical change, and decline. Thus, fulfillment goes beyond oneself, extending to a sense of active participation in the family, community, and national life (Benedict & Ganikos, 1981, p. 16).

One might raise the question, Who are the elderly disabled? We must remember, as stated previously, that only a small percentage live in nursing homes, but most are individuals who live around the corner and up the street. They are people with more chronic health problems, lower income, and less education than most. They are individuals who have experienced more losses than most—the loss of a spouse, the loss of employment, the loss of peers, the loss of good health, and the loss of self-reliance. They are the age group for which disability is most common and rehabilitation service is least.

ASSESSMENT OF PHYSICAL DISABILITY

There is a tendency for health professionals not to make note of impairments and disabilities that effect rehabilitation. Needed is more emphasis on functional disabilities that relate to activities of daily living included in all health professional programs. The orientation toward diagnostic assessment must be supplemented by functional assessment.

Physical health is one of the most important areas for evaluation in determining the overall functional status of an individual at any age. Mental health and socioeconomic resources are likewise vital factors. In dealing with older individuals, these three areas are further involved in an assessment of activities of daily living.

In considering physical disabilities and functional capacity in older persons, the state of spiritual health may be an important factor in rehabilitation. This is an area that is apart from emotional health, religious affiliation, and other support systems. It is apparent that geriatric assessment and rehabilitation are of a multidisciplinary nature.

DHHS ROLE IN DEALING WITH
REHABILITATION PROBLEMS OF THE ELDERLY

Alzheimer's disease, a devastating disease that affects the cells of the brain, is now regarded as a major form of old age senility and presents serious problems of rehabilitation of the elderly. In recognition of the special attention that Alzheimer's disease deserves, DHHS Secretary Margaret Heckler established the Health and Human Services Task Force on Alzheimer's Disease in April 1983. The report of the task force (1984) has recently been released and is available.The task force addressed nine main areas in the problem-oriented approach aimed at better defining research needs and options, as well as the training, service, and policy issues relevant to Alzheimer's disease. The nine areas are (a) research on epidemiology; (b)research on etiology and pathogenesis; (c) research on diagnosis; (d) research on clinical costs; (e) reserach on treatment; (f) research on the family; (g) research on systems of care; (h) training of research and clinical personnel; and (i) educational materials and information dissemination for professionals and the public.

In conjunction with this departmental effort, the Administration on Aging (AoA) has launched a major campaign for the development of support groups for families of older persons with Alzheimer's disease. The goal of this effort is to inform the aging network about the nature of Alzheimer's disease and to encourage the development of support groups to help families cope with the problems created by the disease. AoA has developed a four-volume technical assistance handbook on Alzheimer's disease, to provide background materials and to assist states and local governments, professionals, and families in grappling with this problem.

The recommendations represent the best judgment of leading authorities on Alzheimer's disease from both inside and outside of government, including agency directors, scientists, educators, and clinicians.

PHS/AoA HEALTH PROMOTION
AND PREVENTION INITIATIVE

Within DHHS, several health promotion efforts for the elderly are now in progress. In the forefront is the joint Public Health Service (PHS) and AoA health promotion initiative, which is drawing attention to the need for health promotion for older persons and is helping national, state, and local agencies and organizations create their own programs. Initiated by Surgeon General C. Everett Koop and Commissioner on Aging Dr. Lennie-Marie Tolliver, several DHHS agencies are involved in this campaign. Some of their efforts will be described, but first a brief review of the background that led to the development of this initiative.

Healthy People: The Surgeon General's Report on Health Promotion and Disease Prevention, published in 1979, states that "the long term goal of health promotion and disease prevention for our older people must not only be to achieve further increases in longevity, but also allow each individual to seek an independent and rewarding life in old age, unlimited by many health problems that are within his or her capacity to control." A more specific objective concerning the quality of life was also developed: "by 1990, to reduce the average annual number of days of restricted activity due to acute and chronic conditions by 20 percent, to fewer than 30 days per year for people age 65 and older."

In 1983, the National Institute on Aging (NIA) published a health promotion agenda that had similar goals for the elderly. Though many activities are underway to achieve these goals, special attention is currently being given to health promotion. Activities directed toward this goal include issuing a general prevention-oriented program announcement to solicit research designed to specify how psychosocial processes, interacting with biological processes, influence health and effective functioning in the middle and later years. More recently, two new program announcements have been released to increase knowledge on factors related to health promotion and disease prevention.

NIA is calling for research and research training to specify how particular behaviors and attitudes influence the health of people as they age, and potential modification of these behaviors and attitudes. Not only are the health behaviors and attitudes of middle-aged and older people themselves involved, but also those of formal health care providers and of family and friends. These behaviors and attitudes include medical beliefs about the nature of the aging process. They also include behaviors believed by older people to promote health and functioning, as well as "illness behaviors" that involve how older individuals monitor their bodily functioning; how they define and interpret symptoms perceived as abnormal; whether they take or fail to take remedial action, utilize formal health care systems, comply with prescribed regimens; and how they approach death.

MARKET RESEARCH ON ELDERLY HEALTH CONCERNS

PHS and AoA are working to find out what activities have the most potential for improving the health of people in this age group. A study entitled "Aging and Health Promotion: Market Research for Public Education," conducted by the Office of Disease Prevention and Health Promotion, NIA, and the National Cancer Institute in the PHS and AoA, was undertaken to help provide answers. That study reviewed the literature on the health problems of older people and assessed, through qualitative research, the actual concerns reported by older people. The study also examined the interest of older people in their health and their ability and desire to change their behavior. Focus group discussions were held with older people from different parts of the country to understand their views and to learn from their insights.

The results revealed that although older persons are very interested in maintaining and improving their health, knowledge about specific habits and their association with chronic diseases and conditions was limited. Six primary areas were identified as significantly related to conditions prevalent in the elderly and having the potential for change: fitness/exercise, nutrition, safe and proper use of medicine, accident prevention, prevention services, and smoking.

We have learned a great deal about how to address those issues. Physical fitness improved cardiovascular fitness, strength, and flexibility while reducing the risks of heart attack, falls, broken bones, and lower back pain. Because physical activities make people feel better in general, they often adopt many other healthful behaviors as well. Unfortunately, too few older Americans know about proper exercise and the accompanying benefits. According to national surveys, 57% of those 65 years and older do not exercise on a regular basis. Some programs have already been developed that address the exercise needs of older Americans, including those who are confined to wheelchairs and beds.

The importance of nutrition in maintaining good health applies for all age levels. Recently, many links have been established between diet and disease. For example, osteoporosis or brittle bones is associated with a lack of calcium and exercise. More than 30% of cancers have been linked to diet. In the focus groups, it became evident that many people knew what not to eat, but that they were unable to describe what constituted a balanced diet. Some education programs have been created, but there is a need for simple and well-integrated information on what a healthy diet is, rather than only what ingredients or foods are to be avoided. We suspect that this is true for all age groups, not just older people.

Proper use of drugs and alcohol is another crucial factor in the maintenance of health. Older Americans consume 30% of all prescription drugs and a disproportionate amount of over-the-counter medicines. Several people in the focus groups expressed concern over the interactive effects of the different drugs they are taking. They expressed a need for more information and guidance from health care providers. Efforts should be directed toward the training and education of health professionals about the special needs of the elderly. More research is needed that focuses on the effects of drugs on the elderly, and prescription guidelines need to be developed.

Another major cause of disability and death is accidents, particularly falls and automobile accidents. One of the reasons that the elderly sustain so many injuries during automobile accidents is that only 10% of them report that they regularly use their safety belts. Although the exact cause of the many falls that result in, or are associated with, hip fractures has not been established, falls are attributable in part to unsafe living environments and poor physical condition. Although there is clearly a need for improvement in the utilization of seat belts, many older people are aware of the risk of falling and have taken steps to make their home environments safe. Community programs should be created to reinforce such behavior and to provide additional information, especially to those persons who may not be aware of their high risk for accidents.

There are two other areas of importance in health promotion for older people—prevention services and smoking. Guidelines with respect to screening procedures and tests are developed by various professional groups. The appropriate application of those recommended procedures should be encouraged. All people should be advised to stop smoking and never to start the habit at any age. Evidence now suggests that even if people quit smoking at age 50 their risk for cancer decreases.

Another central purpose of the survey was to determine whether old people are a suitable audience for health promotion activities. The focus groups revealed that older persons are very conscious of their health and that they try to figure out ways to stay healthy. Other studies also indicate that when educated about health habits, older persons had higher levels of compliance and behavior change than the other age groups. This leads us to the conclusion that older people are an interested and enthusiastic audience for health information.

Special Features of the Health Promotion Initiative

At the request of Secretary Heckler, the governors of every state have named individuals in their state to coordinate health promotion activities for older people. Generally based in the state health department or state office on aging, these individuals will receive resources to help make programs in their states a reality.

To provide support and technical assistance to state and local agencies, the AoA, with assistance from the AoA/PHS Health Promotion Steering Committee, developed a publication distribution plan consisting of more than 30 publications in the four priority areas of injury control, proper drug use, better nutrition, and improved physical fitness. One document, *A Healthy Old Age: A Source Book for Health Promotion with Older Adults*, has already been printed for this initiative. AoA sent more than 15,000 copies to state agencies on aging, community and migrant health centers, Indian tribes, service units of the Indian Health Service, and OASIS projects (mini senior centers located in department stores). Other materials will be distributed during the coming year as they are issued by AoA and PHS. AoA has developed two documents for this initiative. The first is a process guide for use by state and local health aging units to set up health coalitions and programs. The second is an annotated bibliography on health promotion.

AoA sponsors nutrition programs that provide meals to older persons: more than 3½ million people participated in 1983. In that same year, AoA served more than 9 million older persons through its programs, many of which include health promotion activities. In addition, AoA supports numerous health-related projects through its discretionary funding of education and training programs in gerontology as well as in its research and demonstration grants.

In conjunction with several other agencies, the Food and Drug Administration has created a seminar series addressing the issue of geriatrics and drugs. Also, a series of articles on the elderly and nutrition is now appearing in their magazine, *The FDA Consumer*. Guidelines for geriatric drug testing are under development. A coordinated effort to investigate many of the issues related to geriatric drug use is ongoing. In addition, they are involved in major consumer education initiatives on sodium labeling, patient education on prescription medications, and health fraud. The agency conducted two consumer outreach programs designed to teach economically disadvantaged black elderly how to reduce sodium in their diets and to make the rural elderly more aware of health promotion messages on nutrition, medications, and medical devices. With regard to health fraud, a special unit is being established to address this specific issue in the drug area at FDA's Consumer Affairs Offices, located throughout the country. Staff continue to work with state and local organizations to bring priority health education messages to the elderly.

Accident prevention for older Americans has received attention from the Centers for Disease Control (CDC). They recently produced *Prevention of Injury for Older Adults*, a selected bibliography providing an overview of the magnitude of injuries among older adults and the types of health education methods and programs being conducted to reduce them. CDC also has initiated a project with the Dade County, Florida, Department of Public Health to assist the county in designing and conducting an epidemiologic population-based study of the elderly to determine the causative factors of non-work-related injuries. This project will develop, implement, and evaluate a model prevention program designed to reduce the incidence of injuries and their associated costs.

As part of the initiative, the Department of Health and Human Services has just awarded over $1 million in grants for health education projects aimed at the elderly to 51 community and migrant health centers in 29 states.

As a centerpiece of this initiative, we will be providing materials and technical assistance to states to assist them in conducting public education programs on health promotion for older adults in their states. Under the direction of the PHS, a variety of radio, television, and print materials will be produced for local distribution, including public service announcements and broadcast materials for talk shows. Printed materials will provide in-depth information on specific health topics and alert the public to the campaign. Regional workshops will be convened to familiarize participants with public education materials and to give assistance on how to work with the media and provide health promotion services for older people.

SUMMARY

In this brief chapter, I have tried to provide a consciousness-raising experience concerning successful and unsuccessful dealing with problems of the aging, common health and mental health problems of the older person, and treatment strategies and implications. I have tried to convey that aging is a developmental stage of life rather than a disability or a handicap.

Because older people are becoming more numerous in our society and their concerns must be addressed, it is important that health professionals concerned with rehabilitation of the elderly be familiar with problems associated with aging and some possible treatment strategies. It is also evident that we need much more research, better epidemiological data, and more information about the morbidity of elderly individuals and its effect on functional disabilities. We also need to address our concerns to the elderly individual with less education and convey to those individuals the importance of prevention activities.

If we support the concepts of equal opportunity and quality of life, then it would seem imperative that as long as people live, they should have equal opportunities for maintaining as high a quality of life as possible.

Rehabilitation services must be offered to persons of all ages. The costs of institutional care are high. Older people want to remain in the community. Rehabilitation services should be extended to disabled older people in areas of physical restoration, physical management reeducation, and psychological services.

Let us accept the assumption that health is a function of physical, social, and mental well-being and is a basic human right. The goal of assisting our ever growing elderly population to achieve the highest level of health is one toward which we all need to work.

REFERENCES

Benedict, R. C., & Ganikos, M. L. (1981). Coming to terms with ageism in rehabilitation. *Journal of Rehabilitation, 47* (4).

Brody, J. A. (1984). Facts, projections, and gaps concerning data on aging. *Public Health Reports, 99* (5), 468–475.

Long, J. M. (1972). *Caring for and caring about elderly people: A guide to the rehabilitative approach.* Philadelphia: J. B. Lippincott.

Rehabilitation Services Administration, DHHS. (1980). *Summary by age 1979.* Washington, DC: RSA.

U. S. Department of Health and Human Services. (1984). *Alzheimer's disease.* Report of the Secretary's Task Force on Alzheimer's Disease. (DDHS Publication No. ADM 84-1323). Washington, DC: U.S. Government Printing Office.

Williams, T. F. (Ed.). (1984). *Rehabilitation and the aging.* New York: Raven Press.

7

Impact of the Formal Support System on Rehabilitation of the Elderly

Stanley J. Brody

Rehabilitation is a philosophy and a set of therapeutic techniques oriented toward the restoration of disabled persons to a maximum level of function and competence (Williams, 1984). Functional integrity (social, physical, and psychological) is the goal of rehabilitation and requires an integrated combination of medical, health care, and social interventions. Yet public resources are typically channeled through disease and/or interest-group-specific programs—that is, separate medically oriented or social service programs or programs that group the disabled and the elderly into a broadly defined population of economically disadvantaged persons.

The fragmentary, compartmentalized nature of publicly supported rehabilitation programing suggests the difficulty of developing a comprehensive treatment program. Rehabilitation programs respond to the interest of a broad spectrum of advocacy and professional groups. Disease-oriented interest groups focus variously on mental health, mental retardation, dementia, blindness, hearing impairment, and different developmental disabilities. Other professional groups interested in rehabilitation include those from the fields of physical medicine; occupational, physical, recreational, and speech therapy; and vocational counseling. These groups share common concerns in the areas of income maintenance, medical care coverage, therapy, housing, transportation, and other (social) services for the disabled, as well as training and research support for rehabilitation professionals. But their priorities differ. Their different ordering of priorities reflects the demographics and pathologies of specific disabling conditions or the context and auspices of care. The different interest groups are pre-eminent in influencing policy formulation.

The formal care system is the product of a pluralistic democracy and embodies both the strengths and weaknesses of such a political system. The democratic process provides an opportunity for interested groups to participate in government; it also encourages those groups to focus on single issues as a means of mobilizing support and power. Separate programs and bureaucracies form around these issues and eventually become entrenched in policy formulation and budgeting.

Although rehabilitation calls for a comprehensive treatment effort involving medical, health, welfare, and social support services, in general, the nature of government does not allow for such an approach. Rather, the formal system is a collection of separate income maintenance, medical and health insurance, housing, education, transportation, and other social programs that address program-specific eligibility groups and goals. Rehabilitation programs are administered through a myriad of layered governmental agencies and auspices. Indeed, social and medical programs are treated as oil and water and carefully funded so as to enforce the separation. For this conference it is necessary to mobilize 20 different federal agencies to achieve, for the first time, a national discussion of the rehabilitation of the disabled elderly.[1]

The values of society are reflected in the program selection and resource allocation decisions that evolve from the political process. Public policy derives from value judgments, screened through the electorate, to which the legislative and administrative arms of government subscribe. Chief Justice Oliver Wendell Holmes included the judicial branch when he observed that the common law reflected the "felt necessities of the time" (Holmes, 1963). All three aspects of government function within the value system so aptly phrased. In short, public policy rationalizes "as much as possible . . . the irrational perception of felt needs" (Brody, 1976).

Governmental attitudes toward disability are reflected by legislative definitions that are usually expressed in medical or provider terms and couched in economic concerns. Thus, the Social Security Act defines disability as "Inability to engage in substantial gainful activity because of any medically determinable permanent physical or mental impairment" (Social Security Administration, 1982a).

Similarly, rehabilitation legislation focuses on the "handicapped individual . . . who has a physical, or mental disability which for such individual constitutes or results in a substantial handicap to employment" (U.S. Congress, 1973).

The legislative image of the elderly parallels that of the disabled or handicapped. That is, the primary needs of older people also have been viewed in medical and economic terms. In another context, Binstock (1983) has described this as scapegoating the elderly. Those perceptions of the disabled and of the aged suggest that there is a series of attitudes on which public policy is based. Specifically:

1. The physically sick role has been assigned to the disabled elderly.
2. Health needs of the disabled elderly require high-tech medical response.
3. Disability relates to medical diagnostic categories.
4. Independence is good and dependency is bad.
5. Disability is a personal limitation.
6. The elderly disabled are a disadvantaged minority.

The consequences of those attitudes, in terms of program development, have been substantial federal support that provides the disabled elderly access to rehabilitation through medical insurance for acute care and, for the older disabled worker, social insurance as an alternative to rehabilitation. Comparatively meager sums of federal money are allocated to the support of rehabilitation of the disabled elderly for long-term care in the home, in institutions, or in the community. No distinction is made as to whether the disability of the older adult is developmental or the result of impairment of later onset.

There is little funding of preventive or chronic care. Except for a modest tax deduction under the IRS and a small Veterans Administration assistance program for wives, the family—which is a key therapeutic agent for the elderly disabled—receives no public support. There is no national program of social support, respite care, or adult day care for the elderly disabled and their caregivers. Services to the disabled elderly are provided through income maintenance programs, medical insurance programs, and social programs including housing, education, and transportation. These will be considered here in turn.

INCOME MAINTENANCE

Income maintenance, to be understood, must be seen in historical perspective. A common policy approach to disability is one that views disability as an economic problem. A disabled person is seen as an individual whose physical or mental condition deprives him/her of the capacity to work and results in economic hardship. Economically oriented disability programs emphasize either income or vocational rehabilitation concerns. Although these programs are based on a shared definition of disability, their orientations and implementation are quite different and, for the elderly, somewhat contradictory.

Income maintenance programs represent a major investment of federal dollars for the support of disabled persons. In 1983, federal expenditures for income maintenance programs for disabled persons totaled nearly $37 billion (Roth, 1984).[2] The Social Security Disability Insurance (SSDI) program and the Supplemental Security Income (SSI) program are the two largest federally administered income maintenance programs. Other federal programs include the VA pension; Social Security benefits for disabled coal miners; the Department of Labor's compensation programs for longshoremen, harbor workers, and coal miners; and the Railroad Retirement Board compensation program for disabled railroad workers.

The SSDI cash benefit program was enacted in 1956—21 years after the enactment of the Social Security retirement program and 17 years after the enactment of Survivors Insurance (U.S. Senate, 1984, p. 295). The delay in legislating disability coverage stemmed from fear that the receipt of such a benefit would discourage rehabilitation and workforce re-entry and that the determination of disability as a cause of unemployment would be subjective and difficult to administer (U.S. Senate, 1984). Such fears persist today.

Initial eligibility requirements for SSDI were narrowly defined and originally limited beneficiaries to severely disabled older workers, 50 years of age or older, with a substantial and recent history of employment covered by Social Security. Disability was defined as inability to engage in any work because of a medical impairment that was expected to continue indefinitely (U.S. Senate, 1984, p. 296). Although eligibility was conditioned by the vocational consequences of severe disability, benefits were contingent on the recipient's participation in vocational rehabilitation services (U.S. Senate, 1984).

The SSDI program was expanded by the Social Security Act amendments of 1958, 1960, and 1965. In 1958, benefits were added for dependents of disabled workers and the work requirement was liberalized; in 1960, the age requirement of 50 was dropped and a trial work period without termination of benefits was instituted; and in 1965, the definition of disability was expanded so that persons whose disabling conditions were expected to last at least 12 months or end in death could be eligible for benefit coverage (U.S. Congress, 1958, 1960, 1965; U.S. House of Representatives, 1983). Under the 1965 amendments, eligibility continued to be tied to a disabled applicant's inability to engage in substantial work. In the 1967 amendments to the Act, Congress responded to rising program participation based on vocational factors by tightening the statutory definition of disability. States were advised that, to be considered eligible for SSDI benefits, a disabled individual's physical or mental impairment must be of

sufficient severity to prevent him/her from engaging in any kind of substantial gainful employment "available in the national economy" irrespective of the availability of appropriate job placements. Amendment provisions also based the disabled-widow benefit, which began at age 50,
solely on medical criteria (U.S. Congress, 1967).

Today, to be considered disabled under SSDI, an individual must have a
physical or mental impairment that prevents him/her from doing any
"substantially gainful activity," and the disability must be expected to last or
have already lasted at least 12 months or be expected to result in death. As
in the beginning, program eligibility continues to be tied to a determination
of an individual's capacity to work and to the expected duration of disability
(U.S. House of Representatives, 1983).

Although the SSDI program is open to all qualified disabled persons of
working age, for the most part it is, as it was originally, an older worker's
disability program. Nearly 80% of SSDI beneficiaries are between the ages
of 45 and 64; of these, more than half are 55 to 64 years of age. The average
age of new SSDI beneficiaries is 53 (Curdette & Baker, 1982; Social
Security Administration, 1982c). SSDI is described in some quarters as an
early retirement program for the elderly (Barfield & Morgan, 1976;
Campbell & Campbell, 1976; Quinn, 1977; U.S. House of Representatives, 1981).

During its first 20 years, the SSDI program experienced a steady growth
in numbers of beneficiaries and program expenditures (Social Security Administration, 1976, 1984). After 1976, the growth in SSDI case load was
reversed, but program costs continued to rise (Social Security Administration, 1982a). In 1978, the General Accounting Office (GAO) issued a report
that criticized the review process used to determine the continuing eligibility of SSDI recipients. The GAO estimated that up to 20% of SSDI
recipients were, in fact, ineligible to continue to receive benefits (U.S.
General Accounting Office, 1978; U. S. House of Representatives, 1983). A
1981 GAO report supported this finding.

Although periodic review of disability insurance (DI) eligibility was a
component of the SSDI program from the beginning, continuing disability
investigations (CDIs) were usually done only when a beneficiary's medical
condition suggested the possibility of improvement or the beneficiary was
reported as having returned to work (U.S. House of Representatives, 1983).
In 1980, Congress expanded the scope of CDI reviews and required the
review of the disability status of DI recipients every 3 years (U.S. Congress,
1980). At the direction of Congress, a step-up in the eligibility review activity was to begin in 1982. However, in response to a variety of pressures,
the Social Security Administration (SSA) implemented its CDI program a
year earlier (U.S. House of Representatives, 1983). Between March 1981
and June 1983, 946,000 CDI case reviews were done, and 421,000 bene-

ficiaries were dropped from DI benefit rolls, thus terminating benefits for 48% of the cases reviewed (U.S. House of Representatives, 1983).

Subsequent Congressional investigations of the CDI process have indicated substantial discrimination against mentally disabled beneficiaries (U. S. Senate, 1983). The vulnerability of this population to SSA review and benefit termination is attributed to the fact that the evaluation of mental impairments is largely subjective and based on symptomological or behavioral, rather than physiological, evidence. Furthermore, state agency disability determinations often are made without the benefit of qualified psychiatrists or psychologists. Protests from some state officials and consumer groups, committee hearing testimony, the high CDI termination rate, and the high rate of benefit reinstatement following Administrative Law Judge appeal led Congress and the states to impose a moratorium on CDI review (Noble, 1984).

The bias of both administrators and practitioners against the legitimacy of mental illness in the older worker was expressed in the CDI process. Although Congress attempted to modify this attitude by enacting corrective legislation in late 1984, the ambivalence toward the mentally ill continues to be expressed through SSA-instituted court actions proposing to restrain the reinstatement of those removed as SSDI beneficiaries.

Modifications in the SSDI program have often been in response to changes in demand and cost, reflecting the changing demography of disability. As the recipients of SSDI have aged and their levels of disability have increased, there has been a shift in the philosophy of providing services (U.S. DHHS, 1982; U.S. DHHS, 1974). In the past, substantial Social Security funds were directed toward the provision of state rehabilitation services for SSDI beneficiaries (U.S. Congress, 1965).[3] Recent reductions in such funding are traceable in part to a belief that rehabilitation is ineffective among older disabled workers receiving income support tied to their disability status, an inadequate referral process from SSA to state vocational rehabilitation agencies (SVR), or to a perceived lack of SVR training effort (Trietel, 1979; U.S. Dept. of Education, 1983). However, the success rate of rehabilitation programs involving older disabled persons suggests that neither age nor the receipt of SSDI benefits is predictive of vocational rehabilitation outcome. Thus, age-based exclusion of older persons from rehabilitation and inadequate funding of rehabilitation services for SSDI recipients may be inappropriate and may result in unnecessarily increased dependency and increased costs of long-term income support (Morrison, 1984; U.S. Dept. of Education, 1983).

In discontinuing SSDI funding of state rehabilitation services, Congress may have been reacting to the attitudes of SVR agencies and corporate employers toward the disabled older worker (Locke-Connor & Walsh, 1980). In an economy with high unemployment, the vocational counselor is faced with at least two major disincentives for restoring the disabled, older worker to the work force. First, the worker may risk substantial monetary loss if he/she is declared rehabilitated, gives up disability insurance coverage, and returns to work. Second, the lack of placement opportunities for older disabled workers (real or imagined) contributes to pessimism about their rehabilitation potential. The uncertainty of continuing employment options open to physically and mentally disabled persons does not compare favorably to the greater security of the income and health benefits program. This negativism is reinforced by the history of the SSA program itself, which was initiated, in part, to provide employment opportunities for younger workers by removing the older worker from the employment market; and confirmed by Congress when, in recently extending the retirement age to 70, the Medicare benefit for the worker who opts to work past age 65 was disallowed.

The Rehabilitation Act did not recognize the older population as a legitimate concern until 1978 when the phrase "handicapped individuals who are aged sixty or older" was added, but only to the research and training program (U.S. Congress, 1978). The term *vocational* was part of the Act's title until 1973 (U.S. Congress, 1973). Two research and training (R&T) centers focusing on the aged were added to the National Institute on Handicapped Research (NIHR) program in 1980. Yet, while more than one-half of all disabled people are elderly, those two centers are among the least funded of the 33 R&T centers. At the same time, as though to accentuate the lack of clear policy toward the older worker, the Older Americans Act provides special employment opportunities that are funded so minimally as to be rhetorical; typically, 8 voluntary agencies, the Forestry Service, and approximately 40 states administer $300 million designated for this purpose (U.S. Senate, 1984, p. 505).

For those not eligible for SSDI benefits or who receive a small disability benefit and are without other minimum income or assets, SSI provides monthly income support to the needy aged (age 65 and over), the blind, and the disabled. SSI is primarily a federally administered income assistance program authorized by Title XVI of the Social Security Act. The SSI program replaced the former Federal Grants to States for Old Age Assistance, Aid to the Blind, and Aid to the Permanently Disabled. Although administered by the Social Security Administration, SSI is a joint federal–state program. Its purpose is to guarantee a minimum level of income to the covered groups. Eligibility is based on financial need, but the minimum level of income and assets allowed to qualify as needy under SSI rules is below federally established poverty levels. Nevertheless, SSI eligibility is important because it often qualifies recipients for significant noncash benefits such as Medicaid, food stamps, rehabilitation, and home care programs.

Veterans Administration (VA) pensions represent the third major source of income support for disabled persons. VA pensions to veterans with non-service-connected disabilities amounted to $2 billion in fiscal year 1983 (Office of Management and Budget, 1983; Roth, 1984). That same year, veterans compensated for service-connected disabilities received an estimated $8 billion (Roth, 1984). The VA pension system supports veterans under 65 who are disabled by service-connected impairments. *All* veterans over 65, are considered disabled *by definition* and are eligible for pension and health care services (U.S. Veterans Administration, 1984a). Today, there are 4 million aged veterans representing more than 15% of the elderly population. By the turn of the century, as many as two-thirds of all males over 65 years will be veterans—37% of all veterans (U.S. Veterans Administration, 1984a, pp. 6, 10). Thus, a significant proportion of older citizens will have a support system that parallels SSI, is more generously administered, and provides roughly half again the SSI benefit.

These three main support programs for older disabled are complemented with a few smaller programs responding to special constituencies. These programs include the Social Security benefits for disabled coal miners, the Railroad Retirement Board compensation for disabled railroad workers, and the Department of Labor's compensation programs for longshoremen and harbor workers and for coal miners. Although these income-maintenance programs have not yet completely resolved the issues of the disabled older worker, particularly those who are mentally ill, they represent 50 years of creditable planning and implementation of a concern for the economic needs of the disabled. The role of the disabled elderly as productive participants in the work force who therefore are entitled to public rehabilitation services is yet to be consistently determined by either legislative or administrative action.

MEDICAL/REHABILITATION SERVICES

Rehabilitation services for the elderly are addressed by the formal system, primarily from a medical perspective. Disability is defined as a medical problem—"an organic defect or deficiency which is located exclusively within the individual."[5] Thus, it is assumed that the resolution of disability lies in medical treatment. Personal problems arising from disability are the responsibility of the individual, and society adapts a neutral role.

The medical orientation of rehabilitation care reflects the absence of a handicap role for older people and an emphasis on disability. The most significant change in federal medical insurance programs for the elderly disabled has been the 1984 implementation of a diagnosis-related group (DRG)–based prospective reimbursement system for inpatient Medicare services that exempts inpatient rehabilitation and psychiatric care (*Federal Register*, 1983).

As an entitlement program, Medicare provides the base for the support of medical care for the aged. Medicare funds inpatient and outpatient rehabilitation care and rehabilitation services in the home under the rubric of home health care. Day rehabilitation hospital care and some rehabilitation service delivered during a short-term nursing home stay may also be funded under Title XVIII (SSA).

Medicare was originally designed to address the acute medical care needs of the elderly. For a stay in a skilled nursing facility (SNF) of less than 100 days to be eligible for Medicare coverage, the admission must be certified as medically necessary. Whereas rehabilitation services may be provided in hospital and SNF settings, medical services are directed primarily toward disease-oriented curative interventions and not necessarily toward the resolution of the disabling consequences of chronic illness.

Post-hospital long-term care was not in the Medicare agenda, nor was full support for psychiatric treatment of the mentally ill. Despite the chronic needs of elderly mental health patients, they are eligible only for minimum inpatient days and ambulatory visits, reflecting the view of Medicare as an acute-care program focused on physical illness. Yet, recent changes in hospital financing under Medicare promise far-reaching changes in the availability and scope of long-term care and rehabilitation services. Those changes suggest the reallocation of the acute-care dollar to cover continuity of care at least for short-term, long-term (STLTC) care (i.e., post-hospital care for approximately 90 days) (Brody & Magel, 1984). In addition to the acute care system, the health care system is made up of two other aspects of continuity of care: a short-term one, STLTC providing services for those who need less than 90 days of care (usually post-acute hospital care) and whose needs are primarily transitory; and a long-term, long-term care (LTLTC) system that provides services for those who need more than 90 days of care and whose needs are permanent (see Figure 7-1).

Both arrays of service, STLTC and LTLTC, are developed by social, health, and medical personnel and organized into auspices reflecting those orientations (Brody & Magel, 1984).

For most of its history, Medicare reimbursed hospitals through a cost-based reimbursement scheme. The prospective DRG system provides hospitals with a financial incentive to shorten inpatient lengths of stay. In one sense, Congress has assigned to the hospitals the responsibility for reallocating the Medicare dollars between acute care and STLTC. A responsible strategy for doing this is for the hospital to discharge patients to appropriate stepdown services, many of which are funded by Medicare. These short-term step-down services include inpatient rehabilitation services, convalescent care (short-term skilled nursing and intermediate care

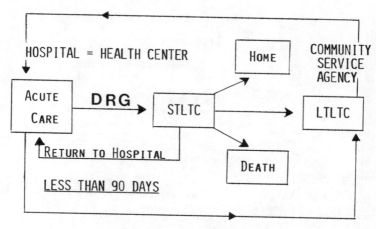

Figure 7-1 Continuity of Care

facilities), rehabilitation day hospitals, home health care (including re-habilitation therapy) and other home support services, and inpatient hos-pice care.

The growing utilization of hospital facilities by the aged, coupled with the incentive of the DRG program to contain lengths of stay, is accelerating the provision of alternative care settings. The flow of these services is ex-pressed diagramatically in Figure 7-2.

Step-down services provide support during convalescence and, where funded by Medicare, currently fall outside the prospective payment system. Developing and/or expanding rehabilitation and other STLTC services allows the hospital to be responsive to the needs of its patients, to cultivate markets for both inpatient and outpatient services, and to assist physicians in securing appropriate services for their patients. Medicare reimburse-ment "gains" realized by hospitals that are successful in containing in-patient lengths of stay may be used to finance an expansion of alternative STLTC discharge options (Brody & Magel, 1983).

From a benefit perspective, the Medicare program had remained largely unresponsive to the dramatic changes that have occurred in the health care needs of the aging elderly population. The Medicare program still primarily addresses the catastrophic short-term *medical* care needs of the elderly.

The long-term health care needs of the poor, permanently frail elderly and disabled that go beyond 90 days are addressed in part by Medicaid (Title XIX of the Social Security Act). Whereas Medicare is an entitlement program, Medicaid is needs-based. A federal–state matching program, Medicaid benefits and eligibility criteria differ from state to state. Eligibility

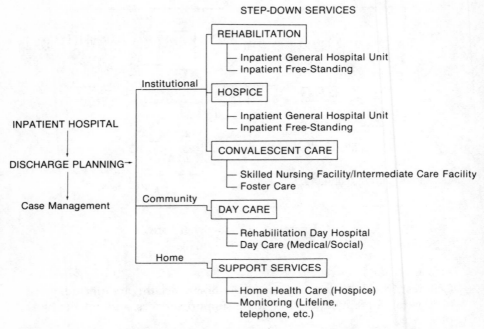

Figure 7-2 A model of a hospital-based system of short-term long-term care. Reprinted from "DRG—The Second Revolution in Health Care for the Elderly" by S.J. Brody & J.S. Magel with permission of *Journal of the American Geriatrics Society*, 32(9), 676–679, © 1984.

is tied to income standards for identifying the categorically needy or to a determination of medical need. Many states use the income eligibility rules of the federal SSI program to determine eligibility for Medicaid.

Although a variety of services may be covered under Medicaid, inadequate federal support and state budgetary eligibility cutbacks have limited Medicaid support for long-term care services. Limitations take the form of restrictions on physician reimbursement, arbitrary limits on the per diem for SNFs, the number of home care visits, or the nonprovision of services such as day care or respite.

The SNF is the major long-term-care institution serving older disabled persons, and more than half of its costs have been covered by Medicaid. The SNF, as a category of medical service, was created by the 1972 SSA Amendments to the Social Security Act (U.S. Congress, 1972). The amendments authorized Medicare and Medicaid coverage for skilled care benefits for individuals in need of skilled nursing care and/or skilled rehabilitation services on a daily basis. The legislation identified SNFs as appropriate medical settings for the provision of extended care and physical, occupational, or speech therapy services to qualifying Medicare and Medicaid recipients (U.S. Congress, 1972, p. 1025).

Despite this legislative mandate, few SNFs offer significant rehabilitation services. Among Medicare or Medicaid-certified SNFs, physical, occupational, or speech and hearing therapies are routinely provided by 24.9%, 24.8%, and 27.1%, respectively (U.S. National Center for Health Statistics, 1979, p. 16). During 1977, although 75% of SNF residents were dependent in one or more activities of daily living (ADL) only 13.7% received physical therapy; 1.4%, mental health counseling; 6.6% reality orientation; 5.9%, occupational therapy; and less than 1%, speech or hearing therapy (U.S. National Center for Health Statistics, 1979, p. 56).

SNF populations are composed of both short-term (less than 90 days of care) and long-term (90 days or more of care) residents. In the course of a year, approximately one-third of SNF residents are short-term and the remaining two-thirds experience longer lengths of stay (U.S. National Center for Health Statistics, 1979, p. 64). Short-term SNF stays are covered partially under the Medicare program (Health Care Financing Administration, 1982). Most rehabilitation services provided in SNFs are probably received by short-term residents who experience high turnover, and about one-third benefit from Medicare coverage (Brody, 1985; U.S. General Accounting Office, 1983).

Long-term SNF stays are covered under the Medicaid program, which is characterized by low reimbursement levels. Rehabilitation or psychiatric services in SNFs are usually not covered under state-administered Medicaid programs. Most long-term SNF residents suffer from chronic mental illnesses of which the dementias are the most prevalent. The "deinstitutionalization" movement of the 1960s and the 1970s resulted in a massive transfer of the mentally disabled elderly from state hospitals to SNFs, boarding homes, or the streets. Of the nursing home residents experiencing stays of more than 6 months, 78.6% suffered from chronic mental disorders and dementias without psychosis (U.S. National Center for Health Statistics, 1979, p. 53). This figure reflects the advanced age of nursing home residents, the positive relationship between age and incidence of dementia in the elderly population, and the lack of community supports for families caring for demented relatives. Thus, it may be said that, because of the lack of payment for even minimum custodial services, dementia patients are "holocausted" by public programs.

Most disabled older persons are not in institutions but live in the community, often receiving care from family members and other informal support providers. Community-based services for the disabled elderly are severely limited. Those who suffer from chronic mental illnesses or dementias typically do not participate in or benefit from community mental health programs, despite repeated Congressional mandates (U.S. General Accounting Office, 1982). Poor, disabled persons suffering from physical and/ or mental impairments may benefit from maintenance-oriented services such as homemaker, meals-on-wheels, and home health care. Rehabilitative services—that is, services designed to preserve and promote mental as well as physical function—are not widely available. Day care, respite care, and attendant care are not provided under any national mandate. Rehabilitation therapy in the home is available only for a short post-hospital period.

A federal survey of long-term care facilities pointed out that, since 1974, "federal regulations for Medicare and Medicaid patients require that participating facilities not admit or retain patients in need of specialized rehabilitation services unless they are provided, either directly or under arrangements with outside resources" (Office of Nursing Home Affairs, 1975). The survey concluded that this requirement was not being met and that the quality of services was deficient. Poor reimbursement levels and a lack of trained rehabilitation personnel in SNFs further preclude the provision of rehabilitation services to disabled residents. Some states specifically deny Medicaid coverage for rehabilitation care in an SNF setting. Although the statutory language defining SNFs has not changed, reimbursement policies and administrative interpretations have encouraged a limited-focus, custodial-care role for these institutions (Brody, 1985). The scope and nature of service delivery in nursing homes reflect a de facto national and state policy of excluding older disabled persons, and in particular, older persons suffering from mental impairments, from rehabilitation services.

The VA system is the third major medical support program for the disabled elderly and contains the largest single group of physicians practicing physical medicine and rehabilitation. Developed largely in isolation from other public-sector programs, there is a general lack of understanding or appreciation of the size, scope, and importance of the VA system. The VA provides free or highly subsidized medical and health care services to eligible veterans. Services include hospital, ambulatory, and nursing home care provided through 172 VA hospitals and medical centers, 226 outpatient clinics, 95 VA nursing home units, and 16 domiciles. Most long-term care services are provided under contract in community nursing homes or subsidized in state veterans' homes. Within the limits of the VA's bed capacity, veterans with non-service-connected disabilities receive care after it has been certified that they are unable to defray personally the cost of inpatient care (U.S. Veterans Administration, 1984b, pp. 37–64).

The quality, focus, and comprehensiveness of physical, psychosocial, and vocational rehabilitation services varies from VA medical center to VA medical center. Forty-three VA medical centers have no organized Rehabilitation Medicine Service (RMS), some medical centers have no rehabilitation beds allocated, and some have neither occupational nor physical therapists (DeLisa, 1984; U.S. Veterans Administration, 1980).

In addition to RMS and other medical center–based rehabilitation programs, the VA provides a broad spectrum of noninstitutional long-term care programs. These include residential home care, adult day health care, mental hygiene clinics, day hospitals, day treatment centers, hospice care, respite care, geriatric evaluation units, and geriatric research, education, and clinical centers. The VA medical system has placed increased emphasis on outpatient and alternative care services, including residential and hospital-based home health care, adult day health care, and ambulatory psychiatric care (U.S. Veterans Administration, 1984a, pp. 37–64).

The Medicare, Medicaid, and VA programs are designed to address the medical needs of broadly defined populations of disabled persons. Medical support for the disabled is also found in programs designed to address the needs of specific classes of disabled persons. For example, the developmentally disabled (persons suffering from conditions such as cerebral palsy, autism, and mental retardation) are covered by Medicaid and by the Developmental Disabilities Assistance Bill of Rights Act, P.L. 95-602, as amended by the Omnibus Budget Reconciliation Act of 1981. P.L. 95-602 provides formula grants to states and territories for planning, services, and administration of programs for residential, personal, institutional, and specialized nursing care (Oriol, 1985; Golley, 1980; Larkin, Bruninks, Doth, Hall, & Hauber, 1982).

SOCIAL SERVICE

The needs of the elderly are different from those of younger patients, not only because of the multiple physical and psychosocial insults they suffer but also because of their older and more fragile psychosocial support systems. The legislatively mandated and administratively reinforced separation of medical and social programs inhibits rehabilitation efforts on behalf of the disabled elderly. Many of the services that enable the dysfunctional elderly to move from the acute-care bed to the community require social support services such as medical/social day care, sheltered housing, foster care, homemaker, and transportation.

Beyond the need for STLTC services is the need for a broad array of services to comprise a comprehensive LTLTC system. These are services that support informal caregivers and help individuals to maintain as much independence as possible whether at home, in the community, or in institutions over long periods of time (see Figure 7-3) (U.S. Senate, 1984; Vogel & Palmer, 1983).

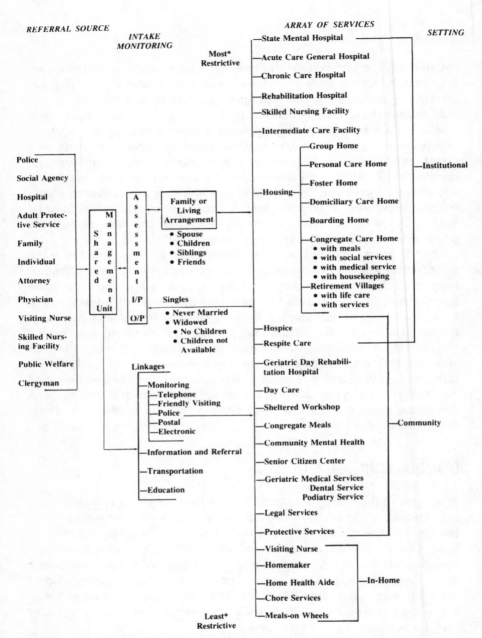

Figure 7-3 Inventory of recommended available services, appropriate to a long-term care/support system. The classification of from most to least restrictive is a general view of services and may vary within each service. Reprinted from "Data for Long-Term Care Planning by Health Systems Agencies" by S.J. Brody & C.M. Masciocchi, with permission of *American Journal of Public Health, 70* (11), 1197, © 1980.

Social service needs of older disabled persons are addressed through a plethora of federal, state, and community programs. Public support for older disabled persons comes from programs whose primary mission is service to handicapped or disabled persons—programs that are legislatively mandated to spend a certain percentage of funds on the disabled (e.g., HUDS's elderly and handicapped program) and handicapped, and/or programs for the elderly benefitting the disabled among a larger, more grossly defined eligible population. Most social programs for the elderly disabled are administered by state and local agencies using federal formula grant monies.[5] Programs funded through discretionary grants are directly administered by federal agencies and usually involve research and demonstration projects. Federal demonstration efforts in long-term care have focused on case management issues, the expansion of Medicare and Medicaid coverage to include nonmedical services, and the use of waivers to permit states to experiment in coordinating long-term care programs characterized by separate funding streams (Roth, 1984).

Despite the vast array of service programs involving disabled persons, the total amount of resources allocated to them is relatively modest compared to federal allocations for medical services. Federal reimbursement restrictions for noninstitutional services and a bias favoring the support of medical as opposed to health and/or social programs further compromise the development of a comprehensive support system for the disabled elderly (Brody, 1979).

Most long-term policy activity and programming is initiated at the state level. The accent on federalism in the last two administrations has resulted in increased delegation of responsibility for all long-term care to states while continuing the federal role in financing acute care. In the face of funding cuts and growing demands for services, many states have established income eligibility standards that are lower than the federal maximum income eligibility limits under the old Title XX law (Social Services Amendment, Social Security Act) (U.S. Congress, 1981).[6]

Social services under Title XX include case management; counseling; day care; employment; education and training; foster care; homemaker; chore and home health–related services; home-delivered and congregate meals; protective services; residential care treatment; socialization; special services for the blind, deaf, and disabled; and transportation (U.S. Senate, 1984). However, the majority of Title XX monies go to programs and services for children and youth. In 1979, day-care, protective, and foster-care services for children accounted for 37% of federal funds spent for Title XX. Day-care, protective, and foster-care services for adults accounted for 5%; special services for the disabled claimed 1.08%. Homemaker and chore services provided elderly and disabled persons with assistance in meal preparation, cleaning, and personal care, enabling some to remain in their own homes and to avoid institutionalization, and accounted for 16% of Title XX funds expended during that time (U.S. House of Representatives, 1980).

All of Title XX social services are carefully monitored, together with those of Medicaid, to assure that social and medical services are not mingled. Thus, two day-care programs can exist side by side; one supported by Title XX, the other by Title XIX (Medicaid). The day-care program funded by Title XX must be headed by social service personnel and cannot pay for any medical rehabilitation services. The program funded by Title XIX must be headed by a nurse or other medical personnel and must have a medical orientation. The existence of both programs is dependent on whether states elect to include either form of day care in their Title XIX or Title XX plans. This kind of administratively enforced separation of services constrains the delivery of comprehensive rehabilitation services whose essence is the integration of medical and social services (Brody, 1973; U.S. House of Representatives, 1982).

The Older Americans Act of 1965 (and its amendments) is another major piece of legislation in the area of community social services for older persons. Compared to Title XX, it represents a more modest outlay of federal dollars, but unlike Title XX, the Older Americans Act is specifically targeted to older persons. The services covered by the Older Americans Acts include social services; nutrition services; multipurpose senior center facilities; training, research, and demonstration activities; and public service employment projects (U.S. Senate, 1984, p. 497). The 1981 amendments to the Older Americans Act modified the 1978 amendment, requiring that states spend at least 50% of Title III funds on supportive and access services. Under the amendment, states are now required to expend only "an adequate proportion" for such services, allowing states greater latitude in allocating funds among nutrition, senior centers, and social services. In fiscal 1981, 350.3 million federal dollars were for Title III supportive services. Federal support for congregate nutrition during 1983 was $365.3 million; $68.7 million was allocated for home-delivered nutrition (U.S. House of Representatives, 1982).[7]

Other major social programs relevant to older disabled persons include modest federal demonstration programs in social/health maintenance organizations, channeling projects, housing, transportation and independent living programs, and a variety of state and local initiatives in long-term care. Social/health maintenance organizations (S/HMOs) are proposed managed systems of health and long-term care services designed to serve the needs of older clients. Services include a full range of acute inpatient, ambulatory, rehabilitation, nursing home, home health, and personal care services. These proposed services are to be provided under a fixed, prospectively determined budget financed through Medicare, private payments, and Medicaid payments. At present, the S/HMO program is a modest demonstration program supported by the Health Care Financing Administration (HCFA). Four S/HMOs were scheduled for development and operation during 1985. The program provides a model for a "comprehensive health care delivery system responsible to the medical *and* social service support needs of older persons" (U.S. Senate, 1984, pp. 433–434).

The channeling program represents a long-term care demonstration project funded by the Department of Health and Human Services. This program provides community-based, long-term-care services to persons 65 years of age and older who are functionally impaired, unable to perform essential ADLs independently and without adequate informal support. Two service models are being tested under the channeling program. One model focuses on the management of services currently available to clients; the other approach seeks to expand the range of publicly financed services, to support informal caregivers, and to add cost-control features. Ten channeling sites began operation in 1982. The program is scheduled to run 4 years, with a final report to be published in the fall of 1985 (U.S. Senate, 1984, p. 434).

TRAINING

At least six agencies offer training for rehabilitation professionals, four of them requiring a focus on the geriatric population. The Rehabilitation Services Administration (RSA) supports physical medicine residents, as well as training for nurses and the full range of therapy professionals. Election of geriatric content is optional. The National Institute of Mental Health (NIMH) has a growing program of funding for psychogeriatric personnel, including psychiatrists and nurses. The National Institute on Aging (NIA) provides career support for physicians committing themselves to geriatric service or research. The Administration on Aging (AoA), too, has funding for medical educational center geriatric programs. Rehabiliation content is not spelled out in these and other programs. The VA system supports geriatric medicine research and training through Geriatric Research, Education, and Clinical Centers (GRECCs).

SUMMARY AND CONCLUSION

The formal system for older disabled persons is oriented toward medical and income support needs, and it is in those areas that the system has realized its major achievements. Although 15% of the elderly remain in poverty, and 25% in near poverty, significant income gains have been realized for the others, thanks largely to SSDI, SSI support, and VA programs. Similarly, Medicare and Medicaid have insured access to catastrophic acute care medical services. Despite such achievements, significant gaps in service remain.

The complex array of direct and indirect programs that comprise financial support for the formal system are organized along narrowly defined categories of need. Public resources are unevenly distributed among income-maintenance and medical and health/social service programs, and between the physically and the mentally disabled. Income and medical insurance programs are viewed as primarily a federal responsibility and receive the largest share of federal appropriations for the disabled. Health/social programs are largely the responsibility of state and local governments and voluntary community-based organizations. They receive a more modest share of federal appropriations and are more vulnerable to federal budget cuts and state and local belt-tightening. Sharp differences in resource allocation reflect federal policy bias against funding services for older persons that relate to personal maintenance and quality of life. Yet personal maintenance and quality of life are central to the philosophy and the practice of rehabilitation.

In a program context, rehabilitation is the way society channels provider services and public resources to eliminate or modify disability. For the most part, comprehensive rehabilitation services are not available to the disabled elderly or to those with chronic mental illness who are not seen as employable, productive members of society. Virtually the entire rehabilitation system is directed at restoring economic independence and therefore has not been relevant to the needs of those two groups. To a substantial degree, the income-maintenance disability program of SSA is a substitute for the vocational rehabilitation of the older worker. This is reinforced by RSA's negative attitudes toward the older worker—attitudes that are shared by state rehabilitation agencies. Rehabilitating the older worker is not a high governmental priority, nor is it of interest to most corporate employers.

The major medical program geared toward the rehabilitation of the elderly (Medicare) is based on an acute-care medical model and is designed to deal with physical problems. The DRG system is emerging as a major incentive for making rehabilitation programs available to older persons because it encourages the development and expansion of STLTC and rehabilitation services.

In the area of mental health care the state hospital has been replaced by the nursing home. The Medicaid reimbursement program does not contemplate any rehabilitation within that setting. There are few federal programs that address elderly disabled persons in need of social service support. There are few day rehabilitation hospitals. Only a few state Medicaid programs support day-care centers providing rehabilitation services. Attendent care is virtually unknown outside of the small VA program. Similarly, publicly supported homemaker services do not exist except for services to the impoverished provided under Title XX and Title III of the Older Americans Act. Whatever attempts have been made to address systematically the social support needs of the disabled elderly have been restricted to demonstration projects such as channeling and S/HMOs, both of which have been challenged by the Office of Management and Budget.

In summary, physical rehabilitation for disabilities encountered within the framework of the acute-care medical model is being provided through Medicare. However, there are few social support programs for the physically and mentally disabled. Income-maintenance needs have been addressed through entitlements and needs-based federal and state programs. But rehabilitation services for the older disabled and the chronically mentally ill are sparse beyond the medical treatment of physical impairment.

Public programs are a direct result of society's value judgement, which has welfarized the aged and stigmatized the disabled because of a bias that may be called "age disabilityism." The policy arena needs the rehabilitation field's attitude of therapeutic otpimism. The attitude should permeate not only the acute-care medical model but community-based services and institutional programs as well. The goals of rehabilitation policy for the disabled elderly should not be couched in the either/or terms of dependence and independence but in terms that recognize the legitimacy of disability in the elderly. The needs of the caring unit—the family—should be recognized and supported. Public policy should not "blame the victims" of disability. When the individual needs a new environment such as service-supported housing, such facilities should be available.

Major strides toward solving the economic independence needs of the disabled were made during the four decades following 1940. In the last 20 years, significant gains have been made in meeting the acute-care medical needs of the elderly and the elderly disabled. What remains to be accomplished in the years left to this century is to build on the accomplishments that have been achieved in lengthening life by improving the quality of the lives that have been lengthened. Comprehensive rehabilitation embedded in adequate psychosocial supports is one path that leads to that objective.

REFERENCES

Barfield, R. E., & Morgan, J. N. (1976). *"Early retirement" in the pre-retirement years*, pp. 193–194. Washington, DC: U.S. Department of Labor, Employment and Training Administration.

Binstock, R. (1983). The aged as scapegoat. Gerontologist, 23 (2), 136–143.
Brody, S. J. (1973). Comprehensive health care for the elderly: An analysis. Gerontologist, 13 (4), 412–418.
Brody, S. J. (1976). Public policy issues of women in transition. Gerontologist, 16 (2), 181.
Brody, S. J. (1979). The thirty-to-one paradox: Health needs and medical solutions. National Journal, 11 (44), 1869–1873.
Brody, S. J. (1985). Rehabilitation and nursing homes. In E. L. Schneider, C. J. Wendland, A. W. Zimmer, N. List, & M. Ory (Eds.), The teaching nursing home: A new approach to geriatric research, education, and clinical care (pp. 147–156). New York: Raven Press.
Brody, S. J., & Magel, J. S. (1983). Diagnosis related groups. Center for the Study of Aging Newsletter, University of Pennsylvania, 6 (2), 6–8.
Brody, S. J., & Magel, J. S. (1984). DRG—the second revolution in health care for the elderly. Journal of the American Geriatrics Society, 32 (9), 676–679.
Campbell, C. D., & Campbell, R. G. (1976). Conflicting views of the effect of old age survivors insurance on retirement. Economic Inquiry, Fall, 382.
Curdette, M. E., & Baker, S. (1982). Characteristics of social security disability insurance beneficiaries, 1976. (pp. 3, 4, 6). U.S. Department of Health and Human Services, Social Security Administration, Office of Policy, Office of Research and Statistics. [SSA Pub. No. 13-11947 (Revised)] Washington, DC: Government Printing Office.
Delisa, J. A. (1984). Rehabilitation medicine within the veterans administration: report of a survey. Archives of Physical Medicine and Rehabilitation, 65 (7), 388–392.
Federal Register. (1983). 48 (171), 39755.
Golley, E. (1980). Long-term care for developmentally disabled citizens: An overview of relevant policy issues (Appendix G). National Association of State Mental Retardation Program Directors.
Health Care Financing Administration. (1982). The Medicare and Medicaid data book, 1982. Health care financing program statistics.
Holmes, O. W. (1963). The common law. Boston: Little, Brown.
Larkin, K. C., Bruninks, R. H., Doth, D., Hall, B. H., & Hauber, F. (1982). Source of long-term care for the developmentally disabled people. Minneapolis: University of Minnesota, Department of Educational Psychology.
Locke-Connor, C., & Walsh, R. P. (1980). Attitudes toward the older job applicant: Just as competent, but more likely to fail. Journal of Gerontology, 35 (6), 920–927.
Morrison, M. H. (1984). The disabled older worker: Factors influencing employment. Rehabilitation Research and Training Center in Aging Newsletter, 2 (1), 1–3. Philadelphia: University of Pennsylvania.
Noble, J. H., Jr. (1984). Rehabilitating the SSI recipient—overcoming disincentives to employment of severely disabled persons. In Special Committee on Aging, United States Senate (98th Congress, 2nd Session) (Ed.), The Supplemental Security Income Program: A 10-Year overview. Washington, DC: U.S. Government Printing Office.
Office of Management and Budget. (1983). Catalog of federal domestic assistance. Washington, DC: U.S. Government Printing Office.

Office of Nursing Home Affairs, PHS, DHEW. (1975). *Long-term care facility improvement study. Introductory report* (p. 56). Washington, DC: U.S. Government Printing Office.

Oriol, W. (1985). *The Complex Cube of Long Term Care* (p. 76). Washington, DC: American Health Planning Association.

Quinn, J. F. (1977). Micro-economic determinants of early retirement: A cross-sectional view of white married men. *Journal of Human Resources, 12* (3), 338–340.

Roth, H. (1984). The federal dollar in the disability field. *Programs for the handicapped*, No. 3 (May-June).

Social Security Administration. (1976). First findings of the 1972 survey of disabled: General characteristics. *Social Security Bulletin, 39* (10), 6.

Social Security Administration. (1982a). 1954 Social Security Act amendments. *Social Security Bulletin Annual Statistical Supplement, 3.*

Social Security Administration. (1982b). Current operating statistics: Monthly tables. *Social Security Bullletin, 45* (8), 30.

Social Security Administration. (1982c). Current operating statistics: Quarterly tables. *Social Security Bulletin, 45* (6), 80.

Social Security Administration. (1984). Old age, survivors, disability, and health insurance. *Monthly Benefit Statistics.* No. 8:1.

Trietel, R. (1979). Recovery of disabled beneficiaries. A 1975 followup study of 1972 allowances. *Social Security Bulletin, 42* (4), 3–23.

U.S. Congress. (1958). Social Security Act Amendments of 1958 (P.L. 85-840) 72 Stat. 1013, August 28.

U.S. Congress. (1960). Social Security Act Amendments of 1965 (P.L. 86-778) 74 Stat. 924, September 13.

U.S. Congress. (1965). Social Security Act Amendments of 1965 (P.L. 89-97), 79 Stat. 286, July 30.

U.S. Congress. (1967). Social Security Act Amendments of 1967 (P.L. 90-248), 81 Stat. 821, January 2.

U.S. Congress. (1972). Social Security Amendments of 1972. Report of Committee on Finance, U.S. Senate, to accompany H.R. 1, Senate Report No. 92-1930, 92nd Congress, 2nd Session, September 26.

U.S. Congress. (1973). Rehabilitation Act of 1973 (P.L. 93-112), Sec. 7, Subsection 6, a.

U.S. Congress. (1978). Rehabilitation Act of 1978 (P.L. 95-602).

U.S. Congress. (1980). Social Security Disability Amendments of 1980 (PL. 96-265).

U.S. Congress. (1981). Omnibus Budget Reconciliation Act of 1981 (P.L. 97-35).

U.S. Department of Education, Office of Special Education and Rehabilitative Services, Rehabilitation Services Administration. (1983). Characteristics of Persons Rehabilitated in Fiscal Year 1981.

U.S. Department of Health and Human Services, Social Security Administration, Office of Policy. (1982). *1978 survey of disability and work.* Washington, DC: U.S. Government Printing Office.

U.S. Department of Health and Human Services, Social Security Administration, Office of Policy, Office of Research and Statistics. (1974). *Disability survey 1972.* Washington, DC: U.S. Government of Printing Office.

U.S. General Accounting Office. (1978). *Report to the Congress of the United States,* HRD-78-97, April 18. Washington, DC: Author.

U.S. General Accounting Office. (1981). *Report to the Congress of the United States,* HRD 81-48, March 3. More diligent followup needed to weed out ineligible SSA disability beneficiaries. Washington, DC: Author.

U.S. General Accounting Office. (1982). *Report to the Congress of the United States,* HRD 82-112, Sept. 16. The elderly remain in need of mental health services. Washington, DC: Author.

U.S. General Accounting Office (1983). GAO/IPE 84-1, October 21. Medicaid and nursing home care: Cost increases and the need for services are creating problems for the states and the elderly (p.4). Washington, DC: U.S. Government Printing Office.

U.S. House of Representatives. (1980). Committee on Ways and Means. *Background data on programs within the jurisdiction of the Committee on Ways and Means* (p. 419). Washington, DC: U.S. Government Printing Office.

U.S. House of Representatives. (1981). Select Committee on Aging, 97th Congress, 1st Session. *The early retirement myth: Why men retire before age 62* (Comm. Pub. No. 97-978). (pp. 6–27, 57–64, 89–91). Washington, DC: U.S. Government Printing Office.

U.S. House of Representatives. (1982). Select Committee on Aging, 97th Congress, 2nd Session. *Older American Act: A staff summary.* Washington, DC: U.S. Government Printing Office.

U.S. House of Representatives. (1983). Select Committee on Aging, 98th Congress, 1st Session. *Social Security disability reviews: A federally created state problem* (Comm. Pub. No. 98-395) (pp. 228–289, 381, 564). Washington, DC: U.S. Government Printing Office.

U.S. National Center for Health Statistics. (1979). National nursing home survey: 1977 summary for the United States. *Vital and health statistics,* Series 13, Number 43. NCHS, PHS, DHEW, Pub. No. 79-2794. Washington, DC: Government Printing Office.

U.S. Senate. (1983). Special Committee on Aging. April 7 and 8. *Social Security reviews of the mentally disabled.* Washington, DC: U.S. Government Printing Office.

U.S. Senate. (1984). Special Committee on Aging, 98th Congress, 2nd Session. *Developments in aging: 1983 Vol. 1* (Rept. 98-360). Washington, DC: U.S. Government Printing Office.

U.S. Veterans Administration. (1980). *Task Force on Rehabilitation, report.* Author.

U.S. Veterans Administration. (1984a). *Caring for the older veteran.* Author.

U.S. Veterans Administration. (1984b). *Federal benefits for veterans and dependents* (p. 3). Author.

Vogel, R. J., & Palmer, H. C. (1983). *Long-term care: Prospectives from research and demonstration.* (Pub. No. 0-391-555). Washington, DC: Health Care Financing Adminstration, U.S. Department of Health and Human Services.

Williams, T. F. (1984). *Rehabilitation in the aging* (p.xiii). New York: Raven Press.

NOTES

1. These agencies are National Institute of Handicapped Research, National Institute on Aging, National Institutes of Health, National Institute of Mental Health, Administration on Aging, Veterans Administration, Administration on Developmental Disabilities, Rehabilitation Services Administration, National Institute of Neurological and Communicative Disorders and Stroke, Department of Health and Human Services, Department of Transportation, National Council on the Handicapped, Social Security Administration, National Academy of Sciences, National Institute of Arthritis, Diabetes and Digestive and Kidney Diseases, Department of Housing and Urban Development.

2. Federal expenditures for income maintenance for disabled persons are allocated among the following programs and agencies:

Social Security benefits for disabled coal miners	$ 1,077,000,000
Social Security disability insurance (SSDI)	17,584,000,000
Social Security supplemental security income (SSI) for disabled persons including the blind	6,500,000,000
Labor Department, longshoremen's and harbor workers' compensation	4,000,000
Labor Department, coal miners' compensation	446,563,000
Veterans Administration, pensions for non-service-connected disability for veterans	2,522,552,000
Veterans Administration, veterans compensation for service-connected disability	8,030,434,000
Railroad Retirement Board, compensation for disabled railroad workers	665,000,000
	$36,829,549,000

3. The 1965 amendments to the Social Security disability program sought to encourage rehabilitation efforts by allowing DI trust fund monies to be used to reimburse state vocational rehabilitation agencies for the cost of providing services to SSDI beneficiaries.

4. These programs include the Older Americans Act, Title XX of the Social Security Act, Community Service Block Grants, Developmental Disabilities programs, Urban Mass Transit Act, National Mass Transportation Assistance Act, Surface Transportation Assistance Act, Section 202 and Section 8 of the Federal Housing Act, Sections 515, 504 and 521 of farmers home programs, Department of Education programs, and VA programs.

5. Title VI of the Social Security Act.

6. State discretionary authority was expanded by the Omnibus Budget Reconciliation Act (OBRA) of 1981 (P.L. 97-35), which amended Title XX of the Social Security Act to establish a "Block Grant to States for Social Services." Section 2176 of OBRA combined funding for social services for states and

territories and social services staff training. States are allowed to transfer up to 10% of their Title XX social service allotment to one or any combination of block grants for community services, low-income home energy assistance, preventive health services, primary health care, and maternal and child health services. States can offer waivers for case management, homemaker, home health aid, personal care, adult day health, habilitation, and respite care. While federal funds were made available to states without matching requirements, OBRA reduced Title XX funding ceilings. In fiscal 1981, Title XX funding levels reached a peak of $2.9 billion. In fiscal 1982, appropriations dropped to $2.4 billion. In fiscal 1983, 1984, 1985, and 1986 the levels remained below the 1981 level. In October 1983 the Title XX ceiling was increased by $200 million for fiscal 1984 to $2.7 billion and by $100 million for fiscal 1985 as part of a federal supplemental compensation program (P.L. 98-135).

The Act eliminated the federally mandated priority that at least 50% of federal Title XX funds be expended on services to AFDC, SSI, Medicaid recipients, or low-income individuals and families. Technically, states were no longer required to set eligibility standards.

7. The Older Americans Act is composed of six Titles. The largest is Title III, which provides for the development of programs to assist older persons through grants to states. Important social services provided under Title III include meals-on-wheels and congregate feeding programs, supportive services, access services, and senior centers. Supportive services include homemakers, home health aide, visiting services, telephone assurance, chore maintenance, and legal services. Access services include transportation, outreach, and information and referral services.

Other titles under the Older Americans Act provide for area planning and multipurpose senior centers (Title III); training, research, and discretionary projects and programs (Title IV); senior community service employment programs (Title V); and the Administration on Aging (Title II). Federal appropriations for Title II, Title III, and Title IV programs have stayed essentially the same since 1982. Between 1983 and 1984, appropriations for nutrition programs under Title III increased by $2.5 million, whereas appropriations for Title V programs declined by $2.2 million.

8

Informal Supports Systems in the Rehabilitation of the Disabled Elderly

Elaine M. Brody

The impact on the family of having a disabled family member and the role of the family in the disabled person's rehabilitation are well-mined themes in the rehabilitation literature. In the main, however, that literature focuses on the effects of a parent's disability on young children and on the effects of a child's disability on young parents. Similarly, the substantial body of gerontological literature about family care of the disabled elderly does not deal specifically with the family's role in their rehabilitation. Thus, despite the fact that older people constitute at least half of the population in need of rehabilitation, there is a virtual absence of attention to their families' roles in their rehabilitation.

Though the fields of gerontology and rehabilitation have proceeded independently (S. Brody, 1985), there are many common themes. Both fields identify effects on family caregivers such as increased emotional, physical, and financial strains; being caught by competing demands on their time and energy; and loss of educational and social opportunities. Both fields have described profound effects on the family system such as role modifications, shifts in the family homeostasis, and changes in the family's social, leisure, and recreational activities, and overall life style. Both fields emphasize the importance of psychosocial factors in determining families' adaptations and recognize the importance of a family systems approach to helping them. In keeping with the historical focus of each field, however, the rehabilitation literature describes the stressors and the strains incurred from the perspective of young families, whereas the gerontological literature does so from the perspective of families at the opposite end of the life cycle.

There is consensus among professionals in both fields about their responsibility to address the needs of all the people affected by the disability. Apart from ethical considerations, a family focus is a practical necessity if only because professional prescriptions for rehabilitation procedures rely on the family for implementation. Lack of attention to the experiences and needs of family members can sabotage the most meticulous, sophisticated rehabilitation plan. Therefore, assessment of the patient's capacities, potential, and service needs—a procedure that is fundamental to rehabilitation— must be matched by assessment of the family's capacities and resources. No matter the stage of the family's life cycle, its role and professionals' expectations should be viewed in the context of those capacities and resources, the caregivers' characteristics, the effects they experience, and the inner meaning to them of providing care—all of which speak to what professionals' expectations can be.

WHAT FAMILIES DO

In turning to consideration of the families of those who become disabled in old age, there is a body of information so well known to gerontologists that it is no longer a scientific issue. Its summarization remains mandatory, however, because the nature of older people's family relationships continues to be subject to widely held biases based on myths and misinformation.

Popular notions to the contrary, families of the aged have an excellent track record. Thirty years of research has established unequivocally, and without a shred of contradictory evidence, that families do indeed care for and about their elderly family members. Older people are not alienated from their families. Rather, intergenerational ties are strong, viable, and characterized by affection and mutual exchange of services throughout the life span. The main flow of intergenerational services goes from the old to the young, but the direction of that flow changes when the old become disabled.

As chronic illnesses replaced the acute diseases accounting for most deaths early in this century, the nature of the needs of older people shifted from short-term acute care to long-term chronic care. People live longer today after the onset of chronic disease and disability. The number of years of active life expectancy decreases with advancing old age (Katz et al., 1983), and few people reach the end of life without experiencing some period of dependency. More years of dependency mean more years during which there must be someone on whom to depend.

Families responded to the needs of a large population of older people for chronic care—a situation that is new to our time—by inventing long-term care long before that phrase was professionally articulated. Families, not the "formal" system of government and agencies, provide 80% to 90% of medically related care and home nursing, personal care, household maintenance, transportation, and shopping. They link the older person to existing formal services provided by the government and agencies. They respond in emergencies, provide intermittent acute care, and receive the elderly when the latter are discharged from hospitals, rehabilitation facilities, and nursing homes. They do the triage, participating in making decisions about calling the doctor and which doctor to call. The family also provides the expressive support—the concern, affection, and sense of having someone on whom to rely—that is the form of family help most wanted by the elderly. And the family—the informal support system—does all of this with relatively little help from what is euphemistically called the formal support system.

CAREGIVERS

A significant way in which families of elderly rehabilitation patients differ from those of younger patients is in the nature of their relationships to the disabled person. With younger patients, caregiving patterns are comparatively clear-cut; in general, parents care for disabled children, and husbands and wives care for each other if need be.

There is a rough hierarchy of people in the informal support network who are likely to be called on for care of disabled older people (Cantor, 1979). As with younger people, a spouse (when there is one) is the first-line caregiver but most often is assisted by adult children. Most of the disabled elderly are very old, however, and most very old people are widowed. Therefore, most of their caregivers are adult children—predominantly daughters and, to some extent, daughters-in-law. In addition to providing the vast majority of the personal care and instrumental services needed, daughters share their homes when the elderly cannot manage on their own. (An older person is three times as likely to live with a married daughter as with a married son.) Sons also sustain bonds of affection, perform certain gender-defined tasks such as money management, and (helped by their wives) become the "responsible relatives" when they do not have a sister who lives close by (see E. Brody, 1978, for review).

Other relatives become prominent as caregivers when a spouse or a child is not available, though this pattern is less frequent. Some are the disabled person's siblings who themselves are older people; others are members of younger generations in the family—nieces, nephews, and grandchildren. There is little information about care by grandchildren, though it is becoming much more common for such young people to assume responsibility when deaths or disability in a generation leave a gap in the family support system. Some young adults have the responsibility for disabled members of two generations—their parents and grandparents.

Friends and neighbors play an important and special role, but in general they do not provide intensive or long-term care (Cantor, 1979).

Caregiving Spouses

Because of the discrepancy in life expectancy between the sexes and the tendency of men to marry women younger than they are, a disabled elderly man is much more likely than an elderly woman to have a spouse on whom to rely. Most of the 9 million widowed older people are women; at age 65 and over, most older women (52%) are widowed and most older men (77%) are married. Since rates of widowhood rise steeply with advancing age, the imbalance in the ratio of women to men increases accordingly. Between the ages of 65 and 74, there are 131 women to 100 men; between 75 and 84, the ratio is 166:100; and at age 85 and over, there are 224 women to every 100 men (Allan & Brotman, 1978).

Aged husbands and wives exert extraordinary efforts to care for each other, but their capacities to do so are limited by their reduced energy and strength and because most have one or more age-related chronic ailments. They are especially vulnerable to financial, physical, and emotional strain (Horowitz & Shindelman, 1981). Elderly wives caring for disabled husbands, for example, have been found to suffer from low morale, isolation, loneliness, economic hardship, and "role overload" due to multiple responsibilities (Fengler & Goodrich, 1979).

The dependency/independence homeostasis couples have achieved in the course of many decades of living together is disturbed when one spouse becomes disabled. The more dependent spouse may need to become the one who is depended on. They may need to do unaccustomed tasks. Husbands may assume homemaking responsibilities, for instance, while some wives learn to manage money and to do chores. Their physical and emotional strains may be accompanied by acute anxiety and by fear of losing one's partner in a marriage that may have endured half a century or more. Caregiving elderly spouses therefore require careful attention to their own physical and mental health and their needs for respite, concrete helping services, and emotional support.

Adult Children as Caregivers

Most older people have an adult child available to assist the "well" parent who cares for a disabled partner and to provide the bulk of care for those who are widowed (Shanas, 1979a; Sussman, 1965; Tobin & Kulys, 1980). In the main, the elderly realize their preference to live near, but not with their children (Shanas, 1979b), sharing households primarily when reasons of health or economics make it necessary. Overall, only about 18% of the elderly live with children, though rates of such shared living arrangements rise with the advancing age and increasing disability of elderly parents (Shanas, 1979a).

Responsible filial behavior has persisted despite the exponential increase in the demands for parent care that has occurred in the past few decades. Changes in family structure illustrate how it came about that parent care is now a normative experience—expectable, if unexpected (E. Brody, 1985a).

The radical changes in family structure have resulted in the four-generation family becoming a common phenomenon. Thus, 82% of people 65 years of age and older have at least one adult child, and of those, 90% have a grandchild; almost half of the elderly have a great-grandchild (Shanas, 1979a). When one looks at the family tree from the opposite perspective—that of younger family members—it is apparent that at every age people have many more old people in their families than used to be the case. To illustrate, as recently as 20 years ago only 25% of people over the age of 45 had a surviving parent. By 1980, 40% of people in their late fifties had a surviving parent, as did 20% of those in their early sixties, 10% of those in their late sixties, and 3% of those in their seventies (NRTA-AARP, 1981). Seventy-eight percent of women age 40 have a surviving mother, and 16% have a surviving maternal grandmother (Soldo, 1980).

Because parents and children age together and because most older people who become disabled are in advanced old age, most of the children on whom they depend are in their forties and fifties. However, approximately one-third are either under 40 or over 60 years of age. A startling statistic is that 10% of all older people—2.5 million individuals—have an adult child 65 years old or older!

Not only are caregiving children increasingly older, but there are fewer of them in families to share caregiving responsibilities than used to be the case. While the population of older people was increasing numerically and in proportion to the total population, the birth rate fell sharply. The result is a marked alteration in the ratio of those potentially in need of care to adult children who are available to provide it.

In short, all of the evidence indicates that nowadays more adult children provide more care to more older people over longer periods of time than was ever the case in the past (E. Brody, 1985a).

EMOTIONAL ASPECTS OF CAREGIVING

The emotional aspects of caregiving are extremely complex. When an elderly person becomes disabled, the family is confronted with a dramatically new situation—a shift from a long history, often as long as 50 years, during which some workable homeostasis in dependency/independence issues has been achieved. Upsetting that delicate balance is a radical change with profound emotional implications. The older patient and family members are equally ill-prepared for their new roles and there is much ambiguity in their role expectations.

Just as dependency—the erosion or loss of autonomy after a lifetime of independence—is a central issue for the disabled older person, being depended on is a central issue for the caregivers. People vary widely in their capacities to be depended on (though growth and change are possible, of course), and different families react differently. To put the matter in perspective, genuine concern and affection for the older person are generally at work. Most family members help the older patient willingly when need be and derive satisfaction from doing so. At the same time, there is concern about themselves, other family members, and the duration and intensity of the caregiving efforts they will need to exert. Anxieties about their own aging are stimulated. No matter their relationship to the older person, many family caregivers are angry and resentful (though they may not be aware of such unacceptable emotions and/or be unable to express them) at finding themselves in the predicament of needing to do more than they feel able.

Substantial minorities of caregivers have been shown to experience financial strain or physical strain as a result of caregiving. But study after study has identified the most pervasive and most severe consequences as being in the realm of emotional strains. Mental health symptoms such as depression, anxiety, frustration, helplessness, sleeplessness, lowered morale, and emotional exhaustion are related to restrictions on time and freedom, isolation, conflict from the competing demands of various responsibilities, difficulties in setting priorities, and interference with life style, socialization, and recreation (e.g., see Archbold, 1978; Cantor, 1983; Danis, 1978, Frankfather, Smith, & Caro, 1981; Gurland, Dean, Gurland, & Cook, 1978; Hoenig & Hamilton, 1966; Horowitz, 1982; Robinson & Thurnher, 1979; Sainsbury & Grad de Alercon, 1970). The entire family is affected by changes in its life style, privacy, socialization, vacations, future plans, and income when the caregiver's time and attention is diverted from other family members.

The strains of providing care also are intimately connected with the physical and emotional state of the disabled older person who is the recipient of care. For example, chronic physical disability is strongly implicated in the etiology of depression (Gurland, 1976), and Gurland speaks of the "contagion of depression." He found the incidence of depression to be significantly higher than normal in people whose households include a depressed older person (Gurland, et al., 1978). Inevitably, a disabled person's distress is communicated to caregivers. It is difficult to imagine that family members are left untouched by the chronic pain and emotional distress that are the most frequent, pervasive, and bothersome symptoms experienced by the old (E. Brody, Johnsen, Fulcomer, & Lang, 1983).

Such emotional currents are at work in the care of disabled people of any age. But there is a fundamental difference when the recipient of care is the parent and the provider is an adult child. Psychologically, the elderly parent cannot be child to his own child, and the child cannot be parent to her parent. Although the same tasks may be performed—lifting, turning, personal care, constant monitoring, and changing the incontinent, for example—the emotional meaning of and reactions to those tasks are very different.

Though most adult children care deeply, the nature of their commitment is different from the shared and total commitment that young parents have to a disabled child's care and rehabilitation. The priorities of competing demands on the caregiver's energy may need to be ordered differently from those of a caregiver to young children or to a spouse. Adult children often feel guilty about not doing enough for the parent, even if they are devoting themselves to his/her care at great personal cost to themselves (E. Brody, 1985a). When an adult child focuses so intensely on the disabled parent's needs that her own needs and those of other family members are disregarded, there is cause for professional concern and intervention, rather than encouragement of further efforts.

Caregiving daughters or daughters-in-law often experience multiple competing demands on their time and energy. But the nature of such women's personal situations and other responsibilities varies greatly because they may be at many different ages or stages of the family life cycle. When they are relatively young, for example, they may have young children at home and/or be working uphill on a career.

Daughters who are in their middle years or the early stages of aging may be experiencing age-related interpersonal losses (these are the years during which rates of widowhood rise steeply), the onset of chronic ailments, and lower energy levels. They or their husbands may be looking forward to retirement or may already be retired. They may have anticipated a responsibility-free "empty nest" stage of life, only to find those empty nests refilled with disabled elderly parents either literally or in terms of increased responsibility (E. Brody, 1978).

A finding from a Philadelphia Geriatric Center (PGC) study illustrates the way in which the demands of parent care on some older women increase at a time of life when their capacities to provide that care are declining. In comparison with caregiving daughters under 50 years of age, those over 50 had older and more severely disabled mothers, spent much more time providing help, did more difficult caregiving tasks, more often shared their households with their mothers, and more often were widowed and had lower incomes (Lang & Brody, 1983).

At whatever age or stage the need for parent care arises, there is enormous variability in factors that qualify the caregiver's capacities—in their health, marital status, living arrangements, geographic distance from the parent, socioeconomic and ethnic backgrounds, personality, adaptive capacities, and the quality of parent–child relationships.

To add to the complexities of these situations, some caregivers have responsibilities to more than one disabled person. A middle-aged couple, for example, can have four elderly parents between them, more than one of whom is disabled. Many caregivers help other elderly relatives such as aunts and uncles in addition to their parents and parents-in-law. In another recent PGC study, for example, we found that many women in our sample of daughters who were providing care to disabled elderly mothers were in the midst of "caregiving careers." Half of them had helped elderly fathers before they died, one-third had helped other elderly relatives in the past, 22% were currently helping another elderly relative as well as the parent, and two-thirds had children under the age of 18 in their households (10% of them under the age of 6) (E. Brody, 1985a).

In recent years, there has been concern about whether the rapid entry of middle-aged women, the traditional caregivers, into the work force would affect their capacity to provide care to the disabled elderly to the same extent as in the past. Sixty-nine percent of women between the ages of 35 and 44 now work, as do 62% of women between the ages of 45 and 54, and 42% of women between the ages of 55 and 64 (U.S. Bureau of Labor Statistics, 1984). Though out-of-home employment places an additional demand on those who are caregivers to a disabled older person, research to date indicates that they do not neglect any of their various responsibilities. What they do give up is their own free time and opportunities for socialization and recreation (E. Brody, 1985a; Cantor, 1983; Horowitz, 1982; Lang & Brody, 1983).

Some of the women in the PGC study, worn down from prolonged periods of care to extremely disabled parents, had experienced negative effects on their own health and had quit their jobs to take care of their disabled parents; others, who were still working, were considering quitting for the same reason, and some had already cut back on the number of hours they worked. (See E. Brody et al., 1983 for a detailed report on these findings.) Apart from the emotional and social costs of such decisions, there are economic costs to the caregiver's family when she leaves her job. The women who had left their jobs had much lower family incomes than any of the other women in the study. Since that study was focused on daughters, it did not include wives of elderly disabled people. Evidence is now emerging that many wives leave their jobs to care for disabled husbands. (See E. Brody et al., 1983, for review.).

Emotional support from spouses (Sussman, 1979), siblings (Horowitz,

1982), and other relatives (Zarit, Reever, & Bach-Peterson, 1980), mitigates the caregivers' strains. But when changes in the family homeostasis stimulate interpersonal conflicts, relationships can be affected negatively between husbands and wives, among adult siblings, and across the generations. The disabled person does not remain unaffected by such emotional currents. Being the storm center of family conflicts undoubtedly has an impact on the older person's response to the rehabilitation process.

When a disabled older person moves into a child's home, the extreme difficulties of such an arrangement are not always fully anticipated. It is not surprising that shared living arrangements have been found to be a powerful predictor of caregiver strain. The introduction of the disabled older person into an adult child's home (often after parent and child have lived separately for half a century or more) is a potent force in upsetting the family homeostasis, changing its routines, affecting privacy, and affording an opportunity for differences in personalities and values to come to the surface.

Moreover, when a disabled elderly person has more than one adult child, the question of which of them is to assume the main responsibility may become a major issue. Even acceptance by one child of the role of principal caregiver does not settle all problems regarding the allocation of caregiving responsibilities. Tensions may arise about matters such as doing one's fair share and differing views about the kind of care that should be given and where it should take place.

All of these considerations require careful appraisal by the rehabilitation team as it plans for rehabilitation procedures and the subsequent ongoing care of the older patient.

SPECIAL CAREGIVING SITUATIONS

Though care of elderly spouses by each other and parent care are the main patterns, there are several other caregiving situations on which attention should be focused as well.

Double Dependency

First, some caregivers provide help to both a disabled elderly spouse or parent and to their own child whose disability may be developmental or due to trauma. Though data are lacking on the prevalence of such situations, the number of them cannot be negligible. Given the reality that parent care has become a normative experience (E. Brody, 1985a), a large (but unknown) proportion of parents of disabled young people can expect that at some point they will be confronted with double dependency—that is, they will be depended on by both disabled children or spouses *and* disabled parent(s). An illustrative case is that of a widow in her fifties who is caring for an elderly mother with Alzheimer's disease; also in her household are a mentally disturbed adult son, another son whose wife left him when his legs were amputated as a result of an automobile accident, and the latter's 6-year-old child.

Sodo and Myllyluoma (1983) provide some information regarding a small subset of such situations. In their analysis of a national data set, they found that when an older couple lived with others in caregiving households, approximately one in nine of the caregivers provided assistance to two or more disabled persons, one of whom is an elderly person and the other most often being an impaired adult child of the older couple.

Growing Old as a Disabled Person

A second underattended and underresearched intergenerational caregiving situation is that of the increasing population of disabled younger people who have grown old and have lost their caregivers or face that prospect. Such situations are illustrated by the retarded man of 62 who was applying for admission to the institutional facility of the PGC. "My mother and father are dead," he said, "so I am an orphan and have no one to take care of me." Variations on the same theme are: the weary 85-year-old woman who was admitted to our nursing home together with the paraplegic daughter for whom she had cared for 62 years, and the 82-year-old woman who could no longer care for her 75-year-old mentally retarded brother and a schizophrenic sister who had been "deinstitutionalized" from a state psychiatric facility. In some instances, the caregiver herself becomes disabled. The anxiety and fear of the future of both the caregivers ("Who will take care of my child when I am gone?") and the care recipients ("Who will take care of me when my parents die?") in such situations have a special poignancy.

The Disabled without Family Caregivers

A third special situation is that of disabled elderly people who do not have family members available. In addition to the 9 million widowed older people (68% of women and 24% of men), 9% of women and 7% of men over the age of 65 are divorced or had never married. About 20% of older people either have never had a child or are childless because they have outlived their children (Allan & Brotman, 1981). Approximately 11% (or almost 2 million old people) do not see a child as often as once a month (Shanas, 1979a); for most of these, geographic distance precludes the availability of a child for supportive care; for a minority, little or no help can be expected due to long-standing alienation.

Friends and neighbors are particularly important to those without kin. But they do less, do what they do voluntarily, and cannot have the commitment or sense of obligation that characterizes family members. Their concrete helping activities are significant at times of temporary illnesses or emergencies but are sporadic and short-term. However, as Cantor's study (1979) showed, friends and neighbors equal kin in relieving loneliness. The value of that role should not be underestimated.

In short, elderly individuals without family or who do not have family close at hand, and whose disabilities are severe or prolonged, are at high risk. Meeting their needs for support in rehabilitation deserves our special concern, attention, and creativity.

The Disabled Who Are Institutionalized

A fourth special rehabilitation situation is that of the severely disabled older people for whom institutionalization becomes necessary. Weighing the possibility of institutionalization is a particularly delicate decision-making process. The number of older people in need of nursing home care will increase in the future as the number of very old, impaired people increases. At present, more than a million older people are in institutions at any one time; between 23% and 38% of people 65 or older will spend some time in a nursing home during their lives (Liu & Palesch, 1981).

Older people and their families suffer intensely when permanent care in a nursing home becomes necessary. Despite their recognition of the realities that make such placement necessary, the elderly patient experiences anxiety, fear, and feelings of rejection and abandonment, and family members have painful emotions such as guilt, conflict, sadness, and shame. Anxieties about separations—including the ultimate separation—are stimulated. Well-meaning families may deny the patient the opportunity to participate to the fullest extent possible in making that decision.

Because the behavior of families of the institutionalized elderly is widely misunderstood, a special word about them is in order. Thanks to a consistent body of research, it can be stated flatly that families do not dump their elderly into institutions. Rather, they exert strenuous efforts to avoid institutional placement of the old, often exhausting their physical, emotional, and financial resources in the process. Nursing home placement is sought when they reach a breaking point.

Old people in nursing homes are not representative of the total elderly population. They are a decade older (with an average age of about 83) and have many more physical and mental impairments. Fifty to sixty percent of them have some degree of Alzheimer's disease or a related disorder, for example, compared with 5% to 7% of noninstitutionalized older people. The role of families is highlighted by the fact that, in contrast to the total elderly population, the vast majority of the institutionalized aged (88%) are not married (being widowed, divorced, or never married), more of them (approximately one-half) are childless, and those who have children have fewer children (E. Brody, 1981). In fact, each additional child one has reduces the chances of being institutionalized in one's old age (Soldo, 1980).

Not only do the vast majority of families exert effort to avoid nursing home placement of the disabled elderly, but they continue to visit and to sustain their interest and concern after admission takes place and are deeply affected by the older person's condition and experiences. Such continued relationships with family members have been found to be central to the well-being of institutionalized older people (see E. Brody, 1985b for review). Given those sustained bonds, family members should be involved in the rehabilitation of those who are in nursing homes to the fullest possible extent. They need explanations no less than families of older people who live in the community. For example, some family members of the institutionalized elderly complain that not enough rehabilitation is being done whereas others request that rehabilitation be discontinued ("My mother is so old and frail. Leave her in peace").

THE HEALTH PROFESSIONAL AND THE FAMILIES OF THE DISABLED AGED

Because family members are the main providers of help, their encouragement and support are critical to the motivation of the disabled elderly. Moreover, the efforts the family members need to exert provide them with a strong incentive for helping the older people to achieve their maximum possible levels of function. The realization of even modest rehabilitation goals that reduce dependency can make major differences in the caregiver's lives. Shifts from wheelchair to walker, from incontinence to continence, or from an inability to communicate to the ability to make themselves understood and provide feedback to the caregiver can significantly reduce the efforts family members must make and ameliorate their strains.

It bears repetition that the capacities of family members must be appraised most carefully by the professional rehabilitation team. Many caregivers expect more of themselves than their realistic capacities indicate, even at the risk of their own health and well-being. And the disabled older person, in focusing on his/her own needs, may expect too much of the caregivers.

In that context, there are some special considerations to which health professionals must be sensitive in dealing with the family of the aged disabled patient.

Balancing their relationships with the patient and with family members who are their partners in the elderly patient's rehabilitation makes special demands on professionals. Although family members need to feel that their feelings and efforts are appreciated, it is important to treat the patient (no matter how disabled) as a dignified adult and to preserve his/her right to manage his/her own life to the fullest possible extent. Some families, with the best intentions, tend to infantilize the disabled older adult and to "take over" too much. Any implication that control over his/her own life has been transferred to others can be detrimental to the patient's rehabilitation, intensifying feelings of helplessness, hopelessness, negative self-image, and loss of autonomy, all of which already have been stimulated or intensified by the loss of function. Professionals' attitudes can set the tone in communicating the respect due the patient and foster his/her motivation to take responsibility for his/her own rehabilitation program.

It is particularly difficult for the professional to avoid being drawn into an alliance with either the caregiver or the patient (Rosow, 1981). The patient and the family caregiver may unite against the professional in expecting— even demanding—that magic be performed to restore the patient to full functioning level. The patient may be left out if the professional and family member talk together about him/her. The caregiver, wanting to control the situation, may try in subtle ways to enlist the professional in supporting his/her position. Or the patient may try to enlist the professional's help in defending against the caregiver's power and control.

Because many people confuse pathological processes with the intrinsic processes of aging, family members often misunderstand the nature of the elderly person's disability. Attributing disabilities to intrinsic aging— "nothing can be done"—leads to therapeutic nihilism and to discouragement that can sabotage the rehabilitation program. At the other extreme, family members may have unrealistic fantasies that the older person's previous level of functioning can be fully restored. The therapeutic optimism so essential to successful rehabilitation of the aged (S. Brody, 1985) is a critical ingredient of what Williams (1984) has called the "rehabilitation philosophy," but that optimism must be in the framework of the patient's realizable potential.

The role of the rehabilitation team often includes becoming the focal point of decision-making and planning. Professionals are looked to as knowledgeable and understanding people who are not caught in the emotional upset of patient and family. This is an exceptionally demanding role for which there are not simple guiding rules, since each patient and family presents a unique set of personal and social circumstances.

The legitimate goal of maintaining the patient in his/her own home as long as possible depends on involving family members in the planning process at the earliest possible moment and in training them in the actual tasks they will need to carry out. Implementing an appropriate plan also relies on each family's particular situation and on the formal (government and agencies) services that can be mobilized to supplement its efforts. In the light of the limited capacities of many families of older people, their efforts often must be supported by such services if the goals of rehabilitation are to be achieved. In contrast to the notion that formal services encourage family shirking, families have been found to be extremely modest in their requests; formal services strengthen the family's caregiving capacities (Horowitz, 1982; Sherwood, Morris, & Morris, 1984; Zimmer & Sainer, 1978), and help them to do what they have been trying to do more effectively. A lack of needed services can lead to breakdown of overburdened family members and can increase their mental and physical health problems.

The rehabilitation team can act as the gatekeeper to introduce patient and family to the complex and confusing array of programs that constitute the "formal" support system (see S. J. Brody, *this volume*). Of particular importance are family-focused services such as respite care (to give the family temporary relief when needed), day hospitals, and day-care centers, for example (though all of these are in short supply). If the critical counseling role cannot be performed by the rehabilitation team, patients and families can be referred to agencies in the community that can provide that service and whose job it is to be informed about the complete range of available services and facilities, to connect older people and their families with those services, and to help to mobilize them. Such organizations include Area Agencies on Aging, family counseling agencies, information and referral services, and hospital social service departments.

CONCLUSION

In conclusion, it is recognized that the most skillful and dedicated rehabilitation effort cannot do it all, and goals must be realistic. But achievement of those goals depends on our viewing family members from two perspectives. The family is our "patient" in a real sense because family members are at risk of mental and physical problems if their caring roles become unduly stressful. If that happens, we lose them in their other role—that of full partner and indispensable ally in the rehabilitation of the disabled elderly individual.

REFERENCES

Allan, C., & Brotman, H. (1981). *Chartbook on aging in America*. Compiled for the 1981 While House Conference on Aging. Washington, DC: Government Printing Office.

Archbold, P. (1978). *Impact of caring for an ill elderly parent of the middle-aged or elderly offspring caregiver*. Paper presented at the 31st Annual meeting of the Gerontological Society, Dallas, TX. Abstract, *The Gerontologist, 18* (5, Part II), 44.

Brody, E. M. (1978). The aging of the family. *The Annals of the American Academy of Political and Social Science, 438,* 13–27.

Brody, E. M. (1981). The formal support network: Congregate treatment settings for residents with senescent brain dysfunction. In N. E. Miller & G. D. Cohen (Eds.), *Aging; Vol 15: Clinical aspects of Alzheimer's disease and senile dementia* (pp. 301–331). New York: Raven Press.

Brody, E. M. (1985a). Parent care as a normative family stress. *The Gerontologist, 25* (1), 19–29.

Brody, E. M. (1985b). The role of the family in nursing homes: Implications for research and public policy. In M. S. Harper & B. Lebowitz. (Eds.), *Mental illness in nursing homes: Agenda for research,* NIMH (pp. 234–264). Washington, DC: U.S. Government Printing Office.

Brody, E. M., Johnsen, P. T., Fulcomer, M. C., & Lang, A. M. (1983). Women's changing roles and help to the elderly parents: Attitudes of three generations of women. *Journal of Gerontology, 38* (5), 597–607.

Brody, S. J. (1985). Rehabilitation and nursing homes. In E. L. Schneider, C. J. Wendland, A. W. Zimmer, N. List, & M. Ory (Eds.), *The teaching nursing home: A new approach to geriatric research, education, and clinical care* (pp. 147–156). New York: Raven Press.

Cantor, M. H. (1979). Neighbors and friends: An overlooked resource in the informal support system. *Research on Aging, 1,* 434–463.

Cantor, M. H. (1983). Strain among caregivers: A study of experience in the United States. *The Gerontologist, 23* (6), 597–603.

Danis, B. G. (1978). *Stress in individuals caring for ill elderly relatives*. Paper presented at the 31st Annual Meeting of the Gerontological Society, Dallas, TX. Abstract, *The Gerontologist, 18* (5, Part II), 63.

Evans, J. G. (1981). Care of the aging in Great Britain: An overview. In M. A. Lewis (Ed.), *The aging: medical and social supports in the decade of the 80's* (pp. 13–19). New York: Center on Gerontology, Fordham University.

Fengler, A. P., & Goodrich, N. (1979). Wives of elderly disabled men: The hidden patients. *The Gerontologist, 19* (2), 175–183.

Frankfather, D., Smith, M. J., & Caro, F. G. (1981). *Family care of the elderly: Public initiatives and private obligations*. Lexington, MA: Lexington Books.

Gurland, B. (1976). The epidemiology of depression in the elderly. Paper presented at Conference on Depression in the Elderly, Philadelphia.

Gurland, B., Dean, L., Gurland, R., & Cook, D. (1978). Personal time dependency in the elderly of New York City: Findings from the U.S.–U.K. cross-national geriatric community study. In B. Gurland, L. Dean, R. Gurland, & D. Cook (Eds.), *Dependency in the elderly of New York City* (9–45). New York: Community Council of Greater New York.

Hoenig, J., & Hamilton, M. (1966). Elderly patients and the burden on the household. *Psychiatra et Neurologia* (Basel), 152, 281–293.

Horowitz, A. (1982). *The role of families in providing long-term care to the frail and chronically ill elderly living in the community.* Final report submitted to the Health Care Financing Administration. Washington, DC: U.S. Department of Health and Human Services.

Horowitz, A., & Shindelman, L. W. (1981). *Reciprocity and affection: Past influences on current caregiving.* Paper presented at the 34th Annual Meeting of the Gerontological Society of America, Toronto. Abstract, *The Gerontologist, 21* (Special Issue), 312.

Katz, S., Branch, L. G., Branson, M. H., Papsidero, J. A., Beck, J. C., & Greer, D. S. (1983). Active life expectancy. *The New England Journal of Medicine, 309* (20), 1218–1224.

Lang, A., & Brody, E. M. (1983). Characteristics of middle-aged daughters and help to their elderly mothers. *Journal of Marriage and the Family, 45,* 193–202.

Liu, K., & Palesch, Y. (1981). The nursing home population: Different perspectives and implications for policy. *Health Care Financing Review, 3* (2), 15–23.

NRTA-AARP (National Retired Teachers Association-American Association of Retired Persons). (1981, July). *National survey of older Americans.* Washington, DC: Author.

Robinson, B., & Thurnher, M. (1979). Taking care of aged parents: A family cycle transition. *The Gerontologist, 19* (6), 586–593.

Rosow, I. (1981). Coalitions in geriatric medicine. In M. R. Haug (Ed.), *Elderly patients and their doctors* (pp.137–146). New York: Springer.

Sainsbury, P., & Grad de Alercon, J. (1970). The effects of community care in the family of the geriatric patient. *Journal of Geriatric Psychiatry, 4* (1), 23–41.

Shanas, E. (1979a). The family as a social support system in old age. *The Gerontologist, 19* (2), 169–174.

Shanas, E. (1979b). Social myth as hypothesis: The case of the family relations of old people. *The Gerontologist, 19* (1), 3–9.

Sherwood, S., Morris, S., & Morris, J. N. (1984). *Relationships between formal and informal services provision to frail elders.* Paper presented at 37th Annual Scientific Meeting of the Gerontological Society of America, San Antonio, TX. Abstract, *The Gerontologist, 24* (Special Issue), 81.

Soldo, B. J., & Myllyluoma, J. (1983). Caregivers who live with dependent elderly. meeting of the Secretary's Advisory Committee on Rights and Responsibilities of Women, U.S. Department of Health and Human Services, Washington, DC.

Soldo, B. J. & Myllyluoma, J. (1983). Caregivers who live with dependent elderly. *The Gerontologist, 23* (6), 605–611.

Sussman, M. B. (1979). *Social and economic supports and family environment for the elderly.* Final report to the Administration on Aging, Grant No. 90-A-316. Durham, NC: Duke University.

Sussman, M. B. (1965). Relationships of adult children with their parents in the United States. In E. Shanas & G. F. Streib, (Eds.), *Social structure and the family: Generational relations* (pp. 62–92). Englewood Cliffs, NJ: Prentice Hall.

Tobin, S. S., & Kulys, R. (1980). The family and services. In C. Eisdorfer (Ed.), *Annual review of gerontology and geriatrics* (Vol. 1) (pp. 370–399). New York: Springer.

U.S. Bureau of Labor Statistics. (1984). *Employment and earnings.* Washington, DC: Author.

Williams, T. F. (1984). Introduction. In T. F. Williams (Ed.), *Rehabilitation in the Aging* (p.xiii). New York: Raven Press.

Zarit, S. H., Reever, K. E., & Bach-Peterson, J. (1980). Relatives of the impaired aged: Correlates of feeling of burden. *The Gerontologist, 20*(6), 649–655.

Zimmer, A. H., & Sainer, J. S. (1978). *Strengthening the family as an informal support for their aged: Implications for social policy and planning.* Paper presented at the 31st Annual Meeting of the Gerontological Society, Dallas, TX. Abstract, *The Gerontologist, 18*(5, Part II), 153.

Part II

Mental Health and the Elderly

9

Rehabilitation and Alzheimer's Disease

Burton V. Reifler and Linda Teri

There is no cure for Alzheimer's disease. This is hardly new information, but we wish to deal with this issue first so we can set it aside and then give rehabilitation in Alzheimer's disease the attention it deserves, free of any bias that, because it cannot be cured, rehabilitation doesn't matter. For years the public and professionals alike have mentally classified Alzheimer's disease as different from other chronic diseases, and the time-honored concepts of tertiary prevention and rehabilitation have somehow been viewed as less applicable to demented patients than to individuals with, for example, heart disease or stroke. Until the past few years, few people seemed to be giving attention to the problem of what to do after the diagnosis was made.

Times have changed. Rehabilitation, defined as helping someone reach his/her highest attainable level of skill and function, matters in Alzheimer's disease. Concerned families and leading practitioners are now eager to learn more about rehabilitation in Alzheimer's disease. It is no longer sufficient just to make an accurate diagnosis. We now have the knowledge, experience, and resources to make specific recommendations and establish a plan.

Several issues will be addressed in this chapter. First, we will briefly review both the scope of the overall problem of Alzheimer's disease and the curious attitude that many people have toward Alzheimer's disease compared with other chronic diseases. The other topics we will address are the evaluation process of a patient with Alzheimer's disease, the problem of assessing function, and the need for development of educational programs to train health professionals.

Anyone with more than a casual interest in Alzheimer's disease can hardly fail to notice the attention it receives. After one grasps the extent of the problem, the attention seems at least deserved, and perhaps inadequate. Once we do away with the misconception that Alzheimer's disease and senility are two different things—for all practical purposes they are the same—we are faced with the realization that Alzheimer's disease is the most common cause of memory loss in old age, accounting for more than one-half of such cases, thus affecting 2 to 4 million people in this country.

The costs both dollar and human are so enormous that they are hard to grasp. One reason that rehabilitation is so important is the enormous potential savings from even the smallest gains in Alzheimer's disease. If the cost of nursing home care is around $2,000 a month, any treatment that prolongs independent living for 6 months saves $12,000 in one patient. For the estimated one-half million Alzheimer's patients already in nursing homes, that would be a total savings of $6 billion. Postponing admission by 6 months in only 10% would save $600 million. And once in the nursing home, even modest gains can result in savings of hundreds of millions of dollars. Given the extent and expense of Alzheimer's disease, the cost–benefit potential of successful rehabilitation programs is great.

Our initial comment was that Alzheimer's is viewed differently from other chronic illnesses. To explore this point further, a few other chronic diseases should be briefly considered to see if we have learned the etiology and means of prevention or cure. The search for cancer's cause has led in many directions, including genetic factors, exposure to toxic substances, and infectious agents. Some forms of cancer can be prevented or cured, others are thought of in terms of improved 5-year survival, and some are so severe that there are no 5-year survivors. There are numerous forms of heart disease, with atherosclerosis and hypertension the most common causes, but we are far short of a precise understanding of why they occur, and treatment success is measured by reduction in symptoms and sequalae, not cure. Parkinson's disease is frequently mentioned as a model for improved understanding and treatment of Alzheimer's, the possible similarity being identification of a specific chemical deficiency and treatment through supplying this missing substance. However, the result of 15 years of clinical experience with raising brain levels of dopamine is that Parkinson's sufferers have been helped, but not cured. The point is, that whereas our goal is to learn the cause and cure of Alzheimer's disease, we have not yet accomplished that with other major chronic diseases, and rehabilitation efforts in Alzheimer's disease should not be slighted just because Alzheimer's is incurable at the present time.

The opportunities for improving our rehabilitative efforts in Alzheimer's disease are extraordinary—partly because of past attitudes that have interfered with this goal. Imagine for a moment that in individuals over 65, cancer was not considered a disease but "senile deterioration." Never mind that this senile deterioration did not occur in most old people, or that it seemed to occur in several forms, or that there were distinct pathologic changes, or that in younger individuals it was identified correctly as an illness. Although the evidence was overwhelming that it was a disease, many people, including health professionals, regarded it as part of growing old.

This is not a farfetched consideration when applied to Alzheimer's disease. In one study (Barnes & Raskind, 1981), 64 patients, representing three different nursing homes and under the care of a total of 20 physicians, were evaluated. The patients were selected because they met accepted criteria for dementia and, when additional well-established criteria were applied by the investigators to make a more precise determination, more than 90% could be given a specific diagnosis, usually Alzheimer's disease. Of the existing chart diagnoses, 69% contained either no diagnosis of any kind related to dementia, or only a nonspecific diagnosis such as organic brain syndrome or senility. This is analogous to 69% of cancer patients in nursing homes having either no diagnosis at all, or only the general diagnosis of malignancy with no additional details such as primary location, presence of metastases, or degree of differentiation on microcopic examination.

A recent *Journal of the American Medical Association* commentary further explored the adequacy of nursing home diagnoses (Sabin, Vitug, & Mark, 1982). In that report, the investigators confirmed a diagnosis of dementia in 132 nursing home patients (as with the study by Barnes and Raskind, patients were from several nursing homes and from the practices of many different physicians), but on reviewing the charts, they found that "two-thirds . . . had diagnoses such as senility, chronic brain syndrome, or schizophrenia . . . the others had general medical diagnoses that made no mention of neurological or psychiatric ailment."

Unfortunately, those two studies are representative of the "state of the art" with respect to the diagnosis of Alzheimer's disease in the nursing home; it is usually done carelessly or not at all. And since a fundamental rule of medicine is that diagnosis precedes treatment, it is obvious that if a problem is not identified, there can be no plan for dealing with it.

Since making an accurate diagnosis is the cornerstone of rehabilitation, let us take a moment to outline the reasons for the failure to diagnose Alzheimer's disease; for if we can identify them, we can work to correct them. One is precisely the point I have been developing, sometimes expressed in statements such as "Why bother making a diagnosis you can't do much about?" If that argument is valid, then it should also be applied to illnesses such as carcinoma of the pancreas and severe forms of emphysema and cardiomyopathy. Obviously I do not suggest this but offer it to illustrate the perspective many physicians have toward dementia that allows them to justify ignoring it. With cancer and heart disease, we place great emphasis—and rightly so—on detection and classification, so that we can learn more and improve treatment. The same need exists with Alzheimer's disease.

Another reason for inadequate diagnosis may be the confusing terminology in the literature on Alzheimer's disease. We have the following terms: Alzheimer's disease (sometimes modified by the adjectives senile or presenile), dementia of the Alzheimer's type (DAT), senile dementia of the Alzheimer's type (SDAT), primary degenerative dementia (PDD), primary neuronal degeneration (PND), and senile dementia (SD). There is obviously room for simplification, and perhaps it is time to develop a uniform terminology.

Lack of payment for medical services related to Alzheimer's disease, particularly by Medicare, is another factor in not diagnosing it. Payment is inconsistent and seems to depend on the interpretation of the specific Medicare carrier. Many families of patients with Alzheimer's have received denial-of-payment forms containing the explanation that Medicare does not reimburse for counseling related to coping with the normal aging process—a statement families find ironic, enraging, and sometimes demoralizing. To continue the cancer analogy, these rejections of benefits would be similar to refusing payment for services related to cancer on the ground that such services are only to help people cope with the physical changes of normal aging. Support by Medicare of basic psychiatric services for Alzheimer's disease is sorely needed. The recent recommendation to this effect from the Secretary's Task Force on Alzheimer's Disease (1984) will be an important step in accurate diagnosis, and therefore in rehabilitation as well, if it is administered according to the intent of the Task Force.

Having presented the arguments about the need to correct the errors in our attitudes about Alzheimer's disease, the evaluation process itself will be discussed. Rehabilitation requires comprehensive assessment with attention to multiple factors. It is difficult to help victims of Alzheimer's disease reach their highest level of function without evaluating their mental function, physical health, and social and environmental situation.

To illustrate how evaluation and rehabilitation are linked together, the outpatient clinic at the University of Washington in Seattle will be described. Since opening in 1978, the clinic has provided more than 1,200 assessments for mentally impaired elderly, most of whom were diagnosed as having Alzheimer's disease. A representative case example is as follows:

> Mrs. A had required lengthy hospitalizations for depression twice during her adult life. Now at age 73 the possibility came up again. She was fretful, disoriented most of the time, and constantly complained about muscle aches. Her

routine medications included an antidepressant, an antipsychotic, a narcotic analgesic, and a sleeping pill.

Her daughter, Mrs. B., had insisted that her parents accompany her to Geriatric and Family Services. Mrs. B. was unsure not only as to what she should do, but about what was wrong. Her father was shy, unsure of himself around others, and felt the burden of caring for his wife.

Mrs. A. had moderate dementia and was also depressed. The first step was to gradually withdraw as many medications as possible, and, as this was done over a 3-month period, her affect improved and her memory became slightly better. Her diagnosis was established as Alzheimer's disease with depressive features, with the latter in remission.

The next task was to deal with the issues within the family. Mrs. A. was frightened, her husband was frustrated, and their daughter was angry and confused. The team psychiatrist met with Mr. and Mrs. A., and the social worker had individual sessions with their daughter. Mr. A. was explicitly told that his well-being was crucial for his wife and that if he allowed himself some respite he would be better able to care for her. He was finally able to accept this advice when his wife said she could see the need as well, and he took a fishing trip with a cousin. The benefits of this trip extended over several months, during which he became more realistic about the limits of what he could provide, and he successfully enrolled Mrs. A. in an adult day center.

Their daughter needed to discuss past history before she could deal with the present. She had wished for more affection from her parents and resented having had little opportunity to express her feelings to them. She frequently felt angry at her mother and then felt guilty because of that. The opportunity to ventilate, combined with education about the nature of her mother's problem and suggestions as to how to respond to certain situations—such as changing the subject when she became frustrated by the mother's repetitive questions—enabled her to feel more comfortable with her parents. Instead of dreading visits, she began to look forward to them.

One year after their first visit, relationships among the family were stable; Mr. A. allowed himself to pursue some interests of his own, and his wife had adjusted well to the day center. They reduced their clinic visits to every 3 months, then to every 6 months.

Four years later the patient's husband died, and her dementia had progressed to the point that she required nursing home care. The daughter again consulted the clinic staff, this time for recommendations about the best placement for her mother and to help her deal with the re-emergence of her feelings toward her mother.

In our opinion the services of the clinic helped Mrs. A. and her family in several ways: She received an accurate diagnosis, a source of excess disability (overmedication) was removed, the family received advice and counseling on how to best care for her, she was referred to an adult day center, Mr. A. was encouraged to take periodic breaks, and her daughter received help on choosing her mother's nursing home. Thus, this case example provides numerous instances of the potential for rehabilitation in Alzheimer's disease as our interventions aided in keeping her as active and independent as possible.

First presented in the literature in 1980 (Reifler & Eisdorfer, 1980), the evaluation at Geriatric and Family Services consists of a psychiatric assessment, physical examination, social and environmental assessment (done in the patient's home where possible), and psychological testing. After these steps are completed, there is a staff conference to review the findings. Recommendations are given to the family in writing and cover 11 areas: stop medications, begin medications, further medical evaluation or treatment, move to new living situation, modify current living situation, regular treatment for patient, further consultations with family, additional in-home help, participation in specific community programs, respite for family, and other. Each area is checked as strongly recommended, recommended, or not recommended, and space is provided for staff comments. Follow-up care is provided on a case-by-case basis.

There was nothing new about any of the components of this program: the novel aspects were to combine all of the features in a single administrative structure using an integrated data base (Cox, Hanley, & Reifler, 1982), to place equal emphasis on both patient and family, and to pay close attention to program evaluation from the outset. Initially, the research component was descriptive. The average age of our patients was 77 years; women were referred twice as often as men; most of the patients still lived at home; half were homeowners; the referring family member was usually a spouse, daughter, or son; and, as we expected, most of the patients had Alzheimer's disease, depression, or both. Appointment-keeping rates have consistently exceeded 90%. We estimate that the cost of the evaluation currently averages $850 and that Medicare pays for more than half.

One measure of the program's effectiveness is based on the responses of families after the evaluation was completed. Replies to questionnaires sent to a sample of accompanying family members indicated that 90% of respondents would recommend the service to others, and 75% were satisfied with the overall program. Statistically significant changes include an improvement in the ability of the families to handle the stress of the situation and increased utilization of community resources, both of which we had hoped to accomplish.

The improved ability to handle stress was often in the face of worsening behavioral problems. The benefits of the evaluation were that the family now felt they knew what they were facing, had left no stone unturned, and had a place to turn for help. In many instances, the evaluation was the treatment.

We also have been gratified to find out that the model travels well. Directors of eight other programs have acknowledged that they either successfully replicated our program or that the experience from our clinic was useful in shaping their own. We do not see this as a tribute to our ingenuity; rather it confirms that there is an immediate demand in any large city for a comprehensive, family-oriented, outpatient approach to the diagnosis and long-term management of Alzheimer's disease.

Our research over the last 5 years shows a clear link between accurate diagnosis and rehabilitation, in that the diagnostic evaluation often reveals sources of excess disability. We have examined the area of detecting unrecognized or untreated illnesses in patients with Alzheimer's disease and have specifically studied patients with Alzheimer's who are also depressed.

In a study directed by my colleague, Eric Larson, M.D., we looked for coexistent medical illnesses in patients with Alzheimer's disease (Larson, Reifler, Featherstone, & English, 1984). In this prospective study of 107 patients, 74 of whom had Alzheimer's, almost half (45%) had other previously unrecognized diseases (such as hypothyroidism or drug toxicity), and in approximately one-half of those (23% of the total sample) there was objective improvement with appropriate treatment. Only three patients had complete reversal of symptoms: one with a subdural hematoma, one with medication toxicity, and one with rheumatoid cerebral vasculitis. In the first two of those cases the initial mental status abnormalities had been mild. The remaining 22 patients who improved had a treatable condition in addition to an irreversible dementia.

We do not advocate diagnostic laxity, rather realistic expectations. The idea that large numbers of patients with chronic, progressive dementia will have a completely reversible cause has been overemphasized. What has not been sufficiently stressed is the value of looking for treatable illnesses as part of the long-term care of the demented patient.

Our studies on depression and Alzheimer's disease illustrate this. In our initial report on coexisting dementia and depression (Reifler, Larson, & Hanley, 1982), we noted that the study was prompted by two clinical observations. First, like other authors (Liston, 1978; Miller, 1980), we had the impression that dementia and depression seemed to coexist in many patients, and that the concept of pseudodementia was not helpful in dealing with this mixed presentation because it created a misleading "either-or" decision process. Second, depression seemed less common in severely demented patients.

Using the Mental Status Questionnaire (MSQ) (Kahn, Goldfarb, Pollack, & Peck, 1960) and *DSM II* criteria (then the official nomenclature) for dementia, and the Research Diagnostic Criteria (Woodruff, Goodwin, & Guze, 1974) for depression, we judged that of 20 patients with coexisting cognitive impairment, 17 had mixed depression and dementia (usually Alzheimer's disease) and only 3 had cognitive impairment due solely to depression. We also found that the rate of depression decreased as the dementia was more severe; 33% (9/27) of mildly demented patients were depressed, compared to 23% (8/35) of moderately demented and 12%

(3/26) of severely demented. This difference is statistically significant ($x^2 =$ 3.6, $df = 2$, p br 0.05).

The next step was to study the effectiveness of treating Alzheimer's disease patients who were also depressed. In a sample of 154 demented patients, 86% of whom had Alzheimer's disease, 44 (29%) were also depressed. Antidepressant medication was prescribed for 22 of those patients, of whom 18 (82%) showed clinical improvement in affective and/or vegetative symptoms based on chart review.

We are now engaged in a 3-year study supported by the NIMH Center for Studies of Mental Health in the Aging that is a double-blind placebo investigation of the effects of a tricyclic antidepressant in patients with Alzheimer's disease and depression. It is our impression that the depression seen in approximately one-quarter to one-third of Alzheimer's disease patients can be successfully treated. However, we are not yet sure to what extent, if any, their memory improves.

The importance of a thorough diagnostic assessment in rehabilitating Alzheimer's disease patients has been demonstrated. In selected situations, their physical and mental function can improve with treatment. But we are not fully satisfied with the measures we use to gauge improvement. Although the physiologic, cognitive, and affective changes can be measured with some confidence, we are concerned about our ability to measure accurately functional improvement, which may be the most important index of all.

One of the major difficulties facing Alzheimer's patients and their families is the management of day-to-day problems such as finances, legal obligations, household chores, self-care needs, troublesome behaviors, and interpersonal conflicts. Health care professionals from all disciplines agree that caretakers and patients must be helped to cope with such problems, and each discipline offers its own suggestions about strategies that are helpful in managing such problems.

These suggestions are typically generalized statements or idiosyncratic case anecdotes that are written to illustrate a particular   approach or strategy. For example, *The 36-Hour Day* (Mace & Rabins, 1981) and *Alzheimer's Disease: A Guide for Families* (Powell & Courtice, 1983) are two excellent references full of anecdotal reports and suggestions about how family members might deal with the array of problems confronting them. Nursing and social work journals, various agencies, and health care providers also have published suggestions for dealing with problems confronting Alzheimer's patients and their families (e.g., Zarit, Orr, & Zarit, 1984; McDowell & Lincoln, 1980).

This work is useful because it provides ideas for clinicians and researchers. Unfortunately, the usefulness is limited because of the lack of empirical evidence supporting these writings. Thus, although there is a great deal of agreement that such problems exist and that caretakers must be helped to deal with them, there are few data indicating effective methods of measurement or intervention: we do not know how best to measure these problems, how prevalent they are, or which management suggestions are most effective (indeed, we don't know which suggestions are effective at all).

Such lack of empirical data is particularly striking when one realizes that most of the literature on Alzheimer's disease focuses on cognitive functioning to the relative exclusion of social–behavioral areas of function (e.g., self-care, troublesome behaviors, and interpersonal conflicts). An array of measures exists to classify and quantify the cognitive deficits prominent in Alzheimer's disease, varying from brief mental status evaluations, such as the MSQ (Kahn et. al., 1960) and Mini Mental Status Exam (MMSE) (Folstein, Folstein, & McHugh, 1975), to more comprehensive and complete evaluation batteries, such as those conducted at major Alzheimer's centers. These latter batteries typically include measures that assess the seven cognitive areas considered critical to Alzheimer's disease by the NINCDS–ADRDA report: orientation, memory, language, praxis, attention, visual perception, and problem solving (McKhann et al., 1984).

Although the importance of such cognitive assessment is easy to understand, social–behavioral functioning is an equally critical aspect of Alzheimer's disease. We need to evaluate such functioning to understand its relationship to cognitive status in Alzheimer's disease and to provide concrete suggestions for management and rehabilitation.

Let us now review what we do know about such functioning. First, a review of the literature shows five scales that have been specifically designed to measure the problems thought to be associated with Alzheimer's disease (Blessed, Tomlinson, & Roth, 1968; Greene, Smith, Gardiner, & Timbury, 1982; Haycox, 1984; Moore, Bobula, Short, & Mischel, 1983; Zarit, Reever, & Bach-Peterson, 1981). Other attempts at measuring such behavior come from individualized studies that report on behaviors that have been assessed as part of a larger project rather than as an attempt to design a particular scale.

Across these specialized scales and individual project measures, the measurement of social–behavioral functioning varies in several ways, including the number of items assessed (8–40), the type of problems evaluated, the method of evaluation, and whether or not the caregiver's reactions were also assessed. Despite such diversity, those measurement strategies represent significant advances over anecdotal case reports describing such problematic behaviors, are easily adaptable to clinical practice, provide a start at systematically evaluating the functional problems thought to be present in Alzheimer's disease patients, and point to the following directions for future research:

1. Psychometric validation and reliability studies are needed on the measures that currently exist. We need to know (a) whether or not the measures that do exist adequately evaluate the domain of behaviors important to Alzheimer's disease (construct validity); (b) whether they each evaluate the same problems (content validity); (c) whether they yield consistent results over time and across similar populations (reliability); and (d) whether they adequately discriminate problems of Alzheimer's disease from problems of other diseases (discriminate validity).

2. Studies specifically focusing on Alzheimer's disease are needed. The studies reported in the area of assessment have typically identified their patient population as "demented." We need studies that classify the type of dementia under investigation and specifically focus on Alzheimer's disease. We need studies that compare Alzheimer's disease to other dementias and to other problems of normal (and abnormal) aging.

3. Refined measurement strategies need to be integrated into empirical studies. We know little about the complex nature of the functional problems evident in Alzheimer's disease patients. Most of the studies and scales mentioned earlier use a unidimensional approach to assessment (i.e., global ratings of functional abilities as in "how impaired is your husband?"—1 = not impaired at all ... 5 = extremely impaired). Future studies could be strengthened by using more standarized and multidimensional assessment techniques that attempt to take into account the complexity of behavior—e.g., that the problems in Alzheimer's disease influence and are influenced by the patient's cognitive status, physical health, social supports, affect, premorbid personality, and history. We need to understand the relationship between those variables, function, and rehabilitation.

4. The usefulness of measures that were not specifically designed for Alzheimer's disease (but appear relevant to Alzheimer's disease) could be investigated. For example, there are measures that were not developed specifically for Alzheimer's disease patients but may be useful for Alzheimer's disease assessment and rehabilitation because they address many of the problems thought to be critical in Alzheimer's disease. Unfortunately, there is a plethora of such measures, i.e., a recent review by Katz (1983) indicates at least 23 activities of daily living (ADL) measures alone, and Kane and Kane (1981) reviews more than 100 assorted measures for use with "the elderly." Future work could investigate such measures on Alzheimer's disease patients and provide suggestions regarding the differential utility of such measures (as suggested by Katz, 1983; Rossman, 1983).

These suggestions focused on assessment. Obviously, there are treatment directions that we can suggest as well. Specifically, it would be helpful for studies to evelute empirically and to compare different management strategies designed to help patients and their families deal with problems of Alzheimer's disease. As already discussed, despite the array of articles exhorting the importance of such strategies, empirical research is virtually nonexistent. Exceptions to this are (a) the work by Zarit and Zarit (1983), in which family members are trained to deal with problems of Alzheimer's disease by specific intervention strategies tailored to the family's needs; (b) the work by Hussain and Davis (1984), in which, taking a classic behavioral analysis approach, different aspects of wandering behavior and incontinence were identified and then modified by manipulating the environment and stimulus cues; and, finally, (c) the work by Patterson and Eberly (1983) in which a comprehensive behavioral assessment program involving training in social and daily living skills in a token economy was carefully evaluated and found effective in increasing communication and daily living skills of severely demented older adults. Clearly, such research can be done and can provide sound management strategies for families and health care professionals alike.

Let us conclude this section by providing an example of how one research project on functional problems might develop and help in rehabilitation.

A number of books and pamphlets written for family members suggest that family members respond to the affect of repetitive questions rather than the content. They suggest such questions are a function of anxiety and memory loss, and recommend that family members address the emotional inquiry of the question rather than the literal content. For example, in response to "When are we going home?," "I told you, in about an hour" does little to relieve the Alzheimer's disease patient's anxiety. Rather, the family member is advised to respond to the anxiety by touching the Alzheimer's disease patient in a reassuring way and saying, "You are safe here, I love you."

A research protocol might (a) develop a reliable and valid method of assessing such repetitive questions, their antecedents and consequences; (b) develop a method of intervention for such problems; and (c) evaluate change in the problems as a function of such intervention. That type of strategy would allow us to develop reliable, valid, and effective treatment strategies.

The field of rehabilitation of functional problems for Alzheimer's disease patients seems very much hit and miss, trial and error, with each clinician and researcher attempting to evaluate on his/her own the effectiveness of different assessment and intervention strategies. It is time for standardized evaluation strategies to be tied to functional and cognitive status and for controlled studies to investigate the efficacy of treatment strategies.

The points discussed so far, which have included attitudes toward rehabilitation of Alzheimer's disease patients, the importance of the evaluation process, and the need for better methods of assessing function, are vital to progress in the rehabilitation of patients with Alzheimer's disease. But they will do little good unless we can develop successful teaching programs to pass along what we learn. Therefore, the last topic we will address is that of teaching people the skills they need to rehabilitate Alzheimer's disease victims.

Although there has been no educational research on this precise topic, there have been some encouraging general reports on geriatric training programs. A sampling of the literature on geriatric education indicates that well-designed, thoughtful programs can be very effective.

A study at Wright State University (Warren, Painter, & Rudisill, 1983) investigated effects of a 25-h geriatric education component during a family practice clerkship on the attitudes of third-year medical students toward older patients. The 25-h educational program consisted of several activities, including 10 h of direct contact with the elderly, two small group discussions, and an interesting exercise in sensory deprivation whereby students were required to perform some activities of daily living while encumbered with sensory limiting devices.

The student's attitudes improved in all of the categories they measured. Before the clerkship, only half of the students endorsed the statement "I will welcome old people into my practice," compared with 90% afterward. The greatest improvement occurred in the category of sterotypes regarding older people, suggesting that with proper teaching, lingering myths can be quickly dispelled. We are encouraged to think that this might apply to the myths about the lack of applicability of rehabilitation in Alzheimer's disease.

It is proper to raise the question of whether these attitudinal changes are short-lived or enduring. A study at the University of Kentucky (Wilson & Hafferty, 1983) says enduring. First-year medical students who elected a seminar on aging and health were compared to a control group before the seminar and 3½ years later, prior to graduation. Short-term effects of the seminar were quite favorable, with students reporting significantly more positive attitudes on all five measures than did controls. Of particular interest were the long-term effects, which proved favorable, as the differences persisted on three of the measures when they were retested as fourth-year medical students. Despite the limitations of this study, which did not compare educational strategies or use random assignment, it does suggest that improvements in attitude produced early in medical education can persist throughout the course of medical school.

Even if students are not reached during medical school, there is evidence that postgraduate experiences are valuable and effective. Wolf-Klein, Libow, Foley, and Silverstone (1983) reported on a 4-week geriatric rotation for general internal medicine residents at the Jewish Institute for Geriatric Care in New Hyde Park, New York. Each resident was assigned responsibility for 20 patients under the direction of a geriatrician. The overwhelming majority (86%) stated that the experience was positive, and all 28 thought that the team approach could be applied to their future practices.

We believe that these examples prove there are simple well-designed models for educational programs at all levels of training that can effectively convey the knowledge, skills, and attitudes needed to improve rehabilitation of patients with Alzheimer's disease. The challenge we face as educators is how to implement the training programs.

Rehabilitation in Alzheimer's disease is a complex task. The intent of this chapter was to highlight not only the problems but the bright spots as well. Attitudes have been nihilistic, but with education and increased awareness that is changing. In the past, evaluations were less than ideal, but there has been a tremendous growth in programs devoted to Alzheimer's disease and the emergence of a substantial pool of skilled clinicians. True, our ability to measure function accurately is limited, but progress is on the horizon. And although specific educational programs have been few, we have reason to believe new efforts can be highly successful.

Let us conclude with a brief story:

A stranger asked directions to his destination. "Continue along this road and you will come to it," the man replied.

"How far is it?"

The man drew back, insulted. "You have to know how far it is too? Just keep going and you'll get there."

We are on the right path, but we do not yet know how far we must go to reach it.

REFERENCES

Barnes, R. F., & Raskind, M. A. (1981). DSM II criteria and the clinical diagnosis of dementia: A nursing home study. *Journal of Gerontology, 36,* 20–27.

Blessed, G., Tomlinson, B. E., & Roth, M. (1968). The association between quantitative measures of dementia and of senile change in the cerebral grey matter of elderly subjects. *British Journal of Psychiatry, 114,* 797–811.

Cox, G. B., Hanely, R. J., & Reifler, B. V. (1982). An integrated data base for an interdisciplinary geriatric clinic. *Journal of Psychiatric Treatment and Evaluation, 4,* 149–153.

Folstein, M. R., Folstein, S., & McHugh, P. R. (1975). Mini-mental state: A practical method for grading the cognitive state of patients for the clinician. *Journal of Psychiatric Research, 12,* 189–198.

Greene, J., Smith, R., Gardiner, M., & Timbury, G. (1982). Measuring behavioral disturbance of elderly demented patients in the community and its effects on relatives: A factor analysis study. *Age and Ageing, 3,* 121–126.

Haycox, J. A. (1984). A behavioral scale for dementia. In C.A. Shamoian (Ed.) *Biology and treatment of dementia in the elderly.* Washington, DC: American Psychiatric Press.

Hussain, R., & Davis, R. L. (1984). *Behavioral analysis of wandering behavior in institutionalized geriatric patients.* Paper presented at the Association for Advancement of Behavior Therapy Conference.

Kahn, R. L., Goldfarb, A. L., Pollack, M., & Peck, A. (1960-61). Brief objective measure for determination of mental status in the aged. *American Journal of Psychiatry, 117,* 326–328.

Kane, R. A., & Kane, R. L. (1981). *Assessing the elderly,* (pp. 25–76). Lexington, MA: D. C. Heath.

Katz, A. (1983). Assessing self-maintenance: Activities of daily living, mobility, and instrumental activities of daily living. *Journal of the American Geriatrics Society, 31,* 721–727.

Larson, E. B., Reifler, B. V., Featherstone, H. J., & English, D. R. (1984). Dementia in elderly outpatients: A prospective study. *Annals of Internal Medicine, 100,* 417–423.

Liston, E. J., Jr. (1978). Diagnostic delay in presenile dementia. *Journal of Clinical Psychiatry, 39,* 599–603.

Mace, N. L., & Rabins, P. V. (1981). *The 36-hour day.* Baltimore: Johns Hopkins.

McDowell, F., & Lincoln, E. (Eds.). (1980). *Manual for Alzheimer's disease families.* White Plains, NY: The Burke Rehabilitation Center.

McKhann, G., Drachman, D., Folstein, U., Katzman, R., Price, D., & Stadlan, E. (1984). Clinical diagnoses of Alzheimer's disease: Report of the NINCDS–ADRDA Work Group under the auspices of Department of Health and Human Services Task Force on Alzheimer's disease. *Neurology, 34,* 939–944.

Miller, N. E. (1980). The measurement of mood in senile brain disease: Examiner ratings and self reports. In J. Cole & J. Barrett (Eds.), *Psychopathology in the aged.* New York: Raven Press.

Moore, J. T., Bobula, J. A., Short, T. B., & Mischel, M. (1983). A functional dementia scale. *Journal of Family Practice, 16*(3), 499–503.

Patterson, R. L., & Eberly, D. A. (1983). Social and daily living skills. In P. Lewinsohn & L. Teri (Eds.), *Clinical geropsychology,* New York: Pergamon.

Powell, L. S., & Courtice, K. (1983). *Alzheimer's disease: A guide for families.* Reading, MA: Addison-Wesley.

Reifler, B. V., & Eisdorfer, C. (1980). A clinic for the impaired elderly and their families. *American Journal of Psychiatry, 137,* 1399–1403.

Reifler, B. V., Larson, E., & Hanley, R. (1982). Coexistence of cognitive impairment and depression in geriatric outpatients. *American Journal of Psychiatry, 139,* 623–626.

Rossman, I. (1983). *Comprehensive functional assessment.* Paper presented at the NIH Technology Assessment Conference: Evaluating the Elderly Patient: The Case for Assessment Technology, Bethesda, MD.

Sabin, T. D., Vitug, A. J., & Mark, V. H. (1982). Are nursing home diagnosis and treatment inadequate? *Journal of the American Medical Association, 248*, 321–322.

Secretary's Task Force on Alzheimer's Disease. (1984). *Alzheimer's disease.* (U.S. Department of Health and Human Services, Publication No. ADM 84–1323). Rockville, MD: National Institute of Mental Health.

Warren, D. L., Painter, A., & Rudisill, J. (1983). Effects of geriatric education on the attitudes of medical students. *Journal of the American Geriatrics Society, 31*, 435–438.

Wilson, J. F., & Hafferty, F. W. (1983). Long-term effects of a seminar on aging and health for first-year medical students. *The Gerontologist, 23*, 319–324.

Wolf-Klein, G. P., Libow, L. S., Foley, C. J., & Silverstone, F. A. (1983). Training internal medicine residents in geriatrics. *Journal of Medical Education, 58*, 583–584.

Woodruff, R. A., Jr., Goodwin, D. W., & Guze, S. B. (1974). *Psychiatric diagnosis.* New York: Oxford University Press.

Zarit, S. H., Orr, N. K., & Zarit, J. M. (1984). *Families under stress.* Unpublished manuscript, University of Southern California, Los Angeles.

Zarit, S. H., Reever, K. E., & Bach-Peterson, J. (1981). Relatives of impaired elderly: Correlates of feelings of burden. *Gerontologist, 21*, 158–164.

Zarit, S., & Zarit, J. (1983). Cognitive impairment. In P. Lewinsohn & L. Teri. (Eds.), *Clinical geropsychology,* New York: Pergamon.

10

Psychosocial and Mental Health Issues in Rehabilitation of Older Persons

Bryan Kemp

RELATIONSHIP BETWEEN PSYCHOLOGICAL FACTORS, REHABILITATION, AND AGE

Psychological factors play a large role in rehabilitation, both by themselves and in conjunction with physical and social factors. Further, it is quite likely that the extent of interaction between biological, psychological, and social factors increases with age. Clinically, it appears that there is greater inter-dependence between and among these spheres in older persons. Any aspect of an older person's functioning—from ambulation to outlook on life—is a product of these multiple factors, and none can be ignored if a rehabilitation program is to be successful. Improvements in psychological functioning per se can be brought about through biological, psychological, social, or functional approaches. An older depressed person can be aided, for example, by antidepressants, personal counseling, social participation, and the elimination of functional deficits more than he/she can be aided by any single technique alone. Thus, there is a two-way relationship between psychological factors and rehabilitation: psychological factors play a major role in overall rehabilitation success; and a rehabilitation approach focusing on a biopsychosocial–functional model can greatly improve psychological functioning.

PSYCHOSOCIAL CONTEXT OF GERIATRIC REHABILITATION

It is impossible to discuss geriatric rehabilitation without mention of the psychosocial values, beliefs, and practices that prevail in society and that bear on the success of rehabilitation for older persons. Even the most effective techniques of rehabilitation will fail in an environment that is not accepting of the product or the process. Many of the ultimate determinants of rehabilitation success are the responsibility of society as a whole.

This point is illustrated in the now widely accepted distinction between "disability" and "handicap." A disability is a chronic medical (sometimes psychological) limitation imposed by a condition that can be described in anatomical, biological, physical, and sometimes psychological terms. Common disabilities include arthritis, stroke, Alzheimer's disease, mental retardation, or polio. The factors that account for the degree of disability can be described by the amount and location of tissue damage and the extent of physical impairment. On the other hand, a handicap is the degree to which a person is prevented from participating in the physical and social environments. A person may have polio and therefore lack normal walking ability. That is the disability. However, that person is *handicapped* if there is no transportation in the community, if he/she is excluded from employment or normal schooling, if he/she is excluded from social activities, or if other people devalue the person. The factors that account for the degree of handicap are partly intrinsic to the person, such as the disability, but are also largely determined by the degree to which the world is physically and socially handicapping.

Psychosocial factors are some of the most limiting causes of handicap among disabled persons, and it is possible that older persons are even more handicapped by these than are younger persons. Regardless of how much effort is devoted to correcting the "mental health problems" surrounding rehabilitation of older persons, ultimate improvement must come from also addressing the psychosocial factors adding to problems that lie outside the older person's control. Three such factors affect the rehabilitation of older persons.

First and foremost is the process of "devaluation." That is the process of seeing a person who is disabled—particularly an older person—as inferior to, less important than, less valuable than, less attractive than, less worthwhile than a nondisabled person. Unfortunately, older persons possess two attributes that are devalued, their age and their disability. Vash (1980) has described vividly the process of devaluation and its effects on the person who is disabled. Certainly one point emerges: if persons with disabilities do not act the way others think they should, the first place to look is how society—from the family to political parties—prevents better possibilities.

Second, and closely related to the first, has been a general lack of interest in the problems of the elderly and, on the whole, negative attitudes toward older persons. For example, of 49,000 medical school faculty assessed in the United States in 1970, only 20 *persons* indicated that geriatrics was an area of interest (Institute of Medicine, 1978). Older persons frequently have been seen as uninteresting, despairing, incurable, unproductive, and unattractive by faculty members. That attitude in turn affects the attitudes of their students. Clinicians have similar attitudes. Between 40% and 50% of health professionals are reported to have negative attitudes toward older persons (Kosberg & Harris, 1978). Many people, even health professionals, still believe that older persons are *expected* to have impaired health just because they are older. Hence, these "normal" aspects of aging go untreated.

Devaluation and lack of interest help to create the third major psychosocial obstacle: lack of opportunity. Fewer than 5% of the case loads of departments of rehabilitation are persons over age 65 (Benedict & Ganikos, 1981). Less than 2% of all outpatient mental health care goes to older persons (Busse & Blazer, 1980). Perhaps as few as 20% of the older persons who could use it receive comprehensive rehabilitation approaches to their chronic health problems.

Those three barriers can be reduced by demonstrating effective methods of rehabilitating older persons and by widespread dissemination of successful models. The remainder of this paper will address a subpart of the complex rehabilitation process; namely, psychological and mental health issues frequently involved in geriatric rehabilitation, with comments on their assessment and treatment.

ADJUSTMENT TO DISABILITY IN OLDER AGE

Rehabilitation care typically requires a holistic approach to the patient, including an understanding of the psychologic factors that influence him/her. Older persons have many psychologic characteristics that set them apart in rehabilitation. First is the process of adjusting to the disability itself and the changes it produces in the older person's life. In an era when the "syndrome" approach to mental health problems is popular, such as with *DSM III* (American Psychiatric Association, 1980), the "adjustment model" of past decades is often minimized. Often, too much focus is on diagnosis of psychopathology rather than on understanding the intense internal struggle people go through in attempting to cope with the multiple personal, interpersonal, and social consequences of a disability. There is usually little in the background of individuals to help them adjust to the life-changing consequences of disabilities. Therefore, people ultimately adopt some style of adaptation that "works" for them or they succumb to multiple problems that the disability produces. In this context, even disordered behavior after a disability should first be viewed as a *normative* response to the onset of abnormal stimuli, rather than as an abnormal response to more or less normal stimuli (Vash, 1980).

Elderly persons seem to be especially vulnerable to the stresses produced by a disability. Such difficulties appear to involve several processes: (a) attempting to deal with the intense, personal feelings and thoughts that accompany the disability; (b) attempting to preserve self-esteem; and (c) trying to incorporate the changes, losses, and new limitations into an already established life-style. Most people do not consider themselves old as long as they feel reasonably well and can function at most daily tasks. For many older persons, a disability marks when they have become "old." Thinking of oneself as finally being old instills an additional life change that compounds the problems of the disability—the realization that life is finite and the intense reality of death. At this point, many older persons are likely to want to give up, or they may consider life as they know it as pretty much over for them.

By contrast, for most younger disabled persons, death is not as great an issue as is how to deal with a life complicated by a disability. With younger patients, appeals can be made to increase efforts in rehabilitation in order to return to school or work, to return to raising children and the role of spouse. Younger persons may more easily redirect their goals and methods of achieving them. For older persons, it is difficult to establish goals that are meaningful, and setting of goals is strongly related to rehabilitation success (Kemp & Wetmore, 1969). Even though many younger people feel hopeless for some period of time after a disability, for most it eventually passes. Older persons are less likely to have hope of being able to compensate for their losses and may believe that there is not enough time remaining in life; therefore, they become more despairing. This may help to explain the higher prevalence of depression among older disabled persons than among younger disabled persons (Blazer, 1982). Many older persons have a difficult time expressing these feelings or thoughts and may even have a hard time realizing they exist.

Much of the behavior in adjusting to a disabilty also can be seen as an attempt to preserve self-esteem. Self-esteem (being acceptable to yourself exactly the way you are) is the most important outcome of the adjustment process. People who can accept and appreciate themselves after a disability (and therefore their lives) are minimally handicapped by it. People who cannot accept themselves in an altered status are destined for continuous unhappiness. What then helps people to accept themselves? A sense of self-esteem typically derives from three principal sources: (a) what a person *does*, such as occupation or role; (b) what a person *has*, such as good looks, an attractive home, or money; and (c) what kind of person the individual *is*, such as honest, spiritualistic, or humorous. At the peak of one's psychosocial development, all three are important. A disability frequently impairs the maintenance of adequate self-esteem of an older person because what the person now *has* (a disability and an advanced age), what the person *does* (or doesn't), and what the person *is* (different) are not accepted by others. No wonder older disabled persons frequently question their own value. They are only paying attention to what society is saying. It takes an exceptional person to overcome the subtle and not-so-subtle messages communicated by others that reflect this societal attitude. A doctor may hand a prescription to the daughter accompanying the older person to the appointment rather than to the older person. Family members may question the older disabled person's ability to stay at home independently. Senior citizen centers may not readily accept disabled older persons. Older persons may not be referred to or accepted by rehabilitation programs, whereas younger persons are. Maintaining an adequate sense of self-esteem is not an easy task for the older person after a disability.

Another major task is incorporating the disability into a long-established life style. The major issue appears to revolve around pleasure and pain. To incorporate a disability adequately, there still must be an abundance of life's pleasures (either in quantity or quality) over life's pains. A disability in older age all too often has exactly the opposite effect. Learning to create and maintain pleasurable experiences is difficult, especially if multiple disabilities are present. Although it's not true that "you can't teach an old dog new tricks," it can often be a harder process. Living with a disability in later life is more likely to cut the older person off from interaction with others, cause more economic hardships, make the older person more susceptible to other medical problems, and threaten independent living in the community. To survive in the community adequately, the older person has to be able either to utilize his/her own resources or to be adept at utilizing the assistance of others to meet those needs. The method of working out such adaptations varies from person to person but requires using skills the older person possibly never developed. It is here that rehabilitation programs have a great deal to offer through therapy and education.

In summary, dealing with intense personal feelings (including those of death), maintaining self-esteem, and keeping a positive balance of pleasurable experiences are keys to the adjustment of older persons after a disability. At any one time, all three processes may be ongoing simultaneously. Failures to adjust to disability in older age may lead to mental health problems.

ASSESSING MENTAL HEALTH PROBLEMS

Older persons have a high prevalence of mental health problems that affect their success in rehabilitation programs. Those problems may be a reflection of an inability to cope with multiple stressors accompanying a disabled status, may preexist the disability, or may occur concurrently. Proper evaluation, understanding, and treatment of the problems are essential for overall rehabilitation success.

Assessing mental health problems in rehabilitation is done for one or more of the following reasons:

1. To help determine the older person's psychological capacity to improve through rehabilitation.
2. To determine any psychological barriers to improvement (e.g., depression, family conflict).
3. To determine the older person's strengths and assets that will aid in rehabilitation.
4. To plan the necessary psychosocial interventions that will be needed to maintain improvements after discharge from the rehabilitation program.

Although evaluation is necessary, there are dangers inherent in psychological assessment of older persons, and evaluation should not be undertaken without knowledge of some of them. First is the danger of overreliance on psychological tests. Most psychological tests are not fully appropriate for older persons. Although many tests have been developed for older persons (Kane & Kane, 1981), most appear to have limited clinical value and may be more appropriate for research or theoretical reasons.

Second, the purpose of conducting an evaluation can sometimes be corrupted, especially if there is not a specific purpose in mind. It's not always the patient who wants or needs the evaluation, but the staff, to reduce their own anxieties. Time spent on evaluation may interfere with treatment that is needed in trying to adjust to a major life change. One psychologist working with younger persons describes this phenomenon:

> When I worked as a psychologist in a rehabilitation hospital, it occurred to me that my role was to reduce staff anxiety. Somehow, having test data made us feel we had a better handle on something. If I gave a patient a WAIS and an MMPI and could say with assurance that he was normally smart and wasn't crazy, he was just a little upset over being paralyzed all of a sudden and suspected his wife had moved in with his best friend while he was in the hospital, and he had never done any work except manual labor and didn't see how he could get her and the kids back unless he could support them, and he probably

couldn't satisfy her anyway so perhaps he was being selfish to want her back—the anxiety of the staff was relieved. But somehow no one ever said, "Wow! What a heavy trip! I'll do without my evaluations. You should spend your time just talking to people, seeing if you can guide them through this incredible trip, because it seems a lot more important" (Vash, 1980).

Older persons may feel they are failing at tasks involved in the evaluation, and the very assessment, although it can provide some helpful information, can also cause anxiety and worry and even help to undermine an eventual therapeutic relationship. It is well documented that older persons are more susceptible to test anxiety and fears of failure (Botwinick, 1973; Steger, 1976). Somehow, people can accept physical examinations and then turn to the doctor for help more easily than they can accept psychological evaluations and then turn to the psychologist for assistance.

Finally, no replacement has been found for a careful, caring, empathic, and comprehensive interview of any older person. There is a tendency to value (maybe overvalue) "high-tech" methods in the health field because of the lifesaving effects of sophisticated medical test procedures. However, psychology has more to do with the "quality of life" than with the "survival of life," and a technically oriented staff may overrely on psychological tests.

COMMON MENTAL HEALTH PROBLEMS

There are at least seven major mental health problems that are highly relevant to rehabilitation in addition to what has already been described. They are (a) affective disturbances, (b) cognitive impairments, (c) motivation/performance problems, (d) stress-related disorders, (e) family problems, (f) psychotic behavior, and (g) social isolation. Some of the problems also are described in major literature sources (e.g., Birren & Sloane, 1980; Busse & Blazer, 1980; Butler & Lewis, 1977, 1984). However, they are usually described as though they were the primary problem. Their relevance in rehabilitation is somewhat different.

Affective Disorders

Affective disorders include the classic syndromes of dysphoria, depression, and mania. But they also should include other mood-altering states such as excessive worry, discouragement, and passivity. Of those disorders, depression is the most damaging and the most likely to be misdiagnosed and poorly treated in rehabilitation.

The word *depression* is derived from Latin and French and means "to press down upon." Depression is a state that affects many bodily and psychological functions: physical, cognitive, affective, and spiritual. Physical functions of energy, appetite, digestion, sleep, and metabolism are suppressed. Cognitive functions of memory, reasoning, concentrating, and problem solving are affected. Disturbances of mood, sadness, crying, the "blues," lack of interest, helplessness, anger, and lowered frustration tolerance are found. Decreased "spiritual" functioning is reflected in a lack of meaning in life, a dim view of the future, pessimism, hopelessness, and questioning the value of one's own existence.

Among the disabled elderly the rate of depression is 20% to 30% (Blazer, 1980). Among community-dwelling elders the rate is 8% to 15% (Birren & Sloane, 1980; Busse & Pfeiffer, 1969). Older disabled persons have three major factors contributing to their depression: physiological, psychological, and social. Physiological contributors include decreased conditioning and endurance, decreased functional abilities (such as vision or ambulation), and altered neurochemistry (e.g., alterations in brain transmitters). The psychological contributors include multiple unreplaced losses, feelings of helplessness and hopelessness, a belief that nothing can be improved, and a tendency to see life as coming to a close, with limited time to overcome the limitations. Social contributors include isolation, poverty, limited transportation, and social rejection.

Depression in the elderly is frequently mistreated in rehabilitation programs because of faulty diagnostic methods and/or inappropriate therapy. Both kinds of errors are seen: people are labeled as depressed who are not, and older people are not seen as depressed when in fact they are. One reason depression is misidentified is that it often presents itself differently in older persons (Blazer, 1982). The older person may not present with signs of sadness, crying, or a depressed affect. Older persons may have a difficult time admitting to emotional difficulties, talking to a young doctor, or recognizing affective changes themselves. Often memory complaints, digestive disorders, sleep disturbance, anxiety, phobias, feelings of uselessness, or somatic discomfort are the presenting symptoms. Those symptoms are so often associated with depression in the elderly that they have been labeled "depressive equivalents." Such symptoms are often assigned to different causes, and hence many depressions go untreated.

All elderly patients in rehabilitation should be assessed for depression by a careful interview. The most appropriate method is a thorough mental status examination by a trained geriatric mental health professional. Assessment using one of the available depression instruments can be helpful. Those instruments include the Zung Depression Scale (Zung, 1965), the Beck Depression Inventory (Beck, 1967), and the Geriatric Depression

Scale (Yesavage, et al., 1983). However, the assessment scales should never be considered as important as the clinical interview.

Differential diagnoses of depression must be made in chronically impaired elderly persons because depression-like symptoms may be the result of many other problems. Following are the most likely alternative diagnoses to be ruled out:

1. *Physical illness*: cancer, hypothyroidism, infection, dehydration, dementia.
2. *Drug reactions*: analgesics, tranquilizers, antihypertensives, antipsychotics, steroids.
3. *Other psychological states*: grief/mourning, hypochondriasis, schizophrenia, malingering.

The effects of depression on rehabilitation activities are widespread. The rehabilitation process takes effort, the ability to think about alternative living conditions, the ability to develop and utilize the support of others, the willingness to take moderate chances, the ability to weigh alternative decisions, and perhaps most of all, the ability to learn. Those are the very functions that are suppressed by a depression state. Unless properly addressed, depression will thwart all attempts at rehabilitation.

The importance of other affective states should not be underestimated. Sometimes it appears that depression is overpublicized to the detriment of other disorders. Dysphoria, discouragement, worry, and passivity also can damage rehabilitation programs. Such disorders have less of a biological component than does depression, but they can be just as persistent as a biological depression. Butler and Lewis (1977) have described the nature of worries and fears among the elderly, which are considerable. For older disabled persons, worries over money, exacerbations of health impairments, crime in the neighborhood, impact of the disability on family members, and accidents and falls are common (Claremont, 1979). One man of 73 years sustained a stroke that left him with a right hemiopia and an amnestic syndrome. He experienced considerable worry over who could care for his 50-year-old severely disabled son if he were to die. His severe memory impairment made it even more difficult to reassure him and to help him learn ways to solve the problem. Worry of such magnitude is so pervasive that it actually becomes a chronic change in mood. Unfortunately, that can lead to reduced conditioning and further reductions in functioning.

Closely associated with depression is dysphoria—a state of acute unhappiness, sadness, irritability, crying, or sullenness—that can be just as disabling as depression. Dysphoric states are not necessarily self-limiting, and they may mistakenly be left untreated.

All of these affective states are not "normal" responses to a disability, even if they are normative. One question that frequently emerges in clinical work with disabled persons is "Isn't feeling depressed a normal response to having a disability?" Another closely related question is "Isn't depression part of some disabilities, such as multiple sclerosis or dementia?" Prolonged affective states are *not* a normal part of a disability, even in older age. Normative responses reflect a *process* of attempting to accept an altered existence. Affectively, they can range from denial, through grief and anger. However, when responses severely and prolongedly affect self-esteem, restrict activities, or impair the ability to relate to others—as depression can—then a separate condition exists that should be addressed.

Cognitive Impairments

Not uncommonly, the elderly person seen in a rehabilitation program has a cognitive impairment. Cognitive impairments of slight, moderate, or severe degree have a prevalence of 10% to 15% in community-living elderly without other chronic health problems. It is probably higher among people with chronic health problems, especially while in a hospital setting. Cognitive impairments are due either to a reversible condition, such as a drug reaction or medical condtion, or they are irreversible due to a neurological disorder.

Attention to the older person's cognitive abilities and/or impairments in rehabilitation is important for several reasons. First, cognitive limitations may indicate disease states in the brain. They should be fully investigated to determine a diagnosis, to provide what improvements may be possible, and to arrange supportive services. Careful differential diagnosis to rule out reversible causes, such as depression, delirium, metabolic disorders, and pharmacological side effects is important. It appears that dementia (an irreversible condition) is overestimated in the United States. Gurland and Toner (1983) found an approximately 14% misdiagnosis rate. This figure is confirmed by others (Busse & Blazer, 1980). No cures are currently available for such conditions as Alzheimer's disease; the focus should be on minimizing the overly handicapping effect of the illness, improving function, and reducing family burden. Nearly all persons with true cognitive impairment can be assisted through interdisciplinary management. (See Reifler & Teri, this volume.)

Cognitive dysfunction is also important because thinking, memory, and learning abilities act as a kind of "diagnostic window" in elderly persons. Substantial changes in cognitive abilities should be immediate clues that something pathological is occurring, medically, neurologically, or psychiatrically. Aggressive pursuit of the cause is then necessary. Older persons with chronic physical disabilities are at a higher risk of developing acute cognitive impairments because of changes in medical status, greater use of medicines, more hospitalizations, and greater physical restrictions. Health and social service workers should be especially alert to these possibilities and should not assume that all cognitive impairment implies an underlying dementia.

A third reason for concern is the effect cognitive impairment has on the ability to profit from rehabilitation and to live independently. Rehabilitation is in many respects a relearning program. It requires at least minimal abilities to learn and remember new motor and cognitive skills. However, no studies have been conducted to determine the degree of cognitive capacity needed in order to profit from rehabilitation or to live adequately in the community. These data would be invaluable. As it is now, clinicians make educated guesses as to who will be able to profit from occupational or physical therapy, carry out daily activities of living, require supervision with medicines or navigate safely in the home environment.

Cognitive abilities or deficits must be evaluated within the context of the older person's attributes, limitation, and environment. What may be a harmful level of cognitive impairment for one older person may not be for another in a different environment. A supportive family or a well-designed environment with appropriate community supports can often be enough to maintain a person at home. On the other hand, a person with an intact personality, especially if he/she has been socially outgoing, can often disguise even severe cognitive impairments, and that person may wrongly be placed in a dangerously unsupportive environment.

A serious problem common in rehabilitation requires special mention— delirium. Delirium is an acute disruption of cognition characterized by a fluctuating level of consciousness and deficits of attention, wakefulness, memory, and other mental abilities. The source of delirium invariably arises outside the central nervous system—such as an infection or metabolic disorder—and affects brain performance and higher cognitive functions. Older persons who are delirious are often seen as demented (e.g., Plopper & Chui, 1984) and are therefore not seen as suitable rehabilitation prospects. Because of a weakened physical state, excessive immobility, strange surroundings, medical problems, infections, and drug side effects, delirium is fairly common. However, with proper assessment, these persons usually can be restored to their previous cognitive levels.

Motivational Issues

"Motivation," or the lack of it, may be the most frequently used explanation of rehabilitation success and failure in clinical practice. It is generally stated that disabled persons who are well motivated perform well in a variety of situations. Similarly, when people perform poorly, "lack of motivation" is often cited. Despite its widespread use as an explanatory variable, motivation is a poorly understood concept. Age differences are even less well understood in rehabilitation. Hence, attempts at influencing an older person's motivations are frequently misguided.

Often the terms *motivation* and *obedience* (or *compliance*) are confused. Obedience refers to compliance with another person's desires; motivation refers to self-directed behavior. When an older person doesn't act the way someone else believes is best, the older person may be labeled unmotivated. In fact, this is erroneous. When others *disagree* with the older person's behavior, when they can't *understand* it or *control* it, then he or she is likely to be called unmotivated.

Motivation includes two integrated aspects of behavior: the direction/choice aspect of behavior and the intensity/effortfulness of behavior. Persons who are described as motivated are seen as possessing both—they know what they want and they work hard toward attaining it. Persons who are described as unmotivated appear to be passive, indecisive, and easily thwarted.

Motivational theorists from Freud (1901) through Lewin (1935) have stressed the multivariate or dynamic qualities of motivation. McDaniel (1969) has described some of these dynamic processes in rehabilitation. From a practical standpoint, motivation in rehabilitation can be described as a product of four primary variables. Three variables taken as one set, are weighted against one other variable.

The first variable of the set is what someone *wants*; his/her desires, goals, or psychological needs. The second of the set is *expectations*; a person's beliefs, assumptions, or attitudes about that which is wanted. The third is *reinforcement*; the rewards, benefits, and payoffs of the behavior. However, behavior is never as simple as having desires, believing that they can be achieved, and actually receiving rewards for behavior in that direction. These three elements of behavior are also weighted against the *costs* of the behavior in terms of effort, physical pain, emotional discomfort, money, time, not being able to do something else, and so on. Thus, motivation takes into account the factors that encourage or support behavior as well as the factors that discourage or prevent the behavior. Motivation is optimal when the person knows what he/she wants and expects it can be obtained, the rewards associated with it are meaningful and reasonably prompt, and the costs of the behavior are minimal. All of those variables are one person's subjective perception, not what others may perceive as the "facts." Improving motivation generally means improving the circumstances that enhance the person's getting what he/she wants, improving the person's beliefs and expectations that it can be attained, rewarding progress toward it, and reducing unreasonably high costs of the behavior.

Rehabilitation requires a lot of motivation to be successful. The costs of the behaviors required in rehabilitation and afterward must be outweighed by the overall benefits to the individual. The problems of motivation in rehabilitation of older adults can be seen as falling under one of the four variables: There are problems associated with what is wanted (usually there are no goals or shortsighted ones), with what the person believes or expects of himself/herself or the rehabilitation program, with insufficient rewards, or with costs of the behavior required in rehabilitation or afterward. For example, consider the older person who is asked to be compliant with a physical therapy program of daily exercise for 2 h/day while in the hospital. The older patient may demonstrate problems such as not trying hard, being late for therapy, leaving early, complaining a lot. The person is labeled unmotivated. However, it is easy to see that the person *is* motivated because both elements of motivated behavior are present: the person is choosing not to try hard and is giving that a lot of effort. A motivational approach would try to identify which of the four variables is contributing to the problem. Perhaps the older person does not believe exercise helps. Perhaps the rewards of the exercise are minimal; the person does not gain in function in the beginning. Perhaps the costs are too high. The discouraging feeling of being disabled in the first place and then facing a discharge home to a lonely existence in an apartment that is on the second floor may not make the effort worthwhile for the older person. Contrarily, an approach that would try to increase performance through the application of greater obedience would indirectly threaten the person, would withhold rewards, or would point out problems of noncompliance.

Some age-related differences in motivation have been observed that affect the rehabilitation process of older persons. First, older persons need more and different reinforcement from staff than do younger persons. Rehabilitation activities are harder for older persons. It is generally less helpful to make promises of benefit from rehabilitation far in the future for older persons because the onset of a disability may signal the beginning of life termination (Riley & Foner, 1968). Younger persons will respond better to future goals, such as work or educational goals. Older persons respond best to concrete goals that affect daily functioning, especially in the context of a family setting. Existential concerns as well as safety and security needs become more important than a career, future achievements, financial gain, or materialism (Neugarten, 1968). Because they do not have as many of the naturally rewarding activities at home that would continue to support the behavior, special consideration must be given to "reinforcement" practices that will be in effect after discharge.

Fear of failure at difficult tasks and the anxiety associated with new and challenging activities have been observed by many (e.g., Birren & Schaie, 1977). Avoidance of difficult tasks by the older person in rehabilitation or increases in anxiety might therefore be expected. Finally, older persons, as well as the younger staff who treat them, must believe that improvement is possible. Many older persons have lower expectations about their abilities and potential. Without a positive belief in oneself, behavior is tentative and easily thwarted. These and other motivational issues need further exploration through research and demonstration.

Stress-related Disorders

Disability status is usually a distressing personal experience. The physical, emotional, and social consequences of a disability can be so stressful that behavior is not directed toward adaptive relearning but toward reducing the terrible stress, anxiety, and other emotional discomforts to an acceptable level—even if that behavior is maladaptive and unproductive. When this happens, less energy is available for adaptive behavior, improving functioning, and constructive problem solving. At least three such stress-related disorders are common in rehabilitation, and they appear to be more common in the elderly.

One is a complex of excessive bodily concern, sick role behavior, and dependency. Not infrequently these occur for the first time in late life and are often in response to multiple losses. Most older persons have lived with someone most of their lives and have enjoyed relatively good health. A physical disability can rob such persons of the security and safety they have enjoyed for years, especially if other losses have occurred, such as death of a spouse. As a result, they feel stressed, anxious, and insecure. Attention to bodily processes, focusing on real or partial limitations, concerns over care, and requiring repeated reassurance and assistance represents a way of diverting consciousness from the underlying feelings of insecurity. The security of a known disorder and the care believed necessary for it are often better than the insecurity of facing a life alone or impaired (Busse & Pfeiffer, 1969).

Dependency behavior also can be stress-related. Dependency often represents an attempt to control the behaviors of others so that there is more consistency and predictability in their actions. Dependency has several elements. One is attributing causality to others and another is attempting to reduce stress by controlling the actions of others. For example, dependency may be expressed by stating or implying that the actions of other people *cause* the person to feel or act a certain way (such as depressed) and if they didn't act that way (usually the family), then the older person would feel better. Dependency, therefore, can also result in repeated requests for reassurance, assistance, and recognition. Attempts at improvement of dependent behavior are problematic because of the basic fallacy; others actually grow weary of the demand being placed on them. In addition, there are relatively few replacements available for the losses the person has suffered to his/her ego needs, which may have existed for a long time and usually at an unconscious level.

Another stress-related disorder affecting many older persons in rehabilitation is substance misuse. Although much substance misuse in older age is due to iatrogenic causes, a significant amount is due to trying to blunt the painful experiences associated with being disabled. Because older persons are especially susceptible to the effects of medication and because so many medicines have effects on mental or physical functioning in older age, this is an important problem. Medicines that reduce primary stress symptoms of anxiety can obviously be misused. Included in this category would be anxiolytics and hypnotics. However, even substances that treat secondary symptoms of stress, such as physical pain, can be misused. Medicine such as Talwin and codeine can be especially harmful to older persons. A look at the most commonly misused "drugs" in the United States reveals a list composed of substances that people use in order to (a) prepare for being stressed (such as caffeine or sugar), (b) to combat the multiple effects of being stressed (such as antihypertensives, analgesics), or (c) to recover from being stressed (such as sleep medicine). The overuse of food to combat stressors should not be overlooked in the elderly. Food satisfies a basic physiological need, but the act of eating also symbolizes the psychological needs to be cared for, to be comforted, and to be loved. Older persons lacking fulfillment of those needs often overeat, with resultant negative consequences on their physiological status (such as hypertension) or their daily functioning (such as limiting mobility).

Attention to the use of alcohol among older persons is also important. Surveys of general medical wards of older persons indicate a prevalence of alcoholism of 15% to 30% (Atkinson & Schuckit, 1981); in the general population of older persons, the estimate is from 2% to 10%. Alcohol remains the most commonly used "home remedy" for a variety of personal and physical ailments. Alcohol misuse is higher in some subgroups of elderly: depressed persons, widowed, the never-married, and the chronically disabled (Atkinson & Schuckit, 1981). The dangers of alcohol use in the elderly are multiple. Older persons with a disability are already deconditioned to a high extent. Alcohol further depresses them and leads to less activity. The risk of a fracture through a fall is heightened. Older persons take many medicines that interact adversely with alcohol. For example, alcohol can increase the sensitivity to digitalis toxicity and cause increased gastrointestinal bleeding with aspirin. Similarly, older persons already suffer from reduced pain sensitivity, and alcohol can further suppress pain impulses, leading to a masking of potentially dangerous symptoms. Finally, the effects of alcohol on judgment, memory, and attention can lead to disabling conditions through accidents.

Two subgroups of older alcoholics are those with an early-life onset and those with a late (past 55) age onset. The prevalence of late-life onset appears to be higher than previously thought. This group has perhaps been underestimated because they are less likely to have an obvious personality disorder (Rosin & Glatt, 1971).

Use of alcohol is likely to be underassessed in geriatric patients in proportion to the degree of impairment it can cause in trying to overcome the effects of a disability. Assessment of this potential problem should be a routine part of all mental status examinations. Often, rehabilitation of the alcohol problem must precede rehabilitation of many of the physical problems.

Stress-related disorders also include psychotic disturbances in older persons. Although these can certainly be caused by biological abnormalities, such as altered levels of catecholamines, they are also caused by extreme stress. Late-life paraphrenia represents such an example. Roth (1955) found this psychotic-like disturbance to be highest among persons who had sustained a major loss, such as of a spouse, and who could not deal with it. Often, intense ambivalent feelings toward the departed person were present, and the remaining person could not appropriately grieve. Such persons also tended to have a history of social isolation and to have a hearing impairment. Certainly, intense stress such as this can cause an alteration in brain chemistry, which can, in turn, cause the bizarre behavior. Other older persons who have compromised functioning from brain degeneration, respiratory insufficiency, cardiac insufficiency, or metabolic disturbances can easily become psychotic in late life. It is important not to dismiss them as incurable but instead to try to control the symptoms, find the cause, and increase or maintain functional abilities.

Family Problems

The family plays a major role in the life of every individual and continues to be a major factor in the life of older persons (Bengston & Treas, 1982; Butler & Lewis, 1977). Families provide the majority of health and social services to older persons (Butler & Lewis, 1977). Most older persons also help their families as well (Benedict & Ganikos, 1981). Most older persons live within 30 min. of their families and have contact at least weekly. When a person becomes disabled, the family may become even more critical to that person's recovery, attainment of maximum functional abilities, and success in living at home (Power & Del Orto, 1980). Contrary to popular belief, families do not abandon nor neglect their older disabled relatives, and many go to heroic lengths trying to prevent institutionalization (for a full discussion see E. Brody, this volume).

Many investigators have found aspects of family interaction with disabled persons that are highly related to rehabilitation success. Bray (1980) and Kemp and Wetmore (1969) have found family support to be related to adjustment for middle-aged spinal cord injured persons. Drotar, Baskiewicz, Irvin, Kennell, and Klaus (1980) have reviewed the literature on family reactions to children with congenital defects. Falloon, Pederson, McGill, and Boyd (1984) have demonstrated the role of appropriate family interaction with younger schizophrenics. Zarit (1980) has shown the role of families in assisting an older person with Alzheimer's disease.

Bengston and Treas (1982) described some of the major dimensions of family structure that are especially relevant for assessing the nature and "health" of the family. The dimensions are (a) family structure: who is in the family and what are their characteristics; (b) family interaction: the usual and customary pattern of including others in activities; (c) family affect: the quality of affection, warmth, and emotional support; (d) family exchange: practical supportive measures, doing for each other, organizing resources; and (e) family norms: what is believed and expected about the older person's role and behavior. The presence of a disability can change any and all of these dimensions. In addition, an older family member having a disability may bring out earlier family problems that have been dormant for years. The author found 69% of families to have a problem serious enough to interfere with the rehabilitation success of the older person. It does not matter whether the older person actually lives with family members; the family can still be a major help or hindrance.

At least seven adaptive patterns can be discerned in older families. These can be seen to fit within Bengston's dimensions as well.

First is the "uninformed family." This family does not know the difference between normal aging and disease; they do not know how to care for the older person; they do not know how to go about obtaining resources or when a change in the person's status is significant. Often, these families overhelp the older person and inadvertently cause an overhandicapping condition to occur.

Second are families in which there is a "non-identified patient" who is also ill, either from a medical or mental health problem. This person can be the spouse but can also be a younger family member. In the case of older spouses, based on general rates of illness and disability, there is a 40% to 50% chance that the other spouse has a serious health problem as well. This person often resists having it addressed until the more disabled spouse is maximally functional.

Third are families who appear to "demote" the older disabled person— more out of attitude than lack of information. They tend to rob the older person of usual responsibilities and chores. It is as if they say, "Okay, you've had a disability, you better cease being an adult." These families are adept at getting others to collaborate in their misguided actions. For example, when with the doctor, they dominate the conversation, and the physician invariably ends up speaking *to* the family member *about* the older person. The older persons in these families then suffer needless feelings of rejection, uselessness, and decreased self-esteem, yet cannot understand fully why they feel that way because their families seem to be trying so much to help them. Underlying themes of control and power over decision-making are usually evident.

Another problematic family is the "burdened" or stressed one. This is often seen in families where the older person has a dementia, but also where other severely disabling conditions occur. These families, especially the spouses, are faced with multiple problems in physical caregiving, emotional upsets (especially over the severe loss they feel), and decisions regarding legal matters, financial matters, and institutionalization. These persons often feel as though they put in a 36-hour day, such as described by Mace and Rabins (1981). A particular problem recently emerging is that of the middle-aged daughter or daughter-in-law, for it is those persons on whom much of the responsibility rests in day-to-day care, arranging help, and taking the older person to appointments. Such women have been described as the "sandwich generation" or "the women in the middle" because they have responsibilities for a family of their own, including growing children, as well as for older persons and frequently have jobs outside the home as well. Support for these caregivers is therefore of vital importance to the functioning of the older person (E. Brody, this volume).

Fifth are problem families who can be described as "conflicted." In this kind of family there is much internal disagreement and even open warfare over what the course of action should be for the older person with a disability, particularly if the older person is widowed. The family may argue at length over where the older person should live, what the implications of the diagnosis are, whether the older person can live alone safely, and so on. One major issue in these families often unrealized is that of role reversal, which can cause the family conflict. The younger family members change places with older ones in terms of decision-making and problem-solving. Unless specifically agreed on, this change can often result in a "power struggle."

Sixth are families that have problems with "old business"—problems that developed at earlier stages of family life but which emerge later because of the disability. Problems of long-standing resentment, alienation, or conflict between the older person and the other family members could be ignored before. However, now that one person has a disability and requires assistance, the old problems stand in the way of effective cooperation.

Finally, there are families that can be described simply as unaffectionate.

They may provide aid and assistance, but it's done in a businesslike, cold, and clinical manner. The older person may be excluded from activities that are for recreation or fun even though their basic needs are addressed. Although the older person may be helped in some ways, he/she feels isolated and alone.

Because family problems are so common among the disabled elderly and because the family plays such a large role in independent living and proper function, it must be included in all care plans and, when possible, become a unit of care itself.

Social Isolation

Social isolation is a problem for a high proportion of older disabled persons, and it has many ramifications. Living alone does not cause social isolation. Approximately 24% of persons over age 65 live alone (Busse & Pfeiffer, 1969). Social isolation, defined as little or no *positive and meaningful* interaction with relatives, friends, or visitors, occurs in only about 10% of the older population. However, social isolation does increase in the presence of a physical disability (Vash, 1980), due to social rejection, personal mobility problems, lack of adequate transportation, and personal adjustment difficulties. Perhaps as many as 15% to 20% of older persons with a physical disability experience some degree of social isolation.

Social isolation among the elderly has been closely linked to life dissatisfaction (Busse & Pfeiffer, 1969), exacerbation of medical problems, functional deficits (Brummel-Smith, 1984), and psychopathology, especially depression (Blazer, 1982).

Social interaction, on the other hand, is one of the rewards that seem especially helpful in motivating elderly persons. For example, people attending a group treatment program were found to improve their grooming and dress and to miss sessions rarely (Staples, Kemp, Stromberg, & Kleinplatz, 1984). The greater the degree of quality interaction with others, even if it is only a single confidante, the less likely it is that the older disabled person will embark on a downward spiral of debilitation.

Special Subgroups

At least two special subgroups of older disabled persons warrant mention because they often present unique problems. One is the rapidly growing population of older persons who were disabled early in life. This includes people with polio, spinal cord injuries, cerebral palsy, mental retardation, arthritis, schizophrenia, and many other disorders. This populaton is now achieving an older age in higher numbers than ever before. As they do, many are experiencing symptoms that some describe as early aging, both medically and psychologically (Homann, 1980; Laurie, 1979). This is a group that has received comparatively little attention in aging research. Their problems are not typical of the older population disabled late in life because they have had a lifetime of living with a disability. Physically, it is possible that the very rehabilitation procedures and values that were so fervently drummed into them—namely, hard work and perseverance—have now added to a litany of medical problems that are emerging, from neurological to metabolic. Similarly, their mental health problems (also their positive adaptations) should be better understood. Of particular interest would be the topics of substance misuse, depression, family dynamics, and adjustment to disability (See Cotten & Spirrison and Rubenfield, this volume).

The second special group is minority aged. Aging, being a biopsychosocial experience, varies across different ethnic and racial groups. When the presence of a disability is added, the varieties and nature of mental health problems change accordingly. Several studies have shown that minority group older disabled persons have different kinds or amounts of mental health problems (Gelfand, 1981; Lopez, Kemp, Plopper, Staples, & Brummel-Smith, 1984). For example, older Hispanics have a generally higher prevalence of depression and a lower prevalence of social isolation. Older Jewish families have different patterns and customs of interaction. Very few older black persons are institutionalized, with the family working out alternative caregiving. Mental health assessments and treatment need to take these group differences into account.

TREATMENT APPROACHES

The first general principle of care is that mental health problems among the disabled elderly must be seen as bio-psycho-socio-functional phenomena. It is impossible to ignore any one of those areas and effect a lasting improvement. It is the rare older disabled person who does not have problems in each area. Rather than address the psychological problem only through psychological techniques, as one might do with counseling or psychotherapy, it is best to consider the entire range of medical, functional and/or social interventions that also might assist. To use an example from work with younger or middle-aged disabled persons, the issue of self-worth or self-esteem is a common topic in psychotherapy. However, rather than trying to convince a young disabled man that he still has self-worth, a better solution may be to help him get a job and let him discover it for himself. Similarly, an older person with depression can be assisted through psychotherapy, but the need for better mobility, improved eyesight, and enhanced socialization should not be ignored.

A second principle of intervention is that the focus should include both the patient *and* the family. Mental health problems can be dealt with by working with a person alone, but they usually can be helped more effectively by including the family in treatment. Family intervention can take the form of anything from providing information to intense working through of emotional difficulties.

Third, mental health care should not be limited to ameliorating psychological deficits. It also should include strengthening, preventing, and enhancing techniques as well. Approaches that focus exclusively on a "medical model" of treating only deficit conditions while ignoring ongoing adjustments are bound to fall short of what is needed. A disabled person, young or old, will never lead a completely normal life. Intervention to prevent or reduce the impact of likely problems in the future is important. Vash (1980) has made an excellent case for the need for "psychogogic" approaches. These are designed not simply to reduce or replace a deficit but to enhance the disabled person's long-term success.

This section will not focus on specific techniques for every mental health problem that may exist for an older person. For that purpose, the reader can review any of the established texts (e.g., Busse & Blazer, 1980; Birren & Sloane, 1980; Butler & Lewis, 1977, 1984). Instead, this section will describe the general treatment approaches that might be considered in all mental health problems affecting the elderly in rehabilitation.

There are six major approaches available to treating mental health problems of older people. The utilization of more than one of them will be most beneficial to the majority of persons. Each of these approaches assumes that the older person has first received a complete physical examination and that any purely medical problems contributing to mental health problems (e.g., hypothyroidism, tumors, medicines) have been eliminated. The six major approaches include (a) biological/physical, (b) individual psychotherapeutic/counseling, (c) group treatment programs, (d) family-oriented treatment, (e) community-oriented services, (f) psychogogic methods.

Biological/Physical

Three subtypes of approaches are available: psychoactive medications, improvements in endurance and conditioning, and reducing functional problems in daily living.

One of the major advances in the last 30 years has been our understanding of the biochemical correlates of mental health problems and the resultant advent of medicines to counteract these biochemical alterations. There is not sufficient evidence to say that the biochemical abnormalities *cause* the mental health problems, but certainly there is enough proof to state that psychoactive medicines help to reduce the symptoms of mental health problems through restoring a biochemical balance. Older persons frequently develop biochemical deficits through the relatively normal aging process and these deficits can make them more susceptible to psychosocial stressors. For example, there is evidence that monoamine oxidase increases with age and norepinephrine decreases, potentially making older persons at higher risk for depression (cf. Busse & Blazer, 1980).

The usefulness of antidepressants, anxiolytics, antipsychotics, and hypnotics to control the symptoms of major mental health problems cannot be minimized. These agents have proved effective, often in cases where no amount of interpersonal intervention could help. Antidepressants appropriate for the elderly—such as nortriptyline, desipramine, and trazadone—which do not have as many of the unwanted anticholinergic side effects—are readily available. Their ability to improve sleep, reduce fatigue, improve mood, and address other symptoms of depression is well documented. As with other medicines used with the elderly, the general rule of dosage is to "start low and go slow" because drugs last longer in the bodies of older persons. Similarly, appropriate anxiolytics are available for the elderly, particularly lorazepam, oxazepam, and alprazolam, all of which are relatively short-acting. Even for major disruptive behavior such as hallucinations and extreme agitation, older persons can be appropriately medicated. Such drugs as haloperidol and thioridazine help to control those symptoms.

It is not clear whether medicines by themselves will *cure* mental health problems. For obvious ethical reasons, it is impossible to separate people from their usual environments in order to discern the difference between the biological effect and the improvement due to greater interaction with the natural environment. The view here is that drugs such as antidepressants restore a chemical balance that makes the person capable of learning again. With the extreme imbalance of neurotransmitters that occurs in depression, for example, the older person has a harder time learning new information (such as how to adjust to a changing life) or utilizing past learning. The whole area of state-dependent learning focuses on this point. Given that the chemical imbalance can be corrected, it is then still necessary to ensure that the patient learns things that will best assist him/her to adjust to a different life style, one that now includes a disability. The practice of prescribing antidepressants alone for older persons may give the clinician a false sense of assurance. Most older people will also need psychological intervention. Some people have intact enough families and reasonably good prior adjustments so that they need minimal professional guidance. However, many do not, and they will require individual or group intervention of a psychological nature for longer periods.

The effects of exercise and conditioning on mental health have been explored in younger persons. Some evidence suggests that regular jogging can be effective treatment for depression and may even serve as a prevention for relapse—perhaps through the role of endorphins or through development of higher levels of overall physical resistance to stressors. Older persons are notorious for being deconditioned, especially if they have a disability. In fact, it is one of the major problems associated with disability in older age. Deconditioning impairs the older person's mobility, therefore restricting activities, and may add to mental health problems such as mood disturbances. The conditioning status of older persons can be improved with the help of physical or occupational therapy with dramatic results.

Improvements in the ability to do daily activities also can improve mental health. Many older persons, for example, suffer from visual and hearing disorders. This separates them further from their previous activities for recreation and pleasure, such as reading or sewing. In turn, this leads to discouragement and may lead to further disengagement. Other older persons have given up driving after suffering a disability. Many times it is given up inappropriately, as such people could be assisted to drive with hand controls if necessary. Driving could again open up avenues of independence and reduce feelings of isolation. Many older persons suffer from aches and pains that they needlessly accept as part of the disability. These further remind them of their disabled status and lead to feelings of discouragement, if not depression. Physical and occupational therapy may reduce those pains and allow a more functional range of activities, often resulting in improved outlook. The ability for self-toileting is also important to self-concept. Persons who cannot perform that task invariably feel demeaned and discouraged. Thus, attention to functional abilities is of vital concern.

Individual Psychotherapy and Counseling

These approaches remain the cornerstones of psychological intervention. Several persons have reviewed the role of psychotherapy with older persons, including Rechtschaffen (1959), Goldfarb (cited in Busse & Pfeiffer, 1969), Butler and Lewis (1977, 1984) and Schinle and Eiler (1983). A few have explained psychotherapy in relation to disabled elderly (e.g., Steger, 1976). What emerges in regard to older persons in general is that the principles and outcomes are more similar to those of younger persons than they are different. Busse and Pfeiffer (1969) point out some needed modifications, including a need for more exploration by the therapist, a greater focus on here-and-now problems rather than the past, establishing clear-cut goals, and special emphasis on the transference phenomena. However, the essence of psychotherapy remains the same. It requires establishing a safe and supportive interpersonal environment where the expression of feelings and thoughts can be constructively examined, where alternative ways of thinking, feeling, and acting can be explored to create a more satisfactory method of adjustment. Once an appropriate interpersonal environment has been established, improvement through psychotherapeutic intervention depends on (a) becoming aware of unrecognized feelings and thoughts; (b) expression of those experiences to someone who won't make the patient feel wrong for having them; (c) recognition of the self as a major factor in the problem and in change; and (d) exploring, choosing, and creating an alternative set of behaviors. These principles apply to older persons as well as they do to younger persons.

The themes in psychotherapy with older persons are often different from those for younger persons (even though the psychotherapeutic *process* is highly similar). Older persons with a disability frequently have themes of cumulative losses in life, preparation for life's end, a struggle to maintain personal independence, concern over bodily health and family relations, and the preservation of self-worth and self-esteem.

Psychotherapy with older persons in rehabilitation need not be a pessimistic endeavor, even though the themes have more to do with termination of one's life cycle rather than the expansion or unfolding of new life stages. Older persons in rehabilitation can be assisted not to be overly stressed by these multiple concerns, to increase and maintain daily functioning, and to have a high degree of life satisfaction.

Counseling differs from psychotherapy in that it is less focused on clearly maladjusted behavior. Counseling is concerned with assisting individuals whose psychological functioning is more or less normal by providing information, advice, resources, and referrals to reach concrete goals. Counseling is conducted by all disciplines for one purpose or another. For example, many older persons need a better understanding of their medicines or their nutrition. Psychological counseling with older persons can focus on sexual relations, vocational or productive roles, the creation of a living will, stress reduction/relaxation techniques, living arrangements, and divorce and marriage, to a name a few. Clearly, such topics have a different nature from problems of major depression, family conflict, paranoia, agitation, dementia, and bereavement. Salmon (1981), Engram (1981), and Loesch (1981) have discussed various aspects of counseling with older persons around personal, leisure, and communication skills.

Family Therapy

The family plays such a large role in the well-being of older disabled persons that it cannot be left out of the treatment options. Some persons, such as Power and Del Orto (1980), stress it as *the* most important treatment approach. Certainly, treatment of the whole family is both an effective and efficient form of therapy. Herr and Weakland (1979) discuss excellent methods for family counseling and therapy using techniques such as

Hayley's metacommunication model and Virginia Satir's systems approach to family therapy.

In terms of increasing overall functioning and life satisfaction, families can be either very helpful to the disabled older person or very harmful. For example, one family whose mother had Alzheimer's disease was severely divided on whether or not she really had such an illness. The patient had an intact social personality and could converse well enough to fool some of her family. The daughter believed the diagnosis and had seen the mother's problems of leaving the gas oven on, being unable to prepare a meal, and not being able to count money. The son, however, who had always been dominant over his sister, did not believe anything was wrong with his mother because when he visited her the apartment was clean and neat and she seemed very pleasant. During several sessions the only interchanges were each accusing the other of being wrong. The son would say, "It's always been you! You never liked mother! It's you who has the problem, not her!" The daughter would cry and try to reason. It was not until the two of them could deal with the past that appropriate care could be arranged for the mother.

In another situation, a 67-year-old man became severely disabled through spinal arthritis that caused impingement on the cord, with resultant paralysis. He had married only 4 years earlier. The strain of the disability and his resultant discouragement was causing severe marital problems. The wife was upset because she thought he didn't do enough for himself each day when she was at work. He felt she nagged him and didn't believe that he exercised during the day. They had stopped having any fun, and their affection for each other diminished. One thing that emerged by seeing both of them together was evidence that he was staying active, especially by exercising, which meant to the wife that he still cared about her. Although this might have been resolved by seeing him alone, it was more quickly resolved by seeing both of them.

Families justifiably go through many emotions when an older person becomes disabled—whether it is a spouse, a sibling, or a parent. Some of the emotions are due to the current situation, part are due to old, unresolved issues. A family member may feel the loss of opportunity to express affection when the older relative has had a stroke, or may wish he or she had expressed it more and earlier, thus feeling guilty. Another family member may feel guilty for somehow "causing" the disability. A spouse of a disabled older person may feel helpless and overwhelmed by anxiety because he/she is now faced with not being the passive, dependent one in the relationship. A granddaughter may feel angered at having to look after her grandmother each day but unable to express it because others will disapprove of her attitude. Unexpressed emotions will be a source of family conflict and borderline quality care for the older person as long as they exist. The goal of counseling for that kind of problem should be to get feelings out in the open in order to achieve more effective interaction.

In the case of some special problems, such as Alzheimer's disease, families may need therapy and education for themselves. Recently, Kahan (1984) completed a controlled study comparing the effects of a time-limited education-therapy group for such families. The control group came from people on the waiting list to come into the program. As compared to the control group, the experimental subjects showed significantly less burden and stress after the eight-session program, significantly less depression, and a greater understanding of the illness. Such family-oriented treatment programs offer great promise for older persons.

Group Approaches

Group approaches to psychological difficulties (and other difficulties as well) are beneficial for several reasons. First, they are economical; many people can be treated at one time. Second, group approaches facilitate socialization with and learning from *peers* and, hence, promote a cameraderie and a problem-solving atmosphere that is supportive. Third, group approaches are more readily multidisciplinary. They can include physical exercise, psychotherapy, education, and recreation.

Groups for older persons vary, depending on whether they have a psychotherapeutic focus or a broader rehabilitation one. Busse and Pfeiffer (1969) reviewed the history of group psychotherapy with older persons. They cite work by Lichtenberg, Linden, and Wolff on therapy with older hospitalized psychiatric patients. Work by Burnside, also cited (Busse & Pfeiffer, 1969), supports the benefit of group approaches. Lazarus and Weinberg (1980) demonstrated the value of group approaches with the elderly on improving self-esteem, increasing motivation, and expanding interpersonal relations. As with individual psychotherapy, little empirical evidence exists that rigorously supports the effectiveness of group therapy with persons of any age. Eisdorfer and Stotsky (1977) conclude that it is difficult to determine the exact mechanisms of improvement or successful factors in a group program, although they do lead to improvement. Few programs of group therapy have been developed specifically for persons with disabilities, let alone for older persons with disabilities. One approach developed by Lasky (1977), termed structured experimental therapy in rehabilitation (SETR), was used with younger persons with a disability. Although labeled a therapy, it is more akin to a broader rehabilitation group. Its central theme was the reduction of interpersonal stress between disabled and nondisabled people. The sessions included both disabled and nondisabled members. The group explored specific problems in a structured formal setting and reportedly was productive.

With older disabled persons, Kemp et al. (1984) used a control group design to determine the effectiveness of persons attending a group treatment program in terms of improvements in mood, daily functioning, and socialization. The group was not psychotherapeutic but included group problem-solving, recreation, education, exercise, and socialization. Over a 9-month period, older persons in the group improved on those measures.

It is apparent that group approaches to psychosocial problems can be useful and efficient. They cannot be substituted for individual counseling or therapy with older persons for all problems. For persons who have a difficult time trusting others, those who cannot wait until the next group session to discuss a crisis, those who have language difficulties, or those who have phobias of being around other people, individual sessions are still best.

Community-Oriented Approaches

It is well known that rehabilitation success must extend beyond the hospital or rehabilitation center doors. Success in living independently in the community is the best criterion of success. Recognition of this fact has lead to the development of many programs to assist disabled persons in "making it" in a nondisabled world. Although few have been designed specifically for older disabled persons, their development is imminent.

One such approach is centers for independent living (CILs). These are human-service organizations begun *by* disabled persons. They provide a variety of psychological, social, and daily living services. The first was the Center for Independent Living in Berkeley, California, and was essentially an expansion of the Physically Disabled Students Program at the University. Unable to find jobs in the community—even with a college degree and wanting to avoid institutionalization—these severely disabled persons began a program for their own survival. Since then, CILs have appeared elsewhere. One Rehabilitation Research and Training Center in Kansas is devoted to this important topic.

Several characteristics of CILs are important. First, they are organized, administered, and operated by disabled persons. Second, they are not primarily mental health organizations, even though more positive mental health is a common result. Third, they exist in the community, usually free-standing from any institution. To date, CILs have not dealt heavily with problems of the disabled elderly. Their main clientele have been younger disabled persons. However, because there is much that CILs can offer older persons, this approach will probably become a regular part of services for older persons in the future, particularly as the current generation of younger disabled persons become older.

The CIL approach includes a number of helpful techniques. Peer counseling is one of them. As Vash (1980) points out, certain rehabilitative tasks can be better done by life-experienced helpers than by formally trained professionals. She explains that the peer approach to counseling is in many respects life "coaching." Coaches don't assume that their "players" are sick. They assume that they need to be coached to bring out their best performance. Peer coaches of disabled persons employ a variety of methods. They instruct; that is, they provide factual information. They counsel; that is, they motivate and provide emotional support. They also provide role models. They demonstrate how given activities should be performed. In addition to peer counseling/coaching, CILs provide direct help with attendant selection and training, housing, financial aid, transportation, legal aid, crisis intervention, and recreation.

A large role is frequently played by CILs in advocacy for persons with disabilities. The staff of CILs lobby politically and administratively to improve the status of disabled persons. This advocacy may include getting regulations changed at the local, state, or federal level. It may include working with individual politicians to effect a new law. It may even include dramatic actions that call attention to certain grievances. The life-threatening and life-ending actions of a few disabled individuals that recently called attention to the overzealous termination of government disability benefits is such an example.

One center of a related nature for older persons is the Senior Health and Peer Counseling Center in Santa Monica, California. Although not based on the same premises as most CILs, it does offer peer services to older adults. The usual senior citizen center does not fit the requirements to qualify as an independent living center. Although there are now about 5,000 multipurpose centers, their services are primarily professionally administered. Their emphasis has not been on the problems of disability, but they do provide a variety of services that help promote the independence of older persons in the community. Gatz (1980) has demonstrated the value of older persons in a paraprofessional–peer counseling mode. She reports that improved knowledge of community resources, increased life satisfaction, and an increased sense of personal control were some of the positive outcomes.

Psychogogic Approaches

Vash (1980) describes a variety of differences in technique and philosophy that distinguish psychogogic (a term coined by Abraham Maslow) approaches from psychotherapeutic approaches. This approach has much to offer mental health services to older persons with disabilities. "Psychogogic approaches strive to strengthen the individual against the onslaughts of stress, in order to *avoid* or *prevent* mental/emotional/behavioral disorders. On the other hand, psychotherapeutic approaches strive to redress or correct disorders that have already occurred" (Vash, 1980, p. 185; italics added).

All therapeutic approaches, whether they are physical or psychological, are attempts to restore a person to an "equilibrium" from a deficit caused by an illness, injury or trauma. A bone is broken; surgery stabilizes the problem. The person has an infection; medicine cures it. A person is depressed; therapy eases the depression. The underlying, unspoken assumption is that if treatment stops there, the person will spontaneously resume his/her previous life. However, people with a disability already suffer from a *permanent* deficit. Treatment that stops with only restoring an equilibrium without addressing the long-term effects of the disability may result in people who are not ill but not well either; not depressed but not happy either; not dysfunctional but not ready for the future either. What these people also need, and often fail to get, is something to strengthen and enhance themselves.

As applied to the disabled elderly, three classes of psychogogic work are important: (a) education, (b) self-responsibility counseling, and (c) goal refocusing.

It is unfortunate that few older persons receive education about their disability and its implications or about the interaction of their age and disability. Educational opportunities must be arranged to teach about warning signs of acute illness, drugs and their side effects, legal rights, nutrition, family relations, stress, avoiding depression, safety, living wills, doctor-patient relationships, exercise, sexuality, and death. Rehabilitation programs which do not provide for these preventive educational opportunities will probably see limited long-term benefits. Education of family members is equally important, since it is families who provide most of the care and emotional support (or hindrance).

Helping older persons to develop or strengthen a sense of self-responsibility has similarly been ignored. Somewhere along the line, it appears that society, families, professional staffs, and even older persons themselves are prone to develop a point of view that older disabled persons are not or should not be as responsible for themselves as they were when they were young. This can be seen in the language people use in talking about the elderly. In a family conference with the patient present, a family member may say to the doctor, "They develop many mental problems, don't they?" Or a doctor may address an older person as "him" or "her" instead of by his/her name, even if he/she is present. It also is evident when a doctor gives a prescription for medication to a family member instead of to the patient, and the older person allows it! Another vivid example is when a family member wants the older disabled person to stop driving just because he/she is 70 years old and has had a disability. However, families and health professionals are only partly to blame. No one can be robbed of his or her freedom and responsibility without partially allowing it. Therefore, older persons are responding to the social atmosphere which seems to encourage this and are accepting it as the norm rather than objecting to it.

Self-responsibility doesn't stop at a certain age. The capacity to learn and to choose (except possibly for the severely demented) is present at any age. Many older patients present themselves as just "waiting," being "resigned," or "accepting," even in the absence of mental illness, because they and/or others decided not to be self-responsible, not to continue choosing their own life direction, and choosing not to experience it fully. Although this may be a "good" decision, in the sense that it takes less energy, requires fewer risks, and meets certain dependency needs, it leads to a "lifeless" life. Older persons could benefit from viewing themselves as controlling their own lives, choosing how they want to live, and taking charge of it. People who are more self-responsible take the preventive, precautionary steps that help them avoid many stressful problems to which others fall prey. Self-responsible individuals are more likely to utilize their resources better and not to be passive recipients of services.

Goals and goal-setting play an important part in human life, especially in an achievement-oriented society. Although appropriate goal-setting is related to long-term success (Kemp & Wetmore, 1969), this process seems to be impaired in some disabled persons. Refocusing of goals in late life and with a disability appears to be related to more positive adjustments. Erikson (1959) describes the late-life task of being able to make sense of one's life, to feel comfortable about what one has done and the kind of person one has been. Vash (1980) describes the need to "transcend" a disability, to renounce materialism (as in physical matter, i.e., the body), and to develop spiritualistic and other aspects of personality. The same can be said for older persons with a disability. Refocusing of life goals is an important part of rehabilitation. Life goals can be grouped into three kinds: doing, getting, and being. Doing goals are those concerned with achievements and accomplishments—a person's roles. Goals of getting are related to acquiring, collecting, and having. They include college degrees, research grants, houses, furniture, friends, or money. They can also include power, influence, and fame. Goals of being relate to what kind of person the individual wants to be: humanistic, courageous, helpful, or loving. Older age and a disability seem to foster a need for looking at goals differently. Not as many goals are considered feasible after a disability, and even the process of establishing goals is difficult when all of the barriers to achieving them are considered. It is important, though, to help disabled persons of any age realize that the disability or the age need not interfere with goal-setting, and certainly not with attaining goals of being. An older person with multiple disabilities can still *be* a person of dignity, wisdom, humor, self-responsibility, and love.

Research and Training Needs

The needs for research and training in the area of psychosocial aspects of geriatric rehabilitation are tremendously varied. Rather than list all research projects or investigations that might be conducted (an endless task), the broad areas of investigation that appear most promising and applicable will be outlined. Only a few examples of each will be listed.

1. Accessing rehabilitation services.
   a. The process of decision-making among caregivers and professionals regarding referral of older persons for rehabilitation.
   b. Policy and attitudinal barriers to rehabilitation of older persons.
   c. Special adaptations of services to make them more amenable to older persons.
2. Assessment of mental health problems.
   a. Improved assessment methods for depression, cognitive impairment, and other major mental health problems correlated with functional outcomes.
   b. Biological correlates of mental health problems.
   c. The improved recognition by primary care physicians of mental health problems among the disabled elderly.
   d. Development of age-suitable measures of self-esteem and self-worth.
   e. Improved understanding of family patterns that interfere with functional achievements in older persons.
3. Treatment issues.
   a. Improved biological treatment of depression.
   b. Improved individual psychotherapy techniques for older persons with disabilities.
   c. Methods of family therapy which are best for older persons with a disability.
   d. Experimental programs to improve motivation toward independence.
   e. Best methods of promoting self-responsibility, self-esteem, and psychological independence.
   f. Methods to develop improved peer counseling for disabled older persons.
   g. Counseling the marginally cognitively impaired person.

    h. Developing or integrating older disabled persons into Centers for Independent Living.
    i. The effects of specialized nutritional and exercise programs on mental health of older disabled persons.
    j. Preventive approaches ("psychogogic") to mental health problems.
4. Special subgroups.
    a. Patterns of adjustment to disability in minority groups.
    b. Family therapy changes required in minority families with a disabled person.
    c. The adequacy of community practices in treating mental health problems in minority disabled older persons.
    d. The long-range psychological effects of an early life disability.
    e. Family preparation for continued care of a severely disabled child after death of the aged caregiver.
    f. Depression among late-life persons disabled early in life.
5. Effectiveness of mental health care.
    a. The value of mental health services in physical rehabilitation of older persons.
    b. Effectiveness of interdisciplinary approaches to mental health problems.
    c. Long-term adjustment of older persons treated in a rehabilitation format.
6. Linkages
    a. Improving rehabilitation demonstrations between NIA, NIMH, and NIHR.
    b. Improved linkages between each state's long-term care system for older persons and rehabilitation services.
    c. Improved linkages between primary care physicians and specialized geriatric rehabilitation services.
    d. Improved selection of patients/clients by the state departments of rehabilitation, the state departments of aging, and local mental health services for the elderly.

Training needs are equally broad. With the strong interplay of psychological, physical, and social factors in the overall well-being of the older disabled person, several different populations should be addressed. Training needs can be separated into *who* ought to be taught, *what* ought to be taught, and *how* it should be taught. Who should be taught includes professionals and future professionals in all key health disciplines. This includes physicians (especially primary care physicians), nurses, psychologists, social workers, occupational and physical therapists, rehabilitation counselors, and others. Students, such as medical students, generally have neutral attitudes toward the elderly. Unless faculty members incubate negative attitudes, future generations of practitioners will probably approach older patients more positively. A novel approach by the Pacific Geriatric Education Center at USC (Sloane & Leibig, 1983), as well as three other similar centers, is confronting the problem of current faculty members' underknowledge of aging by exposing them to a variety of aging topics.

Families should also be a forum of training and teaching. Families need basic information on what constitutes normal aging and pathological behavior in old age, how to care for and support older persons, and how to obtain resources.

Judging by the results of the first four years of experience of the Research and Training Center on Aging at USC/Rancho Los Amigos Medical Center, the content of mental health training for health disciplines that appear to be best received includes several areas. First are the unique mental health problems encountered in geriatric rehabilitation. This includes much of the material already covered in this chapter. Second is a need to stress the biopsychosocial nature of mental health problems of older disabled persons. Third are the altered presentations of such problems that older persons can have and the best methods of determining the correct problem—for example, methods that determine the nature and cause of cognitive problems. Finally, treatment options for older disabled persons, from biological treatment of depression through family therapy techniques and community programs, should also be included.

The question of how best to train others is also important. Here at least four considerations are important. Firsthand exposure to older disabled persons outside an institution is important. Students and others need to see that older persons, even those severely disabled, can live independently. In this regard, all first-year medical students at USC are brought to the Rancho R&T Center and go on home visits to interview an older person. The students report overwhelmingly positive experiences from this practice. Second, teaching must demonstrate by effective rehabilitation methods that the mental health of older persons can be improved. Attitudes toward older persons are an important issue in teaching others. It is difficult to treat and change attitudes directly. However, positive examples of change through the correct approaches to care *do* change attitudes.

Older disabled persons as teachers themselves should not be overlooked. Recently, one group, called the Rancho Owls (1984) and composed of older disabled persons, has developed teaching materials and methods for educating health providers about the needs and concerns of older disabled persons.

Finally, the dissemination of information should be considered. Information is only as good as the number of people who have it and can use it. In order to disseminate mental health/rehabilitation information to as broad an audience as possible, such techniques as telecommunications, computer-assisted learning, and audiovisual tapes should be further developed to promote the adoption of the latest information in this important area.

REFERENCES

American Psychiatric Association. (1980). *Diagnostic and statistical manual III.* Washington, DC: APA.

Atkinson, J. H., & Schuckit, M. A. (1981). Alcoholism and over-the-counter and prescription drug misuse in the elderly. *Annual Review of Gerontology and Geriatrics, 2,* 225–284.

Beck, A. T. (1967). *Depression: Causes and treatment.* Philadelphia: University of Pennsylvania Press.

Benedict, R. C., & Ganikos, M. L., (1981). Coming to terms with ageism in rehabilitation. *Journal of Rehabilitation, 47,* 19–27.

Bengston, V., & Treas, J. (1982). The changing family context of mental health and aging. In J. E. Birren & R. B. Sloane (Eds.), *Handbook of mental health and aging.* Englewood Cliffs, NJ: Prentice-Hall

Birren, J. E., & Schaie, K. W. (1977). *Handbook of the pschology of aging.* New York: Van Nostrand Reinhold.

Birren, J. E., & Sloane, B. R. (1980). *Handbook of mental health and aging.* New York: Van Nostrand Reinhold.

Blazer, D. (1980). The epidemiology of mental illness in late life. In E. Busse & D. Blazer (Eds.), *Handbook of geriatric psychiatry,* New York: Van Nostrand Reinhold.

Blazer, D. (1982). *Depression in late life.* St. Louis: C. V. Mosby.

Botwinick, J. (1973). *Aging and behavior.* New York: Springer.

Bray, G. (1980). Reactive patterns in families of the severely disabled. In P. W. Power & A. E. Dell Orto (Eds.), *Role of the family in the rehabilitation of the physically disabled.* Baltimore: University Park Press.

Brummel-Smith, K. (1984). Training health professionals: A rehabilitation orientation could improve the gerontology field. *Generations, 8,* 47–50.

Busse, E., & Blazer, D. (Eds.). (1980). *Handbook of geriatric psychiatry.* New York: Van Nostrand Reinhold.

Busse, E. W. & Pfeiffer, E. (1969). Functional psychiatric disorders in old age. In E. W. Busse & E. Pfeiffer (Eds.), *Behavior and adaptation in late life,* New York: Little-Brown.

Butler, R. N., & Lewis, M. (1977). *Aging and mental health: Positive psychosocial approaches* (2nd ed.). St. Louis: C. V. Mosby.

Butler, R. N. & Lewis, H. (1984). *Aging and mental health: Positive psychosocial approaches* (3rd ed.). St. Louis: C. V. Mosby.

Claremont Graduate School. (1979). *A survey of health concerns of residents of Los Angeles County.* Los Angeles: Area Agency on Aging.

Drotar, D., Baskiewicz, A., Irvin, N., Kennell, J., & Klaus, J. (1980). The adaptation of parents to the birth of an infant with a congenital malformation. In P. W. Power & A. E. Dell Orto. (Eds.), *Role of the family in the rehabilitation of the physically disabled.* Baltimore: University Park Press.

Eisdorfer, C., & Stotsky, B. A. (1977). Intervention treatment and rehabilitation of psychiatric disorders. In J. E. Birren & K. W. Schaie (Eds.), *Handbook of the psychology of aging.* New York: Van Nostrand Reinhold.

Engram, B. (1981). Communication skills training for rehabilitation counselors working with older persons. *Journal of Rehabilitation, 47,* 51–56.

Erikson, E. R. (1959). *Psychological issues I: Identity and life cycle.* New York: International Universities Press.

Falloon, I. R. H., Pederson, J., McGill, C. W., & Boyd, J. C. (1984). The social outcome of family management of schizophrenia. *New England Journal of Medicine 117,* 47–54.

Freud, S. (1901). *The psychopathology of everyday life* (standard ed., Vol. 6). London: Hogarth Press.

Gatz, M. (1980). Enhancement of individual and community competence: The older adult as community worker. *American Journal of Community Psychology.*

Gelfand, D. (1981). Ethnicity and aging. *Annual Review of Gerontology and Geriatrics 3,* 91–117.

Gurland, B., & Toner, J. (1983). Differentiating dementia from non-dementing conditions. In R. Mayeux & W. G. Rosen (Eds.), *The dementias.* New York: Raven Press.

Herr, J., & Weakland, J. (1979). *Counseling elders and their families.* New York: Springer.

Homann, G. (1982). *Fifth annual John S. Young lectureship.* Denver: Craig Hospital.

Institute of Medicine. (1978). *Aging and medical education: Report of a study.* Washington, DC: National Academy of Sciences.

Kahan, J. (1984). *The effects of a psychoeducational group program on levels of stress in families of persons with Alzheimer's disease.* Unpublished dissertation, International University, San Diego.

Kane, R. A., & Kane, R. L. (1981). *Assessing the elderly.* Lexington, MA: D. C. Heath.

Kemp, B., Stromberg, L., Kleinplatz, F., & Staples, F. (1984). *Effects of a multidisciplinary group program on functioning of older persons.* Unpublished manuscript, Rehabilitation Research and Training Center on Aging, Downey, CA.

Kemp, B. J., & Wetmore, C. L. (1969). Productivity after injury in a sample of spinal cord injured persons: A pilot study. *Journal of Chronic Disease, 24,* 2.

Kosberg, J., & Harris, A. (1978). Attitudes toward elderly clients. *Health and Social Work, 3,* 66–90.

Lasky, R. (1977). Structured existential therapy: A group approach to rehabilitation.

In D. Marinelli & A. E. Dell Orto (Eds.), *The psychological and social impact of physical disability.* New York: Springer.

Lazarus, L. W., & Weinberg, J. (1980). Treatment in the ambulatory care setting. In E. W. Busse & D. G. Blazer (Eds.), *Handbook of geriatric psychiatry.* New York: Van Nostrand Reinhold.

Laurie, G. (1979). Rehabilitation Gazette polio/respiratory resources. *Rehabilitation Gazette, 24,* 36.

Lewin, K. (1935). *A dynamic theory of personality.* New York: McGraw-Hill.

Loesch, L. C. (1981). Leisure counseling for disabled older persons. *Journal of Rehabilitation, 47,* 58–63.

Lopez, W., Kemp, B. J., Plopper, M., Staples, F., & Brummel-Smith, K. (1984). Health needs of the Hispanic elderly. *Journal of the American Geriatrics Society, 32.*

Mace, N. L., & Rabins, P. V. (1981). *The 36-hour day.* Baltimore: Johns Hopkins.

McDaniel, J. (1969). *Physical disability and human behavior.* Elmsford, NY: Pergamon Press.

Neugarten, B. (1968). Perspectives of the aging process. *Psychiatric Research Reports, 23,* 42–48.

Plopper, M., & Chui, H. (1984). *Dementia in the elderly: A workbook.* Los Angeles: University of Southern California.

Power, P. W., & Dell Orto, A. E. (1980). *Role of the family in the rehabilitation of the physically disabled.* Baltimore: University Park Press.

Rancho Owls. (1984, Summer). Stop, look and listen. *Generations.*

Rechtschaffen, A. (1977). Psychotherapy with geriatric patients: A review of the literature. In M. Steurry & M. Blank (Eds.), *Readings in psychotherapy with older people.* Rockville, MD: National Institute of Mental Health.

Riley, M. W., & Foner, A. (1968). *Aging and society.* New York: Russell Sage Foundation.

Rosin, A. J., & Glatt, M. M. (1971). Alcohol excess in the elderly. *Quarterly Journal of Studies on Alcohol, 32,* 53–59.

Roth, M. (1955). The natural history of mental disorder in old age. *Journal of Mental Sciences, 101,* 281.

Salmon, H. (1981). Theories of aging, disability and loss. *Journal of Rehabilitation, 47,* 44–50.

Schinle, D., & Eiler, J. (1984). Clinical intervention with older adults. In M. G. Eisenberg, L. C. Sutkin, & M. A. Jansen (Eds.), *Chronic illness and disability through the life span: Effects on self and family.* New York: Springer.

Sloane, R. B., & Leibig, P. (1983). *The Pacific Geriatric Education Center: Annual report.* Los Angeles: University of Southern California, Department of Psychiatry and Behavioral Sciences.

Staples, F., Kemp, B., Stromberg, L., Kleinplatz, F. (1984). *A multidisciplinary group program for older disabled persons.* Los Angeles: Rancho Los Amigos Medical Center Rehabilitation Research and Training Center on Aging.

Steger, R. (1976). Understanding the psychologic factors in rehabilitation. *Geriatrics, 27,* 68–73.

Vash, C. (1980). *The psychology of disability.* New York: Springer.

Williams, T. F. (1982). *Rehabilitation in the aging.* New York: Raven Press.

Yesavage, J. A., Bring, T. L., Rose, T. L., Lum, O., Huang, V., Adey, M., & Leirer, D. (1983). Development and validation of a geriatric depression screening scale: A preliminary report. *Journal of Psychiatric Research, 17,* 37–49.

Zarit, S. (1980). *Aging and mental disorders.* New York: Free Press.

Zung, W. W. K. (1965). A self-rating depression scale. *Archives of General Psychiatry, 12,* 63.

11

The Elderly Mentally Retarded (Developmentally Disabled) Population: A Challenge for the Service Delivery System

Paul D. Cotten and Charles L. Spirrison

The demographic information pertaining to the aging of the American population has been presented in previous sections of this publication. This section will focus on one portion of the American population that also is growing older—mentally retarded persons. Unlike the populations discussed in other sections, these people have been mentally retarded since the developmental period (usually age 18), so their condition is one with which they have had many years of experience. One could discuss whether the training of this group constitutes rehabilitation or habilitation. However, the important point is to insure that service systems have a philosophical base on which to develop programs for the elderly mentally retarded individual that will assist that person in either developing new skills or maintaining the ones that have been developed. The goal is that elderly mentally retarded persons may continue to maximize the quality of their lives.

Much of the literature to be reviewed was written using the developmentally disabled population as the subjects for discussion. The present authors recognize that the term *developmental disability* is not synonymous with the term *mentally retarded*, but because the vast majority of developmentally disabled individuals are, at least, functionally retarded, it was felt that the inclusion of this literature was appropriate.

To ensure communication in meanings of terms to be used in this paper, the terms *mental retardation* and *developmental disability* are defined as follows:

Mental retardation: "Mental retardation refers to significantly subaverage general intellectual functioning existing concurrently with deficits in the adaptive behavior, and manifested during the developmental period" (Grossman, 1977, p. 11).

Developmental disability:
The term developmental disability means a severe, chronic disability of a person which—

(A) is attributable to a mental or physical impairment or combination of mental and physical impairments;

(B) is manifested before the person attains age twenty-two;

(C) is likely to continue indefinitely;

(D) results in substantial functional limitations in three or more of the following areas of life activity: (i) self-care, (ii) receptive and expressive language, (iii) learning, (iv) mobility, (v) self-direction, (vi) capacity for independent living, and (vii) economic self-security; and

(E) reflects the person's need for a combination and sequence of special, interdisciplinary, or generic care, treatment, or other services which are lifelong or extended duration and are individually planned and coordinated. (Developmental Disabilities Act of 1984)

The mentally retarded individual is expected to have a longer life today, relative to the retarded person of earlier generations, because of improvements in medical and social conditions (DiGiovanni, 1978; Segal, 1977). Infants born prematurely or with low birth weight now survive in greater numbers (Puccio, Janicki, Otis, & Rettig, 1983). The trend toward increased longevity for mentally retarded people indicates a need for the assessment of skills and then the development of programs and services designed to meet the demand confronting older mentally retarded individuals (Segal, 1977).

SEARCHING FOR A DEFINITION

Traditionally, one of the first steps in assuring that the needs of a segment of the population are met is to define the parameters of the specific group in question. With the elderly mentally retarded group, defining *elderly* has proved to be more problematic than finding a consensus for *mentally retarded*.

Several factors may account for the lack of consensus concerning the term *elderly*. Puccio and his colleagues (1983) note that a uniform chronological age has not been used to define *aged* in the normal population. They note that different age criteria are used for the senior community service programs (55 years), the Older Americans Act of 1965 (60 years), and the Social Security Act of 1935 (65 years).

Definitions of *elderly* usually entail the specification of a certain chronological age at which point one is considered to be "old." Authors addressing the current need of elderly mentally retarded individuals have differed on which chronological age should be used for defining the onset of old age. Kriger (1975) suggests that retarded people experience many of the same changes that nonretarded people incur with old age but at a much earlier age. She cites dependency, physical impairment, impairment of mental functioning, low income potential, family rejection, and unenjoyed leisure time as experiences shared by elderly and retarded people.

Segal (1977) reports that during a 1975 conference on the gerontological aspects of mental retardation, age 55 was used to define the onset of being "aged." This age, Segal reports, was chosen because it is consistent with the age requirement set by some federal agencies that fund programs for the elderly. Cotten and Merritt (in preparation) in a survey of state agencies serving mentally retarded people, used aged 55 as the beginning age for collecting data on this population. It was felt that planning should begin at age 55 to ensure appropriate services for people at age 60. In the same survey, age 60 was selected for defining elderly because 60 is specified by the Older Americans Act. It is suggested that if the generic service system is to be involved in the provision of services to the elderly mentally retarded, a consistent age definition must be maintained.

Elderly mentally retarded people have only within the past 7 years become a segment of the subpopulation of mentally retarded individuals to be subjects of research. Though Bair and Leland (1959) and Dybwad (1962) wrote of older mentally retarded citizens over two decades ago, the recent interest in the elderly mentally retarded person appears to have been generated by DiGiovanni (1978) and Segal (1977). Because the interest in the elderly mentally retarded population is still in an early developmental stage, it is understandable that no firm definition exists as to who these elderly mentally retarded individuals are. The first text concerning this population will be published this year (Janicki & Wisniewski, 1985).

Another possible source contributing to the lack of a unified definition concerns the premature aging issue. It has been suggested by several authors that mentally retarded individuals tend to age sooner than those in the nonretarded population (Bair & Leland, 1959; Gordon, 1978; Kriger, 1975; Thompson, 1951). In spite of some evidence to the contrary (Tiat, 1983), it remains unclear why this may occur. An example of accelerated aging of some mentally retarded individuals is the early evidence of Alzheimer's symptomatology seen at an earlier age in people who are are diagnosed as having Down's syndrome.

When one attempts to ascertain the age at which mentally retarded individuals are to be considered "elderly," it is imperative that the heterogeneity of the population be recognized. The larger portion of individuals labeled as mentally retarded is the group diagnosed as such during their school years. These people are quite often incorporated into the general population following completion of school. Most often the only time that a previous diagnosis of mental retardation comes to light is when such individuals experience periods of stress requiring the administration of psychodiagnostic instruments or a review of developmental records. Otherwise they may be considered to be "ignorant," "slow," etc., but rarely would they be considered by the lay person as mentally retarded. A minority of mentally retarded individuals are diagnosed quite early in their lives and continue to be considered mentally retarded throughout their lifetimes. Such individuals frequently have accompanying medical and physical problems in addition to their severe to profound mental retardation. It is within the latter group that the evidence of premature aging would be more prevalent.

Elderly Mentally Retarded Defined

For the purposes of this paper, the elderly mentally retarded individual is that individual within the larger mentally retarded population who is 60 years of age or older. Although we urge against classifying any mentally retarded individual under age 60 as elderly, we suggest that those individuals of any chronological age within the larger mentally retarded population who are experiencing a constellation of losses or ability relative to their individual, previous level of functioning and life situation as a function of an abnormal process of aging (Puccio, et al., 1983) be eligible for those programs that serve elderly mentally retarded people. Though the principle of normalization may dictate inflexibility in the use of the term *elderly* there must be some flexibility concerning who is eligible for specific programs. Flexible requirements are needed if the heterogeneity of this population is be taken into account.

Searching for a Data Base

Historically, 3% of the total population has been the figure used in planning the services designed for mentally retarded persons. However, it is necessary to remember that approximately 2% of that 3% would be considered mentally retarded due to psychosocial factors, and as adults or elderly people they may or may not be recognized as mentally retarded.

Cotten, Purzycki, Cowart, and Merritt (1983) report that estimates of the elderly mentally retarded population range from 50,000 to 315,000. The wide range of estimates correctly implies that current techniques for appraising the size of this population are inexact. The traditional procedure for estimating total mentally retarded populations in any given area has been to assume a given percentage of the total general population in the area (Hanf & Keiter, 1978). The actual percentage of the general population used to derive these estimates has varied from author to author. Regardless of the discrepancies among different estimates, it appears clear that many elderly mentally retarded people are unknown to service providers (Flumenbaum, 1979; Sweeney, 1979).

Where Have All the Mentally Retarded Gone?

There are many reasons why elderly mentally retarded individuals are difficult to find. Several authors indicate that few agencies arrange records in a manner which readily identifies their elderly mentally retarded clients. In an analysis of services to aging and aged developmentally disabled persons in Ohio, Ackerman (1979) found that only 28.1% of the agencies surveyed categorized their clients by age and/or disability type. He reports that "the excuse most frequently given was that records were not maintained by these categories" (p. 222). Ensor (1979) suggests that when an individual is transinstitutionalized (that is, tranferred from one institution to another), individual records are frequently not transferred to the new facility. Individual records are often altered in order to ensure that particular people will be considered eligible for placement in alternative environments (Hartig & Carswell, 1978). DiGiovanni (1978) indicates that many elderly mentally retarded people are able to go undetected with the help of a protective spouse or familial support system. Furthermore, the caretakers and guardians of older developmentally disabled individuals often do not seek contact with existing services. Thus, the existence of those older developmentally disabled persons is unknown to the service delivery system (Gordon, 1978).

Cotten and Merrit (in preparation) found that only 12 of 45 reporting states could readily locate the elderly mentally retarded persons living in institution (public and private) and community settings. A number of the states could locate the elderly mentally retarded residents of institutions and community facilities operated by the state but were unaware of the current whereabouts of many former residents of those facilities.

Because many elderly mentally retarded individuals are not identified as such, it is difficult to ascertain the number of elderly mentally retarded individuals in America. Without comprehensive demographic data concerning this population, it would be difficult to plan a comprehensive service delivery system unique for this segment of the population. Service delivery planners may well be left to ponder such questions as "Who are they? What are their needs?" (Cotten, Sison, & Starr, 1981) without the necessary information to answer these questions. This point, when coupled with the known heterogeneity of the population, strongly suggests that a coordinated, cooperative interagency approach to service delivery might best meet the needs of the elderly mentally retarded population.

A BILL OF RIGHTS FOR THE ELDERLY MENTALLY RETARDED PERSON

Perhaps the largest dilemma encountered when developing programs and service delivery strategies for the elderly mentally retarded individual is finding an appropriate balance between protecting these individuals from exploitation and protecting them from overprotection (limiting their personal freedoms). They must have the "right to risk" if they are to be seen as respected adults.

While attempting to discern the appropriate amount of protection, it is important that one be aware that the needs of many aging and aged developmentally disabled persons are not so different from those of the general elderly population (Cotten, Sison, & Starr, 1981; Mims, 1983; Puccio et al., 1983). Elderly individuals who are retarded have much in common with their nonretarded peers; for, as DiGiovanni (1978) reports; "The intellectual functioning of the elderly mentally retarded follows a similar aging process that the non-mentally retarded face, but from a lower baseline. The emotional and social aspects of the aging process faced by the elderly retarded are also similar to those of the nonretarded" (p. 264).

In total life planning with the elderly mentally retarded individual, a set of principles should guide decisions. The following bill of rights for the elderly mentally retarded person has been suggested, based on the Bill of Rights for the Elderly and the Bill of Rights for the Mentally Handicapped (Cotten, 1976). They are presented for consideration.

1. The right to an adequate standard of living, economic security, and protective work.
2. The right to humane services designed to help them reach their fullest potential.
3. The right to live as independently as they are able and wish in the community of their choice, in as normal a manner as is possible.

4. The right to an array of services that is generally available to other elderly groups.
5. The right to choose to retire. In addition, the opportunity to retire "to something" rather than just "from something."
6. The right to participate as a member of the community, having reciprocal interdependency.
7. The right to be considered a person and not merely "elderly" or "retarded."
8. The right to protected personal well-being, and to a qualified guardian, when required.
9. The right to be involved in setting one's goals and making one's decisions. The right to fail if necessary.
10. The right to a positive future, having enough involvement with life to prevent a preoccupation with death.
11. The right to be romantic, not asexual.
12. The right to sufficient activity and attention to permit continued integrity of self, individual identity, and purpose.
13. The right to an interesting environment and life style, with availability of sufficient mobility to provide a variety of surroundings.
14. The right to live and die with dignity.

THE JARGON OF CLIENT PLACEMENT

When the array of necessary services to meet the needs of this population is reviewed, there are two terms that are often encountered. The term *normalization* has been used frequently in the past few years. It may be defined as the belief that all individuals are entitled to the most normal (mainstream) life style that they can feasibly have. Normalization implies integration into the general population. The individual who must, as a result of his/her disability, have a limited degree of integration is still entitled to the provision of services in the least restrictive environment possible.

Another term frequently utilized is *deinstitutionalization*. It is often used with different meanings, depending on the user. For purposes of this paper, deinstitutionalization will be defined as a process: (a) preventing unnecessary admission and retention in institutions; (b) locating and developing community resources for housing, treatment, training, education, and rehabilitation of those mentally disabled persons not requiring institutional care; and (c) improving the conditions, treatment, and care of those who need institutional care (General Accounting Office, 1976). Deinstitutionalization, then, not only requires that individuals who need not reside in an institution be discharged, it necessitates active efforts to ensure that the needs of institutionalized as well as formerly institutionalized people are met.

On a conceptual level, normalization dictates that services be delivered to elderly mentally retarded people in the least restrictive environment through age-appropriate care, activities, and treatment (Puccio et al., 1983). Yet one of the alarming, albeit inadvertent, results of the deinstitutionalization zeitgeist is transinstitutionalization. All too commonly, institutionalized residents (particularly the older ones) are depopulated in the name of deinstitutionalization, only to be transferred to another institution. Elderly mentally retarded people are frequently transinstitutionalized to nursing homes, regardless of whether those nursing homes actually constitute the least restrictive environment.

SERVICE NEEDS

Because of the heterogeneity of people who are assigned the label *elderly mentally retarded*, it is apparent that there must be a broad array of services available to meet the service needs of this group.

The array of services needed by the elderly mentally retarded person is outlined in Table 11-1. They will be discussed in more detail in the following sections of this paper.

In attempting to ascertain the current availability of services to mentally retarded individuals 55 years of age and above, Krauss and Selzer (in preparation) are in the process of surveying agencies that purport to provide services to this population. The figures that represent programs identified by a variety of sources note that, tentatively, there are 150 residential services available in the USA, 128 day/vocational services, 50 social/recreational services, and 50 support services. These figures do not include the final count of institutionally based programs. As Krauss and Selzer emphasize, these are only tentative figures and may be an overestimate of specialized programs in which at least 50% of the mentally retarded persons are over age 55.

Functional Assessment

The service that is needed prior to the arranging of other services is a functional assessment of the individual in which not only the areas of deficit are reviewed but also assets on which to build skills are identified. The functional assessment is conducted by an interdisciplinary team so that all aspects of the individual are evaluated. The recommended approach is

Table 11-1 Necessary Service for Elderly Mentally Retarded People

Service	A	B	C	D	E	F	G	H	I	J	K	L	M	N	O	P
Functional Evaluation	*		*		*	*		*					*			*
Case Management					*	*		*		*			*			
Medical	*	*	*			*									*	*
Dental	*	*	*			*								*		
Nursing	*	*	*											*		
Counseling	*	*	*			*		*		*			*			*
Housing:																
Skilled Nursing	*		*		*											
ICF/MR	*		*		*											
Group Home	*	*	*		*											
Supervised Apartment	*	*	*		*	*	*									
Personal Care Home	*	*	*		*	*										
Independent Living/																
Shadow Supervision	*	*														
Transportation	*	*		*	*			*	*		*					*
Meals:																
Own Home	*	*								*						
Nutrition Site				*	*	*										
Socialization	*			*							*	*	*			
Religious Nurture													*			
Day Services:																
Adult Day Care		*	*	*	*				*		*		*			
Work Activity Center					*	*			*		*		*			
Sheltered Work Shop				*	*				*		*		*		*	
Competitive Employment				*					*		*				*	*
Volunteer/Other												*	*		*	*
Legal (Advocacy)	*	*		*				*					*			
Service	A	B	C	D	E	F	G	H	I	J	K	L	M	N	O	P

Source of Funding:

A. Personal Income
B. Supplemental Security Income
C. Medicaid
D. Older American Act/ State Council on Aging

E. Local Government
F. State Government
G. Housing and Urban Development
H. Department of Transportation
I. Developmental Disabilities Act
J. Food Stamps

K. Title XX
L. ACTION
M. Religious Groups
N. Community Mental Health Funding
O. Other (includes Medicare)
P. Vocational Rehabilitation

to evaluate the individual from a dependency/interdependency continuum rather than the traditional psychological, diagnostic categorical one. The IQ score obtained is not nearly as important as the person's social and coping skills. Emphasis should be placed on skills possessed rather than deficits. It is imperative that a comprehensive evaluation be conducted with the ultimate goal being an appraisal of the person's ability to function within the least restrictive environment. At times it is obvious that the dominant needs of an individual may require skilled nursing care, prohibiting the individual from living in a community setting unless such services can be provided there.

The term *interdependency* is used rather than *independency* because the person who is mentally retarded will never be fully independent (nor will we). It is most important to allow the person to be involved in an interdependent relationship in which there is reciprocal interdependency with nonretarded individuals. Having others dependent on the retarded individual for meeting certain needs enhances the perceived worth of that individual since he/she is being seen not only as a receiver of services but also as a provider.

Housing

Because housing services have received the most attention in the literature, that particular area will be discussed in more detail than the other services. The emphasis on least restrictive environment and deinstitutionalization has centered around the housing arrangement for the person. The array of alternative living arrangements is presented to provide an understanding of the components necessary to facilitate the continued growth and development of the heterogeneous mentally retarded population. The support services to the living arrangements would be applicable regardless of living arrangement.

ISSUES CONCERNING CLIENT PLACEMENT

Institutionalization and Deinstitutionalization

Several decades ago institutions for the mentally retarded were more installations for segregation than habilitation. The old custodial care plantation-like institutions seemed to be governed more by policies rooted in horticulture than human development. Twenty-five years ago (Bair & Leland, 1959) most of the geriatric patients in institutions were described as first coming to the institution at an early age. Many were unjustly placed there for juvenile delinquency and illegitimacy. The custodial care policies exacted a high price from many institutionalized residents:

> It does not take the new staff long to recognize that most of the geriatric population fits into one of two categories—those who sit and those who wander. The "sitters" have a routine consisting of getting up in the morning, caring for their needs or having them cared for, and moving to a chair in the dayroom. There they remain until lunch time. The same routine is followed after lunch, uninterrupted except to eat and retire for the night. The wanderer, on the other hand, never sits down, once his personal needs are cared for. In the "locked" institution, he will be found pacing in the dayroom from wall to wall and back again. If he is in an "open" institution he will be allowed on the grounds to walk all day, with no destination in mind, but fulfilling his need to keep moving. (Bair & Leland, 1959, p. 9).

During the last two decades there has been a change in the institutional philosophy of treatment. A shifting focus from custodial care to habilitation has made integration with society the goal rather than segregation from society. An effort to help the older resident obtain or regain independent living skills has been made in order to render community placement as an appropriate alternative to institutional living for some individuals (O'Connor, Justice, & Warren, 1970).

Beyond the negative effects of a segregation-style institutional experience are the positive effects of resident contact with or placement in the community. Zigler and Balla (1977) state that "an institutional policy of encouraging many contacts with the community does promote psychological growth" (p. 4). There is also evidence to suggest that individuals placed in group homes develop and exhibit more independent functioning and show increases in adaptive behavior (Cotten et al., 1983).

Deinstitutionalization and the Elderly Mentally Retarded Person

Under the guise of deinstitutionalization, people have tended to be trans-institutionalized. There is little to suggest measurable progess toward normalizing the service system's approach. Fifty to sixty percent of known elderly developmentally disabled persons reside in institutions, as compared to 5% of the nonretarded elderly (Janicki & MacEachron, 1984). The elderly mentally retarded group comprises approximately 5.2% of the total institutionalized retarded population (Cotten et al., 1983).

When strides are made toward placing retarded elderly people in the community, several issues arise. For example, given that many nonretarded aged individuals live in poverty, and knowing that more mentally retarded people will reach old age in the community, it can be anticipated that the quality of life for community-placed elderly mentally retarded individuals could potentially be rather dismal (Kriger, 1975). How the elderly mentally retarded people will fare depends on how the service delivery system copes with community attitudes, public opinion, limited resources, and a lack of appropriate facilities (Cochran, Sran, & Varano, 1977).

Housing

Appropriate Range of Alternatives

The principle of normalization inherently implies placement of mentally retarded individuals in the least restrictive environment. Several authors have underscored the need to match the individual with appropriate community placement (e.g., O'Connor, et al., 1970). A functional assessment should facilitate such placements. Because there are a wide range of needs and wants among the elderly mentally retarded population, as with any group of people, there must necessarily be a wide range of alternative living arrangements with appropriate support services available.

An appropriate continuum of alternative living arrangements would necessarily include, but not be limited to, the following:

1. *Skilled nursing facilities* (SNFs) offering continuous skilled nursing care or other rehabilitation care under the supervision of a professional nurse. This setting is appropriate for individuals requiring constant medical supervision.

2. *Intermediate-care facilities* (ICFs) offering an array of services that can be provided only in an institutional setting. The rehabilitative nursing approach aims to maintain and improve skills relating to daily living. These facilities are usually arranged to serve 60 or more clients at a time. Though the ICF should not be used indiscriminately for the elderly mentally retarded person, it may be an appropriate setting in some instances, based on a functional assessment by an interdisciplinary team. Certainly the facility selected should possess a strong rehabilitative nursing foundation for services.

3. *Intermediate-care facility for the mentally retarded* (ICF/MR)—with less than 15 beds (ICF/MR15)—providing 24-h supervised residential living with individualized habilitation services. It is established primarily for the diagnosis, treatment, and habilitation of the developmentally disabled person. The goal of the ICF/MR15 programming is to promote placement in a less restrictive environment. The majority of ICF/MR15s are located within the community, often operating as transitional group homes. ICF/MR facilities with more than 15 residents are frequently found on the grounds of state mental retardation centers. The SNF, ICF, and ICF/MR settings are funded through the Medicaid reimbursement program.

4. *Personal care homes* providing a homelike setting. These homes are usually owned by the person who supervises the clientele. The goal of such a home is to provide housing, meals, laundry, and the like for individuals who need supervision and assistance. Training is provided in self-help and activities of daily living.

5. *Group homes* designed to train the clients to become more independent and/or maintain their current level of independence. Self-help and daily living skills are given particular importance here. These homes are typically operated by a community coordinator or houseparents who are employed by public or private agencies.

6. *Supervised apartment complexes* providing minimal supervison of the client's daily activities. A community-living coordinator residing in the apartment complex provides training to polish existing skills, offering assistance as needed.

7. *Shadow supervision,* where the client lives alone or in a setting that maximizes the ability to function with little or no day-to-day supervision. Case managers are available to those clients requesting such services.

The availability of these living situations, as well as foster homes and halfway houses, makes the implementation of normalization plausible. Because the literature indicates that the majority of elderly mentally retarded individuals housed in institutions would be more appropriately placed in the community, such community placements must be made available.

In addition to the agency-operated alternative living arrangements, homes of the elderly retarded individual's family also may serve as an appropriate community placement.

Actual Range of Alternatives

A review of the literature reveals that several authors call for a continuum of alternative living arrangements and day services. There is, however, little documentation regarding the types of alternatives actually available. As Dickerson, Hamilton, Huber, and Segal (1979) note, most agencies have little to say about programs for the elderly mentally retarded person. Without such programs, and given the difficulty in identifying members of this population, it is nearly an impossible task to identify (a) where the majority of elderly mentally retarded individuals live, and (b) where they may have an opportunity to live.

A recent survey (Cotten & Merritt, in preparation) provides some illumination with regard to (b), above. Each of the states responding to this survey (45 in all) reported that they were using the full continuum of alternative living arrangements mentioned earlier. Fifty percent of those states indicated that they also were utilizing housing for nonretarded elderly individuals as placement alternatives for the elderly mentally retarded individual. These data indicate that elderly mentally retarded individuals are being placed in a variety of settings, but it is not clear whether appropriate criteria are being used to determine who is being placed where. It also should be emphasized that the survey results do not imply that there are an ample number of openings within each alternative living arrangement for elderly mentally retarded individuals, but merely that those individuals have been scattered across an array of settings.

Group Homes   In a recent study (Janicki, Mayeda, & Epple, 1983), the prevalence of group homes was explored. Agencies in all 50 states and the District of Columbia responsible for overseeing group home programs for mentally retarded/developmentally disabled persons were surveyed. The survey results indicate that 85.3% of those residing in group homes are over 18 years of age. Unfortunately, the data did not provide information on the percentage of elderly adults served. The data do, however, provide encouraging evidence of a rapid growth in the number of group homes; there has been a growth rate of 900% over the past 10 years. This indicated that strides are being made toward providing alternative environments. The current fiscal climate in our country will probably result in the abatement of the group home growth rate despite an ever increasing need for group home beds.

Research by Nihira and Nihira (1975) and Windle (1962) suggests that older retarded persons are less prone to difficulties adjusting to community setting than are younger individuals. However, group home placement becomes less common as the age of the client increases (Janicki & MacEachron, 1984). This suggests that in spite of their suitability for community placement, elderly mentally retarded individuals are being overlooked for group home living.

Nursing Homes   Flumenbaum (1979) asserts that several institutionalized clients are inappropriately transinstitutionalized to nursing homes for lack of alternative community placements. That appears to hold true for the elderly mentally retarded. Lyon and Bland (1969) suggest that nursing homes are an improvement over state hospitals as placement sites for elderly mentally retarded people. They assert that the state hospital's ratios of patients to staff and physical facilities tend to be less ideal than those offered by most nursing homes. Also cited are client preferences for the nursing homes over state hospitals. This has been taken as evidence that the patient population of the state hospital can be reduced through discharging residents to nursing homes without damaging the patients placed (Lyon & Bland, 1969).

Other authors have concurred with the observation made by Lyon and Bland (1969) that elderly mentally retarded individuals quickly adapt to the nursing home setting (Cotten, Sison, & Starr, 1981; DiGiovanni, 1978; Sayder & Wollner, 1974). However, most apparently disagree with the notion that nursing homes are a panacea for elderly mentally retarded institutionalized people.

Dickerson and her colleagues (1979) suggest that mentally retarded people residing in nursing homes tend to be grouped with people labeled senile. Often the behaviors of the two groups are not differentiated, and the aged mentally retarded person "becomes invisible." Zigler and Balla (1977) conclude that nursing homes are not suited to the needs of the aged developmentally disabled individual, due to the philosophical basis of nursing homes (i.e., "sick person"). Finally, not all elderly mentally retarded people require the comprehensive medical supervision provided in nursing homes. To place people in such settings inappropriately not only violates the principles of normalization, it is also unnecessarily expensive.

Again, when one considers the heterogeneity of this population, there are elderly mentally retarded individuals for whom nursing home placement may be the least restrictive alternative based on their functional assessment. The placement selected should have a strong rehabilitative rather than custodial emphasis.

Implications of Current Alternatives

Because home health care is being presented as an alternative to nursing home placement for the general elderly population, more nursing home space may become available to the mentally retarded person (DiGiovanni, 1978). The current lack of needed group home beds and the relatively infrequent placement of elderly mentally retarded persons in existing group homes further suggest that more elderly mentally retarded individuals are destined for nursing homes. Obviously, the effects of nursing home placement on elderly mentally retarded people must be studied further, in order to judge the appropriateness of such a service delivery policy. Efforts must be made to ensure that nursing home services are structured in a manner that provides their elderly mentally retarded clients with nourishing life experiences.

In addition, the greater use of group homes and foster family care may fulfill the current need for alternative living arrangement housing for the elderly developmentally disabled population (Janicki & MacEachron, 1984). This would enable the disabled population to maintain links with the community while at the same time utilizing a cost-sharing approach in the provision of services. Leading the older institutional resident to community living, when appropriate, will not be inexpensive. Yet the high cost of institutional care in and of itself suggests the importance of making alternative living arrangements available to the elderly mentally retarded person—perhaps not to prevent institutionalization but at least to delay placement in a too restrictive, inappropriate environment.

The discussion of alternative living arrangements has emphasized the necessity of an array of environments so that elderly mentally retarded people have the opportunity to live in their least restrictive environment.

Community Placement: The Relocation Syndrome

Cochran and his colleagues (1977) identify a "relocation syndrome," which involves profound depression, refusal to eat, weight loss, and frequent crying. This syndrome manifests itself in some retarded individuals who move to new environments and is likely to occur with those individuals who were strongly attached to their previous place of residence. Several suggestions are made to avoid the relocation syndrome: site visits to the new environment, family involvement, involving the client in actual preparation of his/her belongings for the move, and assigning an advocate responsible for provision of advice, support, and friendship.

Given that many elderly mentally retarded people have spent much of their lives in institutional settings, it may be expected that they are especially vulnerable to difficulties associated with relocation. Relocation may not be appropriate, particularly where it is a case of transinstitutionalization. Measures must be taken to insure that the person to be transferred is comfortable with the idea of leaving the current placement.

Even if this group is made to feel comfortable about relocating, there remains a real and serious potential for jeopardy in community placement. Nihira and Nihira (1975) conceptualize three main types of difficulty: jeopardy to health or safety, jeopardy of general welfare, and legal jeopardy. Their study identified several difficulties and special relationships:

1. The health and safety of moderately, severely, and profoundly retarded people tend to be at a greater risk than that of mildly retarded people.
2. Inappropriate placement in a facility may jeopardize the general welfare of clients.
3. Greater risks concerning health and safety are associated with younger ages.
4. Borderline intellectual functioning and mild mental retardation are related to greater risks of legal difficulties than are the moderate, profound, and severe levels of retardation.
5. Community placed clients may exhibit inappropriate heterosexual behavior.

ARRAY OF SOCIAL SUPPORT SERVICES

The availability of support services is imperative to ensure continued opportunity to maintain skills, if not to continue to develop skills. It is possible to live in a lovely home without necessary support services and be much more institutionalized than if living in an ICF/MR15 that provides more options for growth and development. In essence, to have the most appropriate placement requires the availability of services to assist in the development of the individual 24 h/day.

Medical Care

Twenty percent of the total national resources of the United States are devoted to the care of elderly persons (Janicki & MacEachron 1984). Medical costs are generally three times greater for persons over the age of 65 as compared to the non-elderly group. For the older developmentally disabled person, medical costs may be as much as 25% greater than for the nondisabled person (Jackson, 1979).

Gordon (1978) found that only 22% of adult and older developmentally disabled persons have their medical and health service needs met. Strides must be made to ensure that the elderly mentally retarded population has ample health care service. Because costs will be high, a prudent strategy for acquiring funding must be designed. The emphasis on fitness and preventive procedures must be featured as one aspect of their habilitation. This topic was a major concern discussed at the Kennedy Conference (Kelly, 1984). The availability of professionals in the fields of medicine, dentistry, nursing, and psychology, who are oriented to see, in some instances, the possibility of rehabilitating the elderly mentally retarded person and, in others, continued habilitation, fosters a quality life experience for this population.

Counseling Services

Counseling is often considered to be synonymous with case management or case coordination by service providers (Thomas, 1978). That is an incorrect assumption. Given that psychopathology is four to five times more prevalent in the retarded population than in the nonretarded population (Matson, 1984), it is clear that psychotherapy and psychological evaluation are important services to have available for some elderly retarded people. Having the labels "mentally retarded" and/or "elderly" does not ensure mental health or imply an inability to profit from psychological interventions.

Historically, the providers of counseling services have been hesitant to interact with the mentally retarded population because it was felt that group was a poor risk for treatment. It is hoped that through training and successful experience these providers will see the importance of this service being available to the elderly mentally retarded person as well as to their informal support groups.

Many of the families of this population did not receive necessary counseling services in earlier years, and thus, they continue to perceive their family member as the "eternal child." To stimulate the opportunity to make individual choices by the elderly mentally retarded person will require the support of professionals who can help the family to realize that the opportunity to take "good sense" risks is directly related to the respect and value shown to the person.

Day Services

Puccio and his colleagues (1983) indicate that day activities for the aging developmentally disabled person should be goal-directed. They stress the importance of scheduled, structured, supervised, and substantiated activities. Interesting and stimulating activities are needed to improve the quality of life for elderly retarded people. Because 6 h of active treatment is one of the requirements promulgated by Medicaid regulations, the mentally retarded individual who resides in an ICF/MR has not been allowed the privilege of nonparticipation. This may be appropriate for the person residing in such a setting, in view of the philosophical foundation for the ICF/MR—the developmental model; but for those of retirement age interested in choosing how they want to spend their day, a more appropriate alternative living arrangement should be found. Among day service choices should be the following:

1. *Adult day care* in which the skills currently available are emphasized, ensuring that the level of debilitation is only that which cannot be rectified. The opportunity to engage in social interaction with others is certainly one of the strong points of this service, as is its ability to provide respite services for the caregiver. Involvement in a senior center may be quite appropriate for some elderly mentally retarded individuals.

2. *A work activity center* in which the person is involved in a productive endeavor such as subcontract work for an industry. Again, social interaction is important, as is the money made from work produced.

3. *Sheltered workshop* in which work is by far the more important aspect when work and social activities are both considered. The person is more productive from a financial standpoint.

4. *Competitive employment* in which the person has the opportunity to

compete with the nonretarded person, regardless of age, in securing and holding a job.

5. *Voluntary services* in which the person has the opportunity to function in a voluntary situation where emphasis can be on the service provided and the feelings of satisfaction. There have been examples of successful involvement of elderly mentally retarded individuals in the Foster Grandparent Program as well as the Retired Senior Volunteer Program (RSVP), both of which are sponsored by the federal agency ACTION. These experiences in being involved with other elderly, though nonretarded individuals, have helped to foster the acceptance of the elderly mentally retarded person as a person first, who happens also to have a diagnosis of mental retardation.

Fengler and Goodrich (1980) report on an RSVP. The participants were elderly physically handicapped clients. The authors suggest that the activity of helping was highly valued by the participants. "Rehabilitation does not need to have a wage attached to it. . . . Through volunteer activities for the client the community acquires important new resources while the volunteer gains a new understanding of his own capabilities and usefulness" (p. 640).

The primary consideration, as in housing, should be on disabled persons having the opportunity to choose from a variety of alternatives so that their needs and desires are met. The most frequently provided day services are work activity centers, sheltered workshops and senior centers for the elderly. The latter may include congregate meals (Cotten & Merritt, in preparation).

As the large state institutions have released their residents, the need for sheltered workshops in the community has increased. Workshop programs for the elderly mentally retarded person have evidenced some increases recently (Cotten & Merritt, in preparation), but more programs are required.

Case Management

Case management services designed to alert elderly mentally retarded individuals and their facilitators to available generic services in the community may help to increase the number of families housing an elderly mentally retarded relative. Only a small proportion of the known elderly developmentally disabled population presently live with their families. In-home support services, health care services that are fully accessible, and social/recreational services that may be a more appropriate substitute for vocational programs would benefit such families, and perhaps encourage others to consider keeping elderly retarded relatives at home (Puccio et al., 1983).

It should be noted here that there is a difference between a social service provider and a mental health facilitator. The provider may help the "patient" to food, shelter, clothing, and such (and a low sense of self-esteem), whereas the facilitator allows the individuals to do as much as they can do for themselves and others, providing only those services that they can not provide for themselves. "Consideration of age appropriate normative patterns of older citizens and a realistic assessment of their capacity and needs may advise against the singleminded pursuit of independence as a goal of services for the elderly. Certainly we wish to reduce dependence and helplessness, but a positive interdependence, a sense of community and friendship, and a supportive environment may be more appropriate service goals for both the aged and the retarded" (Pezzoli, 1978, p. 208). The case manager, then, serving as a facilitator rather than a provider, gives necessary services and opportunities for the client to gain a sense of accomplishment.

Transportation

Gordon (1978) underscores the importance of transportation to service delivery. The lack of adequate transportation services, he reports, may account for the 84% gap in services delivered to the rural aging and aged developmentally disabled populations. Gordon suggests that mobile units providing physical therapy and other specialized medical services could help bridge the service gap. Having access to the transportation services provided by the support of the U.S. Department of Transportation through the local Area Agencies on Aging (AAA) is an excellent way to meet this need.

Meals

The availability of meals can be made through a variety of arrangements. Certainly the opportunity to eat in the living situation is and always will be the primary source of meals. There are often opportunities for meals in the day service setting which the person chooses. For many elderly mentally retarded individuals, the congregate-meal sites for elderly individuals sponsored by AAAs provide another possibility not only to help meet the nutritional needs of the individual but also to facilitate opportunities for socialization.

Advocacy/Legal

Developmental disabilities legislation and the Older Americans Act both emphasize the importance of advocacy services and mandate each state to provide such services. Representation can begin with a friendly advocate who helps to facilitate the involvement of the person into services to which he/she is eligible. Unfortunately, there are situations in which an adversarial posture must be taken to insure that the person is able to access such services. When this is done, it is often the Developmental Disabilities Office of Advocacy and Protection or an ombudsman of the AAA who assumes the role. Certainly this is the route of last resort, and least desired.

STRATEGIES FOR MEETING THE CHALLENGE OF THE ELDERLY MENTALLY RETARDED

Policy Considerations

Dickerson and her colleagues (1979) suggest that elderly mentally retarded people are in double jeopardy. They suggest that the elderly mentally retarded group is often abandoned, ignored or inadequately supported by the community and decision-makers. Though the needs of the elderly mentally retarded are not dissimilar to the needs of other segments of the general population, it is as if the double diagnosis (elderly and mentally retarded) serves to alienate this group from mainstream America. The major problem for any elderly mentally retarded individual lies not in physical or cognitive limitations, but rather in the largely inadequate and segregating manner in which society has dealt with both retarded individuals and elderly individuals.

DiGiovanni (1978) notes that many mentally retarded people are being educated for independent living. Many of the mildly and moderately mentally retarded individuals who were living in institutions in the 1960s were trained by Vocational Rehabilitation and placed in employment in the community. Some of these people do not have informal support systems and are dependent on either themselves or agencies for supportive services. They are now reaching the age of retirement, when the informal support given by employment will be less concentrated. It is important that the support system discussed earlier be available to these individuals so that they will not again enter an inappropriate residential setting, such as a nursing home or a boarding home, without adequate supervision and case management services.

Disagreements regarding the most appropriate political strategy to assure such a program are apparent. Burr (1975) suggests that advocates for the mentally retarded aged must inevitably be prepared to compete for funds with advocates of other groups, such as mentally retarded children and adults, blind persons, and nonretarded elderly. He suggests that funding for elderly mentally retarded people will not occur unless the needs of this group are specifically defined and rigorously asserted. Yet McAllister (1975) points out: "Federal, legal entitlements can be orchestrated and programmed to meet the needs of the elderly retarded person without identifying a special population and coming up with a whole new cause. This last tends to fragment the efforts in Congress and certain of the administrative agencies" (p. 133).

Given the fact that both the retarded and nonretarded elderly populations exhibit a large amount of heterogeneity in both physical and cognitive functioning, there must be significant overlap among the needs of the two groups. At times, the elderly mentally retarded person functions at a higher level than the nonretarded elderly person with senile dementia. Thus, many of the needs of elderly mentally retarded people could well be met through the same service system as that used by the nonretarded elderly person. The emphasis must be placed on a functional assessment of the strengths and needs of the individual with services selected that will complement the strengths and help to meet the needs of the individual regardless of prior diagnosis.

Public Opinion

If public opinion is to be mobilized in favor of programs designed to serve elderly mentally retarded people, positive attitudes regarding the elderly mentally retarded population must be enhanced. The public's attitudes regarding mentally retarded people are improving (DiGiovanni, 1978). In order to foster a more favorable view of the elderly mentally retarded person, interactions between the general community and the elderly mentally retarded person should be governed by rules of common sense. The entrance of large groups of elderly mentally retarded people into generic programs should be avoided because a large and sudden enrollment of these people might be greeted with resentment and concern by the public at large (Puccio et al., 1983). It appears that integration with the community must be carefully orchestrated with emphasis on the person's ability to function within that setting.

Though there are service systems already in existence that can meet some of the needs of elderly mentally retarded people, this does not mean there are programs to meet all of these needs. Lopez (1979) argues that the lack of pressure exerted by the community, clients, and social and legal groups on the government may well account for a general lack of service programs (both in quality and quantity) for adults who are mentally retarded. The creation, development, and implementation of innovative programs closing service gaps to the elderly mentally retarded are, in Lopez's view, related to the amount of public pressure brought to bear on the government agencies.

One of the realities of life is that services are provided only where there are resources available. The elderly mentally retarded population may be considered to be either the responsibility of the providers of services to the elderly or the responsibility of the providers of services to mentally retarded individuals. One of the hazards of such a situation is that either group of providers can be exclusionary, holding that the other agency is responsible and thus absolving itself of any responsibility.

Approaching Geriatric Service Providers

Generic programs for elderly people often do not recognize the elderly retarded person as being part of their responsibility (Puccio et al., 1983). Arguments suggesting that elderly mentally retarded people are more different from elderly nonretarded people than they are similar only serve to reinforce the field of gerontology's reluctance to serve anyone with a diagnosis of mental retardation. Not only are the arguments made from the diagnostic, difference-oriented perspective damaging to the cause of the elderly mentally retarded, there is an overall lack of empirical data to substantiate this notion. Indeed the largest difference between the elderly mentally retarded and other groups may be that the elderly mentally retarded have a chronic condition and that their needs are not as often met.

It may be argued that research and training are not altogether necessary, though desirable. The most pressing need appears to be familiarizing administrators and practitioners with the elderly mentally retarded person. The necessity for familiarity comes more from a need to desensitize the service deliverer to this population rather than to educate. We suggest that most practitioners and administrators who possess a working knowledge of service delivery to mentally retarded and/or elderly people, and common sense, already possess the vast majority of skills needed to serve the elderly mentally retarded person.

Advocates for the mentally retarded aged should attempt to reassure and desensitize service delivery system providers regarding the provider's ability to adequately relate to those who are both aged and retarded. For such advocates to assert the need to educate providers of services to the uniqueness of the elderly mentally retarded person tends only to exaggerate the provider's lack of confidence regarding the ability to provide adequate services. There may well be a need to educate service providers about funding of services and the necessity of a continuum of services to meet the needs of a heterogeneous population. When the elderly person diagnosed as mentally retarded is considered to be an individual, first and foremost, the needs of the elderly retarded people are not inherently different from the needs of other elderly individuals.

Reorganizing Program Eligibility Criteria

Present Criteria

If we acknowledge that there are limited resources available to provide services, it would appear important to maintain cost effectiveness while insuring the array of services necessary to provide for varied needs. Organizing funding sources via diagnostic (DSM-III) categories allows for, and perhaps encourages, overlapping services and the duplication of bureaucratic administrative positions.

Need for New Criteria

Elderly mentally retarded people simply cannot afford to be segregated. That is because they are, essentially, already "a minority group within a minority group" (Thurman, 1979). Compared with the general mentally retarded population or the elderly nonretarded, there are a relatively small number of elderly mentally retarded persons. Most of them do not have living parents to serve as advocates. It is in their best interest that their cause be combined with efforts to enhance appropriate generic services available to the general elderly and mentally retarded populations. If adequate generic services are available to meet the needs of the retarded and elderly populations, then such generic services also will be sufficient to meet the needs of the elderly mentally retarded.

CONCLUSIONS AND RECOMMENDATIONS FOR MEETING THE CHALLENGES OF ELDERLY MENTALLY RETARDED PEOPLE

Several conclusions can be drawn from experience and the literature reviewed above:

1. There is significant heterogeneity among all individuals who are 60 years of age and above.
2. There have been relatively few empirical investigations specifically focusing on elderly mentally retarded individuals.
3. Those providing services to the mentally retarded and the elderly nonretarded populations tend to be unaware of the elderly mentally retarded person.
4. Data are available to suggest that there are similarities among dependent elderly people, regardless of whether those individuals have been given a prior diagnosis of mental retardation.

5. Under the guise of deinstitutionalization many people have been in-appropriately transinstitutionalized or depopulated.
6. The fields of mental retardation and gerontology must necessarily combine and coordinate their efforts if the elderly mentally retarded population is to be effectively and efficiently served. Advocates must advocate for people and not labels.
7. Cross-training opportunities of professionals in the fields of mental retardation and gerontology must be stimulated in order to improve services by having each staff person feel more comfortable providing services to elderly mentally retarded persons.
8. Assessments based on a functional dependency/interdependency continuum, as opposed to the traditional psychological diagnostic categorical one, are needed to insure appropriate placement and ser-vice programs.
9. The provision of services to this long-ignored segment of the pop-ulation allows the service provider to exercise creativity while developing a truly unique service system responsive to individual abilities, wants, and needs. Emphasis must be placed on helping the elderly mentally retarded person to maintain skills obtained through the years, learn new skills, and develop procedures for com-pensating for the losses they may be experiencing, in order to cope with life more effectively.
10. Mentally retarded persons are living longer than ever before because of the advancements made in the manner in which their needs are met. It is now our task to ensure that there are opportunities avail-able to enhance the quality of their lives.

Editor's Note: During the discussion following the presentation there was concern expressed by providers of service to nonretarded elderly people regarding the availability of funds to serve this subpopulation of elderly people. A suggestion was made that perhaps one approach might be the purchase-of-service model, in which the agency serving the mentally retarded person purchases from the agency serving elderly people services appropriate for the elderly mentally retarded person.

REFERENCES

Ackerman, J. (1979). Ohio: Analysis of services to AADD persons. In D. P. Sweeney & T. Y. Wilson (Eds.), *Double jeopardy: The plight of aging and aged developmentally disabled persons in mid-America—a research monograph* (pp. 196–234). Ann Arbor, MI: University of Michigan, The Institute for the Study of Mental Retardation and Related Disabilities.

Bair, H. U., & Leland, H. (1959). Management of the geriatric mentally retarded patient. *Hospital and Community Psychiatry, 10*(5), 9–12.

Burr, J. (1975). From the perspective of the social rehabilitation services. In J. C. Hamilton & R. M. Segal (Eds.), *Proceedings: A consultation Conference on the Gerontological Aspects of Mental Retardation,* (pp. 114–128). Ann Arbor, MI: University of Michigan.

Cochran, W. E., Sran, P. K., & Varano, G. A. (1977). The relocation syndrome in mentally retarded individuals. *Mental Retardation, 15,* 10–12.

Cotten, P. D. (1976). Retarded Mississippians grow old with dignity. In E. L. Butler (Ed.), *Proceedings: A Consultation-Conference on the Gerontological Aspects of Mental Retardation.* Jackson, MS: Mississippi Department of Mental Health, Mississippi Council on Aging.

Cotten, P. D., & Merritt, F. (in preparation). *The aged mentally retarded population: A national survey of state programs.*

Cotten, P., Purzycki, E., Cowart, C., & Merritt, F. (1983). Alternative living arrangement for elderly mentally retarded people. *Superintendent's Digest, 2,* 35–37.

Cotten, P. D., Sison, G. F. P., & Starr, S. (1981). Comparing elderly mentally retarded and non-mentally retarded individuals: Who are they? What are their needs? *Gerontologist, 21*(4), 359–365.

Daniels, P. L. (Ed.). (1979). *Gerontological aspects of developmental disabilities: The state of the art.* Omaha, NE: University of Nebraska.

Developmental Disabilities Act of 1984. Public Law 98-527.

Dickerson, M. U., Hamilton, J., Huber, R., & Segal, R. (1979). The aged mentally retarded: The invisible client: A challenge to the community. In D. P. Sweeney & T. Y. Wilson (Eds.), *Double jeopardy: The plight of aging and aged developmentally disabled persons in mid-America—a research monograph (pp. 8–35).* Ann Arbor, MI: University of Michigan, The Institute for the Study of Mental Retardation and Related Disabilities.

DiGiovanni, L. (1978). The elderly retarded: A little known group. *Gerontologist, 18,* 262–266.

Dybwad, G. (1962). Administrative and legislative problems in the care of the adult and aged mental retardate. *American Journal of Mental Deficiency, 66,* 716–722.

Ensor, D. (1979). Michigan: Assessment of community services for the older/aged developmentally disabled population. In D. P. Sweeney & T. Y. Wilson (Eds.), *Double jeopardy: The plight of aging and aged developmentally disabled persons in mid-America—a research monograph* (pp. 156–164). Ann Arbor, MI: University of Michigan, The Institute for the Study of Mental Retardation and Related Disabilities.

Fengler, A. P., & Goodrich, N. (1980). Money isn't everything: Opportunities for elderly handicapped men in a sheltered workshop. *Gerontologist, 29*(6), 636–640.

Flumenbaum, R. (1979). Minnesota: Analysis of the data. In D. P. Sweeney & T. Y. Wilson (Eds.), *Double jeopardy: The plight of aging and aged developmentally disabled persons in mid-America—a research monograph* (pp. 165–195). Ann Arbor, MI: University of Michigan, The Institute for the Study of Mental Retardation and Related Disabilities.

General Accounting Office. (1976). Improvements needed in efforts to help the mentally disabled return to and remain in communities. *Morris Associates Report, 13*(21).

Gordon, J. E. (1978). A report of a study of a needs assessment of the adult and older developmentally disabled person and its implication for service delivery. In R. M. Segal (Ed.), *Consultation-Conference on Developmental Disabilities and Gerontology: Proceeding of a conference* (pp. 107–144). Ann Arbor, MI: University of Michigan, The Institute for the Study of Mental Retardation and Related Disabilities.

Grossman, H. J. (Ed.). (1977). *Manual on terminology and classification in mental retardation* (rev. ed.). Washington, DC: American Association on Mental Deficiency.

Hanf, C., & Keiter, J. (1978). The Oregon aged developmentally disabled population: Getting it all together from a data base. In R. M. Segal (Ed.), *Consultation-Conference on Developmental Disabilities and Gerontology: Proceeding of a conference* (pp. 68–92). Ann Arbor, MI: University of Michigan, The Institute for the Study of Mental Retardation and Related Disabilities.

Hartig, S. A., & Carswell, A. T. (1978). A perspective on service delivery to aged developmentally disabled adults. In R. M. Segal (Ed.), *Consultation-Conference on Developmental Disabilities and Gerontology: Proceeding of a conference* (pp. 27–37). Ann Arbor, MI: University of Michigan, The Institute for the Study of Mental Retardation and Related Disabilities.

Jackson, A. (1979). Wisconsin: Analysis of the data. In D. P. Sweeney & T. Y. Wilson (Eds.), *Double jeopardy: The plight of aging and aged developmentally disabled persons in mid-America—a research monograph* (pp. 235–262). Ann Arbor, MI: University of Michigan, The Institute for the Study of Mental Retardation and Related Disabilities.

Janicki, M. P., & MacEachron, A. E. (1984). Residential health and social service needs of elderly developmental disabled persons. *Gerontologist, 24*(2), 128–137.

Janicki, M. P., Mayeda, T., & Epple, W. A. (1983). Availability of group homes for persons with mental retardation in the United States. *Mental Retardation, 21*, 45–51.

Janicki, M. P., & Wisniewski, H. M. (1985). *Aging and developmental disabilities.* Baltimore: Brookes Publishing Co.

Kelly, F. P. (1984). Summary of recommendations. In *Elderly mentally retarded individuals: Developing innovative and creative programs.* Washington, DC: Joseph P. Kennedy, Jr. Foundation.

Kleitsch, E. L. (1981). The increase of verbal interaction among socially isolated elderly mentally retarded (Doctoral dissertation, University of Notre Dame, 1981). *Dissertation Abstracts International, 42*(3), 1179B.

Krauss, M. W., & Seltzer, M. M. (in preparation). *National survey of programs serving elderly mentally retarded persons.*

Kriger, S. F. (1975). On aging and mental retardation. In J. C. Hamilton & R. M. Segal (Eds.), *Proceedings: A Consultation-Conference on the Gerontological Aspects of Mental Retardation* (pp. 20–32). Ann Arbor, MI: University of Michigan.

Lopez, S. (1979). Illinois: Factors affecting the response of human service organizations to AADD clients. In D. P. Sweeney & T. Y. Wilson (Eds.), *Double jeopardy: The plight of aging and aged developmentally disabled persons in mid-America—a research monograph* (pp. 89–124). Ann Arbor, MI: University of Michigan, The Institute for the Study of Mental Retardation and Related Disabilities.

Lyon R., & Bland, W. (1969). The transfer of adult mental retardates from a state hospital to nursing homes. *Mental Retardation, 7*, 31–38.

McAllister, J. (1975). From the perspective of the President's Committee on Mental Retardation. In J. C. Hamilton & R. M. Segal (Eds.), *Proceedings: A Consultation Conference on the Gerontological Aspects of Mental Retardation* (pp. 129–134). Ann Arbor, MI: University of Michigan.

Matson, J. L. (1984). Psychotherapy with persons who are mentally retarded. *Mental Retardation, 22*(4), 170–175.

Mims, J. (1983). *A comparison of speech, language and hearing performance among elderly retarded and non-retarded subjects.* Paper presented at the meeting of the American Association on Mental Deficiency, Dallas, TX.

Nihira, L., & Nihira, K. (1975). Jeopardy in community placement. *American Journal of Mental Deficiency, 79*(5), 538–544.

O'Connor, G., Justice, R. S., & Warren, N. (1970). The aged mentally retarded: Institution or community care? *American Journal of Mental Deficiency, 75*(3), 354–360.

Pezzoli, J. J. (1978). National association for retarded citizens and the aged developmentally disabled persons. In R. M. Segal (Ed.), *Consultation-Conference on Developmental Disabilities and Gerontology: Proceeding of a conference* (pp. 202–212). Ann Arbor, MI: University of Michigan, The Institute for the Study of Mental Retardation and Related Disabilities.

Puccio, P. S., Janicki, M. P., Otis, J. P., & Rettig, J. (1983). *Report of the Committee on Aging and Developmental Disabilities.* Albany, NY: New York State Office of Mental Retardation and Developmental Disabilities.

Sayder, B., & Wollner, S. (1974). When the retarded grow old. *Canada's Mental Health, 22*, 12–13.

Segal, R. (1977). Trends in services for the aged mentally retarded. *Mental Retardation, 15*(2), 25–27.

Sweeney, D. P. (1979). Denied, ignored, or forgotten? An assessment of community services for older/aged developmentally disabled persons within HEW Region V. In D. P. Sweeney & T. Y. Wilson (Eds.), *Double jeopardy: The plight of aging and aged developmentally disabled persons in mid-America—a research monograph* (pp. 54–88). Ann Arbor, MI: University of Michigan, The Institute for the Study of Mental Retardation and Related Disabilities.

Talkington, L. W., & Chiovaro, S. S. (1969). An approach to programming for aged mentally retarded. *Mental Retardation, 7*(1), 29–30.

Thomas, N. (1978). Programming for older and aged developmentally disabled adults. In R. M. Segal (Ed.), *Consultation-Conference on Developmental Disabilities and Gerontology: Proceeding of a conference* (pp. 38–61). Ann Arbor, MI: University of Michigan, The Institute for the Study of Mental Retardation and Related Disabilities.

Thompson, C. W. (1951). Decline in limit of performance among adult morons. *American Journal of Psychology, 64,* 203–215.

Thurman, E. (1979). Teaching and learning: The educational role of the UAF and implications for serving the AADD client. In D. P. Sweeney & T. Y. Wilson (Eds.), *Double jeopardy: The plight of aging and aged developmentally disabled persons in mid-America—a research monograph* (pp. 263–311). Ann Arbor, MI: University of Michigan, The Institute for the Study of Mental Retardation and Related Disabilities.

Tiat, D. (1983). Mortality and dementia among ageing defectives. *Journal of Mental Deficiency Research, 27,* 133–142.

Windle, C. (1962). Prognosis of mental subnormals. (Monograph). *American Journal of Mental Deficiency, 66,* 1–180.

Zigler, E., & Balla, D. A. (1977). Impact of institutional experience on the behavior and development of retarded persons. *American Journal of Mental Deficiency, 82*(1), 1–11.

12

Community Status of the Elderly Disabled: Implications for a Developmental "Gatekeeping" Model

Howard L. Garber

The growing national awareness concerning the needs of elderly Americans has, fortunately, encouraged a similar interest in the needs of the elderly disabled—specifically elderly mentally retarded individuals (Cotten, Sison, & Starr, 1981; DiGiovanni, 1978; Sweeney & Wilson, 1979). The unfortunate aspect of this new interest is that focusing on the elderly disabled may result in another fragment being added to a care-provider system that is already in disarray. The chronically disabled elderly, i.e., those whose impairments originated during their early development, reveal needs while living in their local community that are both similar to the elderly population in general but also uniquely related to their earlier developmental experience (Hamilton & Segal, 1975; Segal, 1978).

Among the population in general, and even for some professionals in the service system, it is often incorrectly presumed either that there are no elderly disabled living in the community or that these individuals are already receiving appropriate services in some form of institutional setting. In fact there are a considerable number of elderly disabled residing in the community, with a wide range of variation in the nature of their living conditions (Segal, 1977; Sutter, 1980).

At the University of Wisconsin Research and Training Center, we have been studying the community status of the elderly as part of a larger research interest in developing a developmental risk model that is based on understanding how features of the psychosocial support system (viz., family and community) influence general functioning among the disabled. Attempts by disabled persons to move toward independent status in life must begin early. Successful achievement of that independence varies as a function not only of the individual's own disability but also of the nature and extent of support received through family and community. In other words, as is the case with all of us, we move from dependence toward independence. But for the mentally retarded that movement is very difficult and requires considerable encouragement. Within our developmental model, the rate of movement from dependence to independence is a function, in part, of unique family characteristics. Therefore, by expanding our understanding of the nature of the familial psychosocial support for independence, we expect to be able to derive implications for the treatment of the disabled in general, and for the elderly disabled in particular.

For the larger population of elderly, it is presumed, and often correctly so, that they can and have achieved independence in life, created a family, and prepared for old age. In the case of the elderly mentally retarded, particularly the severely involved, such life-long independence is not likely (Dickerson, Hamilton, Huber, & Segal, 1979; Myers & Drayer, 1979). Instead we often find the elderly handicapped with no available family support, with elderly parents, or with siblings as old or older (Sweeney & Wilson, 1979). These family caretakers usually have their own personal demands that limit their ability to support the handicapped family member (Cotten, Sison, & Starr, 1981; Ensor, 1979; Harting & Carswell, 1979).

There are a number of factors that act to limit the maintenance of an independent life style among elderly clients, particularly for the elderly handicapped (Atchley, 1972; Hardman, Drew, & Egan, 1984; Sayder, 1974; Scheerenberger, 1975; Sutter, 1980). These factors include the following:

1. Deteriorating health precipitates concern among previously independent elderly who fear that their medical care needs will not be met if they attempt to maintain an independent living status apart from institutional medical or social support (Sweeney, 1979). The issue of medical care is especially important for elderly handicapped who may require unique medical supervision (Harting & Carswell, 1979; Mather, Jacob, Thompson, & Cox, 1981).

2. Some elderly clients become apathetic, perhaps due to boredom, and, as a result, suffer from further erosion of their already impaired social and

interpersonal competencies. The handicapped have a special need for an extended social support system of peers (Harting & Carswell, 1978).

3. Extended family members question their competence in caring for their disabled elderly relatives. This is especially true of elderly parents who are the only source of social support for their elderly handicapped off-spring (Myers & Drayer, 1979; O'Connor, Justice, & Warren, 1970).

4. The financial resources of the elderly client or his/her extended family are often inadequate to cover extensive health care and other related medical costs (Rice & Lobenstein, 1975).

5. Federal administrative initiatives are beginning to place limitations on personal insurance coverage which prevent payments for some types of care service needed to maintain independence (National Center for Health Statistics, 1975).

6. Community-based social service agencies have limited budgets and therefore may encourage institutionalization as a means of reducing the number of handicapped clients they are required to serve (Mather et al., 1981).

7. Nursing homes in the United States are a lucrative business which currently attracts many private investors (Ham, 1980; Myers & Drayer, 1979; Sayder & Woolner, 1974). This influence increases the number of nursing homes which, in turn, promotes the need to find elderly clients to place in these institutions. But who will pay for the elderly handicapped (Intagliata & Willer, 1982; Janicki & MacEachron, 1984; Myers & Drayer, 1979; Pratt, Sellar, Anderson, & Arcand, 1977; Segal, 1977)?

It is difficult to estimate the prevalence of handicapped elderly having serious problems with independent living without a comprehensive epidemiologic survey. Even then such a survey would be fraught with methodologic problems from the start.

DEFINING OLD AGE

For the general population life expectancy is in the 70s but for the mentally retarded it was once regarded to be in the 40s—at most (Bureau of the Census, 1977). Many mentally retarded citizens are now living longer lives and experiencing old age (Cutler, 1981). There is some argument as to whether the handicapped age at the same rate as the nonhandicapped elderly. In fact, there is some suggestion that the aging process may be slowed by the supportive environment of benign custodial care. Suggestions for what age the disabled become "elderly" range from 30 to 60 (Segal, 1978). Although at present we cannot resolve the actual age—particularly for the biologic aspects of aging (Cobb & Fulton, 1981)—what is true is that there are normative social events of aging that occur earlier for the handicapped. If aging is a process of changing dependency, by definition, the handicapped are always at risk for dependency and aging merely exacerbates that process.

DEFINING HANDICAPPED

The group we have focused on is the chronically handicapped, viz., the mentally retarded, whose intellectual and social handicaps were manifested during the early developmental period. Although this focuses on particular population, it is likely that there are similarities in the needs of this group of elderly and those whose impairments occur later (Thomas, Acker, Choksey, & Cohen, 1979).

There is also a major problem in achieving consensus on the definition of mental retardation. A Rand Corporation report found that there are 31 different definitions of mental retardation in the 50 states (Brewer & Kakalik, 1979). There are, therefore, problems with valid and consistent indentification, e.g., for some individuals IQ was the sole diagnostic criterion and for others it was socially inappropriate behaviors. In the case of those individuals who are most obviously and severely affected and who are forced into a dependent life style, they are often most available as candidates for a survey. This group is relatively small. The larger group of mentally retarded typically suffers from a disability which enables them to achieve camouflage more successfully (Clarke & Clarke, 1974). From a previous survey of ours (Garber, 1980), upward of nearly 50% of mildly disabled young adults are "lost" shortly after school and of the remainder, only those who maintain Department of Vocational Rehabilitation (DVR) or other community organization contact would remain obvious to any survey. Of course, we can hope that many of those who are lost to the survey do in fact achieve independence and successfully adjust to society, but we are not sure. We know that some run into trouble with the law or become the chronically mentally ill and are prey to the dangers of our inner cities.

There is, therefore, a discrepancy of considerable magnitude between the early and later prevalence figures for the mentally retarded population (Baird & Sadovnick, 1985). As a result, we do not know if the elderly in general and the elderly disabled are elderly at the same age, if they age at the same rate, or if the rate of increase in functional disabilities for them is similar to the elderly in general (Dickerson, et al., 1979; Hamilton & Segal, 1975). However, based on the status of identifiable or locatable elderly handicapped in the community, there may be some important and revealing data that relate to the aging process in general and allow us to make inferences about the social-emotional stability of the elderly handicapped (Cotten, Purzycki, Cowart, & Merritt, 1983; DiGiovanni, 1978).

HIGH-RISK SCREENING AS A
GATEKEEPING STRATEGY

A number of suggestions have been made to develop a gatekeeping strategy that would effectively slow the rate of untimely institutionalization of the elderly by closely monitoring functioning during a limited time frame (Health Care Financing Administration, 1981). It can be argued that the time frame of this concept is too narrow for the elderly disabled. Currently the time frame for focused concern is regarded to begin around age 55 to 65 but more specifically when a major functional disability requires medical treatment. A collateral concept of compressing morbidity suggests that by somehow reducing the increase and/or seriousness of functionally disabling illnesses that accompany aging, loss of independence can be delayed and movement toward institutional care would be slowed or eliminated and general quality of life prolonged. The concepts are admirable, but the strategy of addressing primarily functional disabilities is faulty. A recent Health Care Financing Administration (1981) report indicates that the rate of increase of functional disabilities does not adequately explain the rate of movement toward demand for institutional care among the elderly (Pratt et al., 1977; Sweeney & Wilson, 1979). Rather, this statistic suggests that the unavailability or loss of psychosocial support is a prime factor influencing the rate of movement or loss of independence (Segal, 1978; Sweeney, 1979). The fact that 60% of nursing home residents have no immediate family is supportive evidence for this interpretation (Health Care Financing Administration, 1981). It suggests that loss of independence is not exclusively functional and that a major part is attitudinal, i.e., elderly persons become concerned about ability to take care themselves and move toward the apparent security of the institutional setting—this process occurs even with awareness of a loss of quality of life (Seltzer, Seltzer, & Sherwood, 1982; Sweeney & Wilson, 1979).

PILOT STUDY

We undertook a small survey study in order to understand the unique needs of elderly mentally retarded and handicapped individuals residing in the community. The study sought to develop information on how the existing delivery system could be modified to address their unique care demands. Features for this population that influence service delivery include whether they are elderly at the same age as the elderly in general, the nature of their financial and social resources, the nature of their family support systems, the rate of increase of functional disabilities associated with aging, their ability levels described on a dependence–independence continuum, the likelihood of institutionalization, and the implications for independence/dependence for deinstitutionalization efforts.

Our conceptual orientation is to develop a risk model that is based on features of both the general functioning levels of the individual client and the availability of psychosocial support systems (family and community). These data can be used to suggest both the risk of losing independence and what possible "gatekeeping" strategies can be employed to slow the rate of losing independence and with subsequent unnecessary or untimely institutionalization. In effect, this diagnostic model attempts to subsume both an outcome likelihood estimate for rehabilitation therapy and a treatment protocol that determines rehabilitation strategies.

We are trying to characterize the available psychosocial support—mainly the family—within a probabilistic model. For example, if a family is low-risk, it is likely to encourage independence and maintain a support system appropriate to their offspring's needs to achieve successfully in the community. A high-risk family does not encourage independence and exacerbates the difficulties of their disabled offspring's attempts to achieve some measure of adjustment or independence in the community. Knowing that the developmental transition to independence is difficult for the handicapped individual, and knowing that it can be made more or less difficult by the nature of the family psychosocial support system, would provide us with a basis for developing early intervention strategies for such families and thereby prevent the prolonged dependence of the handicapped into old age.

A limited group of about 35 subjects, including community residing elderly mentally retarded persons and their immediate family members, have thus far been interviewed. The parents ranged in age from 50 to 90, whereas their handicapped sons or daughters ranged in age from 30 to nearly 70 years of age. The interviews constitute a pilot phase of a more extensive research effort which will include a treatment manipulation of the immediate support system. This phase, or survey stage, was designed to develop the referral process and test the instruments to be used in the interview procedure.

Two instruments have been developed: one for interviewing the handicapped client and one for interviewing the parents or family support person who is viewed as having primary caretaker responsibility. The parent and client interview schedules required essentially similar kinds of information including basic demographics, family health, parent's rating of offspring's independence (in both daily living activities and social and emotional behavior), parent's attitude, self-concept, as well as family activity patterns, financial resources, and extent of community service involvement and/or usage. The major interest we have is to determine the nature of the family support system as it relates to the degree of independence achieved by the elderly handicapped individual. The observations made on the son or daughter should be viewed as the outcome measures for the support system that the parents or family have provided.

SUMMARY OF PRELIMINARY DATA FINDINGS

Elderly Client and Family Characteristics

The elderly clients who have participated in our survey to date tend to have previous work histories, either through sheltered workshop (53%) or competitive employment opportunities (20%). A portion of the sample (27%) has never been employed. The parents or sibling caretakers of these clients have achieved middle- or upper-middle-class socioeconomic status. They tend to be employed as skilled technicians and/or small business managers. They have on average graduated from high school and completed some university training. Most (65%) of the parents are now retired.

It is interesting to compare the variation in amount of available family support with the extent of dependence among target elderly clients. In general, the number of individuals available to support the elderly clients was four, but this ranged from single caretakers to as many as nine people available for social support. Similarly, the typical frequency of client–family contact was weekly, but this also varied from daily to not more than once each year. These caretakers report that the elderly clients are independent with respect to their personal hygiene (80% independent) and mobility (87% independent). But activities of daily living, including leisure time opportunities, are low, with 67% of the elderly clients rated as needing assistance in this area. Thus, we can observe great variation in the extent of family support available to these elderly clients together with some suggestions that the independence these clients have achieved is generally limited to functional (e.g., hygiene) but nonsocial areas. We have begun to analyze such interrelationships through subsequent data analysis of the family surveys.

Data Analysis of Family Surveys

In general, survey data are scored with respect to risk domains which characterize overall family functioning. Parameters that estimate family process variables include measures of family occupational and educational status, family health, community involvement, caretaker ratings of client independence, and quality of the family home environment. Normal scores are created across families for each of these six risk domains. Domain scores are averaged to yield a composite family risk score. The medium family risk score is used initially as the cutoff that distinguishes high- versus low-risk families. A multivariate discriminant analysis of all six risk domains is then used to classify subject families as high- versus low-risk.

Preliminary survey results suggest that a prescriptive rehabilitation technology initiated earlier in the adult life of the handicapped person would serve as an effective delivery mechanism to enhance independence and ultimately reduce the rate of movement toward dependence as that person ages. In other words, there are important differences in the level of independence that the individual elderly handicapped can achieve. These differences in functioning level include variations in compensatory coping skills, discrepancies in the extent of available family support, and differences in quality of existing local community rehabilitation services. It appears that a three-way interaction among client, family, and local community characteristics—rather than age or disability per se—determines the degree of independence (or dependence) observed among elderly disabled clients.

From our preliminary survey of elderly parents and their elderly disabled offspring, in the context of our earlier work with families of disabled children, there is a beginning suggestion of a developmental model. First, there is a need to define qualitative differences in disabling conditions among mentally retarded populations. The developmental experiences of the more seriously handicapped individual are different from those of the mildly handicapped, and the support system required to maintain independence is also quite different. Although our data are limited at present, they suggest that the more severely handicapped are by necessity prolonged in their early family dependence, whereas the necessity of prolonged family dependence varies greatly among the more mildly handicapped. During early development, the need for support interacts with psychological characteristics of the family wherein either dependency may be encouraged or intense efforts are made by the family to move their son or daughter, despite their serious handicapping condition, toward independence.

This study provided us some confirmation of a family typology that includes at least three types of families: families who naturally encourage independence, families who actively encourage dependence, and families who are mixed but generally do not actively support the transition to independence. We have seen older handicapped individuals who are cared for at home as though they were little children and are dressed and even fed with prechewed food, compared with those older handicapped individuals who have achieved a "normal" independence, where contact with their family is similar to the normal offspring contact with elderly parents. The crucial difference, it appears to us, is in the nature of the family, i.e., the parents and how they view their role in their handicapped child's development.

The risk model of family rehabilitation that we have been working toward indicates that there are observable characteristics among the different ways that families manage their lives and that these family process differences relate to performance measures in their children. These characteristics in what we have termed high-risk families do not enhance offspring performance but may even interfere with the natural development of independent skills. The characteristics of the families change in importance according to the developmental phase that the offspring is experiencing, but the constellation of familial influences appears to remain relatively the same over time.

Delineating these variables within a predictive model allows us not only to suggest the risk for delayed performance in the offspring of certain families but also reveals which aspects of the family's needs require support and thereby provides a basis for a treatment strategy using a case management approach to family rehabilitation.

The developmental model provides a basis on which to observe the handicapped individual's movement along a dependency continuum. Early in life there is a high level of dependency, but with intense training and encouragement the seriously handicapped individual can achieve a measure of independence that facilitates moving into a stable work setting and independent living situation. Our hypothesis is that the level of independence achieved early is directly related to independent status when that person is older. In this model, the gatekeeping strategy requires that prolonging the independence of the elderly handicapped be initiated in the early developmental period, e.g., at adolescence or earlier.

The early school years are a time when observing parents would be easiest and families would also be most accessible. The school years, therefore, are the time when we should try to implement family rehabilitation strategies. Unfortunately, there is no organized active effort to gather the appropriate information and therefore no predictive model that would allow us to foresee the need of an individualized parent training program. Such a preventive rehabilitation approach would move the families to encourage and even foster independence in their handicapped sons or daughters.

It is hoped that additional analysis of survey data for elderly handicapped clients living in their local communities would provide further suggestions regarding the importance of community or family social support for independence and indicate how the provision of that existing support system may be modified to encourage the independence of all, including aged handicapped clients, for example, by providing training to the family of the elderly client either through the parent or parent groups or through the provision of surrogate family support. Which families are more (or less) likely to profit from this "gatekeeping" rehabilitation strategy will be examined by this continuing research effort.

REFERENCES

Atchley, R. C. (1972). *The social forces in later life: An introduction to social gerontology.* Belmont, CA: Wadsworth.

Baird, P. A., & Sadovnick, A. D. (1985). Mental retardation in over half-a-million consecutive livebirths: An epidemiological study. *American Journal of Mental Deficiency, 89*(4), 323–330.

Brewer, G. D., & Kakalik, J. S. (1979). *Handicapped children: Strategies for improving services.* New York: McGraw-Hill.

Bureau of the Census. (1977). *Projections of the total population by age and sex for the U.S.: Selected years 1980–2050. Current population reports.* (Series P-25, No. 704). Washington, DC: U.S. Government Printing Office.

Clarke, A. M., & Clarke, A. D. B. (Eds.). (1974). *Mental deficiency: The changing outlook* (3rd ed). New York: Free Press.

Cobb, S., & Fulton, J. (1981). An epidemiologic gaze into the crystal ball of the elderly. In S. B. Kiesler, J. N. Morgan, & V. K. Oppenheimer (Eds.), *Aging: Social change.* New York: Academic Press.

Cotten, P. D., Sison, G. F. P., & Starr, S. (1981). Comparing elderly mentally retarded and non-mentally retarded individuals: Who are they? What are their needs? *The Gerontologist, 21*(4), 359–364.

Cotten, P. D., Purzycki, E., Cowart, C., & Merritt, F. (1983). Alternative living arrangements for elderly mentally retarded people. *Superintendents' Digest, 2,* 35–37.

Cutler, N. E. (1981). Political characteristics of elderly cohorts in the twenty-first century. In S. B. Kiesler, J. N. Morgan, & V. K. Oppenheimer (Eds.), *Aging: Social change.* New York: Academic Press.

Dickerson, M. V., Hamilton, J., Huber, R., & Segal, R. M. (1979). The aged mentally retarded: The invisible client—a challenge to the community. In D. P. Sweeney & T. Y. Wilson (Eds.), *Double jeopardy: The plight of aging and aged developmentally disabled persons in mid-America—a research monograph.* Ann Arbor, MI: University of Michigan Press.

DiGiovanni, L. (1978). The elderly retarded: A little known group. *The Gerontologist, 18,* 262–266.

Ensor, D. (1979). Assessment of community services for the elderly/aged developmentally disabled population: A report on services in Michigan. In D. P. Sweeney & T. Y. Wilson (Eds.), *Double jeopardy: The plight of aging and aged developmentally disabled persons in mid-America—a research monograph.* Ann Arbor, MI: University of Michigan Press.

Garber, H. L. (1980). The post-secondary school adjustment of mentally retarded individuals. In *Implications of recent rehabilitation legislation for handicapped children and adolescents,* chaired by R.T. Goldberg. Symposium conducted at the 88th Annual Convention of the American Psychological Association, Montreal.

Ham, R. (1980). Alternatives to institutionalization. *American Family Physician, 22*(1), 95–100.

Hamilton, J. C., & Segal, R. M. (Eds.). (1975). *Proceedings of a Consultation—Conference on the Gerontological Aspects of Mental Retardation.* Ann Arbor, MI: University of Michigan, Institute for the Study of Mental Retardation and Related Disabilities.

Hardman, M. L., Drew, C. J., & Egan, M. W. (1984). Adult and aging factors in exceptionality. In M. L. Hardman, C. J. Drew, & M. W. Egan (Eds.), *Human exceptionality: Society, school and family.* Boston: Allyn and Bacon.

Harting, S. A., & Carswell, A. T. (1978). A perspective on service delivery to aged developmentally disabled adults. In R. M. Segal (Ed.), *Proceedings of a Consultation Conference on Developmental Disabilities and Gerontology.* Ann Arbor, MI: University of Michigan, Institute for the Study of Mental Retardation and Related Disabilities.

Harting, S. A., & Carswell, A. T. (1979). Older developmentally disabled persons: An investigation of needs and social services. In *Research project on aging.* Athens, GA: Georgia Retardation Center.

Health Care Financing Administration. (1981). *Long-term care: Background and future directions.* Washington, DC: Government Printing Office.

Intagliata, J., & Willer, B. (1982). Reinstitutionalization of mentally retarded persons successfully placed into family-care and group homes. *American Journal of Mental Deficiency, 87*(11), 34–39.

Janicki, M. P., & MacEachron, A. E. (1984). Residential, health, and social service needs of elderly developmentally disabled persons. *The Gerontologist, 24*(2), 128–137.

Kriger, S. F. (1975). On aging and mental retardation. In J. C. Hamilton & R. M. Segal (Eds.), *Proceedings of a Consultation—Conference on the Gerontological Aspects of Mental Retardation.* Ann Arbor, MI: University of Michigan, Institute for the Study of Mental Retardation and Related Disabilities.

Mather, S., Jacob, G., Thompson, S., & Cox, M. (1981). *Older developmentally disabled persons: The invisible senior citizen. An investigation of needs and implications for service delivery in Dane County, Wisconsin.* Madison, WI: Dane County Developmental Disabilities Services Board.

Myers, J. M., & Drayer, C. S. (1979). Support systems and mental illness in the elderly. *Community Mental Health Journal, 15*, 277–286.

National Center for Health Statistics. (1975). *United States life tables: 1969–1971.* Washington, DC: U.S. Government Printing Office.

O'Connor, G., Justice, R. S., & Warren, N. (1970). The aged mentally retarded: Institution or community care? *American Journal of Mental Deficiency, 75*, 354–360.

Pratt, J., Sellar, K., Anderson, D., & Arcand, M. (1977). *Needs of and services to the elderly mentally retarded: Report of a project in Dane County, Wisconsin.* Madison, WI: University of Wisconsin, Waisman Center on Mental Retardation and Human Development.

Rice, B., & Lobenstein, J. (1975). Income provision and maintenance. In J. C. Hamilton & R. M. Segal (Eds.), *Proceedings of a Consultation—Conference on the*

Gerontological Aspects of Mental Retardation. Ann Arbor, MI: University of Michigan, Institute for the Study of Mental Retardation and Related Disabilities.

Sayder, B., & Woolner, S. (1974). When the retarded grow old. *Canada's Mental Health, 22,* 12–13.

Scheerenberger, R. C. (1975). Generic services for the mentally retarded and their families. In J. Dempsey (Ed.), *Community services for retarded children.* Baltimore: University Park Press.

Segal, R. M. (1977). Trends in services for the aged mentally retarded. *Mental Retardation, 15*(2), 25–27.

Segal, R. M. (1978). The aged developmentally disabled person: A challenge to the service delivery system. In R. M. Segal (Ed.), *Proceedings of a Consultation—Conference on Developmental Disabilities and Gerontology.* Ann Arbor, MI: University of Michigan, Institute for the Study of Mental Retardation and Related Disabilities.

Seltzer, M. M., Seltzer, G., & Sherwood, C. C. (1982). Comparison of community adjustment of older vs. younger mentally retarded adults. *American Journal of Mental Deficiency, 87,* 9–13.

Shanas, E. (1979). Social myth as hypothesis: The case of the family relations of old people. *The Gerontologist, 19*(1), 3–9.

Soldo, B. (1981). The living arrangements of the elderly in the near future. In S. B. Kiesler, J. N. Morgan, & V. K. Oppenheimer (Eds.), *Aging: Social change.* New York: Academic Press.

Sutter, P. (1980). Environmental variables related to community placement failure in mentally retarded adults. *Mental Retardation, 18,* 189–191.

Sweeney, D. P. (1979). Denied, ignored or forgotten? An assessment of community services for older/aged developmentally disabled persons within HEW Region V. In D. P. Sweeney & T. Y. Wilson (Eds.), *Double jeopardy: The plight of aging and aged developmentally disabled persons in mid-America—a research monograph.* Ann Arbor, MI: University of Michigan Press.

Sweeney, D. P., & Wilson, T. Y. (Eds.) (1979). *Double jeopardy: The plight of aging and aged developmentally disabled persons in mid-America—a research monograph.* Ann Arbor, MI: University of Michigan Press.

Thomas, N., Acker, P., Choksey, L., & Cohen, J. (1979). Aging and aged developmentally disabled people: Defining a service population. In D. P. Sweeney & T. Y. Wilson (Eds.), *Double jeopardy: The plight of aging and aged developmentally disabled persons in mid-America—a research monograph.* Ann Arbor, MI: University of Michigan Press.

Part III

Sensory Impairment

13

Rehabilitation for the Blind and Visually Impaired Elderly

Anthony F. DiStefano and Sheree J. Aston

Changes in vision inevitably accompany the aging process. Almost all of us regardless of sex, race, ethnicity, or socioeconomic status, will experience some deterioration in vision as we get older. The degree to which this visual impairment becomes a disability or a handicap is a function not only of the nature and severity of the impairment, but just as important, a function of the psychological, economic, and technological context within which the individual functions.

With the growing proportion of elderly, the prevalence of the leading causes of blindness and visual impairment will increase. The latter include diabetic retinopathy, senile cataract, senile macular degeneration, and glaucoma. The clear relationship between visual problems and aging underscores the growing need for serious attention to the rehabilitation of the elderly with visual problems.

The purpose of this paper is to provide a broad overview of the state of rehabilitation for the blind and visually impaired elderly. It will include a brief outline of the epidemiology of visual impairment in the elderly and its functional implications, the major causes of disability and their impact, as well as a review of a model rehabilitation program for the visually impaired elderly. In addition, the role of technology will be reviewed, with a listing of the most commonly used visual aids that help the blind and visually impaired elderly. Very importantly, the status of service delivery, with particular emphasis on third-party reimbursement, will be reviewed. The paper will conclude with a summary of key recommendations to launch a comprehensive attack on the problems of the visually impaired elderly.

DISTRIBUTION AND IMPACT OF VISUAL IMPAIRMENT

The 1977 Health Interview Survey of the National Center for Health Statistics (NCHS) estimated that there were approximately 1.39 million individuals in the United States with severe visual impairment (inability to read normal newspaper-size print with conventional spectacles) (Kirchner & Peterson, 1979). These severely impaired persons comprised about 4% of the elderly, noninstitutionalized population. The 1977 National Nursing Home Survey of NCHS estimated that about 3% of the residents in nursing homes were unable to see and another 26% were partially to severely visually impaired. This would add approximately 344,000 home residents who are visually impaired to the national total. Notwithstanding the difference between the two NCHS surveys, it can be estimated that approximately 1.3 million elderly have some level of visual impairment (NCHS, 1979).

In 1980, the National Society to Prevent Blindness (NSPB) estimated that there were approximately 11.4 million people with some level of vision impairment in the United States (NSPB, 1980). Of these, approximately 500,000 were legally blind (best corrected central visual acuity equal to or less than 20/200 in the better eye, or a field of vision no greater than 20 degrees in its widest diameter). Figures from the Model Reporting Area for Blindness Statistics (MRA) have indicated that approximately 67% of the legally blind persons in the United States are over the age of 50 years, 52% over 60, 37% over 70, and 20% over 80 (U.S. DHEW, 1973). Given the significant shifts in the demography of the aging population and the clear association between visual impairment and aging, the rehabilitation of blind and visually impaired elderly is becoming a problem of great national significance. Because the vast majority of the visually impaired elderly have some remaining vision, early and appropriate intervention will help maximize the visual abilities of these individuals with the goal of greater independence and self-sufficiency.

FUNCTIONAL IMPLICATIONS OF VISUAL IMPAIRMENT

Ocular changes, such as nuclear sclerosis of the lens, pupil constriction, loss of accommodation (focusing ability), diminished depth of focus, contrast, and visual acuity are normal in the aging eye. A variety of vision changes affect most older people. Specifically, these range from sensitivity to glare, scattering of light, increased need for illumination, difficulties in night driving and performing activities of daily living to severe visual impairment as a result of ocular disease (Sekular, Kline, & Dismukes, 1982; Wolf, 1964).

In a 1975 American Optometric Association survey of senior citizens, it was reported that nearly one-third of those surveyed felt their inability to see well prevented them from performing activities such as household chores and engaging in recreation. Approximately 40% reported problems going up and down stairs, and an alarming 30% had difficulty reading the newspaper (AOA, 1977). A dramatic number of elderly persons are affected by ocular disease, and all individuals 60 years and older experience reduced near vision due to age-related changes in the eye. Additionally, distance visual performance is affected due to reduction of depth perception, and reduction in visual acuity from loss of contrast, scattering light and glare. It has been estimated that the average acuity of a person in his/her late seventies and older is approximately 20/70 (Pastelen, Mantz, & Merrill, 1973).

A vision loss severely impairs one's ability to interact with the environment and hampers performance of even the simplest everyday tasks. Visual losses can seriously affect the mobility of older persons. Often their narrow world becomes smaller with the addition of chronic health problems. The everyday functional limitations of visual changes in elderly individuals are as extensive as they are limiting. Examples of the problems persons age 70 years and older encounter on a daily basis include inability to see the temperature scale on an iron, oven/stove dials, face of a clock, station on a radio or to read newspaper print, street signs, bus schedules, and store directories. Safe independent travel may be impeded due to glare and shadows reducing the elderly persons' ability to see obstacles in their path. The reduction in contrast and depth perception often makes stairs difficult, if not dangerous, to climb. These normal deteriorations in visual performance not only inhibit performance of these activities of daily living but can adversely affect the social and psychological well-being of the aged individual.

MAJOR CAUSES OF VISUAL IMPAIRMENT

Although there are a wide variety of causes for visual impairment in the elderly, cataracts, senile macular degeneration, diabetes mellitus, and gluacoma are most often identified as the leading causes of vision loss in the over-65 population (Podgor, Lesley & Ederer, 1983). In many cases, the visual impairment occurs gradually over time, providing some opportunity for adaptation and/or rehabilitative intervention.

Cataracts are the most frequent cause of reduced vision in the elderly. In general, a cataract can be described as an opacity or clouding in the lens, which can be slight or dense. The presence of cataracts presents a twofold problem for the patient. First of all, depending on the degree of cataract development, a significant amount of light is unable to reach the retina, causing dimness in vision that will reduce the individual's ability to see detail. Just as important, the opacity in the lens scatters light, causing varying amounts of ocular glare. This can have a dramatic effect on reducing the visibility of objects. It is not surprising to find that persons developing cataracts frequently experience glare and difficulty in adjusting between light and dark environments. Too much or too little light very often makes it harder to distinguish objects and faces. The effects of glare can be exaggerated when the patient is too close to reading lights or windows. Shadow interpretation for cataract patients is difficult, and ability in a dimly lit room can be difficult if not impossible. Descending stairs in a poorly lit environment can be extremely dangerous, as can be wet surfaces at night under street illumination. Adaptation from light to dark zones and vice versa becomes a major problem for cataract patients. Many of these situations are minor to the normally sighted person but can become a catastrophe to the visually impaired elderly.

At the the present time, cataracts can be treated only by surgery, which is usually indicated when a visual impairment interferes with the individual's daily life. With the significant surgical advances, especially in intraocular lens implants, well over 90% of cataract patients can enjoy a full restoration of vision (U.S. DHHS, 1983).

Macular degeneration is a major cause of blindness among people over 65. Until recently there was very little that eye-care providers could do to save the patient's vision in cases of senile macular degeneration (SMD). In 1982, however, as part of a National Eye Institute national clinical trial, laser beam treatment (technically known as argon laser photocoagulation) proved to be effective in reducing the amount of visual loss if diagnosed early enough and intervention is immediate.

In SMD, the macula—the area of the retina that allows for greatest discrimination of fine detail and color vision—is affected in a degenerative process. Depending on the nature and duration of the SMD, this macular area degenerates significantly. Typically, a blind spot occurs in the center of the individual's line of sight. Very often such an individual will be able to detect little if any detail and must look to one side of an object in order to improve the visibility of the object. Although SMD patients lose central vision or the ability to see detail, they often retain much of their side vision and can see forms and objects and identify their locations.

Patients with macular degeneration report considerable blurring and clouding of vision. Very often it is difficult to recognize another person. Reading becomes a difficult if not impossible task. Text may appear to have words missing, or gaps in words might appear at different points in the text. Grabbing a doorknob or picking up small objects from the floor becomes particularly difficult. Mobility, however, is not greatly impaired because of the retention of significant amounts of peripheral or side vision. Chronic macular degeneration typically does not involve a total loss of vision, so the role of the rehabilitation process is to maximize whatever vision is remaining. Persons with macular degeneration are also very susceptible to changes in illumination. Additional time is required to adjust to changes in ambient lighting. Scanning and searching for visual cues becomes a tedious task. Intervention through the use of optical aids and individualized training programs can significantly aid in the rehabilitation of SMD patients so that they enjoy much more productive and independent lives.

A reduction in visual abilities is one of the complications in people with *diabetes*. This systemic disease can cause transient blurring of vision lasting from a few hours to several days. Uncontrolled or poorly regulated diabetics can demonstrate significant shifts in vision depending on blood sugar levels. Temporary nearsightedness is one common functional impact. In cases where the diabetes is uncontrolled for significant periods of time, diabetic cataracts can occur, with the associated glare and dimness of central vision characteristic of other cataracts. In advanced stages, significant deterioration of central vision may occur, not unlike that caused by macular degeneration. Retinal detachments affecting side vision as well as vitreal hemorrhaging causing severe if not total acuity loss also can occur in latter stages of diabetic retinopathy. Patients will complain of dulling or blurring of vision with appreciable deterioration in their ability to discriminate fine detail and to scan for localized objects. Other complaints that diabetic patients can experience include a shrinking or expansion of objects, visual halos around objects, drooping of eyelids, and doubling of vision. Prompt and continuous medical attention is imperative in the control of the diabetic to reduce or minimize visual impairment. Failure to do so will produce irreversible visual changes that will require more comprehensive rehabilitation strategies.

The last major source of severe impairment for the elderly is *glaucoma*. Unfortunately, the onset of glaucoma is a rather slow and insidious process, so that the patient is not always aware of the deteriorating peripheral vision. Once there is increased intraocular pressure within the eye, it interferes with nerve function, irreversible damage occurs, and permanent visual field losses result. The result is what is commonly referred to as tunnel vision, which is comparable to looking down the barrel of a gun and is associated with severe impediments in the person's spatial orientation, object localization, and mobility. Driving becomes particularly difficult. Patients will have problems spotting moving objects in the side of their field of view, even though they may retain 20/20 central vision. This condition leads to a deep sense of frustration and depression in the elderly, who become increasingly dependent because of the visual disabilities. Early detection and control of glaucoma certainly is the best way to avoid many of these problems. However, once the damage is done, the rehabilitative approach demonstrates the greatest chance for restoring maximum independence.

THE REHABILITATION PROCESS

Because of the multifaceted needs of the visually impaired elderly, a "total rehabilitation" approach is required. This comprehensive approach should include physical, mental, economic, familial, social, environmental, personal, and vocational goals. What does this total rehabilitation mean for the visually impaired elderly individual? It can mean a number of things: the use of optical aids to maximize residual vision; training for independent mobility; vocational services to maintain or regain remunerative employment or gainful work; counseling for greater economic or social independence; services to employers and family members so that they can better understand and, when necessary, modify their respective environments to be more responsible to the visually impaired individual; and stimulation for individual self-expression, opportunity, and personal growth.

A logical corollary to the complex and multifaceted needs of the visually impaired population is the team approach. When professionals work as a team, both the professional knowledge and "gut level" reactions of each team member can result in diagnosis and treatment that is much more likely to be focused on the need of the patient rather than the unique perspective of any individual provider. Very importantly, the interdisciplinary approach must stress careful coordination and communication not only among members of the rehabilitation team but also with the various practitioners and agencies in the community.

A model rehabilitation program for the visually impaired should include such professionals as social workers, rehabilitation counselors, eye care specialists such as optometrists and ophthalmologists, special educators, orientation and mobility specialists, and a variety of consultant specialists. In such a model, the social worker or rehabilitation counselor assesses the patient's potential for benefiting from rehabilitation services. Assessment of these needs typically includes comprehensive, in-depth social, medical, visual, educational, and career histories, along with an evaluation of the patient's health, self-image, motivation, expectations, and general level of functioning. Very importantly, the identification of the patient's support system and co-payment mechanisms are included.

Eye care providers should provide comprehensive examination of the visually impaired person, including a treatment plan that is patient-specific and should provide functional and/or environmental assessment of the patient's level of self-sufficiency. The clinical evaluation should be directed at measuring and describing the impairment and determining the proper treatment options to solve identified problems and to enhance self-sufficiency through the establishment of an individualized rehabilitation plan.

For a large number of partially sighted or low-vision patients, the next step in the rehabilitation process involves patient training with various optical and nonoptical aids. Mobility services should be provided by a certified mobility instructor and include an evaluation of the patient's present travel skills, determining if those skills will handicap the successful use of the optical aids at a distance. The patient must be taught to use an aid with acceptable levels of efficiency to obtain maximum benefit for his/her optical aids. Special educational services to train visually impaired patients to use their residual vision with or without optical aids for near tasks should be provided by specially trained personnel. Teaching a person eccentric viewing techniques to maximize residual vision, instructing the patient in the use of an aid for specific educational, vocational, or independent living tasks, and providing feedback to the examining eye doctor in an effort to design an aid that will uniquely meet the educational needs of the patient are all roles that this education specialist should play.

Follow-up services, typically one of the weakest elements in the services presently available, must be a key component of a comprehensive and responsive rehabilitation program. Periodic follow-up after the rehabilitation program has begun is imperative. The purpose of such contact is to assess the current use or nonuse of optical/nonoptical aids, to explore changes in vision or other concerns, and to channel the patient back into services when and if needed. Also a responsive follow-up program can sometimes require the staff to provide community-based services for visually impaired individuals in their home or their occupational or recreational setting.

There is a critical need for expanded community-based services for the blind and visually impaired. Too often providers wait for patients to come to them rather than providing outreach services to identify those unmet needs in the community. Community-based screening services, orientation and mobility services, and rehabilitation teaching are among the most essential services for the visually impaired population. Often the clinical environment does not offer a real-world context for which to evaluate and train visually impaired persons. Getting out into the community and providing mobility training, as well as assistance in daily living tasks, can be effective in enhancing independence and productivity. Another key aspect of a comprehensive rehabilitation program is to provide special services to those deaf/blind and multihandicapped individuals with severe visual impairments. A significant unmet need exists in this area. Specialized staff should be included within a comprehensive team so that the unique needs of this population are addressed.

THE ROLE OF TECHNOLOGY

A variety of optical and nonoptical technologies have been developed to assist blind and visually impaired persons to cope with visual loss. Although such technologies are not an absolute substitute for reduced or absent vision, they can play a significant role in helping the visually impaired lead fuller lives. The following is a brief review of the major sensory aids that have been developed to assist the blind and visually impaired individuals (Corn, n.d.; Independent Living Aids, 1984; Mellor, 1981; Patorgis, 1984; Sicurella, 1977).

Optical Aids

Often, elderly visually impaired persons can benefit from the use of an optical aid that works on the principle of magnification. The image to be seen is enlarged onto the usable retina. The stronger the magnification (the higher the power) of the optical aids, the shorter the working distance and the smaller the field of view. The closer the aid is to the person's eye, the larger the field of view. Optical aids used in performing near visual tasks include spectacle-mounted (microscopes), hand-held, and stand magnifiers. Hand-held and spectacle-mounted telescopes are used for distance viewing.

Magnifiers: for near tasks

Microscopic spectacles are most commonly prescribed because they provide the largest field of view, leave both hands free, enable the person to read for long periods of time and are cosmetically acceptable. One disadvantage is the short reading distance between the patient and the near visual task.

Hand-held magnifiers are basically a high convex (plus) lens with a handle. They are commonly used for spot visual tasks such as reading price tags, appliance dials, numbers in a telephone book. They are not conveniently used for extended reading because they must be held at a fixed reading distance and have a smaller field of view.

Stand magnifiers are plus lenses in a stand with a fixed distance from the reading material. Because accommodation is required, the elderly person will need a reading prescription in addition to the stand. Stand magnifiers have a greater working distance than is possible with microscopes. Stand magnifiers are the aid of choice for persons with arthritis and hand or head tremors.

Telemicroscopes: for near tasks

Telemicroscopes are specialized telescopes or telescopes with reading caps. They allow near point tasks to be accomplished at a more normal, comfortable reading distance. They are available in full field, bioptic, monocular, or binocular spectacle or hand-held types. They have a lesser field of view than other optical aids of similar power.

Telescopes: for distance

Distance optical aids include hand-held and spectacle-mounted telescopes.

Hand-held telescopes are the most frequently prescribed aid for distance visual tasks. They are smaller, lighter, less conspicuous, and often less expensive than spectacle-mounted telescopes. They are often used for spot viewing of street signs, bus numbers, store aisle names, and recognizing faces.

Spectacle-mounted telescopes are less cosmetically appealing and can be more expensive. These aids are available in clip-on, bioptic, full field, monocular, or binocular models. They allow the patient to perform distance visual tasks for extended periods of time, such as watching television or theater.

A *bioptic telescope* is a minaturized telescope device placed in a pair of spectacles above the normal "straight ahead" line of view. Elderly individuals may use their normal vision and, when needed, spot or continuously view by tilting their chin down and viewing through the telescope. In some states, persons with bioptic telescopes are permitted to drive automobiles. Because the bioptic is a minaturized telescope, the field of view is smaller than other mounted or hand-held telescopes.

Field Expanders

Field-expanding devices are for the persons with constricted visual field (tunnel vision). These individuals can benefit from optical aids that enhance their remaining side vision. The reverse telescope utilizes the principle of minification. Fresnel prisms displace objects from the side to near the central field of view. Field expanding devices considerably improve the mobility and independence of elderly individuals with constricted fields.

Projection Devices

The closed circuit television (CCTV) has a camera that reads printed material and transmits it to a televison-like screen. The CCTV gives a very large magnification of printed material, enabling persons with very poor vision to read. The image on the screen can be reversed to show white print on a black background rather than dark letters on a white background. The viewscan is a portable, lightweight device that generates a highly enlarged image made up of square dots of light when the user guides a small camera over lines of type.

Illumination/Nonoptical Aids

Many visual tasks require the use of nonoptical aids in addition to or instead of optical aids. Illumination/nonoptical aids are devices that provide for improvement of contrast, reduction of glare, proper illumination, correct working distance, and increase in print size or object. In most cases, illumination/nonoptical aids are used in conjunction to increase the effectiveness of optical aids. The following is a list of commonly used illumination/nonoptical aids categorized by function:

1. *Illumination devices.* Stand, table, wall-mounted, or gooseneck high intensity lamps or variable intensity (rheostat controlled) table model or gooseneck lamps.

   Contrast aids: typoscope (black matte paper with aperture cut) for reading, check writing, and signature guides, felt-tipped pens with bold lined paper, yellow and other colored acetate sheets. Clip-on yellow lenses, occluder (for nonreading eye).
2. *Glare control.* Typoscopes, colored acetate sheets, especially yellow and pink, absorptive lenses, sunglasses, clip-on lenses, side shields, visors, and multiple pinhole occluders.
3. *Large print and devices.* Large-print materials (books, magazines, newspapers, music, etc.), large numerical telephone dials, playing cards, measuring tape, ruler, and large-eye threading needles.
4. *Miscellaneous aids.* These devices include adjustable desk and floor-model reading stands and adjustable rack and floor-model music stands.

Many of these illumination/nonoptical aids are available through the American Printing House for the Blind and Independent Living Aids product catalog.

Environmental Modifications

Many environmental modifications and cues can be used to improve the daily functioning of elderly visually impaired individuals. The proper implementation and use of color, intensity, outline, depth, size, and distance as they exist or modified can be used to improve the functional visual abilities of low-vision persons. These techniques described can be applied to the home, work, school, institution, or recreational settings. Even in the absence of glare and with appropriate lighting, objects may not be easily discriminated by the elderly individuals due to the lack of contrasts between objects. The following suggestions all involve the use of increasing contrasts between two objects to improve the functional visual abilities of visually impaired older persons.

1. *Food preparation.* The use of a light-colored cutting board with dark-colored foods or dark-colored cutting board with light-colored foods. Using clear glasses for dark liquids, dark place mats with light-colored dishes, and dark-colored food for easier meal consumption. The use of different-colored masking tapes at commonly used temperatures on the oven and stove dials.

2. *Living areas.* Placing constrasting tape around wall sockets, decorating by combining a dark couch with a light colored carpet and walls, the use of a plant or brightly colored object at the edge of light-colored furniture against a white wall to provide clues to edge and height of the surfaces. It is very helpful to use a contrasting-color or tape to distinguish a doorframe from the wall and from the doorway. The use of contrasting-color tape at the edge of each step on a stairway can aid in the safe movement of elderly individuals.

3. *Personal hygiene.* Especially in the bathroom, a person with light hair should hang a dark towel behind the mirror to aid in contrast for personal grooming. A brightly colored comb is easier to find in a crowded purse than a dark object. A clear plastic shower curtain with or without a design will permit more light to be transmitted into the bathing area than an opaque one.

Sensory Aids for the Blind

A sensory aid transforms information normally seen through the sense of vision to a sensory modality that is still usable. Electronic aids can be divided into two types: travel aids and reading aids.

Travel aids: The Russel Pathsounder is an obstacle detector that transmits a beam of ultrasound ahead of the user. Reflected sound from an oncoming object emits tone to indicate its presence. The laser cane sends out three beams (one below, one directly ahead, and a third at head height) ahead of the traveler. A vibration is felt in the cane if an object is present. The Sonicguide also sends out pulses of ultrasound, with the transmitter in a pair of eyeglasses. An object to the left is transmitted via an auditory tone to the left ear, an object on the right of the traveler to the right ear. The pitch of the sound denotes the distance of the object. The Mowat Sensor is a hand-held device that sends out an ultrasound beam ahead of the traveler. The device vibrates to warn the user of an object ahead.

Reading aids: The Kurzwell Reading Machine uses computers to convert print into synthetic speech. The Optacon translates images transmitted from the camera held in the user's right hand into a vibrating image of the same shape to the index finger of the user's left hand.

Specialized software and hardware are available to translate computer word processing to braille and auditory output.

Despite the availability of braille, reading aids, and optical aids, many visually impaired elderly do much of their reading by means of recordings either on cassette or disc. Other electronic devices helpful to these individuals are talking calculators and talking books.

There are many aids, appliances, and techniques to increase the functional abilities of the elderly visually impaired population. The proper visual rehabilitation of these persons demands the use of an interdisciplinary approach. Optical aids must be prescribed by a qualified eye care specialist (rehabilitation optometrist or ophthalmologist). It is imperative that rehabilitation professionals train the visually impaired elderly in the proper functional use of these devices and techniques.

Professionals serving the aged can help them to adjust to the loss of and perhaps stigma of visual impairment through positive reinforcement of the increased levels of independence and performance of activities of daily living made possible through the technology and knowledge presently available.

Providers of care to the elderly who confront the challenge posed by the visually impaired older adult will make a substantial and necessary contribution to the visual and psychological welfare of this rapidly growing segment of our society.

SERVICE DELIVERY ISSUES

Service delivery for the blind and visually impaired elderly is fragmented and discontinuous. The 1981 Report of the Mini Conference on Vision and Aging (1981) pointed out that while there are a number of public and private agencies providing information on services and problems in vision and aging, large numbers of older people of all income levels have little or no understanding of their own visual problems. This problem is compounded by the inadequate training of the service providers in gerontology and the special needs of the elderly. Historically, greater emphasis has been placed on the needs of the totally blind as opposed to the severely visually impaired or low-vision patient, who represents the majority of the visually impaired elderly. Although this is gradually changing, much more needs to be done to address the multifaceted needs of the low vision elderly.

According to the recommendations of the Mini Conference on Vision and Aging, the public does not clearly understand the implications of "functional vision" and how such vision may be used in daily living activities. Too often, emphasis is placed on the vision that has been lost by the elderly rather than maximizing what remains. In particular, the elderly have little knowledge of the continuum of vision and therefore what their visual expectations might reasonably be. Such lack of knowledge contributes to the lack of coordinated educational and rehabilitation efforts. Public and professional educational programs should attack this lack of awareness of the full range of vision abilities that the elderly retain and focus on ways to maximize them.

The American Foundation for the Blind recently completed a national study of third-party financing low-vision services in the United States (Kirchner et al., 1984). The results revealed a patchwork quilt of private and public programs, each with its own eligibility characteristics, waiting list, or confusing bureaucratic regulations. Too often the result is underutilization of existing services, premature withdrawal from work or activities, unnecessary institutionalization, or reduction in the quality of life. Commercial group life insurance typically will cover acute eye examinations under a medical model, with only about 25% covering low-vision aids and less than 20% covering specialized low-vision rehabilitation services. Varying degrees of coverage exist under Medicaid, state rehabilitation agencies, and community service clubs such as Lions. The report (Kirchner et al., 1984) concluded that (a) there is an extreme diversity of conditions under which payments are approved, generally limiting the scope of low-vision services provided and consequently limiting the effective use of the coverage that does exist; and (b) a significant segment of the population, especially the elderly, poor, and unemployed, who are most vulnerable, does not qualify for coverage. Recent efforts to expand Medicare coverage to include low-vision services were not successful.

RECOMMENDATIONS

Because of the significant gaps in knowledge about visual impairment in the elderly and its rehabilitation, both the National Institute on Aging (NIA) and the National Eye Institute (NEI) have major research initiatives in this area. Research is needed to explain the wide difference in the nature and degree of age-related decline in visual perception. Attention must be given not only to genetic and neurophysiological factors, but also to differences in such characteristics as personal life styles and cultural expectations and opportunities. Visual impairment in the older person must be studied in terms of functioning in real-life contexts.

Although a variety of optical and nonoptical aids have been developed to assist the visually impaired, very little knowledge has been accumulated on how to optimize compensation and rehabilitation in the older population. The NEI has identified this area as a priority for future research. Although most elderly will experience some degree of visual impairment, only a small percentage actually become blind. The goal is to achieve maximal use of residual vision, especially in those patients with degenerative disease of the macula and optic nerve. Research is needed to explore better diagnostic and training techniques for the use of optical aids. New technologies in electro-optics, laser science, fiberoptics, and imaging sciences seem to offer promise for significant advances in improving the quality and range of optical aid available for low-vision elderly patients.

A broad-based strategy is required in order to overcome the barriers associated with the rehabilitation of visually impaired elderly. Consistent with recommendations of the Mini White House Conference on Vision and Aging (1981), the following action agenda should be considered: (a) implement a national public education campaign on vision and aging stressing the need for centralized coordination of information, greater awareness regarding the full range of functional vision abilities, and emphasis on environmental considerations; (b) increase the level and effectiveness of rehabilitation and treatment services available to the elderly visually impaired, especially through greater coordination and use of existing federal programs and comprehensive community-based programs; (c) establish more responsive national policies, especially in the areas of public and professional education, and research and technology; (d) encourage and support expanded interdisciplinary curricula for professional personnel involved in serving the elderly visually impaired; (e) initiate a coordinated broad-based interdisciplinary research program from psychosocial considerations to technological advancements; and (f) amend existing legislation such as Medicare, Medicaid, the Older Americans Act, and the Rehabilitation Act, as well as education and research legislation in order to effect the previously identified initiatives.

Meeting the needs of our aging population must be a national imperative. Periodic national conferences are valuable in maintaining the momentum critical to the realization of the aforementioned goals.

REFERENCES

American Optometric Association. (1977). *Manual on vision services and older persons.* St. Louis: Author.

Corn, A. (Undated). Functional environmental cues for the low vision individual. *The interdisciplinary approach to low vision rehabilitation* (pp. 260-274). Oklahoma Clearing House.

Independent Living Aids—product catalog. (1984). New York: I.L.A.

Kirchner, C., & Peterson, R. (1979). The latest data on visual disability from NCHS. *Journal of Visual Impairment and Blindness, 73*(4), 151-153.

Kirchner, C. M., et al. (1984). Third party financing of low vision services: A national study. New York: American Foundation for the Blind.

Mellor, C. (1981). *Aids for the 80's—what they are and what they do.* New York: American Foundation for the Blind.

National Center for Health Statistics. (1979). *The national nursing home survey summary for the United States. Vital and health statistics* (Series 13, No. 43). Washington, DC: Author.

National Society to Prevent Blindness. (1980). *Vision problems in the U.S.* New York: NSPB.

Pastelen, L., Mantz, R., & Merrill, J. (1973). The simulation of age-related sensory losses: A new approach to the study of environmental barriers. In W. Preiser (Ed.), *Environmental design research* (Vol. 1), PA: Dowden, Hutchinson, and Ross.

Patorgis, C. (1984). In-office care of the visually impaired older adult. *Contemporary Optometry, 3*(1), 23-32.

Podgor, M. J., Lesley, H., & Ederer, F. (1983). Incidence estimates for lens changes, macular changes, open-angle glaucoma and diabetic retinopathy. *American Journal of Epidemiology, 118*(2), 206-212.

White House Conference on Aging. (1981, January). Bethesda, MD. Report of the Mini Conference on Vision and Aging.

Sekuler, R., Kline, D., & Dismukes, K. (Eds.). (1982). *Aging and human visual functioning.* New York: Alan R. Liss.

Sicurella, V. (1977, June). Color contrast as an aid for visually impaired persons. *Journal of Visual Impairment and Blindness,* pp. 252-257.

United States Department of Health, Education and Welfare. (1973). *Statistics on blindness in the model reporting area. 1969-1970.* (Publication No. NIH 73-427.) Washington, DC: DHEW.

United States Department of Health and Human Services. (1983). *Vision research—a national plan* (Vol. 1). (Publication No. 83-2469) 76-77. Washington, DC: DHHS.

Wolfe, E. (1964). Glare and age. *Archives of Ophthalmology, 74.*

14

Rehabilitation for Deaf and Hearing-Impaired Elderly

Laurel E. Glass

To be "old" in this country is not quite synonymous with being "hard-of-hearing." However, so prevalent is hearing impairment in the aging that noticeable loss for high tones occurs in men as early as 32 years of age and in women as early as 37 years (Corso, 1963). Reviews on a variety of studies on a variety of populations with a variety of methods agree that the number of hearing-impaired persons in middle and later life is very large—between 7.2 and 11.5 million, at least (Davis, 1983; Ries, 1982, in press). Over age 65, more than 40% of persons acknowledge they have lost some hearing and that they experience difficulty hearing in a noisy environment, approximately one-half of these have some difficulty even in one-to-one conversation in a quiet room. Some studies on the over-80 population report more than 90% with significant hearing impairment (Chafee, 1967; Miller & Ort, 1965). So frequent is hearing loss in older populations that one otherwise excellent geriatric health care center dropped audiologic testing from its health screening for older adults because "everyone is a little deaf." So seldom is hearing loss considered by health care programs that no assessment of hearing loss is included in a large geropsychiatry research project trying to detect early signs and symptoms of Alzheimer's disease—that hearing loss might exacerbate confusional status in older adults was ignored in both the theoretical and clinical construct of the investigations.

Despite the startling increase in the numbers of hearing-impaired persons from middle age to old-old age, only 12 of 2,445 projects summarized in the *Inventory of Federally Supported Research on Aging* concerned hearing loss (U.S. DHHS, PHS, NIH, 1982). Of those 12, none dealt with the psychosocial implications of hearing impairment in old age.

Such realities form the context for this paper in which the following questions will be considered: (a) what are the characteristics of hearing loss in middle and old age (presbycusis); how does presbycusis differ from hearing loss in the young? (b) what do we know about the human costs of hearing loss—that is, how handicapping is hearing loss for aging persons; (c) which rehabilitation procedures help older people cope most successfully with hearing loss; what are the limits of aural rehabilitation for older persons; how do these differ with age and independent living status; (d) which unresolved questions about age-associated hearing loss seem most accessible to *and* in most urgent need of active research?

Some definitions: Presbycusis can be defined loosely as the "normal" hearing loss associated with aging. *Hearing impairment* is a generic term indicating a hearing disability which may range in severity from mild to profound. *Deaf* means a person born deaf or who became deaf before the acquisition of language or speech. *Deafened* means a person who became deaf after the acquisition of language and speech; a deafened person has "lost" hearing. *Hard-of-hearing* means a person who, with or without the use of a hearing aid, has enough residual hearing to process some speech information through audition. This usually is defined as a loss in terms of decibels (db) at different frequencies in the speech range measured as Herz. Hearing loss may be referred to as "slight" (20 db or less; generally unnoticed, though faint whispers may not be understood); moderate (20–40 db; difficulty hearing when tired or inattentive, in a distant theater seat, or in the noise of general conversation when articulation is soft or poor); marked (40–60 db; considerable difficulty in hearing conversation unless voice of speaker is raised, distance is short, or conversation is with one person); severe (60–80 db; difficulty in understanding even shouted conversation); profound (over 80 db; difficulty in hearing even the sound of a voice). A "handicapping" hearing impairment means that, because of the hearing loss, an individual functions less well (or feels he/she functions less well) in his/her life tasks. Such functional deficiencies may be unconscious or may be consciously perceived by the hearing-impaired person.

CHARACTERISTICS OF HEARING LOSS IN MIDDLE-AGED AND OLDER ADULTS

Persons who are prelingually deaf, persons who become deafened after speech is established or in adulthood, and persons who become hard-of-hearing with increasing age often are, but should not be, lumped together.

Though they have in common a loss of hearing, their life experiences related to the hearing loss are very different. In order to cope well with their hearing impairment, each group has different needs—different needs for understanding and ongoing close relationships with their family and friends, different needs for information and service from health care professionals, different needs for support and training from community resources. It is in the group who are "becoming deaf" or hearing-impaired that the largest number of older hearing handicapped persons is found. It is on this group that attention will be focused in this paper.

Presbycusis

That "normal" age-associated hearing loss is called presbycusis does not mean that the hearing loss of older adults is a single entity with a single cause (e.g., Ordy, Brizzee, Beavers, & Medart, 1979; Schow, Christensen, Hutchinson, & Nerbonne, 1978). In addition to genetic tendencies inherent in the biology of the auditory apparatus, the system is also subject to a variety of other cumulative insults that finally may damage hearing.

The Normal Ear

The ear can be thought of as having three compartments, and hearing difficulty can originate from any of the three. The outer compartment is the ear canal; it is the "ear" parents mean when they tell their children, "Don't put anything smaller than your elbow in your ear."

The outer ear canal is separated from the second compartment, or middle ear, by the ear drum (the tympanic membrane). The middle ear is connected by a collapsible tube (the Eustachian tube) to the throat and is the part of the ear that sometimes feels stopped up when changing altitudes. The feeling results from unequal pressure outside the ear drum and inside the middle ear cavity; yawning or chewing gum usually clears it up by allowing air to pass from the throat through the Eustachian tube and into the middle ear cavity so that the pressure is equalized.

Three tiny bones are also in the middle ear cavity. They form a movable bony chain connecting the ear drum with the inner wall of the middle ear. When sound causes the tympanic membrane to vibrate, its motion makes the bony chain in the middle ear vibrate, and that vibration is transferred to the innermost of the tiny middle ear bones, the stapes. The stapes sits in a small hole in the inner wall of the middle ear; its base is on the membrane separating the middle ear from the inner ear. Vibration of the stapes on the membrane sets up vibrations in the fluid filling the inner ear cavities.

The inner ear is made up of interconnected, membrane-lined, fluid-filled tunnels in bone. The tunnel concerned with hearing is spiral shaped and is called the cochlea from its resemblance to a snail shell. Its complete structure includes the hair cells. Vibration of the cochlear fluid causes motion of the membrane on which the hair cells sit, and these motions are translated into energy that activates the nerves that are also part of the cochlea. These auditory nerves transmit the information received from sound to the brain.

Other fluid-filled funnels are connected to the cochlea but have a very different function. These semicircular canals control balance; when they don't work right, dizziness may result.

Causes of Hearing Loss

Hearing loss in older persons may result from no more ominous a cause than cerumen (the layperson's wax) in the outer ear canal.

Hearing loss in older people also may be due to a kind of locking together of the small bones in the middle ear or to a freezing of the stapes in place. This is thought to be genetic in origin, although some suggest that the tendency is made worse by the residue of intermittent infections in the middle ear that most people have suffered during their lifetimes. When the small bones don't move freely, sound waves are not transmitted properly to the cochlea, and poor hearing results. This pathological condition is called *otosclerosis* and, fortunately, can often be corrected surgically.

Presbycusis also can result from problems in the inner ear. Anatomically, several kinds of lesions are observed (Johnsson & Hawkins, 1979; Schuknecht, 1964). There may be bony overgrowth in the cochlea, for example, which may cause decreased efficiency of hair cell and basilar membrane function. There may be decreased numbers of hair cells. There also are fewer nerve cell bodies and fewer nerve fibers in the cochlea of some older people. The *stria vascularis* is a specialized part of the cochlea and is thought to be responsible for maintaining the unique chemical composition of the fluid in the cochlear channels. The stria has a very rich blood supply, and fibrous changes in these small blood vessels sometimes occur in old age. This results in less oxygen and nutrients for cochlear hair cells and nerve endings; sound localization and speech intelligibility are very sensitive to oxygen deprivation (Menzio, 1972).

Hearing Loss Due to Changes in the Central Nervous System

In some people, changes in the central nervous system (CNS) also may contribute to presbycusis (Bergman, 1980; 1983; Corso, 1977; Ordy et al., 1979). The auditory brain stem is the region in the CNS to which the auditory nerve carries impulses from the ear. Hearing stimuli travel up the brain stem to higher brain centers, passing on the way through clusters of cell bodies and other nerve fibers called ganglia. These are places in the brain where information from several sources interconnect. At these sites, for example, messages from the eye and ear begin the many steps by which they are fitted together to deliver coherent information. Sound also causes stimuli to go up to the highest brain centers in the auditory cortex; here the stimuli are perceived consciously and interpreted as sounds with particular meanings.

Microscopic comparison of the brains of hearing-impaired old and young persons after death shows that often older persons have fewer nerve fibers and fewer nerve cell bodies in the auditory brain stem, particular way-station ganglia, and auditory cortex (Pickett, Bergman, & Levitt, 1979). Some studies indicate that transmission of nervous impulses up the brain stem is slower in old than in young persons (Bergman, 1983).

When the ways living persons process sound are studied, these also suggest that CNS changes may contribute to the hearing loss of old age. In some of these experiments, for example, a different sound was presented to the right ear than to the left. When the two sounds were presented asynchronously—that is, when they were out of step with each other—old persons processed them a little more slowly and in a different sequence than did young persons.

Other Characteristics of Presbycusis

Additional poorly understood changes (e.g., Corso, 1977; Bergman, 1980, 1983) in the auditory and nervous systems of older people often combine to make communication hard and age-associated hearing loss difficult to live with. For example, many older hard-of-hearing people find it difficult to understand the parts of spoken words clearly enough to interpret their meaning even when the volume seems loud enough. They are said to have decreased "speech discrimination." Rapid speech, slowed speech, slurred speech, or words spoken in an echoing room are more difficult for the old than for the young to understand. Ironically, along with their progressive decrease in hearing, some old people also experience an increased sensitivity to particular sounds so the tones of a certain pitch may be painfully loud; this phenomenon is called "recruitment." Continuous or intermittent sounds in the ears ("head noises") of various kinds, due to undefined lesions in the auditory system rather than to external sound, often go with partial hearing loss. This is called tinnitus and may be very distressing to its sufferer.

Each of these characteristics, often associated with presbycusis, makes the use of a hearing aid and other assistive devices more difficult for the deafened older person.

Prevention of Hearing Loss

Little can be done yet to prevent the "normal," age-associated, progressive loss of hearing that happens to most people. If individuals live long enough, more than 9 in 10 will probably have a hearing loss that is handicapping to some degree. We still know too little about the genetics and physiology of aging in general—not just the auditory system but of other body systems also—to intervene wisely (or successfully) to prevent or slow the discomforts associated with the aging process. We still know nothing about effective ways to prevent the "natural" hearing loss of aging.

Nonetheless there are other, sometimes preventable, causes of hearing loss. Whether they are additive, in an arithmatic sense, to the hearing deficit caused by natural, biological processes is controversial. However, they are responsible for substantial decrements in hearing and sometimes for overt deafness.

Repeated trauma from loud noise is the most common cause of preventable hearing loss. This usually is from chronic exposure at work or, more recently, from frequent exposure of the young (and sometimes the old!) to the high volume of rock and other music. Noise-induced hearing loss seems to increase progressively for the first 10 or 15 years of exposure and then to remain relatively stable. Noise-induced hearing loss and the age-associated hearing loss called presbycusis are related in complex and poorly understood ways (Corso, 1977). Differences in the site of lesion caused by each suggests that their effects are not simply additive. In industrial compensation cases it usually is recommended that losses due to age not be estimated (or deducted) when assessing hearing loss due to work-related noise.

A second cause of irreversible, and often severe, hearing loss is medication. The best known ototoxic drugs (medicines which damage the auditory mechanism) are the aminoglycosides, a class of antibiotics which includes streptomycin. These sometimes are life saving. Unfortunately, they also sometimes destroy hearing (Lien, Lipsett, & Lien, 1983).

The effects of the aminoglycosides are known to most physicians who therefore are commendably cautious in their use. However, too little is known about the effects of other drugs that frequently are prescribed for older persons. Furosemide (brand name Lasix®), for example, is the diuretic prescribed most often for persons 65 and older and the third most frequently prescribed diuretic for persons between 45 and 64 years of age (Cypress, 1983). What most physicians, even geriatricians, don't know is that furosemide may cause hearing problems that are irreversible when the drug is administered chronically and at high dose (Rybak, 1982). More research is needed to clarify the range of doses and chronicity at which furosemide is ototoxic and to identify which patients are most susceptible to furosemide ototoxicity. Nor is it known whether furosemide interacts with other drugs used frequently with older patients to increase damage to the auditory system.

As little as is known about furosemide, even less is known about direct and/or interactive effects on hearing (or cognition or affect or the feeling of well-being, etc.) of the multiple drugs many old people are told to use daily. These are issues of major importance, not only for persons already old but also for the middle-aged who are moving daily closer to the health problems often associated with old-age.

Less frequent causes of decreased hearing in the old may be the late-acting results of viral diseases in infancy or childhood, or even of late-appearing developmental dysfunctions.

Since avoidance of preventable hearing loss in later years is related primarily to protective measures taken in earlier ones, it is clear that individuals of all ages need education about how the auditory system works. Only with such understanding can they understand the things they must do if they are to avoid damaged hearing later in life.

PSYCHOSOCIAL EFFECTS OF HEARING LOSS IN MIDDLE-AGED AND OLDER PERSONS

Hearing loss is not benign.

Although universal, hearing loss as one ages is rarely a neutral experience. Often it is negative. Though few research studies address this issue, published anecdotal reports by deafened persons and by professionals working with them and the personal experience of all of us who have older hearing impaired parents and friends confirm this statement.

The real, not projected, deficits often associated with old age in our society—e.g., decreased income, decreased access to intimate relationships, decreased value in the eyes of the world—all are exacerbated by hearing loss (Glass, in press-a, in press-b; Orlans & Meadow-Orlans, 1985; Oyer & Oyer, in press). The hearing impaired-elderly are in a doubly devalued status: that of old age and that of deafness (Wax, 1982).

Intrinsic to hearing loss itself are additional realities. Less information is available if one cannot hear or if one's hearing distorts the radio or television. Less humor and lightness is available if one misses the throw-away comments and asides in casual conversation. Establishing closeness with strangers who might become friends is harder if you miss what words are said or, worse, the nuances of voice that carry meaning.

Moreover, lost hearing may erode the self-confidence of the older person by causing repeated errors of understanding and response in verbal exchanges with others. Such errors result not only in confusion for the person with the hearing loss but also in repeated impatience directed toward them—impatience that feels unjustified to its recipient. The hearing-handicapped person tries and tries again harder, with attendant fatigue and a feeling of defeat.

Perhaps because of the association with getting old and with the negative image old age has had in our society, perhaps because of the threat of increasing isolation implicit in hearing loss, and perhaps because of the common assumption that hearing loss and low function go together (Becker, 1980; Herbst, 1983; Thomas et al., 1983), old persons as well as others often deny that they have a hearing problem. The reasons for denial are complex and not well defined by research. Whatever its cause, denial makes diagnosis and treatment of the hearing impairment more difficult.

A few data suggest that emotional as well as behavioral effects are associated with hearing loss in general and that hearing loss may be especially destructive to the well-being of older persons. In 1965, 1974, and 1982, approximately 7,000 persons representative of the population of Alameda County, California, were interviewed about their health attitudes and practices. Factor analysis defined five independent assessments in the study: a health attitude index, a health practices index, a social network index, a life satisfaction index, and a depression index (Berkman & Breslow 1983). Recently, the 1965 data were analyzed for the effects of hearing loss on several parameters of well-being. *More than twice as many hearing-impaired persons were depressed and had low life satisfaction as persons with no difficulty hearing.* The proportion of hearing impaired persons who were depressed and had low life satisfaction was markedly *higher in persons over 55 years of age.*

Such data about the emotional and behavioral accompaniments of age-associated hearing loss are consistent with the writings of professionals working with hearing impaired older adults (Levine, 1960; Luey, 1980; Ramsdell, 1978; Corso, 1977; Oyer et al., 1976), with statements by their family members (Glass, in press-b; P.K. Ashley, in press), with the moving and insightful comments of deafened persons themselves (Elliott, 1978; J. Ashley, 1973; Albert, 1977), and with the limited number of published studies on the psychological and social effects of hearing loss on its sufferer, especially in old age (e.g., Meadow-Orlans, in press; Kisiel et al., 1984; Myklebust, 1964; Rosen, 1979; Hunter, 1978; Weinstein & Ventry, 1982; Ordy et al., 1979; Orlans & Meadow-Orlans, 1984).

The need for careful research to unravel these biological and psychological complexities and to find ways to alleviate the discomfort the elderly suffer by their hearing loss is apparent.

A different kind of data is available from the studies of Ventry and Weinstein (1982) and Thomas et al. (1983). Ventry and Weinstein devised a

Hearing Handicap Inventory for the Elderly which, unlike so many assessment scales, was developed for older persons. Subsequently a shorter form of the test was derived (Ventry & Weinstein, 1983). The subjects received complete audiological evaluations. They were then asked a series of questions exploring the emotional consequences of hearing impairment and its social and situational effects. As found in previous studies, the degree of pure tone loss as measured by audiologic testing was not identical with the degree of handicap experienced. Some people with more hearing loss reported less handicap and vice versa. Nonetheless, persons with greater hearing loss tended to report more handicap.

The Thomas group (1983) attempted a commendable control of variability within their data by careful definition of population characteristics. Unfortunately, the definition resulted in the selection of a relatively favored population, e.g., middle class, well-educated, economically comfortable, mostly Caucasian, in good health, on no medication, and more than half living with spouses. Hearing aid users were excluded and the subjects had an average hearing loss of less than 20 db, usually considered a "slight" hearing loss. No significant effects of hearing acuity were seen for psychological and social measures. When cognitive test questions were administered orally, cognitive function was slightly lower in the hearing-impaired subjects than in the normal hearing. That is not surprising because they probably did not hear the questions perfectly. It was noted in the discussion that even this favored group were angry because others tended to equate the hearing loss with decreased functional ability.

REHABILITATION PROCEDURES HELPFUL TO OLDER PEOPLE

Hearing Aids

The hearing aid has been described as a "private, portable, public address system." Each small instrument contains an electrical energy source (battery), electronic circuitry, microphone, amplifier, receiver (earphone) and controls. Acoustic energy (sound) is amplified by the addition of electrical energy from the battery and fed through a custom-made mold to the ear canal.

Hearing aids amplify sound; they also distort sound. Herein lies a major problem for hard-of-hearing persons who expect their comprehension of sound to be "made new" by the new contraption, their hearing aid. Unfortunately, the prescription of a hearing aid for hearing loss is not so precise as the prescription of glasses for visual deficit. Until now, the amplification of most hearing aids does not match precisely the "shape" of the diminished hearing of their wearers; that is, neither the pitch (vibration frequencies) of sound that are lost nor the amount of hearing lost at different frequencies can be matched perfectly by the instrument. This is in contrast to the surprising specificity with which glasses fit visual losses.

Not least of the problems caused by great expectations is the reality that voice and other important sounds are not the only things made louder by the hearing aid. Extraneous noises—bangs, squeaks, rustles, rattles, scrapes, roars, and most other environmental noises—are amplified too and interfere with the interpretation of sounds whose meaning is important. Such realities often cause fatigue. They also cause disappointment, and they make the use of a hearing aid difficult for many and intolerable for a few.

Added to technological imperfections are other difficulties. Hearing aids are expensive, and Medicare does not help cover the cost of purchase. Hearing aids are visible and seem to many to be an unwelcome sign of old age, both to the wearer and to others whom they meet. Additionally, hearing aids often are small and require manipulations that can be hard for arthritic hands. Correct placement of the ear mold is not always easy. Batteries wear out and the hearing aid "doesn't work," though the reason may not be detected for an embarrassing while.

Whatever the complex of reasons, many hearing aids, though purchased, are not worn. An audiologist commented recently that the problem of noncompliance (failure to wear the hearing aid) in regard to these appliances was one of the most serious problems facing hearing health care professionals. Research on *why* people don't wear hearing aids is badly needed.

Cochlear Implants

Cochlear implants, by which single or multichannel electrodes are placed surgically into the cochlea, continue to be the subject of active research and of active controversy. Although recently approved by the Food and Drug Administration for nonexperimental use and now paid for by some health insurance companies, the present technology is not yet effective in restoring normal hearing. In particular, research is continuing on less intrusive and therefore less hazardous ways to provide selective, frequency-specific stimulation to the auditory nerve. Although not always included in the workup before cochlear implantation, many university implant teams require a careful psychiatric evaluation before surgery in addition to extensive evaluation of the hearing deficit. Although the multichannel implants have particular promise for the future, cochlear implantation remains very expensive and does not yet provide a panacea for hearing impaired persons in general.

Aural Rehabilitation

"Blindness separates me from things; deafness separates me from persons." That insight is attributed to Helen Keller and states vividly the reality that hearing loss handicaps by introducing a barrier to communication. Rehabilitation, therefore, succeeds as it reduces the communication barrier; it fails when the hard-of-hearing person continues isolated and unable to obtain the information and/or the intimacy needed for comfortable function. Traditionally, aural rehabilitation has been available to older hearing-impaired persons through speech and hearing centers and through community agencies, e.g., hearing societies, senior centers and other community sites where older adults gather. A number of thoughtful, evaluative, and pragmatic discussions of rehabilitation programs for the elderly have been published recently (Alpiner, 1982; Hull, 1982; Kaplan, 1979; Kisiel, Sundaram, Capozzelli, & Taub, 1984, Stephens & Goldstein, 1983; Watts, 1983; Weinstein, 1984). The following touches only the surface of these issues.

If the nature of the hearing loss makes amplification by a hearing aid appropriate, aural rehabilitation must provide training in the effective use of that hearing aid. This is one part, but only one part, of a good aural rehabilitation program. Information about the variety of other assistive devices available for hearing impaired persons should also be an intentional and focused supplement to training in the use of the hearing aid. In particular, television and telephone amplification units should be discussed.

In addition, aural rehabilitation should assess how handicapping the hearing impairment is. Such an assessment should consider whether the person is employed or retired, lives alone or with others, participates actively in a church and other groups or prefers a more solitary life style. Such evaluation should also include sensitivity to symptoms of depression, anger, grief, apathy, poor health, etc. The rehabilitation plan must fit the needs of the client. "Poor motivation" may be a mix of poor fit to the client's need, plus lack of awareness in the rehabilitation professional of other needs which are distracting the client and draining energy.

The best of the aural rehabilitation programs provide the hearing-impaired person with skills and strategies that assist her/him to maintain control of the communication environment. Simple things can be learned, e.g., to be sure the speaker is facing the light, which must be behind the hearing impaired person; to repeat instructions or to ask for them to be written down; to watch the cash register in stores so that one is not embarrassed by misunderstanding the cost of a purchase or to use a bill large enough to more than cover the cost of the item; to turn off the television or the radio if an important conversation is going on. Although people often don't think of such simple coping strategies themselves, they can make very good use of them if they are told about them.

Other kinds of skills can be taught. Although only approximately 40% of speech sounds can be seen on the mouth, lipreading (sometimes called speechreading) can be very helpful, especially for a person who has a slight or moderate hearing loss and even for some persons with a severe loss. The residual hearing plus the speechreading combine, especially in noisy environments, to allow the hearing-impaired person nearly full participation and communication. Not infrequently, one finds that people are embarrassed to look at another's mouth when that person is speaking. Aural rehabilitation can provide appropriate experiences in groups and individually that free the hearing-impaired individual to make full use of her/his remaining hearing and other skills. Lipreading classes also can help hearing-impaired persons become conscious of sounds that look like other sounds on the mouth and to be alert for dissonance between context and what is heard and seen. Such awareness sometimes prevents unpleasant errors.

Research is needed to determine whether a simplified sign language, using English syntax and grammar and shared by the hearing-impaired person with family members and close friends, could alleviate some of the isolation experienced by deafened older people in, for example, family gatherings. Adaptations of cued speech might prove very helpful. Research studies with older clients have not yet tested such suggestions.

Support groups which include other older hearing-impaired persons probably are as effective with the hard-of-hearing as with any other group which shares a disability. A consumer organization called Self Help for Hard of Hearing People, Inc. (SHHH), is an effective example of this. Support groups for hearing-impaired persons are sometimes available at hearing societies, senior centers and other community agencies. While the dynamics of such groups deserve study, their effectiveness deserves emulation within the aural rehabilitation framework.

Rehabilitation is always more successful if family members and close friends can be involved in the process. Their understanding of the reality imposed by the hearing loss is important because they must adapt their behaviors too; e.g., they cannot expect the deafened person to understand them if they talk with their back turned or from the next room. Their human support is needed when the hearing-impaired person is frustrated by the imperfections of a hearing aid or disappointed by being unable to hear well enough to enjoy a movie he/she especially wanted to see. These and other implications for hearing-impaired persons and their families are considered more fully elsewhere (Glass, in press-b; P. K. Ashley, in press; Oyer & Oyer, in press).

Aural rehabilitation tends to be less successful with older persons than with younger (Alpiner, 1982). This lack of success seems related more to client attitudes than to severity of the pure-tone hearing loss. Denial that a hearing problem exists, or an attitude of helplessness or an acceptance of the hearing loss, but without a desire for help in coping with it, all make rehabilitation almost impossible (Alpiner, 1982). One recent study suggests that additional investigation of these questions may be appropriate. In her doctoral research, Nguyen (1984) studied denial in older persons who were found to be hearing-impaired by a screening program. She found, unexpectedly, that their attitude toward the hearing loss had no significant correlation with whether or not they followed through on referral to a physician. Equally unexpected was the finding that the audiologist's *failure to refer* was of primary significance in determining whether or not the individual received further workup. An impression from an experienced investigator working with Rehabilitation Services Administration data also suggests that these problems deserve further examination: older adults entering the rehabilitation system stayed a shorter time, had a higher proportion of successful closures, and had fewer returns to the system because of rehabilitation failure than did their juniors.

The special considerations necessary when aural rehabilitation services are provided for confined elderly clients, e.g., persons in nursing homes and other long-term care facilities, are complex and will not be discussed here.

Technological Developments

In addition to hearing aids, alternative listening devices and other assistive aids are available as part of comprehensive hearing services for the hearing impaired. Some relatively simple and low-cost devices are available. These include headphones for radio and television.

Difficulty using the telephone is a major problem for many hearing-impaired persons. Many have enough hearing to understand direct conversation but do not have enough residual hearing to use the telephone comfortably. Telephones that amplify sound can be of real help to such persons. Recently, small, hand-size amplifiers have been developed that can be attached temporarily to pay and other telephones; these devices, too, are relatively inexpensive.

One device which is familiar to the prelingual deaf but which has not been used much until now by deafened adults, including the elderly, is the Telecommunication Device for the Deaf (TDD). This utilizes the telephone system to transmit printed messages and is increasingly available to deaf and hearing impaired persons. The earliest units operated on the same principle as (and adapted the discarded machines of) railroad teletype systems. Modern units use contemporary electronic and computer technologies; many are portable and battery-operated. In California, legislation sponsored by the California Association of the Deaf mandates that the telephone company shall provide free TDDs to persons certified by a physician as deaf. The costs are shared by all telephone users with a charge of less than 5 cents a month added to every telephone bill in the state. Although many older hearing-impaired persons have a severe enough hearing loss to be eligible for a company-provided TDD, few older adults know that the system is available. Increased use of TDDs by the severely hearing-impaired elderly could benefit many and probably would occur if information were more readily available at speech and hearing centers and at general community agencies working with older adults.

A variety of warning devices and alert systems also are available at relatively low cost for the older hearing-impaired person. Of particular benefit are systems of flashing lights attached to the doorbell, the telephone, fire alarms and the like. Not least important of such warning systems are "hearing dogs." Programs to train the dogs and their potential owners are sponsored by local humane and animal protection societies. The hearing-handicapped older person gains the companionship of a pet and is supplied with a living warning system.

In addition, churches, assembly halls, and large public auditoriums can be equipped with auditory loops, FM or infrared amplification systems. These greatly increase the possibilities for hearing-handicapped persons to continue to participate enjoyably in large group activities. Such systems are particularly useful because they bypass environmental noise and feed the meaningful signal directly into the ear of the hard-of-hearing listener.

The U.S. Office of Technology Assessment has prepared a thoughtful background paper on assistive devices for the hearing impaired titled "Selected Telecommunications Devices for Hearing-Impaired Persons." This probably should be in every rehabilitation facility working with older adults and be distributed more widely to churches and other organizations using amplication systems. SHHH (1984) recently summarized information about assistive devices in particularly usable form. Copies of these pamphlets also need wide dissemination.

Closed-caption television is a technological development increasingly available to deaf and hard-of-hearing persons. Only ABC of the major commercial networks and the Public Broadcasting System (PBS) provides closed captioning for some of their programs. CBS is working to develop a captioning system using quite different principles, but it is uncertain when that will be introduced for public use. A major problem of the system is the cost of decoding equipment. Decoders for the ABC and PBS systems are available from only one national distributor (Sears), which fortunately has many outlets, and cost between $300 and $500. CBS stated recently that its decoder would cost more than $1,000. That is beyond the financial reach of the many older persons living alone and on a fixed, low income.

The additional market opened if the millions of hearing-impaired persons over age 65 were viewers might help decrease the cost of decoders by stimulating additional advertising revenue. Additional publicity about the availability of closed captioning also would increase the demand by hearing-impaired older adults for captioning of more and of more varied programs. Organizations such as the National Association of the Deaf and the California Association of the Deaf watch new programming and legislation and work together to improve service. The active involvement of other organizations concerned more specifically with the needs of older Americans, like SHHH and the American Association for Retired Persons, would be beneficial.

Research Priorities

Four directions for intensive research are implicit in this discussion: (a) biomedical research aimed at the discovery of preventable causes of presbycusis; (b) behavioral science research directed at understanding and ameliorating the handicapping emotional and behavioral responses to hearing loss in middle and later life; (c) rehabilitation research directed toward development of workable rehabilitation techniques for the communication deficits caused by hearing loss in the elderly; and (d) technological research to adapt contemporary and future technologies for use by older, hard-of-hearing individuals.

In the near future, a small, research-focused state-of-the-art conference, made up of persons active in research and service delivery to older hearing-impaired persons, would be invaluable. Gaps in knowledge and practice about presbycusis could be established. Feasibilities and priorities for next research emphases could be specified. It might even be possible to set up collaborations so that useless duplication might be avoided but useful replication might be cooperatively defined.

Basic biomedical research might be directed initially toward discovery of the etiologies, results of, and possible treatments for the several origins of presbycusis. Do the repeated episodes of decreased pO_2 during the sleep apnea of normal, aging persons adversely affect cochlear hair cells? Which drugs and which drug interactions have permanent effects on hair cell function? Does hair cell degeneration precede loss of auditory nerve cells and nerve fibers in the cochlea, or is the reverse true? Do such degenerations and losses occur independently, or is one causal of the other? Which direction is causality?

Similar kinds of questions are appropriate about CNS components of presbycusis. Where are the CNS lesion(s) associated with the slower transmission of auditory stimuli in old persons as contrasted with young? Is such slowing a general characteristic of CNS function in the old or are there components unique to hearing? Is fiber and cell loss in CNS tracts and ganglia greater in the auditory pathways than in other sensory pathways . . . in sensory pathways than in motor . . . than in association networks? How does hearing loss affect cognitive function in middle-aged and older persons? Does hearing loss exacerbate the development of confusional states in older adults? What are the effects on cortical function when auditory (and other sensory input) to the arousal centers are decreased or absent?

Behavioral and psychosocial research should consider the affective and behavioral concomitants of progressive hearing loss with aging. In particular, the interactions between age, hearing loss, and other psychosocial problems, e.g., suspiciousness, depression, low life satisfaction, isolation, stress, confusional states, and so on should be assessed by contemporary research methodologies. Several bodies of longitudinal data include unanalyzed information about hearing loss and its effect on emotions and behavior. Recognizing the constraints introduced by collection methods, by methods of data storage and by the retrospective nature of the analysis, it seems important to retrieve the extensive information buried in these longitudinal data, accessible at relatively low costs. Their systematic analysis can give significant information about correlations between hearing loss and occupation, geographic region, diet, racial and ethnic group, and so on. Insight from such studies can be used to direct the design of prospective research focused on specific aspects of affective and behavioral effects of hearing impairment in older persons. In particular, new instruments to assess psychosocial function in the elderly should be developed and validated on older populations. Instruments designed for and tested with college students are not appropriate for uncritical use with the middle-aged and old.

The effects of hearing loss on family systems and on communication and relationship patterns within the family deserve intense study. Similar scrutiny should be given to the ways in which adult-onset hearing loss affects work and relationships in the work place, particularly for those approaching retirement age.

Rehabilitative methodologies are difficult to study, primarily because personal style—both of the rehabilitation professional and of the hearing impaired individual—are so intimately involved in outcome. Nonetheless, efforts to supplement classical rehabilitation techniques with supplemental skills, e.g., simplified manual languages such as a simplified Signed English or a simplified cued speech, might add significantly to rehabilitation success. Research into the reasons why so many older persons refuse to use hearing aids is imperative.

Technological research should continue to be directed toward making hearing aids more manageable and tolerable by older persons. In particular, an inexpensive hearing aid is needed which can be operated simply and repaired easily. Procedures for the inexpensive provision of custom-made ear molds for hearing aids are also needed. Continued efforts to develop other assistive devices and alternative listening equipment are needed, with emphasis on reasonable cost as well as on electronic state of the art.

CONCLUSION

Hearing loss in adulthood interferes significantly with communication and is not benign in its effects on the emotional, social or vocational life of many millions of older Americans. Though of high prevalence, hearing impairment is of low concern among most health care professionals. This paper considers some causes of hearing loss, some of its effects, and some ways of coping with the impairment. In particular, the discussion focuses on questions needing research—demographic, biomedical, behavioral, technological—if the deleterious effects of this handicapping condition are to be eased.

REFERENCES

Albert, M. (1977). Stop that quiet—it's driving me mad. *Hearing Rehabilitation Quarterly, 2*, 12–13.

Alpiner, J. G. (1982). Rehabilitation of the geriatric client. In J. G. Alpiner (Ed.), *Handbook of adult rehabilitative audiology* (2nd ed.). (pp. 160–208). Baltimore: Williams and Wilkins.

Ashley, J. (1973). *Journey into silence*. London: Bodley Head.

Ashley, P. K. (in press). Deafness and the family. In H. Orlans & R. Trybus (Eds.), *Hearing loss in adulthood*. San Diego, CA: College Hill Press.

Becker, F. (1980). *Growing old in silence*. Berkeley, CA: University of California Press.

Bergman, M. (1980). *Aging and the perception of speech*. Baltimore: University Park Press.

Bergman, M. (1983). Central disorders of hearing in the elderly. In R. Hinchcliffe (Ed.), *Hearing and balance in the elderly* (pp. 145–158). Edinburgh: Churchill Livingstone.

Berkman, L. F., & Breslow, L. (1983). *Health and ways of living: The Alameda County study*. Oxford: Oxford University Press.

Chafee, C. E. (1967). Rehabilitation needs of nursing home patients: A report of a survey. *Rehabilitation Literature, 28*, 377–381.

Corso, J. F. (1963). Aging and auditory thresholds in men and women. *Archives of Environmental Health, 6*, 56–62.

Corso, J. F. (1977). Auditory perception and communication. In J. E. Birren & K. W. Schaie (Eds.), *Handbook of the psychology of aging* (pp. 535–553).

Cypress, B. K. (1983). Patterns of ambulatory care in general and family practice. *The national ambulatory medical care survey, United States, January 1980–December 1981*. National Center for Health Statistics. Series 13, No. 73. Department of Health and Human Services Pub. No. (83) 1734. Public Health Service. Washington, DC: U.S. Government Printing Office.

Davis, A. (1983). The epidemiology of hearing disorders. In R. Hinchcliffe (Ed.), *Hearing and balance in the elderly* (pp. 1–43). Edinburgh: Churchill Livingstone.

Elliott, H. H. (1978). *Shifting gears*. Paper presented at Workshop for Deafened Adults, San Francisco.

Glass, L. E. (in press-a). Hearing impairment and aging: Some research issues in the next decade. Paper presented at the Ninth Congress of the World Federation of the Deaf, June 30-July 5, 1983, Palermo, Italy.

Glass, L. E. (in press-b). Psychosocial aspects of hearing loss in adulthood. In H. Orlans & R. Trybus (Eds.), *Hearing loss in adulthood*. San Diego, CA: College Hill Press.

Herbst, K. G. (1983). Psycho-social consequences of disorders of hearing in the elderly. In R. Hinchcliffe (Ed.), *Hearing and balance in the elderly* (pp. 174–200). Edinburgh: Churchill Livingstone.

Hull, R. H. (Ed.). (1982). *Rehabilitative audiology*. New York: Grune and Stratton.

Johnsson, L. G., & Hawkins, J. R., Jr. (1979). Age-related degeneration of the inner ear. In S. S. Han & D. H. Coons (Eds.), *Special senses in aging: A current biological assessment* (pp. 119–135). Ann Arbor, MI: University of Michigan, Institute of Gerontology.

Kaplan, H. (1979). Development, composition and problems with elderly aural rehabilitation groups. In M. A. Henoch (Ed.), *Aural rehabilitation for the elderly*. New York: Grune and Stratton.

Kisiel, D. L., Sundaram, K., Capozzelli, M., & Taub, C. F. (1984). Hearing health care for seniors: A national model program. Paper presented at the 1984 ASHA Convention, San Francisco.

Levine, E. (1960). Progressive and sudden hearing loss. In E. Levine (Ed.), *Psychology of deafness* (pp. 56–74). New York: Columbia University Press.

Lien, E. J., Lipsett, L. R., & Lien, L. L. (1983). Ototoxicities. *Journal of Clinical and Hospital Pharmacy, 8*, 15–33.

Luey, H. S. (1980). Between worlds: The problems of deafened adults. *Social Work in Health Care, 5*, 253–265.

Meadow-Orlans, K. P. (in press). Social and psychological consequences of hearing loss in adulthood. In H. Orlans & R. Trybus (Eds.), *Hearing loss in adulthood*. San Diego, CA: College Hill Press.

Menzio, P. (1972). Influence de l'hypoxie sur les phenomenes auditifs. *Journal Francais d' Oto-rhino-laryngologie, 21*, 121–127.

Miller, M., & Ort, R. (1965). Hearing problems in a home for the aged. *Acta Otolaryngologica, 59*, 33–44.

Myklebust, H. R. (1964). *The psychology of deafness* (2nd ed.). New York: Grune and Stratton.

Nguyen, M. (1984). *Denial and follow-up as predictors of outcome among elderly clients screened in a hearing outreach program.* Unpublished doctoral dissertation, California School of Professional Psychology, Berkeley.

Ordy, J. M., Brizzee, K. R., Beavers, T., & Medart, P. (1979). Age differences in the functional and structural organization of the auditory system in man. In J. M. Ordy & K. R. Brizzee (Eds.), *Sensory systems and communication in the elderly* (pp. 153–166). New York: Raven Press.

Orlans, H., & Meadow-Orlans, K. (1984, Sept./Oct.). Who are the members of SHHH? A report on the SHHH questionnaire. *SHHH, 5,* 3–5.

Orlans, H., & Meadow-Orlans, K. (1985, Jan./Feb.). Responses to hearing loss: Effects on social life, leisure and work. *SHHH,6,* 4–7.

Oyer, H. J., Kapur, Y. P., & Deal, L. V. (1976). Hearing disorders in the aging: Effects upon communication. In H. J. Oyer & E. J. Oyer (Eds.), *Aging and communication* (pp. 175–186). Baltimore: University Park Press.

Oyer, H. J., & Oyer, E. J. (in press). Hearing loss in adulthood: Implications for family relationships. In H. Orlans & R. Trybus (Eds.), *Hearing loss in adulthood.* San Diego, CA: College Hill Press.

Pickett, S. N., Bergman, M., & Levitt, H. (1979). Aging and speech understanding. In J. M. Ordey & K. R. Brizzee (Eds.), *Sensory systems and communication in the elderly.* New York: Raven Press.

Ramsdell, D. A. (1978). The psychology of the hard-of-hearing and the deafened adult. In H. Davis & S. R. Silverman (Eds.), *Hearing and Deafness* (4th ed.) (pp. 499–510). New York: Holt, Rhinehart and Winston.

Ries, P. W. (1982). Hearing ability of persons by sociodemographic and health characteristics: United States. *Vital and health statistics.* Series 10, No. 140. Department of Health and Human Services Pub. No. (PHS) 82-1568. Public Health Service, National Center for Health Statistics. Washington, DC: U.S. Government Printing Office.

Ries, P. W. (in press). The demography of hearing loss. In H. Orlans & R. Trybus (Eds.), *Hearing loss in adulthood.* San Diego, CA: College Hill Press.

Rosen, J. K. (1979). Psychological and social aspects of the evaluation of acquired hearing impairment. *Audiology, 18,* 238–252.

Rybak, L. P. (1982). Pathophysiology of furosemide ototoxicity. *Journal of Otolaryngology, 11,* 127–133.

Schow, R. L., Christensen, J. M., Hutchinson, J. M., & Nerbonne, M. A. (1978). *Communication disorders of the aged* (pp. 75–93, 161–178). Baltimore: University Park Press.

Schuknecht, H. F. (1964). Further observations on the pathology of presbycusis. *Archives of Otolaryngology, 80,* 369–382.

Self Help for Hard of Hearing People, Inc. (SHHH). (1984). Assistive listening devices and systems (ALDS) and you: A series of six pamphlets. Bethesda, MD: SHHH.

Stephens, S. D. G., & Goldstein, D. P. (1983). Auditory rehabilitation for the elderly. In R. Hinchcliffe (Ed.), *Hearing and balance in the elderly* (pp. 201–226). Edinburgh: Churchill Livingstone.

Thomas, P. D., Hunt, W. C., Garry, P. J., Hood, R. B., Goodwin, J. M., & Goodwin, J. S. (1983). Hearing acuity in a healthy elderly population: Effects on emotional, cognitive and social status. *Journal of Gerontology, 38,* 321–325.

U.S. Department of Health and Human Services. Public Health Service. National Institutes of Health. (1982). *Inventory of federally supported research on aging (selected agencies).* (Administrative Document). Washington, DC: National Institute on Aging.

Ventry, I. M., & Weinstein, B. E. (1982). The new hearing handicap inventory for the elderly: A new tool. *Ear and Hearing, 3,* 128–134.

Ventry, I. M., & Weinstein, B. E. (1983). Identification of elderly people with hearing problems. *ASHA, 25,* 37–42.

Watts, W. J. (Ed.) (1983). *Rehabilitation and acquired deafness.* Worcester, MA: Billing and Sons.

Wax, T. (1982). The hearing impaired aged: Double jeopardy or double challenge? *Gallaudet Today, 12,* 3–7.

Weinstein, B. E. (1984). Management of the hearing impaired elderly. In L. Condit-Jacobs (Ed.), *Gerontology and communication disorders* (pp. 244–279). Rockville, MD: American Speech-Language-Hearing Association.

Weinstein, B. E., & Ventry, I. M. (1982). Hearing impairment and social isolation in the elderly. *Journal of Speech and Hearing Research, 25,* 593–599.

Part IV

Organ Impairment

15

Rehabilitation of the Elderly Cardiac Patient

Hank L. Brammel

Diseases of the heart and blood vessels comprise the major medical problem in the United States at this time (American Heart Association, 1984). Almost a million persons each year die from one of these illnesses, almost as many deaths as by cancer, accidents, pneumonia, and all other causes combined. Approximately 4.6 million persons in the United States have coronary artery disease, the most important cardiovascular disease in terms of mortality. There will be approximately 1.5 million acute myocardial infarctions this year in the United States, and approximately 550,000 persons will die. Most of the deaths, greater than two-thirds, will be in the older population.

Coronary artery disease prevalence increases with advancing age and is the commonest cause of death in old people (Caird & Kennedy, 1976). In large epidemiologic studies in the United States (Epstein et al., 1965; McDonough, Hames, Stulb, & Garrison, 1965), coronary artery disease can be detected in from 10% to 30% of the elderly population. Kennedy, Andrews, and Caird (1977), in a smaller study in Scotland, reported a 22.4% prevalence of coronary artery disease in persons living at home, 65 years of age and older. Mihalick and Fisch (1974), in an electrocardiographic study of elderly persons living free or hospitalized for noncardiac disease, reported evidence of coronary artery disease in 49% of that special population. Coronary artery disease is not the only cardiovascular condition seen in the elderly, but it is the disease that will most commonly result in consideration of, and perhaps referral to, a cardiac rehabilitation program. Other cardiovascular diseases that are seen in the elderly and that might prompt referral to the rehabilitation program include hypertensive heart disease, cor pulmonale, myocardial amyloidosis, rheumatic heart disease, viral heart disease, nonrheumatic aortic valve disease, and thyroid heart disease. Congenital heart disease is rare but not unheard of in the elderly. Older patients who have had cardiac surgery are excellent and appropriate candidates for referral to the cardiac rehabilitation program. The most common cardiac surgery procedures performed on elderly patients are myocardial revascularization through coronary artery bypass grafting, aortic valve replacement, and pacemaker implantation for high degrees of heart block or sinus mode dysfunction.

CARDIOVASCULAR EFFECTS OF AGING

It is often difficult to determine accurately those changes that are due solely to the irrevocable passage of time. Separating disease-related changes from those resulting from age or disuse has been, and continues to be, a challenge for investigators.

Gross morphologic changes that have been ascribed to aging include darkening of the color of the myocardium resulting from an increase in lipofuscin pigment, thickening of the endocardium and valves (greater on the left side of the heart than the right), and stiffening and calcification of the heart's fibrous skeleton. Heart size does not change, or may decrease slightly. Microscopic examination of the aged heart shows an increase in collagen and elastic fibers, and atrophy, fragmentation, and sporadic hypertrophy of individual muscle fibers (Burch, 1975).

Physiologic changes attributed to the aging process are a reduction, at maximal effort, of heart rate (Astrand, Astrand, & Rodahl, 1959), stroke volume, cardiac output (Granath, Jonsson, & Strandell, 1964), oxygen comsumption (Dill, Horvath, & Crain, 1958; Dehn & Bruce, 1972; Astrand, Astrand, Hallback, & Kilbone, 1973), and the arteriovenous oxygen content difference (Julius, Antoon, Whitlock, et al., 1967). As a result, there is a reduced physical work capacity. Although there is an age-related decrease in lung function, this does not seem to be the factor that limits physical work capacity. In addition, there is an increase in peripheral vascular resistance and a failure of the left-ventricular ejection fraction to increase with exercise in normal sedentary persons over the age of 60 years (Port, Cobb, Coleman, & Jones, 1980). The cause of these physiologic changes with aging has not been clarified. Some of these changes, e.g., reduced VO_{2max}, can be partially reversed by conditioning, suggesting that disuse may account for some of the changes attributed to age (Robinson et al., 1973).

Animal studies have shown a reduced inotropic response to catecholamines (Lakatta, Gerstenblith, Angell, Shock, & Weisfeldt, 1975) and reduced left-ventricular compliance (Templeton, Platt, Willerson, & Weisfeldt, 1979). In addition, there is increased impedance to left-ventricular emptying, and prolonged contraction duration with aging. The lower stroke volume response during exercise is minimized by administering propranolol in humans (Conway, Wheeler, & Sannerstedt, 1971), suggesting that a reduced sympathetic response in the elderly is the cause of the decrease in submaximal cardiac output (Weisfeldt, 1980).

CARDIAC REHABILITATION AND THE ELDERLY

Cardiac rehabilitation is the process of restoring and maintaining a cardiac patient to his/her optimal physiologic, psychosocial, vocational, and educational status. Rehabilitation activities are conducted in three phases, and an individual patient may be enrolled in the program at any phase, depending upon the specific clinical situation.

Phase 1 activities occur during hospitalization for an acute cardiac event. Major tasks during this phase of rehabilitation include patient and family education, progressive ambulation, psychosocial and vocational assessment, and intervention, as needed. Current practice dictates early ambulation and discharge, usually within 8 to 14 days following an uncomplicated myocardial infarction (Wenger, Hellerstein, Blackburn, & Castranova, 1982). The goal of progressive ambulation during hospitalization is to have a functionally independent patient, at least for activities of daily living, at the time of discharge. Mock (1977) has complained that elderly patients are kept at bed rest longer than younger patients and that some physicians believe that advanced age renders the patient unfit to participate in an exercise or rehabilitation program. Some (Williams, Begg, Semple, & McGuinness, 1976), but not all (Berman, 1979), authors have noted longer treatment periods in the coronary care unit and longer hospitalizations following myocardial infarction in patients over age 70.

The practice of increasing the duration of bed rest and withholding more aggressive ambulation and exercise programs from elderly patients may lead to a greater degree of cardiovascular deconditioning, an extended convalescence, greater dependency, and, quite likely, may result in an increase in discharges to nursing homes, rather than to independent living. These issues, however, have not been explored in a systematic fashion.

Phase 2 is the early post-hospitalization rehabilitation program, which usually begins within 2 weeks of discharge from the hospital. The program typically lasts 12 weeks. The major activity of Phase 2 is supervised, often telemetry-monitored, exercise conditioning. A comprehensive patient and family educational program generally accompanies the exercise training activity. In addition, stress management, behavior modification, coronary disease risk factor identification and modification, and psychosocial and vocational/avocational assessment and intervention activities may be pursued as indicated.

Phase 3 is the long-term maintenance program, which begins on completion of Phase 2. The exercise program is community-based and is commonly not medically supervised. Other program activities are maintained and reinforced, with the goal of achieving an optimal status in each area of real or potential disability.

COMPONENTS OF CARDIAC REHABILITATION

Activities that occur in all phases of a cardiac rehabilitation program can be assigned to one or more program components. These components define areas of effort which, if properly and comprehensively addressed, will optimize the patient's condition, minimize disability, and lead to what one hopes is the best rehabilitation outcome for each person.

The major components of a cardiac rehabilitation program are (a) physiologic, (b) psychosocial, (c) vocational, and (d) educational. Each component will be discussed briefly, with special emphasis on the elderly cardiac patient.

Physiologic Component

Activities within this component are designed to enhance body function of the person with heart disease. There are three major elements within the physiologic component of a cardiac rehabilitation program: medical and surgical management, activity counseling, and nutrition.

Medical and Surgical Management

High-quality traditional medical and surgical care is necessary if an optimal rehabilitation outcome is to be realized. The efforts of the family practitioner, internist, geriatrician, cardiologist, and cardiac surgeon are directed toward the identification of physiologic sources of disability. These usually include chest pain, heart failure, and symptoms associated with abnormalities of heart rhythm.

In the elderly, the diagnosis of angina pectoris may be difficult. Quite often, a history of classic retrosternal pressure, squeezing, tightness, or heaviness will not be present. Dyspnea with exertion, or pain in the arms, shoulder, back, or hands may reflect myocardial ischemia and not the presence of chronic lung disease, heart failure, or arthritis (Rothbaum, 1981).

Arrhythmias often do not cause palpitations. Symptoms may occur in any organ that is underperfused as a result of a rhythm disturbance. Arrhythmias must be considered in otherwise unexplained central nervous system symptoms, abdominal pain, episodic angina, or heart failure.

In addition to cardiac problems, other associated and complicating conditions such as hypertension and diabetes must be sought. Once these conditions are identified, medical and/or surgical management approaches are decided on and implemented. Quality medical care should remove or minimize symptoms and the attendant disability.

Medical management of the elderly cardiac patient must be approached with some caution, however. Some physiologic changes associated with aging will influence management decisions (Moser, 1982). The net effect of these changes is that the use of drugs must be approached with great care. The elderly patient is sensitive to blood volume changes and sudden changes in blood pressure. In addition, because of the frequent reduction in lean body mass and decreased glomerular filtration, drug doses must be reduced to avoid toxic effects. Whenever possible, it is appropriate to consider nondrug management of specific medical problems of the elderly as the first-line therapeutic effort. If drugs must be used, they should be used with care and caution, and nonpharmacologic management should not be neglected as an important adjunct to drug treatment.

Cardiac surgery may be undertaken in the elderly patient, although with increased risk of mortality (3% to 12%) (Garcia, Cheauvechai, & Effler, 1975; Ashor et al., 1973) and postoperative complications. The major determinant of survival in elderly patients who undergo myocardial revascularization is left ventricular function. Evidence of left ventricular failure is a clear indicator of increased surgical risk (Jolly, Isch, & Shumacker, 1981). Symptomatic improvement occurs in a high percentage of elderly patients who undergo myocardial revascularization and survive the procedure (Garcia, Cheauvechai, & Effler, 1975; Tucker, Lindsmith, Stiles, Hughes, & Meyer, 1977). Data are lacking regarding the effect of revascularization on the natural history of coronary disease in the elderly.

Other cardiac conditions in which surgery may be an important aspect of rehabilitative care include complete heart block (pacemaker implantation) and aortic stenosis (aortic valve replacement).

Activity Counseling

For the person with heart disease, activity is prescribed much like medication. Unfortunately, there is no pharmacopaeia of exercise, and therefore each prescription must be individualized. In order to do this in a rational and safe manner, each patient's response to exercise is observed during functional capacity assessment, usually on a motor-driven treadmill. Once this has been done, an appropriate activity prescription can be written for work, recreation, and exercise conditioning.

Aerobic exercise conditioning is the cornerstone of most, if not all, Phase 2 and Phase 3 cardiac rehabilitation programs. Although many practitioners do not promote exercise for the elderly, interest in exercise for this age group is increasing and its effects are being documented. The 1981 National Conference on Fitness and Aging, sponsored by The President's Council on Physical Fitness and Sports, emphasized the value of fitness for older and aging persons.

It is clear that older persons can obtain training effects similar to those of younger individuals (DeVries, 1970; Kasch et al., 1973; Seals, Hagberg, Hurley, Ehsani, & Holloszy, 1984). Submaximal heart rate and blood pressure is reduced, aerobic capacity (VO_{2max}), stroke volume, cardiac output, physical work capacity, and endurance may increase. The reduction in heart rate and systolic blood pressure is particularly important for patients with angina pectoris, since the rate-pressure product (heart rate × systolic blood pressure) is directly related to myocardial oxygen demand (Kitamura, Jorgensen, Gobel, Taylor, & Wang, 1972). Persons with stable angina pectoris will develop chest discomfort at a reproducible rate-pressure product (Robinson, 1967). Exercise conditioning may not change the rate-pressure product at which angina occurs, but the workload at which the critical value is reached will be greater following training than before. Thus, conditioning increases the workload and therefore the number of tasks that can be accomplished before myocardial ischemia occurs. In this way, the ability to perform self-care tasks and activities may be prolonged if the exercise program is continued.

It is appropriate to consider the exercise conditioning program as an important aspect of the maintenance of independent living for elderly cardiac patients. Almost all activities of daily living can be performed at a workload of 4 METs or less (1 MET = the energy cost at seated rest $\cong$ 3.5 cc/min/kg O_2 consumption). This corresponds to a New York Heart Association functional Class 3 level of activity, a level that is achievable for most elderly cardiac patients. As long as mental competence is sustained, elderly patients who can perform at 4 METs, even for a short time, should be able to live independently and remain out of a nursing home.

Other potential benefits of exercise in the elderly include a decrease in body fat and an increase in lean body mass (DeVries, 1970; Sidney, Shepherd, & Harrison, 1977). Triglycerides and low density lipoprotein have been reported to fall during training after myocardial infarction, and high density lipoproteins may rise (Ballantyne, Clark, Simpson, & Ballantyne, 1982). The effect of these changes in lipids on the natural history of coronary artery disease is not clear. In addition, exercise conditioning improves carbohydrate metabolism (Bjorntorp et al., 1972), may correct glucose intolerance, and typically will improve blood sugar control in diabetic patients.

Psychological benefits of exercise are seen in elderly as well as younger participants. Self-image is improved, a more positive approach toward life is obtained (Council on Scientific Affairs, 1984), and the ability to handle stress may improve as well (Freidrich, 1977). Of particular benefit is the observation that physically fit elderly persons have faster reaction times and more rapid muscular movement than sedentary controls (Spirduso, 1980). Fit older persons should, therefore, be better able to avoid, or to cope with, daily hazards in their environment.

The above discussion of the effect of exercise in elderly persons is based on data largely obtained from subjects who are apparently well. There is very little information on persons known to have heart disease. Of course, because coronary artery disease is so prevalent in the elderly (Caird & Kennedy, 1976; Epstein et al., 1965; McDonough et al., 1965; Kennedy et al., 1977; Mihalick & Fisch, 1974) some of the subjects studied must have had asymptomatic disease. In addition, because younger cardiac patients can obtain a training effect similar to that seen in normal persons (Varnauskas, Bergman, Honk, & Bjorntorp, 1966) it could be argued that most elderly cardiac patients will obtain training benefit similar to their apparently well counterparts.

There are no data regarding the effect of exercise on the development of coronary collaterals, disease progression, or the natural history of coronary disease in elderly patients.

Nutrition

For patients with heart disease, specific nutritional prescriptions or guidelines are often required. The cardiac patient may require a prescription designed to decrease body fat and change body composition, to reduce sodium intake for those with hypertension or heart failure, or to manage specific abnormalities of blood lipids (unusually high blood cholesterol, triglyceride, or both). Diet is an important, and may be the only, management tool required for control of glucose intolerance.

For elderly cardiac patients, vigorous nutritional changes are often not indicated or necessary. Because cholesterol and elevated triglyceride levels are not risk factors for coronary disease in persons 65 years old or older (Kannel & Gordon, 1978), intense efforts to modify these lipids by diet or drugs are not indicated. Any nutritional recommendations should be made on the basis of identified problems whose management can be improved by dietary change: diabetes, heart failure, hypertension.

It is particularly important for the elderly cardiac patient to eat a nutritionally balanced diet. Education activities directed toward insuring a balanced diet and providing tips on how to stretch the food dollar are often helpful for elderly patients.

Psychosocial Component

Psychosocial issues are of great importance in cardiac rehabilitation and can have a significant effect on the rehabilitation outcome. The most common emotional responses to heart attack are anxiety and/or depression (Hackett & Cassem, 1973; Cay, Vetter, & Philips, 1973). For many, these responses are transient and do not impede a return to normal living. Patients who, before the acute illness, were more apt to have an extended untoward emotional response, considered themselves to be more disabled and returned to full normal vocational activity much less often than patients who had demonstrated good coping skills prior to the heart attack (Cay et al., 1973). Inability to cope with stress, financial trouble, marital or job discord, or unhealthful behaviors (e.g., cigarette smoking, poor eating habits) may therefore delay or prevent a successful rehabilitation effort.

Denial has been shown to be a valuable psychological mechanism to cope with the anxiety and depression associated with acute cardiac illness such as myocardial infarction. Patients who are successful deniers have a lower hospital mortality and improved vocational outcome following infarction (Hackett, Cassem, & Wishnie, 1968; Stern, Pascale, & Ackerman, 1977). Areas of potential psychosocial disability must be sought and appropriate management plans developed when needed.

Unfortunately, there is very little information known regarding psychosocial issues in elderly cardiac patients. It is clear that many of these patients do not do well when provided with only routine follow-up care. Gray has observed that a large portion of elderly cardiac patients express passive hopelessness and resignation to a life of dependency and incapacity (Gray, Reinhardt, & Ward, 1969). Peach and Pathy (1978; Pathy & Peach, 1980) documented the degree of disability among elderly patients following myocardial infarction. All patients in the 100-person cohort were over 65 years old, and more than half were over 75 years old. None of the patients were enrolled in a comprehensive cardiac rehabilitation program. At 3 months following the infarction, more than half of the patients admitted feelings of anxiety or depression, fewer than one-quarter could perform the household chores or social activities undertaken prior to the illness, and roughly half (48%) could not walk 100 yards on the flat. Follow-up 3 years after the heart attack revealed that 47 had died. The survivors ranged in age from 69 to 88, with an average age of 79 years. There had been no improvement in the survivors outcome: half were anxious, one-third were depressed, there was no improvement in walking performance, two-thirds were unable to perform household chores or participate in social activities as they would have liked to do.

It seems clear that early disability following myocardial infarction in the elderly will not be corrected spontaneously. The role of comprehensive cardiac rehabilitation or other services in improving this dismal prospect for elderly patients needs to be investigated.

Of the unhealthful behaviors that might lend themselves to management by behavior modification, cigarette smoking deserves a special word. The data regarding cigarette smoking as a risk factor for coronary disease are not consistent. The Framingham study (Kannel & Gordon, 1978) indicates that cigarette smoking is not a risk factor for the development of coronary artery disease in persons over 65 years, whereas hypertension, left ventricular hypertrophy, elevated low-density lipoproteins, and reduced high-density lipoproteins are significant risk factors. On the other hand, Kennedy, et al. (1977), in their Glasgow study, stated that cigarette smoking was the only factor associated with ischemic heart disease events in persons over 65 years. The cholesterol and blood pressure levels had no relationship. However, the evidence that cigarette smoking is a risk factor for sudden cardiac death is more compelling and provides justification for smoking cessation efforts.

Very little systematic work has been done in the area of psychosocial concerns of the elderly cardiac patient. Areas of psychosocial disability need to be defined, management approaches identified and implemented, and changes in outcome documented. Pertinent research questions include the following: What is the usual emotional response to acute cardiac illness in elderly patients? How long does it last? Does it affect the duration of hospitalization or the return to normal activities? Does it affect the attending physician's practice regarding the use of medication, duration of hospital stay, or referral to a rehabilitation program? What are the most effective interventions and when should they be employed? Do personality, mood, and education affect outcome for the elderly cardiac patient? Does modification of certain unhealthful behaviors affect outcome? Is stress important and does stress management help the elderly cardiac patient? What stress management techniques work best? What is the role of the family and community institutions in the rehabilitation process?

Vocational Component

For the younger cardiac patient, return to work often defines a successful rehabilitation outcome. Indeed, it is reasonable to expect the postinfarction patient to return to work. The usual expectation is that 70% to 80% will return to work following infarction (Mitchell, 1980), although percentages approaching (Shapiro, Weinblatt, & Frank, 1976) or exceeding 90% (Brammell, Henritze, Wolfel, & Morton, in preparation) have been noted.

Vocational issues are less important for the elderly cardiac patient and the rehabilitation team. The number of elderly persons in the work force is declining (Woodruff & Birren, 1975). In 1959, 45.8% of those 65 years old and older were part of the work force. In 1971, the figure was 25.5%. The type of work a patient performs will, to a certain degree, affect the probability of the older employee returning to work. After age 60, there is a marked fall-off of return-to-work rates for manual and clerical workers, whereas older businessmen and professionals return to work in substantial numbers (Sigler, 1967). Nevertheless, advancing age alone is a negative factor regarding return to work, at least following acute myocardial infarction or coronary artery bypass grafting (Barnes, Ray, Oberman, & Kouchoukos, 1977; Anderson, Barboriak, Hoffman, & Mullen, 1980).

When the elderly cardiac patient returns to work, the job evaluation and prescription for work should be approached in the usual manner. A work history is obtained, physical and nonphysical aspects of the work are assessed, and often the supervisor is interviewed. Potential modifiers of the work prescription are sought, necessary job modifications are recommended and implemented, the employee is taught to monitor activity intensity at work, and he or she reenters the workforce at an appropriate time. The effect of time off work on return-to-work rates following myocardial infarction, coronary artery bypass grafting, or other major cardiac events, has not been studied. One would expect that the effect would be substantial, as it is in younger cardiac patients who are unlikely to return to work after 6 months' layoff and almost never return to work if out of work 1 year or more (Shapiro et al., 1976).

Vocational questions yet to be answered regarding the employable elderly cardiac patient include: What is the role of the physician, family, employer, medication, complications, and unemployment compensation, in reaching a decision that the elderly cardiac patient will not return to work? What are employee attitudes and practices regarding elderly cardiac employees? Do they need to be changed? If so, how? In the case of cardiac surgery, would preoperative counseling improve the likelihood of returning to work? Should counseling include the spouse/family and employer as well as the patient? Is there a difference in return-to-work rates between self-employed elderly and those employed by others? What psychosocial issues affect reemployment in this group?

Educational Component

There have been no prospective investigations regarding educational needs or best approaches for elderly cardiac patients. It seems fair to assume that the elderly patient has as great a need for information as do younger patients. There is some evidence that providing information or emotional support can help patients handle the crisis of coronary care following heart attack and can reduce the stay in the hospital (Mumford, Schlesinger, & Glass, 1982). Although this analysis did not address the elderly specifically, it suggests the benefit of simple interventions that should be beneficial to all ages.

The goals of the educational program for the elderly cardiac patient should be to enhance understanding of procedures, medications, and so on; to increase compliance with the therapeutic and rehabilitative regimen; and to enhance independence and self-reliance. Topics that should be appropriate for an educational program for older cardiac patients include the following:

Medications—what for, side effects, importance of taking as prescribed, some tricks to help you to take them on time
Warning signals—what they are, what they mean, what to do about them and when, how to get into the health care system quickly
Nutrition—emphasizing items important to the elderly
Staying fit—how, where, when, why; activity in the cold, at altitude, when the air is bad, when it's hot

Some researchable issues regarding education of the elderly cardiac patient are: What is the effect of education on adherence to the medical regimen or recommended life style changes? What are the major educational needs of this group? Are currently available educational materials acceptable to the elderly? Are they relevant? What reinforcement schedules are necessary and work best? Is there a best time/worst time to begin the educational effort? How does emotional status affect retention? What is the minimal content required to achieve educational goals?

SUMMARY

Elderly patients with cardiac disease should not be kept from participating in a comprehensive cardiac rehabilitation program. The goals of cardiac rehabilitation for the elderly are to promote and extend independent living, increase confidence, enhance the quality of the patient's life, and minimize disability from any source. The program is not specifically designed to modify the natural history of the underlying disease (usually atherosclerosis) or to make the disease remit. If this seems to occur, it should be counted as an unexpected benefit. Modification of natural history or disease progression should never be promised a patient.

Much remains to be learned about rehabilitation of the elderly. Important research questions need to be answered in each component area of the rehabilitation program. These answers will permit better use of rehabilitation resources, more client-specific services, and improved outcomes for each person served.

REFERENCES

American Heart Association. (1984). *Heart facts*. Dallas, TX: Author.

Anderson, A. F., Barboriak, J. J., Hoffman, R. G., & Mullen, D. C. (1980). Retention or resumption of employment after aortocoronary bypass operations. *Journal of the American Medical Association, 243*, 543–545.

Ashor, G. W., Meyer, B. W., Lindesmith, G. G., Stiles, Q. R., Walker, G. H., & Tucker, B. L. (1973). Coronary artery disease. Surgery in 100 patients 65 years of age or older. *Archives of Surgery, 107*, 30–33.

Astrand, I., Astrand, P. O., Hallback, I., & Kilbone, A. (1973). Reduction in maximal oxygen uptake with age. *Journal of Applied Physiology, 35*, 649–654.

Astrand, I., Astrand, P. O., & Rodahl, K. (1959). Maximal heart rate during work in older men. *Journal of Applied Physiology, 14*, 562–66.

Ballantyne, F. C., Clark, R. S., Simpson, H. S., & Ballantyne, D. (1982). The effect of moderate physical exercise on the plasma lipoprotein subfraction of male survivors of myocardial infarction. *Circulation, 65*, 913–918.

Barnes, G. K., Ray, M. J., Oberman, A., & Kouchoukos, N. T. (1977). Changes in work status of patients following coronary bypass surgery. *Journal of the American Medical Association, 238*, 1259–1262.

Berman, N. D. (1979). The elderly patient in the coronary unit. I. Acute myocardial infarction. *Journal of the American Geriatrics Society, 27*, 145–151.

Bjorntorp, P., Berchtold, P., Grimby, G., Lindholm, B., Sanne, H., Tibblin, G., & Wilhelmsen, L. (1972). Effects of physical training on glucose tolerance, plasma insulin and lipids and on body composition in men after myocardial infarction. *Acta Medica Scandinavica, 192*, 439–443.

Brammell, H. L., Henritze, J., Wolfel, E. E., & Morton, M. (in preparation). An industrial cardiac rehabilitation program. Preliminary observations.

Burch, G. E. (1975). Interesting aspects of geriatric cardiology. *American Heart Journal, 89*, 99–114.

Caird, F. I., & Kennedy, R. D. (1976). Epidemiology of heart disease in old age. In F. I. Caird (Ed.), *Cardiology in old age* (p. 1). New York and London: Plenum Press.

Cay, E. L., Vetter, N. J., & Philips, A. E. (1973). Practical aspects of cardiac rehabilitation: Psychosocial factors. *Giorn It Card, 3*, 646–655.

Conway, J., Wheeler, R., & Sannerstedt, R. (1971). Sympathetic nervous activity during exercise in relation to age. *Cardiovascular Research, 5*, 577–581.

Council on Scientific Affairs. (1984). Exercise programs for the elderly. *Journal of the American Medical Association, 252*, 544–546.

Dehn, M. M., & Bruce, R. A. (1972). Longitudinal variations in maximal oxygen uptake with age and activity. *Journal of Applied Physiology, 23*, 805–807.

DeVries, H. A. (1970). Physiological effects of an exercise training regimen upon men aged 52 to 88. *Journal of Gerontology, 25,* 325–336.

Dill, D. B., Horvath, S. M., & Crain, F. N. (1958). Response to exercise as related to age. *Journal of Applied Physiology, 12,* 195–196.

Epstein, F. H., Ostrander, L. D., Johnson, B. C., Payne, M. W., Hayner, N. S., Keller, J. B., & Francis, T. (1965). Epidemiologic studies of cardiovascular disease in a total community—Tecumseh, MI. *Annals of Internal Medicine, 62,* 1170–1187.

Freidrich, J. A. (1977). Tension control techniques to combat stress. In R. Harris & L. J. Frankel (Eds.), *Guide to fitness after fifty* (pp. 323–338). New York: Plenum Press.

Garcia, J. M., Cheauvechai, C., & Effler, D. B. (1975). Myocardial revascularization in patients age 65 and older. *Cardiovascular Clinics, 3*(1), 83–91.

Granath, A., Jonsson, B., & Strandell, T. (1965). Circulation in healthy old men studied by right heart catheterization at rest and during exercise in supine and sitting position. *Acta Medica Scandinavica, 176,* 425–446.

Gray, R. M., Reinhardt, A. M., & Ward, J. R. (1969). *Rehabilitation Literature, 30,* 354.

Hackett, T. D., & Cassem, N. H. (1973). Psychological adaptation to convalescence in myocardial infarction patients. In J. Naughton, H. K. Hellerstein, & I. C. Mohler (Eds.), *Exercise testing and exercise training in coronary heart disease* (p. 253). New York: Academic Press.

Hackett, T. P., Cassem, N. H., & Wishnie, H. A. (1968). The coronary care unit: an appraisal of its psychological hazards. *New England Journal of Medicine, 279,* 1365–1370.

Jolly, W. W., Isch, J. H., & Shumacker, H. B. (1981). Cardiac surgery in the elderly. In R. J. Nobel & D. A. Rothbaum (Eds.), *Geriatric cardiology* (pp. 202–203). Philadelphia: F. A. Davis.

Julius, S., Antoon, A., Whitlock, L. S., et al. (1967). Influence of age on the hemodynamic response to exercise. *Circulation, 36,* 222–230.

Kannel, W. B., & Gordon, T. (1978). Evaluation of cardiovascular risk in the elderly. The Framingham Study. *Bulletin of the New York Academy of Medicine, 54,* 573–591.

Kasch, F. W., Phillips, W. H., Carter, J. E. L., et al. (1973). Cardiovascular changes in middle-aged men during two years of training. *Journal of Applied Physiology, 34,* 53–57.

Kennedy, R. D., Adrews, G. R., & Caird, F. I. (1977). Ischaemic heart disease in the elderly. *British Heart Journal, 39,* 1121–1127.

Kitamura, K., Jorgensen, C. R., Gobel, F. L., Taylor, H. L., & Wang, Y. (1972). Hemodynamic correlates of myocardial oxygen consumption during upright exercise. *Journal of Applied Physiology, 32,* 516–522.

Lakatta, E. G., Gerstenblith, G., Angell, C. S., Shock, N. W., & Weisfeldt, M. L. (1975). Diminished inotropic response of aged myocardium to catecholamines. *Circ Res, 36,* 262–269.

McDonough, J. R., Hames, C. G., Stulb, S. C., & Garrison, G. E. (1965). Coronary heart disease among Negroes and whites in Evans County, Georgia. *Journal of Chronic Diseases, 18,* 443–468.

Mihalick, M. G., & Fisch, C. (1974). Electrocardiographic findings in the aged. *American Heart Journal, 87,* 117–128.

Mitchell, D. K., (1980). Principles of vocational rehabilitation: A contemporary view. In C. Long (Ed.), *Prevention and rehabilitation in ischemic heart disease* (p. 316). Baltimore: Williams and Wilkins.

Mock, M. B. (1977). Rehabilitation of the elderly cardiac patient hampered by bias. *Geriatrics, 32*(13), 22–23.

Moser, M. (1982). The management of cardiovascular disease in the elderly. *Journal of the American Geriatrics Society, 30*(11), 520–529.

Mumford, E., Schlesinger, H. J., & Glass, G. V. (1982). The effects of psychological intervention on recovery from surgery and heart attacks: An analysis of the literature. *American Journal of Public Health, 72,* 141–151.

Pathy, M. S., & Peach, H. (1980). Disability among the elderly after myocardial infarction: A 3-year follow-up. *Journal of the Royal College of Physicians of London, 14,* 221–223.

Peach, H., and Pathy, J. (1978). Disability in the elderly after myocardial infarction. *Journal of the Royal College of Physicians of London, 13,* 154–157.

Port, S., Cobb, F. R., Coleman, R. E., & Jones, R. H. (1980). Effect of age on the response of the left ventricular ejection fraction to exercise. *New England Journal of Medicine, 303,* 1133–1137.

Robinson, B. F. (1967). Relation of heart rate and systolic blood pressure to the onset of pain in angina pectoris. *Circulation, 35,* 1073–1083.

Robinson, S., Dill, D. B., Ross, J. C., Robinson, R. D., Wagner, J. A., & Tzankoff, S. P. (1973). Training and physiological aging in man. *Federation Proceedings, 32,* 1628–1634.

Rothbaum, D. A. (1981). Coronary artery disease. In R. J. Nobel & D. A. Rothbaum (Eds.), *Geriatric cardiology* (pp. 105–106). Philadelphia: F. A. Davis.

Seals, D. R., Hagberg, J. M., Hurley, B. F., Ehsani, A. A. & Holloszy, J. O. (1984). Endurance training in older men and women. I. Cardiovascular responses to exercise. *Journal of Applied Physiology, 57,* 1024–1029.

Shapiro, S., Weinblatt, E., & Frank, C. W. (1976). Return to work after the first myocardial infarction. *Archives of Environmental Health, 24,* 17–26.

Sidney, K. H., Shepherd, R. J., & Harrison, J. E., (1977). Endurance training and body composition of the elderly *American Journal of Clinical Nutrition, 30,* 326–333.

Sigler, L. H. (1967). Reemployment of the elderly cardiac. *Geriatrics, 22,* 97–105.

Spirduso, W. W. (1980). Physical fitness, aging and psychomotor speed: A review. *Journal of Gerontology, 35,* 850–865.

Stern, M. J., Pascale, L., & Ackerman, A. (1977). Life adjustment postmyocardial infarction: Determining predictive values. *Archives of Internal Medicine, 137,* 1680–1685.

Templeton, G. H., Platt, M. R., Willerson, J. T., & Weisfeldt, M. L. (1979). Influence of aging on left ventricular hemodynamics and stiffness in beagles. *Circulation Research, 44,* 189–194.

Tucker, B. L., Lindsmith, G. G., Stiles, Q. R., Hughes, R. K., & Meyer, B. W. (1977). Myocardial revascularization in patients 70 years of age and older. *Western Journal of Medicine, 126,* 179–183.

Varnauskas, E., Bergman, H., Honk, P., & Bjorntorp, P. (1966). Haemodynamic effect of physical training in coronary patients. *Lancet, 2*, 8–12.

Weisfeldt, L. (1980). Aging of the cardiovascular system. *New England Journal of Medicine, 303*, 1172–1174.

Wenger, N. K., Hellerstein, H. K., Blackburn, H., & Castranova, S. J. (1982). Physician practice in the management of patients with uncomplicated myocardial infarction: Changes in the past decade. *Circulation, 65*, 421–427.

Williams, B. O., Begg, T. B., Semple, T., & McGuinness, J. B. (1976). The elderly in a coronary unit. *British Medical Journal, 2*, 451–453.

Woodruff, D. S., & Birren, J. E. (Eds.). (1975). *Aging. Scientific perspectives and social issues*, 59. New York: Van Nostrand Reinhold.

16

Stroke and Rehabilitation

Paul E. Kaplan

As the mean life span has increased from 47 to 73 years, complications and sequellae surrounding chronic disease have become major contributors to premature mortality. Once chronic disease develops, it cannot be cured. Therefore, the focus of medical care has shifted toward those measures which in any one population will significantly delay the establishment of the pathogenic processes. Chronic disease will thus be ameliorated or prevented, and morbidity from a specific entity will be lowered. The application of measures to alleviate impairment from chronic disease constitutes rehabilitation. Preventive rehabilitation modifies, delays, or eliminates the onset of the impairment. In time, by enhancing the efficiency of medical and surgical treatment, we further augment preventive rehabilitation effectiveness.

BASIC SCIENCES

Neocortic structures of the central nervous system are the most susceptible to damage as result of stroke because blood vessels, like those of the heart, are relatively small muscular end-arteries. The pyramidal tract generated from the regions most commonly affected sends 55% of its fibers to cervical levels. Anastomotic circulation is regulated by genetic and congenital factors and is not usually noted until after an occlusion has occurred. As a result, when anastomotic circulation does occur, it does so only in response to a dire need and usually presents a byway for anterior cerebral artery circulation to those cells controlling lower extremity control. Mobility activities return best after a stroke, then cognitive/communicative, and last, those self-care functions requiring upper extremity fine motor coordination.

Most reflexes in humans are complex and include feedback circuits. Most physiologic pathways have numerous collaterals so that potential control could possibly be exerted by adjacent and also contralateral areas. Functional and neural return within the first 6 weeks of ictus relies upon ischemic but not necrotic cells within the primary affected areas. Recovery can therefore be dramatic in incomplete lesions. Late significant recovery—often in the 3 or 4 years after ictus—is slower and relies on the plasticity of those other areas of the neocortex which can be recruited into service. Brain plasticity itself works through neuronal sprouting and regeneration, as well as through activation of new alternative pathways. In the neocortex, the latter mechanism is frequently predominant. Plasticity is usually thought of as a characteristic of young people but is also present in older people as well. For example, augmented dendritic length can compensate for the inactivation of some neurons. Synaptic growth and regeneration also occurs, even after massive strokes. The nature of this regeneration is currently one of the many "hot" research topics.

The early ischemic neurological return is usually rapid. The late plastic neurological return is commonly gradual. Both are enhanced in hemorrhagic strokes and retarded in thrombotic events. But these rules are not universal. Sometimes the late return will come suddenly and will be greater than the early ischemic return. The exact relationship of neural and functional return to blood supply and neuronal metabolism after strokes is not well understood. Generally, the smaller the lesion, the greater the return.

Spasticity is not generally recognized as being closely and primarily related to overdrives within the long central tracts—rubrospinal, vestibulospinal, reticulospinal—that are organized by the area of the body controlled or affected. A failure of the spasticity gate within the posterior horn of the spinal cord could also be present. In any event, the muscle spindle and its function has been shown to be a secondary mechanism—an effect rather than a cause of spasticity. Consequently, much of the neurophysiology underlying neuromuscular re-education efforts will have to be reinvestigated.

Sensory deficits in stroke have been shown to be dynamic more than static. They affect stereognosis, two-point discrimination, and relative velocity sensation far more often than they reduce light touch or pin prick sensitivities. The movement of the upper extremity through space is affected. The nature of the altered sensory feedback will have to be more closely studied. It obviously devastates fine motor coordination, but the pathophysiology underlying this deficit has been only superficially delineated (Adams & Victor, 1981; Bach-y-Rita, 1981a; 1981b; Cooper,

Bloom, & Roth, 1982; Cotman & Nieto-Sampedro, 1982; Filskov & Boll, 1981; Kaplan, 1984; Kaplan & Cerullo, 1984; Kaplan & Materson, 1982; Lezak 1983; Licht, 1975; Logemann, 1983; Mayo Clinic, 1981; Merritt, 1979; Trexler, 1982; Wynn-Parry, 1981).

REHABILITATIVE FUNCTIONAL CONSIDERATIONS

Cognition–Communication

Understanding aphasia and stroke is closely linked to appreciation of aphasia in the normal aging population. Similarly, the effects of aphasia that create impairment of people who have had strokes correlate with the extent and location of the stroke itself. To study these relationships, one would formerly have had to wait for the results of clinicopathologic investigations. Even then, the numbers of patients studied might have been relatively small. But this is no longer the case; many new and noninvasive examinations are available.

Computerized axial tomography provides a living picture of the central nervous systemic structure. Nuclear magnetic resonance augments it. Positron imaging will map metabolic function. Evoked potentials demonstrate the patterns of reaction to known electric, visual, and auditory function. Neuropsychiatric and sensory integrative evaluations document psychologic and neural function (Ackerman et al., 1981; Feeney, Gonzalez, & Law, 1982; Gur et al., 1982; Soderstrom, Ericson, Mettinger, & Olivecrona, 1981; Stockard & Rossiter, 1977; Wood, Lukin, Tomsick, & Chambers, 1983; Zawadzki et al., 1983). It is now possible at any one or at any serial period to "slice" the brain noninvasively, using a combination of any of the above tests. At any one point in the rehabilitation process, objective markers can be applied.

This help comes none too soon. The patients now referred to major rehabilitation centers have become more complex. Patients will have dominant rather than nondominant coronary artery disease, renal disease, and severe diabetes. Typically, three or more specialists will be involved, as the physiatrist becomes the family physician for the disabled patient and the central clearinghouse for diverse information.

Uncomplicated nondominant stroke patients will probably not be referred to rehabilitation programs but will be treated as part of the acute-care setting. Yet populations of normals, patients with uncomplicated strokes, and more severely involved stroke patients should all be screened using the new, noninvasive techniques. These could then be compared with the results of testing for aphasia. In this manner, the true patterns of aphasia and of its rehabilitation could be delineated with different areas of central nervous system involvement, in normal versus stroke patients, in aged versus young patients, serially through time, and in dominant versus nondominant strokes.

At present, standard absolute functional outcome scales are not sensitive regarding cognitive–communication disability. For instance, saying that any one patient is aphasic does not describe the type of aphasia. Each has a different rehabilitation potential and prognosis, yet many of the prognostic studies in this area were devised or run before noninvasive studies came into general usage.

The basic natural history of stroke and its rehabilitation will have to be rewritten. Aphasia will probably be observed to be far more frequent and more disabling than now recognized. Nondominant strokes also frequently need aphasic and neurophysiologic evaluation and therapy. Accordingly, even clearly nondominant strokes will benefit from a short, intensive course in a rehabilitation unit. An important and urgent need has already arisen for education about stroke and its rehabilitation in private medical communities. Moreover, the complexity and sophistication of cognitive–communicative testing and therapy dictate that rehabilitation take place in regional and tertiary centers. We have not reached this state. In fact, many third-party carriers do not pay for rehabilitation in this functional area, whether provided on an outpatient or inpatient basis (Adams & Victor, 1981; Bach-y-Rita, 1981a; Filskov & Boll 1981; Holland, 1984; Kaplan, 1984; Kaplan & Materson, 1982; Kottke, Stillwell, & Lehmann, 1982; Lezak, 1983; Licht, 1975; Merritt, 1979; Naeser, Alexander, Helms-Eastabrooks, Laughlin, & Geschwind, 1982; Schuman et al., 1981, 1982; Trexler, 1982).

Dementia

The most feared of all the complications of stroke syndromes, intellectual dysfunction, poses an enormous barrier to rehabilitation. Because they are often associated with organic brain syndromes, bowel and/or bladder incontinence are adverse prognostic factors in stroke rehabilitation. Moreover, dementia is almost universally looked on as something shameful in Western society. People with it are isolated and quarantined. Their very existence is suppressed, much as one would suppress a dreadful family secret. They are not candidates for any sort of rehabilitation. Younger therapists and nurses often want little to do with them. They are, in fact, willfully avoided and it is thought "lucky" when they die.

In past civilizations, senility was held as an honorable condition of old age; a sign of that person having overcome numerous past challenges. More than just tolerated, their presence was prized and their words honored. If there was little day-to-day carryover, they met each day with a fresh attitude. Intellectual dysfunction meant that such people more fully developed emotional sensibilities, much as a blind man uses his hearing.

What a contrast to present-day practice; patients with incontinence are shunned. Even under relatively optimal circumstances, moderately impaired patients are often thought not to respond to a standard rehabilitation program. The solution suggested is that demented patients need a program designed for them. So they do, but that program should be constructed with the view of recording results in a properly controlled fashion. Spontaneous return of memory regression of the organic brain syndrome does occasionally occur with time. Intellectual dysfunction is not monolithic. One type of memory may be affected more than another. Each factor must be specifically characterized. Accurate clinical and basic studies must be conceived and elaborated. Cognitively impaired people can still be functional members of society. Western civilization often inordinately rewards its precociously verbal citizens. What of persons who find it difficult to express themselves appropriately? Much multidisciplinary and multicenter investigation will have to be done. The bigger the population, the more precise the clinical methods need to be. The end results will provide a clearer conclusion (Adams & Victor, 1981; Bach-y-Rita, 1981a, 1981b; Buell & Coleman, 1979; Chow & Stewart, 1972; Feeney et al., 1982; Goodglass & Kaplan, 1973; Gur et al., 1982; Holland, 1984; Kaplan, 1984; Kaplan & Cerullo, 1984; Kaplan & Materson, 1982; Kottke et al., 1982; Lezak, 1983; Licht, 1975; Logemann, 1983; Mayo Clinic, 1981; Merritt, 1979; Rosenback & La Pointe, 1978; Schuman et al., 1981; Terry, 1976; Trexler, 1982).

Mobility Activities

Mobility activities are what the lay person usually means by rehabilitation. Though mobility is usually a high priority with patients at the beginning of the inpatient stay, its popularity declines somewhat as appreciation of the use of self-care therapy is more successful. As the age of the patient increases, however, the plasticity of the response to central nervous system lesions decreases. As a result, the recovery of fine motor coordination necessary for success is more difficult. Strength is less important for gait than coordination. Moreover, coordination is often difficult to treat.

What therapy can be applied to compensate for deficient sensory response and defective motor control? Biofeedback for control after applying electrodiagnostic methodology can be a useful part of specific neuromuscular reeducation (Brudny, Korien, Grybaum, Belandres, & Gianutsos, 1979; Kaplan, 1984; Kottke et al., 1982; Licht, 1975). Another practical method is functional electric stimulation. Both have been made more potent with advances in electrophysiologic equipment. That equipment has now been made more digital and easier to use quantitatively. Its continued application will greatly change orthotic therapy and consequently gait and transfer activities. The hallmark of therapy for balance and coordination is still repetition. These aids make therapy more effective and efficient.

With the advances in neuromuscular reeducation and the intensive continuing efforts in neural and muscular facilitation, the milieu surrounding therapy has been greatly modified. Therapeutic demands in time, energy, and effort in this context mean that one-to-one patient/therapist contact has increased. The effectiveness of group interaction has been modified. Groups of therapists from different therapies can work effectively with small groups of patients. As a result, staffing patterns have changed. Staff turnovers have increased in our more mobile society. The expansion of rehabilitation units has also played its part. The pressure has substantially increased with the diagnosis-related group (DRG) exemption that rehabilitation units now enjoy. Much more work must be done to study staffing requirements in view of the technologic advances alluded to above. Modular administrative control of a central pool of resources is useful. Graduate work in basic scientific disciplines is a practical addition to a professional in this functional area. Availability of therapists with exposure to the discipline of graduate education builds the pool's resources.

Studies are in progress clarifying the nature of spasticity and spastic motor control in patients with stroke (Bach-y-Rita, 1981a, 1981b; Balliet, Shinn, & Bach-y-Rita, 1982; Brunnstrom, 1965; Burke, 1980; Cooper et al., 1982; Cotman & Nieto-Sampedro, 1982; Holland, 1984; Kaplan, 1984; Kaplan & Cerullo, 1984; Kaplan & Materson, 1982; Kottke et al., 1982; Licht, 1975; Roper, 1982; Young & Delwaide, 1981). This investigation will have to be expanded to include the effects of commonly used modalities—heat, cold, and hydrotherapy. Also relevant would be observations on auxiliary contributing factors—lipid profile, platelet activity, conditioning markers— before, during, and after chronic exposure to modalities, therapeutic exercise, and mobility activities. This bedrock of clinical observation of patients involved in the long and often demanding rehabilitative experiences provides solid support for the investigations of the future. The time will come when the average therapist helping stroke patients to augment mobility activities will have had extensive graduate education and work within a sophisticated matrix of group interactions within each rehabilitative team setting (Kaplan, 1984; Kaplan & Cerullo, 1984; Kaplan & Materson, 1982; Kottke et al., 1982; Merritt, 1979; Roper, 1982).

Self-Care Activities

Upper extremity orthotic application is still very much affected by ebb and flux surrounding advances in the technology of plastic materials. Certainly, a wide range of strengths and flexibility is now available within plastics. The clinical application, however, has far outstripped scientific inquiry as to the basis of dynamic and/or corrective splinting in stroke patients. The situation regarding slings is unclear and, accordingly, controversial. Noninvasive measuring templates could standardize the situation by reproducible quantification of position. Stress patterns will have to be thoroughly depicted and compared with orthotic design.

Stroke patients usually lose dynamic sensation (stereognosis), even if static sensation (light touch) is preserved. What happens through time is vital and largely unknown. We do know that in certain select cases, significant recovery of dynamic sensation returns as late as 3 or 4 years after ictus. Why? As these sensations tell where the arm or leg is in space, they underlie success in fine motor coordination and its related self-care skills. Orthoses modify the application of this sensation and also feedback to each patient. Application of orthoses early in the rehabilitation recovery of sensory feedback must still be studied.

Sensory-motor evaluations have attempted to standardize observations. More interdisciplinary work could be performed by relating these examinations to vocational evaluations and to driver's education screening tests. Additionally, the effectiveness and efficiency of sensory reeducation programs varies with the protocols. There is even a muddled uncertainty whether sensory reeducation has been accomplished. It probably can be effective, but the conditions and variables must be clearly delineated. Well-controlled blind studies with large matched populations would greatly help.

Vocational rehabilitation often exists in name only. Work evaluation, counseling, and placement efforts are poorly and inadequately funded by third-party carriers. Few stroke patients are wealthy enough to pay for this therapy on their own. Work alternatives are generally looked on with disfavor by the patient, his/her family, and friends. Grants in this area have not reflected clinical and training needs. Because there is a clinical spectrum from avocational to prevocational to vocational activities, interdisciplinary projects should be nurtured among occupational therapy, vocational rehabilitation, psychology, and speech pathology departments.

Computer/electronic interactions have widened the possibilities but only to those who have been trained appropriately. These requirements are really a form of job retraining. Most stroke patients now retire on disability if they were working prior to ictus. Nonetheless, this present situation does not have to be perpetuated. Regional multicenter, multidisciplinary efforts will be needed to improve retraining possibilities. Private organizations have had success reducing accessibility barriers on a local and focal basis. These efforts should be organized and funded nationally so that basic relative and absolute standards can be set and maintained.

There is a problem in all of these projects of visibility—visibility in the university hospital, the community, and with private industry. For example, facilities connected with modes of public transportation are centered around large cities and, even then, vary in quality and quantity. Transportation difficulties must be solved before vocational efforts will be successful. The lay public is often more sensitive to deficiencies in this special area than is the medical community. Resistance is both active and passive. It ranges from inertia to unrealistic expectation that each acute medical speciality will "take care" of its chronic illnesses. The result is a thin trickle of substandard rehabilitation. For the team concept to work, there has to be at least one medical area in which rehabilitation has a high priority (Adams & Victor, 1981; Bach-y-Rita, 1981a; Balliet et al., 1982; Cailliet, 1980; Kaplan, 1984; Kaplan & Cerullo, 1984; Kaplan & Materson, 1982; Kottke et al., 1982; Lezak, 1983; Logemann, 1983; Mayo Clinic, 1981; Merritt, 1979; Roper, 1982; Rosenback & La Pointe, 1978; Wynn-Parry, 1981).

Bowel and Bladder Activities

Two problems often arise with dysfunction in this area—incontinence or retention. Retention is a medical problem and is relatively rare in stroke patients. Bowels and the urinary bladder are usually hyperactive unless severe peripheral neuritis is also present. Increased spasticity can lead to retention, but this situation generally responds well to medication that lowers spasticity (tranquilizers, dantrolene, baclofen). Retention is not usually a severe functional disability in stroke patients.

Incontinence is a social problem and is also very common in stroke patients. There is little chance of successful disposition to family or community unless it has been first controlled. Society is not forgiving about either urinary or fecal incontinence. Accordingly, many patients are cared for in inpatient situations against their wishes. Whereas a variety of external and internal catheters and disposable diapers are available to aid in urinary incontinence, no such equipment is in standard usage for fecal incontinence.

Relatively little is known about the function of the neurogenic bowel. Even less has been published about the function of the neurogenic bowel in stroke patients. Bowel training regimens are usually based on purely empiric observations. They are provincial and reflect local/focal concerns, old traditions, and myths. Well-controlled blind studies with matched populations will become vital for further progress in this area. Multidisciplinary multicenter efforts assure observations on a large enough population. There are only a very few electrophysiologic, radioimaging, isotopic, or X-ray studies that are applicable. More might be developed. At least theoretically, biofeedback should be successful but could be more thoroughly explored.

Bladder incontinence control is socially desirable, but catheter usage can lead to infection, especially with an open system. One, in fact, "sacrifices" the bladder to maintain kidney function. Nonetheless, the natural history and comprehensive treatment of urinary tract infections in the neurogenic bladder of stroke patients is exceedingly murky for such an important topic. Only the most superficial work involving emptying times, flow rates, and bacterial replication rates has thus far been published. Bacterial viability, host resistance, the nature of bacteremia/bacteruria remains cloudy and controversial. The fact remains that any catheter can lead to infection. Urine is an excellent culture medium. If prostate enlargement is added, along with the prevalent treatment of the infections using bacteriostatic agents, the initial acute urinary tract infection can generate a state of acute and chronic serial urinary infections.

Urinary incontinence can, in some chronic illnesses, lead to skin breakdown and decubitus ulcers. Fortunately, this condition is relatively uncommon in stroke patients. It is a bit more frequent in those confined to wheelchairs, but is still much rarer when compared to incontinent patients in wheelchairs with paraplegia/quadriplegia. Clearly, the normal side of the body is present to generate timely weight shifting. This phenomenon needs more investigation.

Although the workup of the neurogenic bladder is more advanced than that of the neurogenic bowel, the pathophysiology of the neurogenic bladder in stroke patients is still controversial. Extensive urodynamic pyelographic and electromyographic data are available. Noninvasive procedures—evoked potential monitoring, ultrasound, abdominal computerized scanning, renography—add evaluations that are both sensitive and specific. No cookbook approach will uniformly "work" in stroke patients, but one can, at any point, obtain much more information about the status of the neurogenic bladder. Increasingly, there is a scientific, physiologic basis for specific decatheterization protocols. Unfortunately, there is an embarrassment of riches. Almost too much information is being published in too many different journals. A central national and international clearinghouse for sorting the data would be useful.

Women with stroke and neurogenic bladders cannot use an external catheter. Successful decatheterization depends on the patient's ability to undress easily and to transfer swiftly onto a toilet. As these types of urinary bladders are hyperreflexic, urinary frequency is a problem. Anticholinergic medication can help, but frequency/urgency also accompany urinary infections. These variables all interact. The results are frequently devastating to successful management of incontinence in women with strokes. The newer availability of various diaper products has helped, but skin maintenance, odor, and appearance are still concerns. Whether incontinence is actually present or is just a threat, the cost in socioeconomic terms is exorbitant.

Patients are placed in a wide range of institutions instead of remaining at home. Patient productivity as a working member of the community is limited. Instead of producing a living wage, incontinence patients often end up absorbing money to pay for care (Adams & Victor, 1981; Kaplan, 1984; Kaplan & Cerullo, 1984; Kaplan & Materson, 1982; Kottke et al., 1982; Licht, 1975; Merritt, 1979).

Psychosocial Factors

Basically, socioeconomic considerations must be covered as part of rehabilitation. In fact, these actually define how much rehabilitation will actually occur. Not all of the available rehabilitative resources will be funded. Psychologic, vocational, speech, and even occupational therapies might be left out in the cold. At this point, either alternative income must be obtained or the rehabilitation pruned. Because rehabilitation is expensive in space, equipment, and personnel, it will never be a big money-earner up front. The cost benefit is ultimately returned when the former patient returns to work. But as we have noted above, this is uncommon in stroke patients. Can rehabilitation pay for itself? Only if the functional outcome is used to justify institutional costs, and even then, national catastrophic health insurance will still be vital.

Family involvement has its parallel in the nurturing applied to raise infants—nothing can help so much as an involved, enthusiastic family effort. Nothing can undermine rehabilitation so much as active/passive family resistance. The family might not have been particularly close prior to the illness. Our patient might have even been the glue holding it together prior to ictus. Spouses could have frequently fought before ictus. The patient might well have been the dominant partner prior to stroke and now must adjust to a role reversal. Besides the changes taking place within the family, the family and the patient also must weather a series of crises. But stroke often makes the patient more rigid and less able to adjust. Usually these momentous family changes take place in a milieu in which significant family members are "burned out" and unable to perform. Frequently, inpatients have, for the duration of their rehabilitative stay, no other place to go, in any case. They are prisoners of their hospital.

Social adaptation techniques try to modify a given no-win situation, so that the patient is left more flexible and positive after the crisis has passed. No one discipline will succeed. Rather, an informal workshop-type group consisting of nursing therapist, social worker, and psychologist will have to pool information identifying problems and coordinate the appropriate behavioral response. This type of therapy is and must stay behavioral to succeed. Spaced, frequent learning must be provided in an atmosphere that is warm and does not threaten the patient. The family will have to be recruited into this effort so that all of the messages are constant.

To end on a practical note, the family environment to which the patient will return will have to be forgiving and accessible. At an early date, house or apartment plans will be needed for the rehabilitation team to study. Home visits by team members are a valuable asset to the rehabilitative effort. Though they can be done at any time, home visits are most effective at the start of the last third of the inpatient stay, so that discharge planning can be reviewed. Certainly, equipment will have to be ordered for the patient and his/her dwelling. Should the patient be going to an extra-care facility rather than a home, the patient and his/her family should visit the facility prior to discharge—numerous times if necessary. Accomplishing these items in a standard, organized, and efficient method remains an objective for further study (Adams & Victor, 1981; Bach-y-Rita, 1981a, 1981b; Brudny, et al., 1977; Cailliet, 1980; Kaplan, 1984; Kaplan & Cerullo, 1984; Kaplan & Materson, 1982; Kottke, et al. 1982; Licht, 1975; Merritt, 1979).

STRATEGIES FOR OVERCOMING REHABILITATION BARRIERS

Medicaid-financed nursing homes have become vast human warehouses. Within these disposal units, infection rates and subsequent morbidity increase, even if mortality stays level. Although therapy resources are available on paper, these assets are usually dependent on the interest of one or two excellent employees who care for the patients. When these move on (because of pay, benefits, etc.), so does the rehabilitation program.

Although multidisciplinary geriatric rehabilitation medicine programs are being mounted, these efforts are usually limited to facilities closely related to university hospitals. Within such programs, permanent discharges to the community increase, and the mean length of stay decreases. Self-care and mobility activities show dramatic gains within the patient population. The whole concept of the university hospital nursing facility is one that can be effective in providing an example of what can be done. University facilities could become regional units monitoring conditions within a given geographic/demographic area and channeling monetary resources accordingly. The unit itself would handle people with complex conditions. They would be primary halfway houses.

Staffing of Medicaid nursing homes also has to be closely watched. Credentials should be inspected and checked. Because current levels are not adequate for the job at hand, more public money will have to be spent. In exchange, arbitrary and random movement of personnel and also sharp management practices could be regulated.

A wide variety of types of nursing home environments also might be supported within a given general framework. Regulations would provide a safety net, rather than a dome. This particular concept would be valuable in patients who have had strokes because there is frequently a broad spectrum of involvement from people barely affected to those totally disabled. Currently, many Medicaid nursing homes are maintained of, by, and for the extremely aged and disabled stroke patients. Younger and more able patients simply are not provided with outlets for their talents and energy. Within those storage houses, there is often nothing to do and nowhere to go. Alcoholism or boredom provide the only distractions (Kaplan, 1984; Kaplan & Cerullo, 1984; Kaplan & Materson, 1982; Kottke et al., 1982; Licht, 1975; Schuman et al., 1980, 1981).

Graduate Education Programs

Rehabilitation medicine in the United States has usually been primarily a clinical service. The basic science produced has generally lagged behind those advances in functional care. Consequently, physical medicine and rehabilitation is now in the awkward position of having to create its basic science rationale for these applied improvements in clinical care.

The rate-limiting factor, however, will continue to be staffing. If the present momentum of clinical excellence is to continue, many more M.D., Ph.D. physicians will have to be attracted into this field from bioengineering, orthotics and prosthetics, physiology, and pharmacology. Although some residency programs also offer the opportunity to obtain master of science degrees, an organized and combined approach leading to the standardized production of M.D., Ph.D. degrees is relatively uncommon. Moreover, to be accepted in the basic science milieu, rehabilitation programs will have to have the Ph.D. portion come from basic rather than clinical sciences. The increased length of training will be more than balanced by the application of scientific methodology to factors that ultimately generate clinical difficulties.

The proportions of nurses and therapists, other than psychologists or speech pathologists, at the master's level or above are not very high. Yet technological progress has also yielded significant areas for basic science inquiries in these areas. The time is rapidly arriving when most clinicians will require graduate education to the master's level or greater. In order to create a multidisciplinary research rehabilitative effort, a special concentration of minds must coordinate efforts on the subject at hand to produce the "chain reaction." The formation and maintenance of research and administrative rehabilitation teams is a delicate, intricate process. It must have a pool of qualified and interested talents and security of funding.

In order to staff graduate education, funding must be steady and predictable. But it is precisely this last requirement that has been absent in the last 5 years. A well-considered, well-funded effort should last a full decade and have clearly understood, concise ground rules. It should act through a few regional centers that have proven track records in graduate education. As it is, the lack of qualified graduate education is a serious barrier to further progress in stroke rehabilitation as well as in geriatrics (Kottke et al., 1982; Steinwachs et al., 1982).

Integration of Support within the Community

The end result of the rehabilitative process is to create a situation in which the patient will be at a maximal amount of self-sufficiency. Many resources are available within the community, but they have to be organized and coordinated. It isn't a question of mobilizing one person's attention but that of dozens of people, all of whose areas overlap at different points. For example, the problem of the optimal utilization of retraining and of working alternatives involves not only the private sector, but social work, vocational rehabilitation, occupational therapy, and psychological agencies within the hospital and the community. Volunteer and nonprofit citizen agencies are available to act as referral sources on a local and focal basis. They are, however, greatly underfunded, and the quality might be spotty. A natural and standard network of these access organizations should be formed and encouraged. Uniform records of needs/resources should be transferrable, especially if the patient moves.

Follow-up is vital. The system must not lose track of people who still need help. Random and frequent checks should monitor the efficiency and effectiveness of services rendered. The specific matrix of outpatient consultant might have to be adjusted at any one point. Certainly, any one agency of our national system should be flexible enough to modify services and quality if needed, and they should be available 24 hours a day. It is the lack of thorough, quick, and knowledgeable service that constitutes the major barrier in this particular area (Kaplan & Cerullo, 1984; Licht, 1975).

INEFFECTIVE USE OF PRESENT RESOURCES

Although the United States is a world leader in the care of acute medical disorders, it is much less advanced in the care of chronic diseases. Funding, patients, and equipment are available to generate a much more efficient response to chronic illness; but year in and year out, efforts of many medical communities fall short. Why?

Active and passive resistance of the community is one problem. The rationale supporting the resistance is (a) rehabilitation is the concern of every department; and (b) each department—neurology, internal medicine, orthopedic or neurologic surgery—should take care of its own rehabilitation.

Resistance also can be expressed overtly. As one medical school official put it, "Rehabilitation does not belong on a university campus." This position is flawed. Under this rationale, no one area is primarily responsible for rehabilitation. In whichever department rehabilitation lies, it steadfastly maintains a low priority. Acute concerns are always serviced first. The thinking is, therefore, cyclic and the emotion self-defeating. A thin trickle of substandard work is usually generated under these circumstances. Optimal utilization of the talents of physician personnel demands the establishment and maintenance of separate departments of rehabilitation medicine.

With the formation of a separate department of rehabilitation medicine, a second problem can be tackled. It is the distribution of allied professional support and equipment. A daily and intense supervision is not at all necessary. But conflicts will arise over equipment, space, and time between therapies. Priorities will have to be established by an administrative rehabilitation team of which the physiatrist is a vital member. Without his/her participation, the physician member will not necessarily be knowledgeable and will, in any case, have his/her own acute medical agenda.

Rehabilitation is a deficit area in physician and allied professional manpower. More participation from the very top of American training is needed. The problems to be overcome are usually complex and difficult in patients with chronic diseases. A more even geographic distribution is also necessary. Many heavily populated areas are generally understaffed, largely due to socioeconomic factors. A slant toward solving this difficulty will be made through a growing vigorous national specialty of rehabilitation medicine. In fact, about half of the medical schools in the United States have no significant rehabilitation training at all, let alone distinct rehabilitation medicine departments. Space on the medical school curriculum must be made during the sophomore and junior years. Medical school resources now directed at specialties that are oversubscribed should be bent toward rehabilitation medicine departments.

Outpatient care is often spotty. Public transportation is often useless. Orthoses, prostheses, and equipment are difficult to find and obtain. Only the basic therapies—physical therapy and nursing—are funded, and then only partially. It is clear that, along with separate departments of rehabilitation medicine, regional tertiary rehabilitation centers should be supported on a national basis to coordinate outpatient care of patients with strokes. These centers could also, in time, serve as training centers for allied professionals (Kaplan & Materson, 1982; Kottke et al., 1982; Steinwachs et al., 1982).

SPECIFIC RECOMMENDATIONS

These arise out of the literature review and barrier analysis already given.

1. *General rehabilitation medicine research and training centers* should be established on a regional basis. They should be given only to university medical centers with separate and distinct departments of rehabilitation medicine. Their funding should be adequate (at least $1 million per year) and guaranteed for at least 10 years.

2. *Procedural standards* will have to be drawn to monitor the productivity of each research and training center. Due process should be provided, but centers that violate any of the conditions mentioned above should be stripped of their grants. In particular, centers should have (a) geographic location for therapy and also for Commission on Accreditation of Rehabilitation Facilities-accredited inpatient bed units; (b) a department head and at least two other Board-certified physiatrists; (c) an approved residency program; (d) a mandatory place on the medical school curriculum in the second and/or third year.

3. *Peer review*, similar to that of the National Institute of Health, regarding quality and quantity of academic productivity. An appeal mechanism will have to be built into the system.

4. *NIHR fellowships* should be located at regional general research and training centers. They should be given in, but not limited to; central nervous system disorders, spinal injuries, electrophysiology, pediatric rehabilitation, and musculoskeletal disorders.

REFERENCES

Ackerman, A. H., Correia, J. A., Alpert, N. M., Baron, J. C., Gouliamos, A., Grotto, J. C., Brownell, G. L., & Taveras, J. M. (1981). Position imaging in ischemic stroke disease using compounds labeled with oxygen 15. Initial results of clinico-physiologic correlations. *Neurology, 38,* 537–343.

Adams, R. D., & Victor, M. (1981). *Principles of Neurology* (2nd ed.). New York: McGraw-Hill.

Bach-y-Rita, P. (1981a). Brain plasticity as a basis of the development of rehabilitation procedures for hemiplegia. *Scandinavian Journal of Rehabilitation Medicine,13,* 73–83.

Bach-y-Rita, P. (1981b). "Sprouting and unmasking" in the rehabilitation of patients with CNS lesions. *Archives of Physical Medicine and Rehabilitation, 62,* 413–417.

Balliet, J. B., Shinn, J. B., & Bach-y-Rita, P. (1982). Facial paralysis rehabilitation: Retraining selective muscle control. *International Rehabilitation Medicine, 4*(2), 67–74.

Brudny, J., Korien, J., Grybaum, B., Belandres, P.V., Gianutsos, J. G. (1979). Helping hemiparetics help themselves: Sensory feedback session. *Journal of the American Medical Association, 241,* 814–818.

Brunnstrom, S. (1965). Walking preparation for adult patients with hemiplegia. *Journal of the American Physical Therapy Association, 45,* 17–29.

Buell, S., & Coleman, P. (1979). Dendritic growth in aged human brain and failure of growth in senile dementia. *Science, 206,* 854–856.

Burke, D. (1980). A reassessment of the muscle spindle contribution to muscle tone in normal and spastic man. In R. G. Feldman, R. R. Young, W. P. Kowlla (Eds.), *Spasticity: Disordered motor control* (pp. 261–278). Chicago: Year Book.

Cailliet, R. (1980). *The shoulder in hemiplegia.* Philadelphia: F.A. Davis.

Chow, K. L., & Stewart, D. L. (1972). Reversal of structural and functional effects of long-term visual deprivation in cats. *Experimental Neurology, 34,* 409–433.

Cooper, J. R., Bloom, F. E., & Roth, R. H. (1982). *The biochemical basis of neuropharmacology* (4th ed.) (p. 367). New York: Oxford University Press.

Cotman, C. W., & Nieto-Sampedro, M. (1982). Brain function, synapse renewal, and plasticity. *Annual Review of Psychology, 33,* 371–401.

Feeney, D. M., Gonzalez, A., & Law, W. (1982). Amphetamine, haloperidol and experience interact to affect rate of recovery after motor cortex injury. *Science, 271,* 855–857.

Filskov, S. B., & Boll, T. J. (Eds.). (1981). *Handbook of clinical neuropsychology.* New York: Wiley and Sons.

Goodglass, H., & Kaplan, E. (1973). *The assessment of aphasia and related disorders.* Philadelphia: Lea and Febiger.

Gur, D., Wolfson, S. K., Yonas, H., Good, W. F., Shabason, L., Latchaw, R. E., Miller, D. M., & Cook, E. E. (1982). Progress in cerebrovascular disease—local cerebral blood flow by xenon enhanced CT. *Stroke, 13,* 750–758.

Holland, A. (1984). *Language disorders in adults.* San Diego, CA: College Hill Press.

Kaplan, P. E. (1984). *The practice of physical medicine.* Springfield, IL: Charles C. Thomas.

Kaplan, P. E., & Cerullo, L. (1984). *Stroke and neurosurgical rehabilitation.* Boston: Butterworths.

Kaplan, P. E., & Materson, R. S. (1982). *The practice of rehabilitation medicine.* Springfield, IL: Charles C. Thomas.

Kottke, F. J., Stillwell, G. K., & Lehmann, J. F. (1982). *Krusen's handbook of physical medicine and rehabilitation* (3rd ed.). Philadelphia: W. B. Saunders.

Lezak, M. (1983). *Neurophysiological assessment* (2nd ed.). New York: Oxford University Press.

Licht, S. (1975). *Stroke and its rehabilitation.* New Haven, CT: Elizabeth Licht.

Logemann, J. (1983). *Evaluation and treatment of swallowing disorders.* San Diego, CA: College Hill Press.

Mayo Clinic, Mayo Foundation. (1981). *Clinical examination in neurology* (5th ed.). Philadelphia: W. B. Saunders.

Merritt, H. H. (1979). *A textbook of neurology* (6th ed.). Philadelphia: Lea and Febiger.

Naeser, M. A., Alexander, M. P., Helms-Eastabrooks, N., Laughlin, M. A., & Geschwind, N. (1982). Aphasia with predominantly subcortical lesion sites. *Archives of Neurology, 39,* 2–14.

Roper, B. A. (1982). Rehabilitation after a stroke. *Journal of Bone and Joint Surgery, 64B,* 156–163.

Rosenback, J. C., & LaPointe, L. L. (1978). The dysarthrias: Description, diagnosis and treatment. In D. F. Johns (Ed.), *Clinical management of neurogenic communicative disorders* Boston: Little-Brown.

Schuman, J. E., Beattie, E. J., Steed, D. A., Gibson, J. E., Merry, G. M., & Kraus, A. S. (1980). Rehabilitative and geriatric teaching programs: Clinical efficacy in a skilled nursing facility. *Archives of Physical Medicine and Rehabilitation, 61,* 310–315.

Schuman, J. E., Beattie, E. J., Steed, D. A., Gibson, J. E., Merry, G. M., & Kraus, A. S., (1981). Geriatric patients with and without intellectual dysfunction: Effectiveness of a standard rehabilitation program. *Archives of Physical and Medical Rehabilitation, 62,* 612–618.

Steinwachs, D. M., Levine, D. M., Elzinga, J., Salkever, D. S., Parker, R. D., & Weisman, C. S. (1982). Changing patterns of graduate medication education. *New England Journal of Medicine, 306,* 10–14.

Soderstrom, C. E., Ericson, K., Mettinger, K. L., & Olivecrona, H. (1981). Computed tomography and CSF spectrophotometry—diagnosis and prognosis in 300 patients with cerebrovascular disease. *Scandinavian Journal of Rehabilitation Medicine, 13,* 65–71.

Stockard, J. J., & Rossiter, V. S. (1977). Clinical and pathologic correlates of brain stem auditory response abnormalities. *Neurology, 27,* 316–325.

Terry, D. (1976). Dementia. A brief and selective review. *Archives of Neurology, 33,* 1–4.

Trexler, L. (Ed.). (1982). *Cognitive rehabilitation: Conceptualization and intervention.* New York: Plenum Press.

Wood, G. W., Lukin, R. R., Tomsick, T. A., & Chambers, A. A. (1983). Digital substraction angiography with intravenous injection—assessment of 1,000 carotid bifurcations. *American Journal of Roentgenology, 140,* 855–859.

Wynn-Parry, C. B. (1981). *Rehabilitation of the hand* (4th ed.). Boston: Butterworths.

Young, R. R., & Delwaide, P. J. (1981). Drug therapy, spasticity. *New England Journal of Medicine, 304,* 28–33, 96–99.

Zawadzki, M. B., Davis, P. L., Crooks, L. E., Mills, C. M., Norman, D., Newton, T. H., Sheldon, P., & Kaufman, L. (1983). NMR demonstrations of cerebral abnormalities—comparison with CT. *American Journal of Roentgenology, 140,* 847–854.

17

Musculoskeletal Disabilities

John W. Frymoyer

Musculoskeletal disease and injuries are a frequent precursor to disability in our aging population. This paper reviews four topics: (a) the biochemical, physiologic, and biomechanical changes that occur in the aging musculoskeletal system; (b) general differences between the younger and the aging population with respect to the impact of musculoskeletal disorders on them; (c) general principles applied to the treatment and rehabilitative management of those patients; and (d) the most common diseases and injuries affecting the elderly in terms of their epidemiology, clinical presentation, and treatment.

BIOCHEMICAL, PHYSIOLOGIC, AND BIOMECHANICAL CHANGES OF THE AGING MUSCULOSKELETAL SYSTEM

Four structures constitute the musculoskeletal system: bone, ligaments, joints, and muscles. It is well recognized that the changes in these structures that occur with aging represent a continuum of events, often starting in early adulthood or even dating back to childhood.

Bone

Primary osteoporosis is defined as "an age-related disorder characterized by decreased bone mass and increased susceptibility to fractures in the absence of other recognizable causes of bone loss," which affects an estimated

15 to 20 million individuals (National Institutes of Health, 1984). The cost, primarily attributable to associated fractures, is $3 billion per year. The underlying physiologic basis of osteoporosis appears to be an imbalance between bone formation and bone absorption. The bone loss affects both the mineral and organic constituents, so there is a progressive loss of total bone mass as opposed to a selective loss of one constituent. This decline in bone mass starts at age 35 for cortical bone and at a somewhat earlier age for trabecular bone. The rate of loss is greater for females than for males and is particularly accelerated in the postmenopausal female. Paradoxically, the rate of loss appears to diminish after the age of 70 (Barzel, 1983). The average decrease approximates 6% to 8% of total bone mass each decade. In addition to age and sex, other risk factors increase the rate of bone loss, such as low body weight, small skeleton, light skin, lack of physical activity (immobilization), diet (particularly deficient calcium intake), smoking, and some drugs and hormones—particularly corticosteroids.

Loss of bone mass is associated with alterations in the mechanical properties of the affected bones. Mechanical tests demonstrate approximately linear correlation between compressive strength and bone mass (McDonagh, White, & Davies, 1984). Thus, there is a general trend toward age-related diminishment in the strength of bone. The remodeling which accompanies bone loss may partially modify this loss of strength. In diaphyseal, weight-bearing, long bones, endosteal bone resorption loss is accompanied by periosteal new bone formation, which results in an increased total cross-sectional diameter of the bone. This resultant change in geometry increases the cross-sectional modulus (Mazess, 1982; Smith & Walker, 1980). Weakening due to cortical bone loss is thus partially compensated by a more mechanically favorable geometry. Estrogens in high doses appear to promote this process (Horsman, Jones, Francis, & Nordin, 1983).

Despite these and other observations, there remain critical gaps in our knowledge of the basic regulation of bone metabolism, as well as the accompanying mechanical properties of osteoporotic bone. Also, further understanding of the mechanical properties of osteoporotic bone is extremely relevant to the interaction between bone and internal fixation devices and implants in the elderly. Clearly, early identification of the patient at risk for excessive bone loss and osteoporosis and the development of effective therapy, as well as greater epidemiologic knowledge, are important in the development of prevention strategies.

Ligaments and Other Soft Tissues

The basic biochemical constituents of ligaments and other supportive soft tissue structures include collagen, elastin, noncollagenous proteins, proteoglycans, and water. With aging, collagen fibers increase in size and are altered in shape as a result of changes in the cross binding between the molecules. The proportionality of the collagen types is also altered. Often there is a decrease in noncollagenous proteins and proteoglycans, and in some tissues there is a decrease in water content. These chemical events are particularly important to the aging of the intervertebral disc (Pope, Wilder, & Booth, 1980). The mechanical consequences of these biochemical changes are to decrease the elasticity of the collagen fibers, to increase the composite stiffness of the structure, and, thus, diminish the overall elasticity and mobility of the structure. In some ligaments (for example, intraspinous ligaments), these changes are accompanied by diminished tensile strength. It is noteworthy that immobilization of a joint may result in similar changes, a point of particular importance in fracture treatment.

Muscles

Muscle mass decreases as a function of age, although such changes are, in part, favorably modified by exercise (Rothstein & Rose, 1982). The specific morphologic, biochemical, and physiologic events that accompany muscular aging are beyond the scope of this discussion. Although loss of strength accompanies diminishment of muscle mass, there is not strict proportionality between those two variables. Ultimate loss of muscle strength is of the magnitude of 30% to 50%.

Changes also occur in the tendinous portion of the musculotendinous unit. The anatomy of certain tendon structures (best exemplified by the shoulder) contribute to the accelerated degeneration of those structures. In the shoulder, the supraspinatus tendon and the rotator cuff are subjected to mechanical pressures from the adjacent acrominion and ligaments as the shoulder is abducted. These mechanical pressures interfere with blood supply to the tendon, resulting in acceleration of a degenerative process. For reasons ill-understood, degenerate tendons serve as a nidus for the deposition of calcium–pyrophosphate crystals that often are associated with acute calcific tendinitis and bursitis.

Joints

Osteoarthritis (OA) is the most common disabling rheumatic disorder of the elderly. As Hamerman (1983) has observed, "just where normal aging ends and OA begins is an important point, but there is no certain answer." There is no doubt that OA is age-related, although not necessarily age-dependent. In the adult, articular cartilage is avascular and dependent on synovial fluid for nutrition. The mitotic activity of cartilage cells (chondrocytes) is minimal once skeletal maturity is reached. With aging, the water content of hyaline cartilage diminishes, and proteoglycans are altered in their relative proportions, with a decrease in chondroitin sulfate and an increase in keratin sulfate (Mankin & Brandt, 1984). In osteoarthritic articular cartilage, foci of increased chondrocyte activity are identified, the water content increases, there are relative decreases in proteoglycans, and there are alterations in the proportionality of constituent proteoglycans, such that keratin sulfate decreases and chondroitin sulfate increases (Meachim & Brooke, 1984). There is a relative lack of change in collagen, except in the late stage of the disease, although the distribution and size of collagen molecules may be altered.

The underlying mechanical pathogenesis of OA is controversial. One popular theory (the Radin-Rose model) (Radin, 1984) attributes OA to stiffening of subchondral bone resulting from repetitive subcritical impact loads that result in trabecular fractures. Subsequent healing of those microfractures results in stiffening of the subchondral bone, which shifts loads to the articular cartilage. Other investigators attribute the primary changes of OA to chemical changes within the cartilage, which alter its mechanical properties, or possibly to immunologic or enzymatically mediated processes (Howell, 1984). Regardless of what tissue (i.e., bone or cartilage) is primary to pathogenesis, it is well established that any alteration in the congruity or stability of a joint is associated with an increased probability of degenerative change. Examples of this association are periarticular and intra-articular fractures of the hip, childhood congenital hip dislocation, Legg-Perthes disease, slipped capital femoral epiphysis, and aseptic necrosis. In fact, it is suggested that at least 80% of patients with OA of the hip have an underlying, predisposing mechanical abnormality (Harris, 1977). Similarly, OA of the knee occurs after fracture, ligamentous injuries, or malalignment of either the tibial/femoral or patellofemoral joints. Other mechanical factors include immobilization of joints, which can be shown experimentally to produce histologic and biochemical changes consistent with osteoarthritis. These latter observations are particularly relevant to the effects of immobilization in the elderly patient with a fracture.

Summary

During the process of aging, changes occur in all elements of the musculoskeletal system, which can be viewed as "normal aging." Although these changes are associated with alterations in chemical composition, materials, properties, and mechanical function, aging, per se, does not appear to cause disease, with the exception of osteoporosis, which theoretically is a preventable disease. These aging changes have major implications for the treatment of the elderly patient, and indeed are the basis for major differences in treatment of the elderly compared to the younger population.

GENERAL HEALTH

The aging population has many more significant general health problems. The impact of these health problems or treatment outcome has been most extensively analyzed in hip fractures, where there is an increased prevalence of rheumatoid arthritis, diabetes, thyrotoxicosis, malabsorption syndromes, and neoplasms (Gallagher, Melton, & Riggs, 1980). Any condition that increases the possibility of a fall is also important, such a ischemic heart disease, cerebral vascular diseases, parkinsonism, and spinal stenosis.

These factors also influence the outcome of treatment and its effects on rehabilitation, often leading to prolonged hospitalization or the need for institutionalization. Some of the more common additional health care problems are incontinence—which in turn leads to an increased risk for wound infection as well as a decreased resistance of the skin to decubitus ulcers.

Psychosocial Issues

Injuries to the musculoskeletal system often occur in institutionalized patients, and their outcome is often unfavorable with respect to both morbidity and mortality. Niemann and Mankin (1968) documented that patients institutionalized before hip fractures had a 40% mortality at 6 months and a 60% mortality at 1 year, in comparison to the commonly reported mortality figures of 5% to 20% for noninstitutionalized patients. Ceder's study (Ceder, Svensson, & Thorngren, 1980) more clearly demonstrated the effect of preinjury status on treatment outcome. Of those patients admitted from their homes, all but 15% survived a hip fracture, whereas the death rate for institutionalized patients was 45%. Other health factors eventually influence the capacity to walk and be functionally independent, of which three predictive variables are   most significant: general medical health, living with another person, and ability to walk prior to the fracture. Using these three variables, the following probabilities of returning to the home were identified: 0 of 3, 12%; 1 of 3, 50%; 2 of 3, 80%; and 3 of 3, 90%. It remains conjectural whether age is predictive of morbidity and mortality. Some studies demonstrate a close relationship of age to morbidity and mortality following musculoskeletal injuries, whereas others have demonstrated that age is less important than the functional status of the patient at the time of the injury. As will be seen, decisions in treatment of patients are often based on the concept of advanced "physiologic age."

Less well understood is the role of other psychologic variables in the pathogenesis and outcome of musculoskeletal diseases and injuries. There is considerable evidence that the disease activity in rheumatoid arthritis and OA fluctuates as a function of depression, anxiety, and stress. The effect of these psychologic factors on functional outcome and mortality is less well understood, although depression and anxiety, as measured by the Minnesota Multiphasic Personality Inventory, appear to have significant influences on failure to obtain a functional range of motion after reconstructive procedures on the hip (Ritter & McAdoo, 1979). Dementia, broadly defined as a confusional state, also has been associated with a higher rate of complications and prolonged hospitalization in patients undergoing elective joint replacement arthroplasty.

Cost–Benefit

One of the most difficult issues to assess relates to the cost versus the benefit, particularly of elective musculoskeletal surgical procedures in the elderly. This controversy surrounding cost–benefit issues has been explored in depth by Aaron and Schwartz (1984). Because cost–benefit in the elderly population cannot be assessed by such traditional measures as return to work and income generation, a great deal of attention has been related to the issues of "quality of life." These issues clearly are a major factor in elective operative interventions, particularly those involving pain and dysfunction of the musculoskeletal system. Among the newer methods being used to assess this elusive problem are "quality of life adjustments" (Aaron & Schwartz, 1984).

These issues also have major implications for the distribution and allocation of health care costs in the aging population. Although there are incomplete cost data for many musculoskeletal conditions, a number of examples underscore the major economic impact of these diseases and injuries. For example, the mean cost for a fracture of the proximal femur, related to osteoporosis, was calculated to be $5,644.00 in 1976 (Owen, Melton, Gallagher, & Riggs, 1980). Based on a very conservative estimate of 150,000 such fractures annually, short-term direct costs were determined to be in excess of $1 billion. In an attempt to define some of the other costs of hip fractures, Jensen, Tondevoid, and Sorenson (1980) studied the utilization of hospital beds, hospital rehabilitation, and nursing home beds in a Danish population. Based on a population of 5,000 inhabitants, they calculated that 32 hospital beds, 43 rehabilitation beds, and at least 21 nursing home beds were required for the short and longer term treatment and rehabilitation of hip fractures. Kelsey, White, Pastides, and Bisbee (1979) reported that of the 1 million fractures sustained each year in the United States by women who are 45 years old or older, approximately 700,000 were found to occur in relationship to osteoporosis. The calculated cost of osteoporosis, primarily attributable to these fractures, was $3.8 billion per annum. In another study, the rate of total hip arthroplasty was determined on an annualized basis by age as shown in Figure 17-1. It was calculated that more than 120,000 total hip arthroplasties would be required for the population of the United States (Melton, Stauffer, Chao, & Ilstrup, 1982). Based on this analysis, and a conservative estimate of the cost for each procedure, the direct medical cost for total hip arthroplasty was calculated to exceed $1 billion annually. Despite the high cost demonstrated by this study, a benefit-to-cost ratio of hip arthroplasty was calculated to be 4:1, because of increased quality of life and the diminished demand for community health and welfare services (Taylor, 1976).

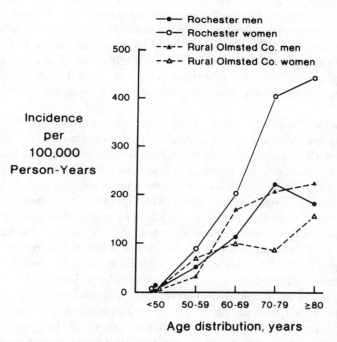

Figure 17-1. The incidence per 100,000 person-years for total hip replacement is plotted for four groups, residents of Rochester, Minnesota, male and female, and residents of Olmsted County, male and female. Note the progressive incidence of total hip arthroplasty beyond the sixth decade, peaking at approximately age 70 to 72. (Reprinted with permission from L. Joseph Melton, III, M.D. and *The New England Journal of Medicine* from Metton et al., "Rates of Total Hip Arthroplasty: A Population-Based Study," Vol. 307, 1243, 1982.)

PRINCIPLES GOVERNING TREATMENT IN THE ELDERLY

If optimal functional rehabilitation is to be achieved with the least mortality and morbidity, a musculoskeletal disease or injury in the elderly demands adherence to a set of principles. The following discussion details some of these principles:

1. *Minimize immobilization.* The basic materials properties of the aging musculoskeletal structures make them particularly susceptible to prolonged immobilization, which results in accelerated bone loss, joint stiffness, and muscular weakness. Experimental data indicate that degenerative changes also may be accelerated. In some instances, open reduction and internal fixation of fractures or arthroplasties can achieve early mobilization. In other instances—for example, severely comminuted fractures adjacent to the joint—compromises may be made that sacrifice some long-term function of the joint for the goal of early mobilization (Rowe & Lowell, 1961). In extreme cases, such as difficult fractures about the knee, amputation may occasionally be chosen as preferable to prolonged immobilization.

2. *Emphasize function rather than anatomic perfection.* Wherever possible, operations and orthotic devices that promote function are chosen. Examples of this approach include ischial weight-bearing quadrilateral braces for the management of femoral fractures not amenable to internal fixation, and the use of cast braces rather than immobilizing casts in upper extremity injuries (Sarmiento & Latta, 1981). Operative interventions often are chosen that promote function at the expense of less than perfect long-term results, such as prosthetic replacements in femoral neck fractures or the use of methylmethacrylate as an adjunct to internal fixation devices.

3. *Treat promptly.* The elderly patient with an acute musculoskeletal injury often has significant associated medical problems. Usually it is preferable to pursue an early operative intervention before all medical problems are resolved, rather than attempting to solve all problems preoperatively. Typically, only those medical problems that are potentially life-threatening, such as uncontrolled cardiac failure or major electrolyte disturbances, are considered as contraindications to operative intervention.

4. *Choose devices applicable to osteoporotic bone.* The materials properties of osteoporotic bone often make them less suitable to stable internal fixation. In general, osteoporotic bone is less satisfactorily treated by devices that depend on screw fixation, although the development of improved cancellous screws has reduced that problem. Generally, intramedullary devices are the preferred method of fracture fixation. The adjunctive use of methyl-

methacrylate may prove beneficial in the particularly difficult fracture patient and is routinely chosen in total joint arthroplasties, despite the availability of the newer prosthetic devices that depend on bone ingrowth.

5. *Do not set unrealistic expectations for functional improvement.* In younger patients, one will often anticipate significant increases in the functional capacity of the patient, after operative intervention, recognizing that the time to achieve that goal may be extensive. In the older patient, particularly those with fractures, functional improvement is less likely to occur. This point has been underscored in statistics relating to fractures of the hip and the prognosticators for return to function. However, total joint arthroplasties often produce substantial gains in function. The elderly patient may often be counseled that the continued use of canes or external assistive devices may be preferable after an arthroplasty because of other health problems (neurologic, vascular) that diminish steadiness of gait.

COMMON MUSCULOSKELETAL DISEASES AND INJURIES—THEIR TREATMENT AND REHABILITATION

The following section is divided according to the underlying pathologic process which produces the disease or problem. Because only those conditions that are widely prevalent or have unusual implication for treatment will be discussed, this presentation should not be considered a comprehensive outline of all musculoskeletal diseases of the aged.

Metabolic Bone Disease

Osteoporosis

The previous sections have reviewed the overall problem of osteoporosis and its associated presentation. Insofar as its major socioeconomic and medical impact relates to fractures, the important fractures associated with osteoporosis will be discussed in that context.

Osteomalacia

Osteomalacia is generally viewed as an uncommon adult bone disease characterized by defects in bone mineralization, in contrast to osteoporosis, which is a total loss of bone mass (Mankin, 1974a, 1974b). Bone mineralization depends on the availability of calcium, phosphorus, and vitamin D. In the child, deficiency of vitamin D on a nutritional or genetic basis results in rickets. The adult counterpart is termed osteomalacia. Some of the causes are as follows: inadequate dietary intake of vitamin D combined with absence of sunlight, which is essential for the conversion of vitamin D to its active metabolite; intestinal disorders that affect absorption (milk-alkali syndrome, total gastrectomy, sprue); abnormalities of urinary excretion of phosphorus (chronic renal disease, congenital abnormalities); and certain drugs (e.g., Dilantin). Histologically, osteomalacia is characterized by areas of unossified osteoid (the organic matrix of bone). When these areas of decalcified osteoid are sufficiently large, the resultant radiographic appearance is described as Looser's zone. Osteomalacia has been viewed as an uncommon disease, but this opinion is rapidly changing. Histologic examinations of bone obtained from elderly patients with femoral neck fractures have shown that 25% have changes of osteomalacia, which appears to result from dietary deficiency (Doppelt et al., 1983). This pathologic finding is important, because osteomalacia, unlike osteoporosis, is a reversible disease through the reinstitution of adequate dietary intakes of phosphorus and vitamin D. In its more florid and less common forms, osteomalacia results in significant bony deformities of long bones, bowing deformities of long bones with pseudofractures, a characteristic collapse of the vertebral bodies (the Rugger–Jersey spine), adult-onset scoliosis, and pain (Chalmers, 1968).

Paget's Disease

Paget's disease is characterized by "excessive and abnormal remodeling of bone." Histologically, one observes areas of intense osteoclastic resorption, intermingled with extreme osteoblastic activity and the formation of abnormal laminated new bone formation. Etiology is unknown, although slow-growing viruses have been implicated. The classic clinical description is a patient with an enlarging hat size, progressive bowing deformities of the lower extremities, and high-output cardiac failure, but the clinical expression may range from asymptomatic radiographic changes in a single bone to the more classic description. Approximately 1% of the population over the age of 50 has radiographic stigmata of the disease. By the age of 80, it is estimated that one of every nine individuals is affected.

The most relevant clinical manifestations of Paget's disease are bone pain, spinal stenosis, pathologic subtrochanteric fractures, and secondary OA of the hip (Arnoldi, Bordsky, & Cauchoix, 1976). Spinal stenosis results from bony compromise of the spinal canal due to excessive osteoblastic activity and poses one of the major challenges of operative spinal surgery (Barry, 1967). Pathologic subtrochanteric fractures are often complicated by a delayed or non-union and failures of internal fixation. OA results from the structural weakening of the acetabulum with progressive tendency toward intrapelvic protrusion of the femoral head (protrusio acetabulae).

Paget's disease undergoes sarcomatous degeneration in 1% of patients. These tumors are suspected by increasing pain in a previously asymptomatic patient with known Paget's disease; they have a notoriously poor prognosis.

Fractures

Fractures represent the single most important musculoskeletal problem of the aging population, with 1,700,000 osteoporosis-related fractures each year (Holbrook, 1984). The socioeconomic impact of some of those fractures, as well as the general principles that guide treatment, have been summarized. Discussion of all fractures observed in the geriatric population is beyond the scope of this paper, but attention is directed to the most common fractures—hip, spine, and distal radius—as well as to some of the principles that govern the treatment of intra-articular and long-bone fractures.

Hip Fractures

Fractures of the hip are estimated to occur in 210,000 to 250,000 patients, with an annual calculated incidence of 98 to 99 per 100,000 (Holbrook, 1984; Lewinnek, Kelsey, & White, 1980). (Note: This figure is much higher than the 150,000 fractures used to calculate annual cost.) The incidence is age-related, with a usual mean age ranging from 70 to 77. Ethnic and geographic factors influence the incidence. Such fractures are less common in blacks and in temperate climates; females are more commonly affected than males. In women, the fracture is most commonly associated with moderate trauma (fall from a chair, bed, or standing position), which accounts for 87% of the hip fractures; whereas in males, trauma is often more severe (Lewinnek et al., 1980). Costs currently are estimated to be greater than $1 billion per annum for acute care. The factors influencing morbidity and mortality have been discussed. Hip fractures are the primary cause of mortality in 2% of the U.S. population.

Fractures of the hip are classified by their anatomic location (i.e., femoral neck, intertrochanteric, subtrochanteric). The relative proportions of these fractures are variably reported, with femoral neck fractures accounting for 30% to 60% of the total. Subtrochanteric fractures are relatively uncommon (Lewinnek et al., 1980). Further subclassification of individual fractures is based on the anatomic pattern, including direction of the fracture, displacement, and the magnitude of comminution. Based on these descriptors, fractures are further classified as stable or unstable, which has major implications for successful adequate fracture stabilization (Garden, 1961).

Femoral neck fractures pose particular challenges because of the compromise of blood flow through the femoral head, which commonly occurs after that injury. Common complications include non-union, variably reported from 0% to 34%, and aseptic necrosis, variably reported from 8% to 84%, dependent on fracture pattern and treatment utilized (Calandruccio & Anderson, 1980). The initial displacement of the fracture, the reduction, and the fixation device used appear to be the most important predispositions to these complications. Because of the high rate of non-union or aseptic necrosis, optimum management of femoral neck fractures has remained controversial. Some authorities recommend primary prosthetic replacement, whereas others recommend primary internal fixation. Common indications for prosthetic replacement include "advanced physiologic age," severe displacement, inability to cooperate with the rehabilitation programs, irreducible fracture, and shortened life expectancy.

The detractors of primary prosthetic replacement point to an increased operative mortality, increased infection rate, risk of prosthetic dislocation, and the longer-term complications of loosening, intrapelvic protrusion of the prosthesis and pain which may necessitate joint replacement. Some studies indicate one or more of these late complications occur in 50% of patients within 5 years after prosthetic replacement. In recent years, the standard prosthetic designs (Austin Moore, Thompson) have been improved on by a bipolar prosthetic design, which theoretically provides a more favorable mechanical distribution of forces and is more easily converted to a total hip replacement if necessary (Long & Knight, 1980). Controversy exists as to whether methymethacrylate fixation of the femoral stem is desirable, but this adjunct is frequently chosen when bone is severely osteoporotic to ensure more stable prosthetic fixation. The proponents of internal fixation point to the lessened morbidity and mortality, as well as the desirability of retaining a normal femoral head. If internal fixation is chosen, the factors important to success include anatomic reduction of the fracture, optimum positioning of the fixation device within the femoral head, and the capacity of the device to slide (impact) as resorption occurs about the fracture site. Provided that adequate stabilization can be achieved, these devices are compatible with early weight-bearing, which does not appear to have adverse effects on the rate of non-union or aseptic necrosis.

Intertrochanteric Fractures

In contrast to femoral neck fractures, intertrochanteric fractures have a high probability of union, and avascular necrosis is a rare complication (Dimon & Hughston 1967). However, adequate stabilization of the fracture, particularly in osteoporotic bone with an unstable fracture pattern, poses major problems. In fact, adequacy of stabilization appears to be the single other most important factor that ultimately determines morbidity and mortality. The most widely used implants incorporate ability of the fixation device to impact with the fracture (i.e., a sliding nail). These devices are preferable to the traditional rigid nail fixation. Because loss of fixation occurs in 30% to 40% of unstable intertrochanteric fractures, alternative methods have been sought to deal with this difficult fracture pattern, including osteotomies to increase the stability, and positioning of the fracture in a more extreme valgus position (Sarmiento & Williams, 1970). In the severely osteoporotic elderly patient, the adjunctive use of methymethacrylate has been used by some to increase stability (Harrington, 1975). The use of intermedullary devices (Ender's nail), introduced from the distal femoral shaft, is receiving increased popularity because of the reported reduction of blood loss and intra- and postoperative mortality (Chapman et al., 1981). Regardless of the device chosen, the concept that prolonged bedrest may reduce later complications due to loss of fracture fixation is not borne out by *in vivo* biomechanical studies using telemetered internal fixation devices and prostheses. These telemetered devices show that the forces at the fracture site and joint are as great for activities required of the bedridden patient, such as getting on and off a bedpan, as the forces that occur with protected weight bearing (Rydell, 1966).

Spinal Fractures

Spinal fractures directly relate to axial osteoporosis and, in the absence of severe trauma, almost exclusively occur in patients with underlying metabolic bone disease. Twenty-seven thousand such fractures occur annually in patients over the age of 65 (Holbrook, et al., 1984). Osteoporotic spinal fractures typically occur with minimal trauma, such as bending, and often follow a sudden cough or sneeze. In such circumstances, pain may be severe and temporarily incapacitating. The usual pattern of fracture is an anterior wedge compression injury; such fractures are rarely unstable and pose no threat to spinal cord function. Other fractures are primarily manifested by chronic spinal pain and the radiographic appearance of either multiple anterior wedging deformities or deformations of the vertebral end plates. Anatomic and biomechanical studies conducted with bone densitometry measurements support the direct relationship of these fractures to the magnitude of osteoporosis (Hansson, Roos, & Nachemson, 1980).

Treatment of acute symptomatic compression fractures is directed toward pain relief. Light supportive corsets and braces may be used but have little if any effect on the healing of the fracture, deformity, or function. The complexities of applying and removing an orthotic device may preclude the elderly patient being able to comply with the prescription.

Distal Radius Fractures

Fractures of the distal radius result from a fall on the outstretched hand and are often associated with underlying medical diseases that make the person unsteady. The most common fracture pattern (Colles fracture) is dorsal displacement of the distal radial fragment, loss of radial length, and radial angulation. For most patients, manipulation and cast immobilization suffice to produce union in 4 to 8 weeks, compatible with function. Functional orthotic devices are useful because they permit earlier range of motion. Internal fixation devices are rarely indicated, and the use of external fixators to maintain radial length and position is largely unnecessary in the elderly population. Regardless of the method chosen for treatment, the overall goal is the avoidance of prolonged immobilization and careful attention to the mobilization of the wrist, as well as to the elbow and shoulder during convalescence. One of the significant complications of these injuries is the shoulder/hand syndrome (Sudek's atrophy) manifested by pain, disruption of vasomotor control, severe joint stiffness, and accelerated osteoporosis.

Intra-Articular Fractures

Fractures involving weight-bearing joints (in particular the knee and ankle) and major upper extremity intra-articular fractures (elbow and shoulder) pose particular problems in management and rehabilitation. The historic teaching advocated sacrifice of anatomic reduction for early mobilization, particularly in those comminuted fractures that disrupt the joint surfaces. These same principles still hold for fractures with modest comminution and minimal disruption of the joint. In more severely comminuted fractures, however, the traditional perspective is now being questioned as new techniques of internal fixation have become available. Although an aggressive operative approach to these fractures is not uniformly accepted, the advocates cite the improved anatomic and functional results that occur when internal fixation procedures are performed by surgeons who have the essential technical skills and equipment to accomplish desired goals. The resultant early motion and continued use of muscles is thought to prevent "fracture disease," which is defined as a stiff, painful, swollen joint associated with muscle contractures and osteoporosis in the affected limb. Certain intra-articular fractures in specific joints may best be treated by primary prosthetic replacement. The best example is in three- and four-part fractures of the shoulder that have a high risk for avascular necrosis (Neer, Watson, & Stanton, 1982). As an adjunct to the treatment of these complex injuries, the use of continuous passive motion is now being advocated as yet another promising method to promote functional rehabilitation.

Long-Bone Fractures

Long-bone fractures of the upper extremities, particularly the humerus, can be satisfactorily treated by braces or alternatively by intermedullary devices. Forearm fractures have the best functional outcome after plating, although functional cast braces are a suitable alternative. Fractures of the femoral shaft pose special problems because of the prolonged immobility that traction treatment requires. Alternatives include the use of functional cast braces, which can result in early mobilization and maintenance of joint function, sometimes at the sacrifice of leg length equality. However, the weight of such devices adds cardiovascular work, which in the patient with significant cardiac disease may be unacceptable. Intramedullary devices are the preferred alternative, and special approaches such as "nested" rods may be necessary to fill up the enlarged medullary canal in the osteoporotic patient. Because of improved radiographic technique, most intramedullary rodding can be done blindly so that the fracture site does not have to be visualized. Consequently, blood loss, tissue damage, and morbidity are reduced. In contrast, tibial shaft fractures are usually amenable to functional cast brace treatments, which permit early weight bearing and are compatible with functional rehabilitation. Particular attention must be directed to the avoidance of ulcers when these casts and braces are used in the vascularly compromised lower extremity.

Degenerative Diseases

The management of OA includes medical, surgical, and rehabilitative approaches. The medical and overall rehabilitative management of osteoarthritis will be discussed elsewhere in this symposium. It should be emphasized that simple measures, such as the use of canes, anti-inflammatory drugs, exercise programs, and splints may suffice for many patients and permit adequate function and pain control. The remainder of this discussion will focus on surgical approaches to the rehabilitation of the osteoarthritic patient. The principles outlined are equally applicable to other disease entities such as rheumatoid disease and aseptic necrosis.

Two joints, the hip and knee, account for the majority of reconstructive surgical procedures performed for arthritis. Although there are many surgical options available for the management of arthritic joints, such as fusion, osteotomy, and hemiarthroplasties, total joint replacement remains the preferred method of treatment for most elderly patients who require surgical interventions. It is estimated that 108,000 total hip arthroplasties are performed annually in the United States and that 50,000 total knee arthroplasties are performed. Elderly patients are the most common group who require such procedures.

The indications for these operations are (a) incapacitating pain in the face of "optimum medical management"; (b) presence of adequate bone stock to allow the procedure to be performed; (c) adequate neuromuscular control of the operated limb; (d) the absence of infection at the local operative site or remote infections; (e) satisfactory overall medical health, which permits the surgery to be performed safely; and (f) reasonable expectation that arthroplastic replacement will at least preserve, if not improve, function. Age *per se* is not a contraindication, although coexistent severe medical diseases may raise the risks of surgery to an unacceptable level. Also, advanced age always raises cost–benefit questions.

The basic components of total joint replacement have remained the same over the past decade and include a polyethylene component, a matted metallic bearing surface, and methylmethacrylate, which acts as a grout to stabilize the prosthetic components. Evolutions in prosthetic designs have improved both the early rehabilitation of patients and later durability of these operations. Metal backing of plastic components has been shown experimentally, by mathematical modeling, and by clinical experience to equalize stress distributions at the prosthesis–bone interface, which is of particular importance in patients with underlying osteoporosis as a means of preventing later loosening (Harris, 1984; Carter, Vasu, & Harris, 1982). Cement retaining devices, the use of pressurization, and cement centrifugation have led to improved fixation and durability of the cement at the bone–cement interface. Advances in metallurgy have led to strengthening of components, with a decrease in the rate of appliance failure due to fatigue fractures. Improvements in the clinical and biomechanical understanding of prosthetic alignment, prosthetic placement, and ligamentus rebalancing also have reduced the risk of later prosthetic loosening and fracture. Other advances in design currently seem less applicable to the elderly population. The most popular of these advances are the porous-coated devices that permit bony ingrowth for the stabilization of the prosthesis, theoretically avoiding the later problems produced by methylmethacrylate. Because such devices require an extended period of protected weight bearing, and also depend on adequate bone stock, these devices seem less applicable to the aging population, particularly those with osteoporosis.

A variety of rating scales has been developed to assess the clinical results that follow joint arthroplasty, scales are based on such factors as pain relief, function, range of motion, and stability (Harris, 1969). Using these clinical criteria, short-term success rates range from 90% to 95%. Early failures are the result of infections that occur in 0.5% to 38%, major medical complications (particularly thromboembolism), interoperative fractures, prosthetic malpositioning and dislocations, stiffness due to ectopic bone formation, and vascular or neurologic complications (Charnley & Cupic, 1973; Stauffer, 1982). The use of perioperative antibiotics has been shown to reduce the risk of infection, and thromboembolic complications can be reduced by a variety of anticoagulant regimens of which graded heparin doses currently appear to be most effective (Leyvraz, Richard, & Bachmann, 1983). Results, as measured by the same clinical criterion, tend to deteriorate over time because of the later prosthetic failures. The 10-year experience indicates 5% to 15% failure rates, and radiographic evidence of potential failure is identified in an additional 5% to 15% of patients. Factors associated with long-term failures include excessive weight (greater than 200 lb.), male sex, age (younger individuals at greater risk for failure than older individuals), prosthetic malpositioning and joint malalignments, osteoporosis, and certain older prosthetic designs. Fractures about the prosthetic devices pose special problems in management, as does late infection.

Although the hip and knee are most commonly treated by replacement arthroplasty, similar devices are available for implantation in the shoulder, elbow, wrist, and ankle. The evolution of prosthetic design is far less advanced in these joints. The most common indication is rheumatoid arthritis rather than OA. Similarly, the small joints of the hands and feet can be treated successfully by arthroplasties, although silastic interpositional devices are the usual prosthetic design.

Spinal OA

It is known that 80% of adults are affected at some time in their life by low back pain. Although radiographic evidence of spinal degeneration, defined as disc space narrowing and spinal osteophytes, increases directly as a function of age, clinical symptoms are less prevalent after age 50 (Frymoyer, Pope, & Costanza, 1980). The most common clinical syndrome—herniated nucleus pulposus—also is uncommon after the age of 50, but the incidence of upper lumbar disc lesions increases (Figure 17-2) (Spangford, 1972). The observation that back pain and disc herniations diminish with age may be explained by age-related loss of proteoglycans, diminished water content of the disc, and relative increases in collagen—all of which may "physiologically stabilize" the disc. Stabilization also may occur by osteophytic overgrowth, which increases overall surface area for load sharing and results in a diminished force per unit area.

Figure 17-3 outlines the various clinical syndromes that may occur (Pope, Lehmann, & Frymoyer, 1984). In the aging spine, the most clinically relevant syndromes are spinal OA (spondylosis) and spinal stenosis. The former is characterized by axial pain, usually increased by weight bearing and sitting and associated spinal stiffness, whereas the latter is usually manifested by peripheral neurologic symptoms. Nerve root symptoms may be due to direct nerve root compression or interference with the vascular supply to the spinal cord and cauda equina. In the cervical spine, spon-

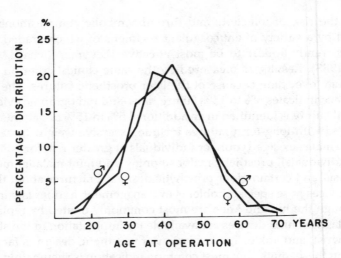

Figure 17-2 This graph depicts the percentage distribution of operations for herniated nucleau pulposus for males and females. Note the relative infrequency of disc herniations as a percentage of the whole after the age of 60. The peak frequently occurs at age 42. (Reprinted with permission from Erik V. Spangford and *Acta Orthopaedica Scandinavica* from "The Lumbar Disc Herniation—A Computer-aided Analysis of 2,504 Operations," Supplementum 142, page 17, 1972.)

dylosis commonly is manifested by peripheral radiculopathies and less commonly by transverse myelopathies where upper motor neuron symptoms and signs predominate (Bohlman, 1984). In the lumbar spine, the clinical syndrome of stenosis results from encroachments by posterior osteophytes at the margin of the discs, hypertrophy of the facets, and sometimes collapse of the ligamentum flavum. These changes may be focal or diffuse. The most common focal lesion is degenerative spondylolisthesis, which is more common in females (risk, 4:1 for males), is most commonly located at the L4-5 level, and appears to be predisposed to by diabetes (Rosenberg, 1975). The common clinical symptoms are claudicatory leg pain, defined as referred pain in the distribution of one or more lumbar nerve roots which is increased by walking and relieved by sitting. Relief of pain by sitting often differentiates claudication due to spinal stenosis from vascular causes, and is the result of the spinal canal dimensions being greater with the spine in the forward flexed position. The available evidence suggests that the neurologic symptoms result from an underlying compromise of the vascular supply to the cauda equina, produced by the bony stenosis (Crock & Yoshizawa 1976). At the present time, the

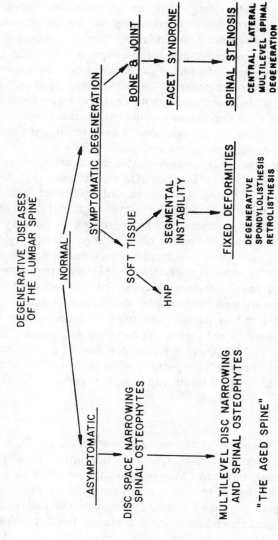

Figure 17-3. This outlines the possible clinical manifestations of degenerative disease. Attention is drawn to the fact that many of the radiographic signs of degeneration such as disc space narrowing and spinal osteophytes are unassociated with symptoms. The "aged spine" is frequently associated with multiple changes characterized as degeneration, but without significant symptoms. Symptomatic degeneration can involve predominantly the soft tissues of the spine leading to disc herniation, abnormalities in motion such as segmental instability, and ultimately fixed deformities of the spine. In other instances, overgrowth, particularly of the facet joints and resultant narrowing of the spine may lead to the syndrome of spinal stenosis.

epidemiology of these various spinal disorders is only poorly understood, but it is commonly believed the annual incidence is increasing proportionally to the aging population.

The treatment of degenerative spinal disease includes conservative measures such as anti-inflammatory drugs, orthotic devices such as cervical collars and lumbar braces, traction, and occasionally the use of epidural blocks. If symptoms become disabling, particularly if there is progressive loss of sensation and motor power, surgical intervention is warranted. In the cervical spine, decompression of affected nerve roots may be accomplished by anterior or posterior approaches. When an anterior approach is used, an interbody fusion is often performed; whereas in posterior decompressions, stabilization is only occasionally required. When there is a transverse myelopathy, indications for operative intervention are much less well defined and the surgical outcome less predictable.

In the lumbar spine, posterior decompression is the usual approach. Adequate decompression may require sacrifice of facets and even pedicles. In the aging population, spinal fusion is less commonly indicated than in the younger population, probably because the "physiologic stabilization" present in the older population reduces the risk for later instability syndromes. Because lumbar and cervical spinal disease have a tendency to coexist, it is not uncommon for patients to require treatment of both their cervical and lumbar lesions by either conservative or operative approaches. Dependent on the criterion used to measure success, the results of such interventions in both the cervical and lumbar spine range from 70% to 90%. Success often may be defined as partial pain relief and prevention of further deterioration in neurologic function, rather than as dramatic improvement in function. At present, there is no direct evidence that defines the numbers of these surgical procedures performed annually and no information relating to either the cost of treatment or cost–benefit.

Infections

Infections of the musculoskeletal system may affect bones, joints, and bursa, as well as the intervertebral discs. Osteomyelitis poses the single greatest challenge in management and may occur as the result of hemotogenous spread from other foci of infection, as the result of the direct extension of an infection from an adjacent structure, or as the sequelae of a penetrating injury or surgical procedure (Cierny & Mader, 1984). Infection of joints may occur through the same routes, and also may follow aspiration or injection of a joint.

The description of osteomyelitis is based on its anatomic site, the location of the process within the affected bone (medullary, superficial, diffuse), and also by underlying host factors, based largely on immune competence.

Staphylococcus aureus, streptococcus, and gram-negative organisms such as Pseudomonas are most common, although organisms traditionally viewed as nonpathogenic frequently are identified in infections that accompany implant surgery. Factors that predispose to osteomyelitis relate to the local tissue competence, as well as to the overall immune status. Local factors include vascular sufficiency, quality of skin, lymphedema, as well as the presence or absence of associated factors such as implants. Systemic factors that predispose to infection include any chronic disease, most particularly renal and liver failure, diabetes, chronic immunosuppression by steroids or antimetabolite drugs, and the presence of other remote foci of infections such as urinary tract disease. These same factors increase the risk of a joint infection, as does any underlying joint disease such as OA and rheumatoid arthritis. Age is a risk factor for both joint and bone infections, probably because of associated medical diseases and alterations in the skin and vasculature.

The clinical presentation of osteomyelitis is varied and depends on the type and location, the organism, and the associated local and systemic factors described above. Particularly relevant to the overall problem of infection is a significant probability that a hematogenous infection will not be considered as part of the differential diagnosis and that significant delay will occur between onset of symptoms and definitive diagnosis and treatment. This delay is variably reported as 60 to 90 days for spinal infections and somewhat less for joint infections (Ho, Toder, & Zimmermann, 1984). The delay in diagnosis is often because the patient frequently has an underlying disease, such as OA, and the increased pain is thought to be a manifestation of the basic disease process. Also, infections are commonly misdiagnosed as neoplasms.

The treatment of infections of bones and joints depends on accurate identification of the infecting organism, the systemic administration of bactericidal antibiotics, and local operative intervention. Many operative techniques are available, but the basic principles of treatment include debridement of all the devitalized, avascular, and infected tissues, removal of all foreign material, and often the administration of high local concentrations of antibiotics through perfusion techniques or implantation of methylmethacrylate beads impregnated with appropriate antibiotics. Stabilization of an infected long bone or spine is important to promoting healing and also to preventing pathologic fractures, which are devastating complications of infection. If there is an associated fracture, this poses special problems in management which, at the extreme, may result in amputation—particularly in the elderly patient.

The ultimate outcome of infections depends on the magnitude of infection, the organism, the associated systemic diseases, and the adequacy of the surgical technique. Although good mortality statistics are not available for all types and forms of osteomyelitis and joint infections, it is known that the death rate associated with vertebral osteomyelitis, or disc space infection in the aged, approaches 50%. Although the socioeconomic impact is small compared with many other diseases of the aged, the individual case cost often can be extremely high. For example, the cost for treatment of an infection of a total joint arthroplasty is estimated to be $100,000.

Neoplasms

Malignant neoplasms affecting the musculoskeletal system are most commonly metastatic rather than primary tumors. The most common sites of origin are breast, lung, kidney, prostate, and thyroid. The most common primary bone neoplasm in the elderly is multiple myeloma, although osteogenic sarcoma, fibrosarcoma, and other tumors may occur, particularly in association with Paget's disease, in areas of previously irradiated bone, or occasionally after long-standing osteomyelitis.

The major clinical problem of metastatic neoplasms and multiple myeloma relates to bone pain and impending or actual pathologic fracture due to the structural weakening of the affected bone. Radiographic criteria have been developed and continue to evolve that attempt to quantify the risk of fracture based on tumor type and anatomic location, size of the metastatic lesion, and presence or absence of cortical bone involvement.

It is well recognized that operative stabilization is less traumatic, initial stabilization is greater, and function is more rapidly restored if treatment is initiated before fracture has occurred. Morbidity and mortality are therefore reduced. The femoral and humeral shafts are the most common long bones requiring stabilization. Intramedullary devices, rather than plates and screws, are the preferred method because intramedullary devices are not dependent on cortical integrity for adequate stabilization (Boland, Lane, & Sundaresan, 1982; Harrington, 1982; Levy, Sherry, & Siffert, 1982; Pugh, Sherry, Futterman, & Frankel, 1982; Sim & Pritchard, 1982). The use of adjunctive methylmethacrylate is controversial.

Impending and actual fractures involving the subtrochanteric region of the femur seem best to be treated by the Zickel intermedullary device, although on occasion severe bone loss may necessitate a proximal femoral replacement arthroplasty. Fractures of the femur proximal to the subtrochanteric region are often treated by cemented endoprosthetic replacement, but hip nails combined with supplemental methylmethacrylate are an alternative method.

Because most other bones can adequately be treated by splints, operative intervention is rarely required. In the spine, the decision to operate is largely based on pending or actual neurologic involvement, rather than pain, which often is controllable by radiation therapy. Decompression through either an anterior or a posterior route combined with operative stabilization, often with supplemental methylmethacrylate, is the usual approach (Clarke, Kessi, & Panjabi, 1984).

Regardless of the anatomic structures involved, the choice to do an operation is based on a reasonable probability of survival for more than 3 to 4 weeks, which in turn will depend on the overall tumor activity and the presence of other metastatic lesions. The benefits of stabilization are to allow functional rehabilitation and relative freedom from pain, particularly when radiation therapy is combined with the operative approach. In the operative management of these patients, particular attention must be paid to actual or impending hypercalcemia, which can be life-threatening if unrecognized.

Primary bone tumors, other than myeloma, pose quite different problems. Here the goal is to eradicate the disease if possible. This goal may be achievable by amputation or radical limb-sparing resections, which in the elderly often are accompanied by prosthetic replacements of the excised parts. Local radiation therapy combined with a variety of chemotherapeutic regimens are further adjuncts to treatment. If metastatic spread has been identified, one nevertheless may elect to perform local resections, or even ablative surgery for the purposes of pain control and preventing local tissue breakdown as the tumor expands in size.

OTHER PROBLEMS OF THE MUSCULOSKELETAL SYSTEM

The principles outlined in the rehabilitation of musculoskeletal injuries are widely applicable to most anatomic structures that make up that system. The foot and hand pose certain special problems that are beyond the scope of this paper. It should be emphasized, however, that in both the hand and foot many of the principles outlined are applicable, and also that there are numerous specific orthotic, prosthetic, and implant devices that can improve hand and foot function in the elderly. It also should be emphasized that diseases of other systems, most particularly neuromuscular diseases, may require musculoskeletal intervention to maintain maximal function. These goals often can also be achieved by orthotic and prosthetic devices, as well as reconstructive surgery. For example, the function of the spastic hemiplegic is often improved by such procedures as tendon transfers, neurectomies, and even joint arthrodeses.

SUMMARY

This article has reviewed selected topics in the epidemiology, patho-physiology, diagnosis, rehabilitation, and operative interventions for aging patients with musculoskeletal diseases and injuries. Many of the principles and procedures identified are applicable to the younger population, par-ticularly those with chronic diseases present since birth or acquired in early adulthood. For example, much of the philosophy detailed for the treatment of fractures is equally applicable to younger patients with chronic neuro-muscular diseases who sustain fractures. Alterations in function resulting from osteoporosis, diminished muscular function, and increased risk of joint stiffness are similar for younger patients with chronic disease. It again is re-emphasized that most musculoskeletal diseases of the aged represent a continuum of events often starting early in life, rather than as diseases specific to the aged. Because of this fact, it is most important that patients at risk for the later development of musculoskeletal disease be identified early in their lives and appropriate preventive measures taken. Currently this aggressive intervention philosophy is being applied to the early prevention of osteoporosis, as well as to the more aggressive management of mus-culoskeletal diseases and injuries that have a high probability of leading to later OA.

The overall philosophy of management in the elderly patients with mus-culoskeletal diseases remains largely unchanged, although the specific methods to achieve these goals are changing. Avoidance of immobilization, maximal attempts at functional rehabilitation, maximal preservation of muscular strength and joint mobility are seen as essential cornerstones of treatment. The major changes in treatment philosophy that have occurred during the past decade have been related to more aggressive operative in-tervention to achieve these goals. This change in approach has been pro-moted by improved knowledge regarding basic nutrition and fluid and electrolyte management, increased awareness of the natural history of dis-eases and injuries in the aging, and improved biomechanical understand-ing critical to implant design.

Although this review is not focused specifically on the longer-term rehabilitation requirements of the elderly patient with a musculoskeletal in-jury or disease, it is apparent that total rehabilitation is a continuum, start-ing at the time of initial treatment and continuing until maximal functional restoration has occurred. This continuum of treatment requires an early and ongoing collaborative effort between physicians, surgeons, nurses, physical and occupational therapists, and social workers. The longer-term rehabilitation requires adherence to the principals of preservation and maximization of muscle strength and endurance, restoration and main-tenance of maximal joint mobility, the maximization of ambulatory and functional status, and the avoidance of medical complications that often delay or prohibit successful rehabilitation. Goals for rehabilitation must be set at the highest attainable level within the realities of the patient's overall health and capabilities. Whenever possible, the goal should be directed toward the patient's functioning independently and in a noninstitutional environment. In each part of this process, the select use of modalities such as heat, cold, ultrasound, and the like may all play a role in achieving specific goals. The physical therapist is invaluable in selecting physical rehabilitative methods most applicable to the patient and seeing that those methods are applied consistently. New devices, such as the continuous passive motion machine, isokinetic exercise machines, and other devices are important treatment adjuncts. The occupational therapist also can make major differences in the patient's function through the selection of assistive devices.

Despite the major advances that have occurred, critical gaps in knowledge remain: much greater information is needed regarding the basic tissue properties (biochemical, physiological, and mechanical) of the aging musculoskeletal system; ongoing research is required in developing better prosthetic and orthotic devices, which will be possible only through improved understanding of tissue properties and by collaborative research with bioengineers; the natural history of diseases and injuries needs far greater definition, as does the outcome of various treatments in both the short and long term; the epidemiology of disease and injuries is incompletely understood and lacks background for addressing critical social issues such as cost, cost–benefit, quality of life, and resource allocations. As our aging population increases, these issues will become of increasing importance to our society.

REFERENCES

Aaron, M., & Schwartz, W. (1984). Rationing hospital care: Lessons from Britain. *New England Journal of Medicine, 310*(1), 52–56.

Arnoldi, C., Bordsky, A., Cauchoix, J. (1976). Lumbar spinal stenosis and nerve root entrapment syndromes. *Clinical Orthopaedics and Related Research, 115,* 4–5.

Barry, H. (1967). Fractures of the femur in Paget's disease of bone in Australia. *Journal of Bone and Joint Surgery, 49-A,* 1359–1370.

Barzel, U. (1983). Common metabolic disorders of the skeleton in aging. In W. Reichel (Ed.), *Clinical aspects of aging* (pp. 360–370). Baltimore: Williams and Wilkins.

Bohlman, H. (1984). Osteoarthritis of the cervical spine. In R. W. Moskowitz et al. (Eds.), *Osteoarthritis: Diagnosis and Management* (pp. 443–459). Philadelphia: W. B. Saunders.

Boland, P., Lane, J., & Sundaresan, N. (1982). Metastatic disease of the spine. *Clinical Orthopaedics and Related Research, 169,* 95–102.

Calandruccio, R., & Anderson, W. (1980). Post-fracture avascular necrosis of the femoral head: Correlation of experimental and clinical studies. *Clinical Orthopaedics and Related Research, 152,* 49–84.

Carter, D., Vasu, R., & Harris, W. (1982). Stress distributions in the acetabular region. II. Effects of cement thickness and metal backing of the total hip acetabular component. *Journal of Biomechanics, 15,* 165–170.

Ceder, L., Svensson, B., & Thorngren, K. (1980). Statistical prediction of rehabilitation in elderly patients with hip fractures. *Clinical Orthopaedics, 152,* 185–190.

Chalmers, J. (1968). Osteomalacia: A review of 93 cases. *Journal of The Royal College of Surgeons of Edinburgh, 13,* 255.

Chapman, M., Bowman, W., Csongradi, J., et al. 1981. The use of Ender's pins in extracapsular fractures of the hip. *Journal of Bone and Joint Surgery, 63-A*(1), 14–28.

Charnley, J., & Cupic, Z. (1973). The nine and ten year results of the low-friction arthroplasty of the hip. *Clinical Orthopaedics, 95,* 9–25.

Cierny, G., & Mader, J. (1984). Adult chronic osteomyelitis. *Orthopaedics, 7*(10), 1557–1564.

Clark, C., Kessi, K., & Panjabi, M. (1984). Methylmethacrylate stabilization of the cervical spine. *Journal of Bone and Joint Surgery, 66-A*(1), 40–46.

Crock, H., & Yoshizawa, H. (1976). The blood supply of the lumbar vertebral column. *Clinical Orthopaedics and Related Research, 115,* 6–21.

Dimon, J., & Hughston, J. (1967). Unstable intertrochanteric fractures of the hip. *Journal of Bone and Joint Surgery, 49-A,* 440.

Doppelt, S., Neer, R., Daly, M., et al. (1983). Osteomalacia and vitamin D deficiency in patients with hip fractures—an unrecognized epidemic. *The Journal of Bone and Joint Surgery, 7*(3), 512–513.

Frymoyer, J., Pope, M., & Costanza, M. (1980). Epidemiologic studies of low-back pain. *Spine, 5*(5), 419–423.

Gallagher, J., Melton, L., & Riggs, B. (1980). Examination of prevalence rates of possible risk factors in a population with a fracture of the proximal femur. *Clinical Orthopaedics and Related Research, 153,* 158–165.

Garden, R. (1961). Low angle fixation in fractures of the femoral neck. *Journal of Bone and Joint Surgery, 43HB,* 647.

Hamerman, D. (1983). Current leads in research on the osteoarthritic joint. *Journal of the American Geriatrics Society, 31*(5), 299–304.

Hansson, T., Roos, B., & Nachemson, A. (1980). The bone mineral content and biomechanical properties in lumbar vertebrae. *Spine, 1,* 46–55.

Harrington, K. (1975). The use of methylmethacrylate as an adjunct in the internal fixation of unstable comminuted intertrochanteric fractures in osteoporotic patients. *Journal of Bone and Joint Surgery, 57-A,* 744–750.

Harrington, K. (1982). New trends in the management of lower extremity metastases. *Clinical Orthopaedics and Related Research, 169,* 53–61.

Harris, W. (1969). Traumatic arthritis of the hip after dislocation and acetabular fractures: Treatment by mold arthroplasty. *Journal of Bone and Joint Surgery, 51-A,* 737–755.

Harris, W. (1977). Idiopathic osteoarthritis of the hip—a twentieth-century myth? *Journal of Bone and Joint Surgery, 59-B,* 121.

Harris, W. (1984). Advances in total hip arthroplasty: The metal-backed acetabular component. *Clinical Orthopaedics and Related Research, 183,* 4–11.

Ho, G., Toder, J., & Zimmermann, B. (1984). An overview of septic arthritis and septic bursitis. *Orthopaedics, 7*(10), 1571–1576.

Holbrook, T. (1984). *Epidemiology and impact of musculoskeletal injuries in the general population of the United States.* Ph.D. dissertation, Yale University.

Holbrook, T., Grazier, K., Kelsey, J., et al. (1984). *The frequency of occurrence, impact and cost of selected musculoskeletal conditions in the United States.* American Academy of Orthopaedic Surgeons, Chicago.

Horsman, A., Jones, M., Francis, R., & Nordin, C. (1983). The effect of estrogen dose on postmenopausal bone loss. *New England Journal of Medicine, 309,* 1405–1407.

Howell, D. (1984). Etiopathogenesis of osteoarthritis. In R. W. Moskowitz et al. (Eds.), *Osteoarthritis: Diagnosis and management* (pp. 129–146). Philadelphia: W. B. Saunders.

Jensen, J., Tondevoid, E., & Sorenson, P. (1980). Costs of treatment of hip fractures. *Acta Orthopaedica Scandinavica, 51,* 289–296.

Kelsey, J., White, A., Pastides, H., & Bisbee, G. (1979). The impact of musculoskeletal disorders on the population of the United States. *The Journal of Bone and Joint Surgery, 61-A,* 959–964.

Levy, R., Sherry, H., & Siffert, R. (1982). Surgical management of metastatic disease of bone at the hip. *Clinical Orthopaedics and Related Research, 169,* 62–69.

Lewinnek, G., Kelsey, J., & White, A. (1980). The significance and a comparative analysis of the epidemiology of hip fractures. *Clinical Orthopaedics and Related Research, 152,* 35–43.

Leyvraz, P., Richard, J., & Bachmann, F. (1983). Adjusted versus fixed-dose subcutaneous heparin in the prevention of deep-vein thrombosis after total hip replacement. *New England Journal of Medicine, 309,* 954–958.

Long, J., & Knight, W. (1980). Batemen UPF prosthesis in fractures of the femoral neck. *Clinical Orthopaedics and Related Research, 152,* 198–201.

Mankin, H. (1974a). Rickets, osteomalacia, and renal osteodystrophy, Part I. *Journal of Bone and Joint Surgery, 56-A,* 101–128.

Mankin, H. (1974b). Rickets, osteomalacia, and renal osteodystrophy, Part II. *Journal of Bone and Joint Surgery, 56-A,* 352–386.

Mankin, H., & Brandt, K. (1984). Biochemistry and metabolism of cartilage in osteoarthritis. In R. Moskowitz et al. (Eds.), *Osteoarthritis: Diagnosis and management* (pp. 43–79). Philadelphia: W. B. Saunders.

Mazess, R. (1982). On aging bone loss. *Clinical Orthopaedics and Related Research, 165,* 239–252.

McDonagh, M., White, M., & Davies, C. (1984). Different effects of ageing on the mechanical properties of human arm and leg muscles. *Gerontology, 30,* 49–54.

Meachim, G., & Brooke, G. (1984). The pathology of osteoarthritis. In R.W. Moskowitz et al. (Eds.), *Osteoarthritis: Diagnosis and management* (pp. 29–42). Philadelphia: W. B. Saunders.

Melton, L., Stauffer, R., Chao, E., & Ilstrup, D. (1982). Rates of total hip arthroplasty. *New England Journal of Medicine, 307,* 1242–1245.

National Institutes of Health. (1984). Osteoporosis, Consensus Development Conference statement, 5(3).

Neer, C., Watson, K., & Stanton, F. (1982). Recent experiences in total shoulder replacement. *Journal of Bone and Joint Surgery, 64A,* 319–337.

Niemann, K., & Mankin, H. (1968). Fractures about the hip in an institutionalized patient population. *Journal of Bone and Joint Surgery, 50-A,* 1327–1340.

Owen, R., Melton, L., Gallagher, J., & Riggs, B. (1980). The national cost of acute care of hip fractures associated with osteoporosis. *Clinical Orthopaedics and Related Research, 150,* 172–176.

Pope, M., Lehmann, T., & Frymoyer, J. (1984). Structure and function of the lumbar spine. In *Occupational low back pain* (pp. 5–38). New York: Praeger.

Pope, M., Wilder, D., & Booth, J. (1980). The biomechanics of low back pain. In *American Academy of Orthopaedic Surgeons symposium on idiopathic low back pain* (section 3, pp. 252–295). Author.

Pugh, J., Sherry, H., Futterman, B., & Frankel, V. (1982). Biomechanics of pathologic fractures. *Clinical Orthopaedics and Related Research, 169,* 109–114.

Radin, E. (1984). Biomechanical considerations. In R.W. Moskowitz et al. (Eds.), *Osteoarthritis: Diagnosis and management* (pp. 93–107). Philadelphia: W. B. Saunders.

Ritter, M., & McAdoo, G. (1979). A method for determining success following total hip replacement surgery. *Clinical Orthopaedics and Related Research, 141,* 44–49.

Rosenberg, N. (1975). Degenerative spondylolisthesis: Pre-disposing factors. *Journal of Bone and Joint Surgery, 57-A,* 467–474.

Rothstein, J., & Rose, S. (1982). Muscle mutability. *Physical Therapy, 62*(12), 1788–1798.

Rowe, C., & Lowell, J. (1961). Prognosis of fractures of the acetabulum. *Journal of Bone and Joint Surgery, 43-A,* 30–59.

Rydell, N. (1966). Forces acting on the femoral head-prosthesis. *Acta Orthopaedica Scandinavica, 37* (suppl. 88).

Sarmiento, A., & Latta, L. (1981). *Closed functional treatment of fractures.* Berlin-Heidelberg-New York: Springer-Verlag.

Sarmiento, A., & Williams, E. (1970). The unstable intertrochanteric fracture: Treatment with a valgus osteotomy and I-beam nail-plate: A preliminary report of one hundred cases. *Journal of Bone and Joint Surgery, 51-A,* 1309.

Sim, F., & Pritchard, D. (1982). Metastatic disease in the upper extremity. *Clinical Orthopaedics and Related Research, 169,* 83–94.

Smith, R., & Walker, R. (1980). Femoral expansion in aging women. *Henry Ford Hospital Medical Journal, 28*(2-3), 168–170.

Spangford, E. (1972). The lumbar disc herniation. A computer aided analysis of 2,504 operations. *Acta Orthopaedica Scandinavica, 142* (Suppl), 1–95.

Stauffer, R. (1982). Ten-year follow-up study of total hip replacement. *Journal of Bone and Joint Surgery, 64-A,* 983–990.

Taylor, D. (1976). The costs of arthritis and the benefits of joint replacement surgery. *Proceeding of Royal Society of London (Biology), 192,* 145–155.

Part V

The Social and Environmental Context

18

Technology for Functional Ability and Independent Living

Dudley S. Childress

> I believe that to deny any human being the freedom of living fully, with dignity is to deny life itself. We are called by the power within us to unite against society's mold of second class citizens and non-persons. We are called into questioning society's value system and therefore we resolve to work for social justice, for ways to maintain independent living, and the strength and courage to live with the one non-variable, change.
>
> *M. Kreager, 1984*

Mildred Kreager was a worker against ageism and for social justice. She saw value in the maintenance of independent living. To the extent that technology can work in ways to maintain independent living and to aid elderly people to live fully and with dignity, it would meet some of her expectations for overcoming problems of aging and rehabilitation. Technology is not a panacea, but, if applied with care and human understanding, it can be a positive factor in the lives of some elderly persons.

Aging is a process of decreasing physical and functional ability. To some extent it includes a gradual diminishment of activities, a fading away. There may be reduced energy, reduced mobility, and even a lowering of expectations concerning one's ability and effectiveness.

Disabilities caused by amputations, strokes, arthritis, and the like often

303

contribute to or accelerate aging by contributing to diminished activity and ability. Vineberg (1961) had concluded: "Rehabilitation, on the other hand, aims at expansion of the individual's life space, at social re-integration, at 're-engagement' of the individual. In this sense, rehabilitation may be viewed as a 'de-aging' process." That idea will be the theme of this paper. The goal of technical devices and technology in aging should be to contribute to the "de-aging" process.

There are no magical devices that will solve all the problems of older people. In fact, I'm not particularly sanguine about technical aids for elderly people. As people grow older, they seem to become less interested in technology and more interested in children, travel, gardening, music, art, and so on. Technology can be confusing to older people. Therefore, we must take care that it is used appropriately.

PREVENTION

We can increase the odds of not requiring technical aids for living through good diet, appropriate exercise, appropriate rest, appropriate health care, by living interesting lives, by not smoking, by controlling blood pressure, by having received appropriate genes, and by experiencing a little luck. This being the case, we can fall apart all at once like the "Wonderful One-Horse Shay."

We can also prevent the need for technical aids for serious health conditions by using simple aids to prevent serious injury. From a physical view point, *auto seat belts* and *balance aids* are probably most important. The *cane* may be one of the most underutilized technical aids for older persons. We need to make it "in style" to use a cane. If canes were stylish, like eyeglasses, much injury-accelerated aging could be prevented by avoidance of falls. If some well-known persons, like Jacqueline Kennedy Onassis or President Reagan, were to use canes (perhaps only for esthetic purposes), their influence might encourage people to use canes and, as a result, reduce the number of injuries caused by falls. President Reagan has already improved the acceptability of hearing aids.

Walkers and *grab bars* are other technical aids that can prevent injuries. Walkers probably will never be stylish, but bathroom designers can certainly make grab bars important and attractive features in the well-designed and beautiful bathroom.

Prevention of the need for aids is the most effective way to use technical aids. Nevertheless, the need for technical assistance cannot always be avoided through prevention schemes.

APPROPRIATE TECHNOLOGY

Schumacher (1973) has pointed out the need for developing countries to use technologies appropriate to their location environment, resources, and manpower. We can apply this same notion to technical aids for aging and handicapped citizens. The *rocking chair* is one of the best examples of appropriate technology for elderly persons. It is an exceptional aid, very acceptable, and usable by people of all ages. The rocking chair provides low-level exercise for the user. Coupled with music, the rocking chair, like dancing, gives the user a certain rhythm to living. The rocking chair also produces dynamic redistribution of seating pressure on the user's body tissues. It is an appropriate technology, relatively inexpensive, and non-complex, yet perhaps not used as widely today as it once was.

Modern chairs often have low seats and are difficult to use, particularly by some elderly people who have trouble getting down into them and up out of them. A friend, whose mother was having this problem, asked me about chairs that mechanically assist with this process. I consulted some occupational therapists about the matter and they suggested special wooden blocks under the chair legs to raise the level of the seat. In this way the woman could move on and off the chair with very little effort. A footstool was required. This simple and straightforward solution avoided complicating technology. It was appropriate technology.

TOOLS FOR LIVING

Wolff (1980a) has suggested that we look upon aids not in the sense of "aids for the disabled" but as "tools for living." He feels there is stigma concerning use of paramedical appliances that are often prescribed by physicians or suggested by persons associated with the medical field. We should encourage an attitude that such tools are as acceptable and ordinary as electric drills or all the other tools that persons commonly use.

Wolff's suggestion for "tools of living" is well illustrated in a new sales catalog called *Comfortably Yours: Aids for Easier Living.* This sales approach presents technical aids in a positive way, without undue association with disability. The aids are attractively designed and presented. Also, not all of the aids relate to functional loss. Undoubtedly, we will see more of this approach to "tools for living." Sears, Roebuck and Company is moving in this direction with some of their catalogs.

Along this line, Wolff (1980b) has suggested a chain of stores where everything could be bought for grandmother. He visualizes them as something like the Mothercare shops of Canada, France, and the United Kingdom. Wolff calls the proposed shops, "Granny-Care" shops. Many Americans with whom I've talked like the idea but not the name.

Through the years, occupational therapists have developed expertise related to aids for disabled persons. Their knowledge and approach, appropriately modified for the older population, should be of great use for people in the field of gerontology. Occupational therapists can effectively help elderly people equip their homes with aids that can greatly extend their ability to live independently. In recent years, engineers trained in rehabilitation engineering have been able to complement the work of occupational therapists. Working together, the therapist and engineer (or appropriately trained technical person) can be an effective team in solving problems of the elderly and the handicapped.

Faletti (1984b) suggests that functional impairment be separated from disability. He feels the disability-oriented view tends to emphasize the characteristics of the person rather than describing the total person-environment system. The approach to technical aids for the elderly should be a nonmedical, nondisability approach. This supports the ideas of Wolff (1980a). It does not rule out use of the knowledge-base buildup by occupational therapists, but suggests the application of that knowledge may need to be modified for aging persons.

Faletti's concept views the environment as often having a handicapping function. This idea is prevalent in the thinking of many disabled consumer groups. He suggests the need for age-responsive environments, and describes how environments can be developed to meet the needs of everyday living for persons with diminished physical and sensory abilities.

Human factors engineering ("ergonomics" in the United Kingdom) looks for better ways to use man-made things or ways to design things so that they may be used better. Lawton (1977) has used this general approach related to problems of aging. Faletti (1984a) has used the human factors approach in studies related to aging (e.g., problems associated with meal preparation and the opening of bottles, jars, cans, etc.).

EXAMPLES OF TOOLS FOR LIVING

It is not possible to identify all items that could be helpful to aging and handicapped persons. However, a few examples may be helpful as an aid to understanding the kinds of tools that are important.

In the *kitchen*, pots and pans may be fitted with large-diameter handles. Faucet handles at the sink may be extended to operate at low force and without the use of finger or wrist force. Lazy Susans and ferris-wheel-type holders may be used in cabinets to make contents easily accessible. Side-by-side refrigerator designs may make access easier. Portable ovens, microwave ovens, and crock-pots may make cooking easier. Electric can openers and special lid removers are often beneficial, as are special implements such as rocker knives for persons limited to single-hand function. It is often helpful if food is packaged in small, easily identified packages. Braille identifiers on food packages can be used by some people. Technical systems are available that will read bar-codes on packages or that will read magnetic cards that have been attached to the packages. These systems provide an auditory output that describes the contents of the package. Devices that assist with identification and dispensing of medicines also may be helpful. This equipment may also remind people concerning their medicine schedule.

Door knobs may be converted to lever-type action. Vertical-bar door openers are available that allow doors to be opened by pushing with the hand, the foot, or the footrests on a wheelchair. Electric-powered doors are available but simpler approaches are better if possible. Floors should be nonskid and easily cleaned and maintained. If there are stairs, small chair-lifts or elevators may be helpful.

In the *bathroom*, grab bars are useful around tubs, showers, and toilets. Elevated toilet seats may be useful. Shower benches, bathtub benches, bathtub lifts, and nonskid mats may be important.

In the *bedroom*, ceiling poles placed near the bed may be useful for getting in and out of bed. Bed rails may be necessary. Pressure-relief mattresses may be needed and, in special cases, dynamic beds that rock to relieve pressure or to assist with breathing may be required. The standard electric bed may be useful. Bedside control of lights and other devices may be advantageous. Simple environmental controllers like the Home Controller sold at electronic retail stores may be helpful for control of lights and appliances. More advanced environmental controllers are available for severely disabled people, but these are seldom needed by the aging person.

Large-button telephones and amplified receivers may be helpful. A "ringing" light may be useful for those with hearing impairments. Electric outlet bars located at waist level may be useful in some rooms. These can eliminate the need for people to bend down behind furniture to plug in electrical devices. Remote-controlled videocassette recorders, televisions, and stereos may be useful for some elderly people if the devices are not too complicated. Electric garage door openers are a great help for those who drive but who have limited strength.

At the personal level, the use of buttonhooks in dressing is sometimes helpful. Velcro replacements for buttons can ease the process of dressing. Large-handled combs and toothbrushes may find acceptance.

MOBILITY

Canes and *walkers* enhance mobility and increase security as aids in walking. The hand grips of these devices frequently need to be large in diameter to make optimal use of hand strength. Typical canes often have handles too small in diameter. They also frequently have poor tips. Large rubber tips with flat bottoms are usually good. Canes should be cut for length so that when the cane tip is on the floor the arm is slightly flexed. One rule of thumb is to cut the cane so that the thumb of the hand holding the cane (tip at feet) is opposite the greater trochanter of the femur.

Wheelchairs frequently do not fit their occupants. This is not serious if a person is only in the chair for short periods of time during transfer from one location to another. If a person uses the chair for sitting for long periods, it must be properly sized and the supporting structure for the seat cushion and back cushion should be firm. Continuous sitting on "sling" seats of fabric, which enable a chair to be foldable, can be detrimental to the user. Also, seat width, depth, height, arm rests, and footrests must be individualized if a person is to use the chair comfortably and safely for long periods of time.

Persons with limited walking ability often find the three-wheeled powered wheelchairs (e.g., Amigo, Lark, Mobie, etc.) to be convenient and helpful. Four-wheeled powered chairs are sometimes necessary. Because sitting in the powered chair may cause difficulty similar to sitting in a manual chair, attention must be given to correct seating if the user is in the chair for long periods. The powered chair must be controlled through some input method. The hand is commonly used to drive powered chairs, but the feet, legs, head, chin, and pneumatic pressure of the mouth also may be used. If a user has a progressive disease, it may be cost-effective to arrange to use the same wheelchair as functional ability diminishes. Only the control modes need be altered. A powered wheelchair may mean that a van with a lift or ramp is needed for wider mobility.

Sidewalks facilitate walking or wheelchair use for disabled or aging citizens. Also, neighborhood shops are beneficial for these people. American suburbia, with its lack of sidewalks and distant shopping malls, is not well-suited for mobility-limited individuals.

SECURITY SYSTEMS

Security for elderly persons living alone is a universal desire. Security systems go beyond door locks and burglar and fire alarms. These are important, but beyond them is the requirement to request assistance in case of a severe fall, a heart attack, or some other emergency.

Several systems have been developed so that a person can signal for help through a small transmitter on the wrist or around the neck. Some of these systems also monitor activity in the house or require the occupant to report regularly. Lack of activity or failure to report will initiate an alarm. Systems are hospital- or community-based. Examples are "Care-Continuity," "Communi-Care," "Companion Service," "Home Town," "Phone-Care," and "Lifeline." Systems available in a local area should be carefully investigated before installation is requested. Sometimes *cost* and *trust* matters must be weighed against each other in a decision about which system to use.

HOME ASSISTANCE AND CARE

Home assistance in the form of cleaning, washing, repairs, and lawn work are important for many people who wish to live alone. Meal preparation and personal attendant care are often necessary. All of these activities can be facilitated with proper technical equipment (e.g., transfer devices, lifts, inflatable bathtubs, etc.). They are also facilitated through effective planning for their availability.

RECREATION

Walking and swimming are excellent recreation for older persons. Cycling and the stationary cycle are also good. Dancing is an activity that many older people find satisfying. From the technical side, television, video movies, radio, and stereo music provide outlets to the world-at-large without leaving the home. Of course, reading is superb activity. It can be facilitated through "talking books" for those people with visual impairments or who are bed ridden and very weak. Also, "page turners" are useful for people who cannot manipulate the pages of a book or magazine. Tape recorders can have extensions attached to their keys so that they may be activated by persons without much strength or dexterity. Some churches have tape ministries and the recorder can be used to play back each week's service.

Gardening can be excellent recreation for some aging or disabled people. Elevated gardening areas can make gardening possible for persons in wheelchairs.

MEDICAL TECHNOLOGY AND HEALTH CARE

Technological devices that are more medically oriented can be of great assistance to older persons. The pacemaker, which is an electrical stimulator for the heart, is probably one of the most successful and effective devices of this nature. Artificial joint replacement and artificial limb replacement are two other areas of effective medical technology for chronic conditions often related to age. Artificial hearts, heart assists, and incontinence controllers are only a few examples of future technological devices in long-term medical care. Other technological advances such as the CT scan, NMR, and ultrasonics are but a few of the diagnostic devices developed to enable physicians to improve the quality of long-term life.

PROSTHESES FOR ELDERLY PERSONS

Glattly (1966) found in 1963 that approximately 52% of all amputees fitted with prostheses for the first time were over 50 years of age. Of these, 82% had amputations because of vascular disease. Hansson (1984) has reported that the amputation rate in Sweden in males over 60 years of age increased from 34 per 100,000 population in 1974 to 129 per 100,000 in 1982. Since the numbers of persons in the older range are increasing, the number of amputations should be increasing unless the rate of incidence has greatly diminished (doubtful). Thirty to forty years ago, relatively few geriatric amputees were given prostheses. Today, age alone should never be the determining factor for not prescribing a prosthesis. If a person can get out of bed into a chair, he/she should be given a prosthesis. Even if the prosthesis only assists with transfer to a toilet, it is useful. Mital and Pierce (1971) point out that geriatric amputees usually have many health problems and that it is desirable from a health standpoint that they be given means for mobility, within reason. These authors also observe that prostheses should be provided early, that they should be simple, light in weight, comfortable, and safe, even at the expense of the best biomechanical principles of prosthetics. Boenick (1980) has reviewed prosthetic technology for geriatric amputees and McCollough, Sarmiento, Williams, & Sinclair (1968) have described management principles for older above-knee amputees.

In my laboratory we recommend the use of rigid, removeable casts, as described by Wu, Brncick, Krick, Putman, & Stratigos (1981), after below-knee amputation. This is followed early with the fitting of a preparatory prosthesis to the cast. Early fitting is good from a physical and a psychological standpoint.

There is a need for nursing home personnel to be better acquainted with prosthetic care. Therapists or other individuals should provide supervised walking for amputee residents and make sure the prostheses are used properly.

As already noted, prostheses for elderly persons need to be simple. They should also be easy to "don" and to "doff," and be as inexpensive as possible. Elderly amputees often wait longer than other amputees to replace worn-out prostheses and they endure socket pain longer because they may not have the money to buy a new one. Expense for a prosthesis may be considerable, even with the assistance of Medicare.

DELIVERY OF AIDS

Page, Galer, Fitzgerald, & Feeney (1980), in a study of some 500 people with technical aids, found that about 50% of all aids were being used (or that 50% were not being used, whatever your viewpoint). The investigators found that aids were not used because (a) they were misprescribed, (b) they did not work or were not safe, (c) the aid was broken, or (d) what the client really needed was personal help. There appeared to be a need for better designed aids, for more information about aids, for better prescription of aids, and for better service, delivery, and maintenance of aids. Most aids are probably obtained for elderly people by friends or family. The next level of assistance may come from self-help groups of aging or disabled organizations. Community organizations, such as churches and service organizations, can frequently provide assistance with funds or manpower to obtain aids or home modifications. In England, Australia, and Germany volunteer engineers, technicians, and craftsmen have been organized to help disabled and aging persons modify their homes or to set up aids in order for the persons to continue to live independently. A few such organizations are developing in America. Of course, the Pioneers, a group of retired Bell Telephone employees, have volunteered their time in such causes for years.

Visits to the homes of aging or disabled persons by occupational therapists and rehabilitation engineers may be necessary and desirable. An aging person would rarely need to enter a medical facility as an inpatient to obtain technical assistance. However, a physician's prescription is required in order to obtain financial assistance for purchase of aids under Medicare. Hospital outpatient services or service at day hospitals are sometimes needed for delivery of technical aids.

The appropriate infrastructure for delivery of assistive aids has not yet been worked out completely. It is one of the most important barriers to optimal use of technical aids by elderly and disabled persons.

INFORMATION ABOUT TECHNICAL AIDS

An excellent information source concerning technology in rehabilitation has been prepared by Enders (1984). Her source book is a relatively comprehensive source on information in this field and informs the reader where further information may be obtained. In it one can find out about ABLEDATA,[1] a computerized data retrieval system for information on rehabilitation products; NARIC (the National Rehabilitation Information Center)[2]; Accent on Information,[3] and other informatioin sources. Books, manuals, and publications on various rehabilitation topics are cited, and locations and phone numbers of manufacturers, research laboratories, and specialists in the rehabilitation technology field are provided.

The Gerontological Society of America and the Western Gerontological Society (now the American Society on Aging) held the First National Research Conference on Technology and Aging in 1981. Conclusions and recommendations of that conference are available from the sponsoring societies. Two European conferences were held in 1979 sponsored by the Commission of the European Communities. The first, "The Use of Technology in the Care of the Elderly and the Handicapped," was held near London and the second, "Technical Innovation in the Service of the Elderly and Disabled," was held in Berlin. A book, *The Use of Technology in the Care of the Elderly and the Disabled* (Greenwood Press, 1980), resulted from these two conferences.

Sources of good information can be a weak link in providing appropriate technical assistance to the elderly people. It would seem that gerontologists could make use of the new networks of information that are being developed in rehabilitation.

CONCLUSIONS

Provision of technical aids for elderly people can be enhanced by using, in modified ways, the knowledge, personnel, devices, and information sources available through the rehabilitation field. This must be done wisely, with common sense, and with an understanding that elderly persons make up a new category of technical aid users who may need to be approached in different ways than other disabled persons. New devices may need to be developed for special problems of elderly persons and new ways of marketing and supplying these devices may need to be devised.

Only appropriate technology should be used by the aging population and such technologies should be used with caution. Emphasis must be placed on the human aspects of aging. Technological assistance should be pursued to the extent that it can improve the quality of life of the aging person, making life more fulfilling and rewarding.

REFERENCES

Boenick, U. (1980). Prosthetic technology for elderly amputees. In J. Bray & S. Wright (Eds.), *The use of technology in the care of the elderly and the disabled.* Westport, CT: Greenwood Press.

Enders, A. (1984). *Technology for independent living source-book*. Washington, DC: Rehabilitation Engineering Society of North America (RESNA, 1101 Connecticut Avenue, N.W., Suite 700, Washington, DC 20036).

Faletti, M. (1984a). Human factors research and functional environments for the aged. In I. Altman, et al. (Eds.), *Human behavior and the environment; Vol. 7: The elderly and the environment*, New York: Plenum Press.

Faletti, M. (1984b). Technology to adapt environments. *Generations, 8*, 35–38.

Glattly, H. (1966). Aging and amputation. *Artificial Limbs, 10*, 1–4.

Hannson, J. (1984). The leg amputee. *Acta Orthopaedica Scandinavica, 69* (Suppl.), 1–104.

Kreager, M. (1984). In L. Coberly (Ed.), *Becoming . . . the voice of Mildred Kreager*. Madison, WI: Francis Wayland Foundation.

Lawton, M. (1977). The impact of environment on aging and behavior. In J. Birren & K. Schaie (Eds.), *Handbook of the psychology of aging* (pp.276–301). New York: Van Nostrand Reinhold.

McCollough, N., Sarmiento, A., Williams, E., & Sinclair, W. (1968). Some considerations in management of the above-knee geriatric amputee. *Artificial Limbs, 12*, 28–35.

Mital, M. A., & Pierce, D. C. (1971). *Amputations and their prostheses*. Boston: Little, Brown.

Page, M., Galer, M., Fitzgerald, J., & Feeney, R. (1980). Problems of the selection, provision and use of aids. In J. Bray & S. Wright (Eds.). *The use of technology in the care of the elderly and the disabled*. Westport, CT: Greenwood Press.

Schumacher, E. F. (1973). *Small is beautiful: Economics as if people mattered*. New York: Harper and Row.

Vineberg, S. (1961). Report of panel of psycho-social implications. In *The geriatric amputee*. (Publication 919). Washington, DC: National Academy of Sciences National Research Council.

Wolff, H. S. (1980a). Introduction: Tools for living. In J. Bray & S. Wright (Eds.), *The use of technology in the care of the elderly and the disabled*. Westport, CT: Greenwood Press.

Wolff, H. S. (1980b). Tools for living, a blueprint for a major new industry. In J. Bray & S. Wright (Eds.), *The use of technology in the care of the elderly and the disabled*. Westport, CT: Greenwood Press.

Wu, Y., Brncick, M., Krick, H., Putman, T., & Stratigos, J. (1981). Scotchcast P.V.C. interim prostheses for below-knee amputees. *Bulletin of Prosthetics Research, 10–36*, 40–45.

NOTES

1. ABLEDATA, 4407 8th Street, NE, Washington, DC 20017.
2. NARIC, 4407 8th Street, NE, Washington, DC 20017.
3. Accent on Information, P.O. Box 700, Bloomington, IL 61701.

19

The Social Context of Arthritic and Rheumatic Disorders

James J. Pattee and Alan M. Jette

This paper will focus on the rehabilitation of the older person who is handicapped by arthritic and rheumatic disease. Four steps will accomplish the task: (a) a presentation; (b) identification of strengths and weaknesses of health care in meeting the needs of the older arthritic; (c) identification of the gaps and opportunities; (d) prioritizing the gaps and opportunities.

An estimated 30 million people in the United States suffer from handicaps of the musculoskeletal system. Twelve million, or 40%, of this group is over age 65. Since the over-65 comprise 11% of our population, there is a marked increase in the symptoms and loss of function due to arthritis with aging. But more important, the severity of the symptoms and the loss of function also increase. Thirty percent of the over-65 group report moderate to severe activity restriction because of arthritis (Cunningham & Kelsey, 1984). As statistics become available for cohorts over 75 and 85 years of age, we can expect these percentages to continue to rise.

While osteoarthritis accounts for a vast majority of symptoms and handicaps, a thorough diagnostic evaluation is fundamental to successful rehabilitation. Hunt (1983) identified this as the first of four principles for successful rehabilitation:

1. *Specific treatment* for control of the underlying disease and disability.
2. *Prevention of secondary disabilities*, that is, of additional impairments resulting from inadequate treatment or neglect of the primary condition.

3. REstoration of temporary impairment or restoration of as much normal function as possible in the case of a permanent handicapping condition.
4. ADaptation of the individual, the family, society, and the environment to cope with the persisting impairment with or without change in the basic underlying condition.

A great need for rehabilitation service exists among the elderly. Sound principles of successful rehabilitation are in place. However, many factors affect the development of a significant program for the arthritic older person. The factors include: (a) the attitude of society toward arthritis; (b) assumptions that are the foundation of our health care system; (c) characteristics of the elderly; (d) characteristics of the health care system; (e) characteristics of the support system in the community.

ATTITUDE OF SOCIETY

Many elderly with arthritic and rheumatic disorders never contact a physician for evaluation or treatment. This reflects the attitude of patients who accept their pain and loss of function from arthritis. They respond to the diagnosis of arthritis with the statement, "You can't do anything for arthritis, can you?" This attitude reflects the "quick fix" mentality of society as well as of many physicians. Our technology has enabled us to remove blindness due to cataracts with a simple operation. Hip joints are replaced with complete rehabilitation of the patient. Antibiotics effectively treat life-threatening infections. Because of the quick-fix attitude, many modalities of rehabilitation have been neglected by the practicing community as well as by the patient. The cost effectiveness of lengthy, labor-intensive modalities has not been accepted by funding agencies. A practicing primary care physician is bombarded with promotion of drug therapy but knows little about physiological bases for the avoidance of painful stress, the use of heat, rest, and passive and active exercise treatment modalities.

ASSUMPTIONS UNDERLYING HEALTH CARE

The mission of health care is to identify and cure disease. The technology of health care is built on this assumption. Health care is frustrated by the elderly patient because of the challenge of identifying multiple diseases in a single individual and the chronic nature of many of the diseases that defy cure. The individual with a chronic disease that cannot be cured wanders from one provider of episodic care to another.

Health care is focused on disease. Perhaps the dichotomy of health versus disease could be replaced with a system that addresses issues of health versus non-health and disease versus non-disease. This would enable health care to address issues of health promotion and issues of disease prevention separately. In the *New England Journal of Medicine*, Anne R. Somers (1984) asks the question, "Why not try preventing illness as a way to control Medicare costs?" This is one of many challenges to health care educators, health care providers, and the health care delivery system to re-examine the basic mission of their programs.

At a time when our potential for developing high technology medicine seems unlimited, we must ask ourselves whether the technology that is possible is indeed, reasonable. The reasonableness will be based on value systems and quality of life issues. Health care is more than identifying and curing disease.

CHARACTERISTICS OF THE ELDERLY

The older person tends to have multiple diseases. Therefore, a rehabilitation program must have the input of a physician knowledgeable in geriatric medicine as well as rehabilitation. Drug/drug, drug/disease, disease/disease and treatment/disease interaction will exist. Rehabilitation of the elderly will address the effects of any modality of treatment on the whole person.

The elderly have multiple symptoms. There are gradual changes which manifest themselves in symptoms that concern the patient. These are manifested by complaints about the inability to sleep, the inability to remember, the inability to drive a car safely, and the presence of pain and stiffness of joints. The physician is challenged by family and patient for the quick-fix, and this often results in polypharmacy with its attending iatrogenic disease. Because of these multiple symptoms, we must be careful not to identify aging as disease or disease as normal aging.

The elderly gradually lose their ability to respond to change. Each organ system has less reserve to overcome stress. This includes the stress of an active rehabilitation program.

The elderly are in delicate equilibrium with their environment. Small changes in the internal environment, due to drugs or infection or external environment, can lead to catastrophes. The hospitalization of an elderly person that leads to confusions, restraints, and marked behavioral changes has a devastating effect on the ability to cope with the environment. These characteristics of the elderly challenge the health care system to respond in a meaningful way.

CHARACTERISTICS OF THE HEALTH CARE SYSTEM

The fragmentation of the medical profession is well known, with relative isolation of the expertise within various specialties and subspecialties. As a result, focusing the expertise of numerous specialists on a patient who has multiple illnesses is a tremendous challenge. The compartmentalization isn't confined to medicine. Minimal communication occurs between the many professionals providing health care. And finally, the facilities and programs in the community providing different components of services to the elderly function in isolation. Perhaps diagnostic-related groups (DRGs) will force the hospitals to begin communication between themselves and services within the community. In the past, it has been almost impossible to obtain a history and physical or a discharge summary of patients from hospitals, let alone any meaningful dialogue. The elderly are the prime utilizers of services across the continuum of care, moving from home to hospital, to nursing homes, to home with home care, and back again. The high utilizers will need case managers to facilitate effective, efficient communication of information across the continuum.

Another characteristic of the system is the lack of knowledge and skills in both geriatric medicine and rehabilitation among practicing physicians. The physician's knowledge of rehabilitation is usually developed in the acute-care system where the focus is on the needs of acute episodic illness. As a result, most physicians have little interest in elderly patients with chronic disease. And the elderly patient doesn't fit the rehabilitation programs in the acute-care settings.

CHARACTERISTICS OF THE COMMUNITY SUPPORT SYSTEMS

Eighty percent of the support for health care of the frail elderly is provided by the family. Family support receives little input from the health care providers. Most self-care and self-help groups are formed outside of health care systems. This occurs because of lack of response of the health care providers to the social, psychological, and nontechnological needs of the family support system.

REFERENCES

Cunningham, L. S., & Kelsey, J. L. (1984). Epidemiology of musculoskeletal impairment and associated disability. *American Journal of Public Health, 74,* 574–579.

Hunt, T. E. (1983). Rehabilitation of the aged patients. In R. J. Ham, M. L. Marcy, &
    R. M. Smith (Eds.), *Primary care geriatrics* (chap. 6). Boston: PSG, Inc.
Somers, A. R. (1984). Why not try preventing illness as a way of controlling
    Medicare costs? [Sounding Board.] *New England Journal of Medicine, 311*(13),
    853–856.

APPENDIX
Occupational Therapy
Arthritis Exercise Program*

PURPOSE

To provide specific exercises three to five times a week to maintain functional abilities.

Arthritis Exercise Group should meet three to five times a week. The group is geared to exercises, however, education and pain support are also important components.

On the following pages you will note a variety of exercises divided into joint location. Each exercise is set up to insure that the following goals are met:

1. Maintain or increase joint mobility.
2. Maintain or increase muscle strength.
3. Maintain or increase physical tolerance.
4. Prevent, correct, or minimize the effects of joint deformity.

Once you begin arthritis group, the leader should monitor the individual members tolerance and base your exercises on this. REMEMBER to always start group with a series of relaxation/warm-up exercises (i.e., deep breathing, neck and shoulder exercises).

Depending on the groups' tolerance, choose one or more exercises from each joint area to make sure that all joints are being exercised and reaching maximal range of motion. (DO EACH EXERCISE 10 TIMES). Exercise should be for approximately 20–30 minute duration with frequent rest. About halfway between group have all residents who are able to stand up and stretch.

Relaxation

Deep breathing, neck and shoulder exercises.

1. Take a deep breath in through nose—out through mouth (5 times).
2. Drop head down—tip to right—straight back—tip to left (repeat 5 times).
3. Bring shoulders up to ears—HOLD—relax (repeat 5 times).

*Used by permission of the North Ridge Care Center, 5430 Boone Avenue North, Minneapolis, Minnesota.

UPPER EXTREMITY

Shoulder

Goal: To move shoulder through all motions. (i.e., flexion, abduction, adduction, rotation).

Active exercises: (Choose one or two exercises and repeat 10 times).

1. Climb fingers up an imaginary ladder; going higher each day.
2. Lift arm forward and bring it over head.
3. Lift both arms sideward and upward—then clasp hands over head.
4. Raise arms to side—shoulder level, make circles, going from smaller to larger—change directions.
5. Alternate arms behind neck and lower back. Keep elbow bent.
6. Arms at sides, with elbows bent, attempt to touch elbows behind you.
7. Shrug shoulder up to ears—hold—down—relax.
8. Begin with hands lying on lap, moving from your shoulders, each up as high as you can.

Elbow

Goal: To improve/maintain elbow function.

Active exercises: (Do all exercises 10 times each).

1. Bring both hands up to shoulders.
2. With palms up, bring hands to shoulders.
3. With thumbs up, bring to shoulders.
4. Back of hand toward shoulder.
5. Hands palm down on table—turn from elbow until palm up.

Wrist

Goal: To improve wrist function through gradually increasing difficulty. To insure smooth movement and full active range of motion.

Active exercises: (Choose two to three exercises and do 10 times each).

1. Rest arms on table, resting on their sides, and turn both wrists in and out (like a gate swinging.)
2. Bend your elbow and support it on the table—drop wrist down—lift back up.
3. Again, bend your elbow and support it on the table—twist palm away from you, not toward you.
4. Move hand to thumb side and then to little finger side.
5. Rotate wrist to one side and then to the other.
6. Hand over table side—let wrist fall down, then raise up.

Hand

Goal: To improve hand function through grasp, release and stretching.
Active exercises: (Both hands together—all exercises 10 times each.)

1. Make into a *loose* fist—straighten fingers completely.
2. Place hands flat on table—palm down, spread fingers apart and back together.
3. Hands palm down on table—beginning with little finger—lift up and down ten times—continue to do with fingers and thumb.
4. Support on table the first joint of fingers, bend second over the edge and straighten.
5. Support first and second joints of fingers, bend last one over edge.

LOWER EXTREMITIES

Trunk and Hip

Goal: To maintain flexibility, and range of motion in trunk and hip motions.
Active exercises: (Do each exercise 10 times.)

1. Sit up straight, hold your arm out in front of you at shoulder level.
2. Lean body forward, trying to touch nose to knees.
3. Raise legs up off floor—knees straight. Spread legs apart—now back together, crossing ankles. (Scissors kick). Repeat.
4. Quad set: Legs straight. Tighten thigh muscles to fully straighten knee. Lift heels off surface.

Knee

Goal: To maintain range of motion in knee flexion and extension.
Active exercises:

1. Start with right knee—slowly straighten it out until knee is straight—hold that position, now bend knee back to floor. Do 5 times, then switch to left knee.
2. Keep knees bent—lift right leg straight, then down. Do the same with left leg. (Marching step)
3. Cross right knee over left knee—do 10 times—then change directions.

Ankles

Goal: To improve range of motion.
Active exercises:

1. Lift your heels about three inches off the floor—then rock back and lift your toes up three inches, repeat.

2. Raise right foot off the floor, about two inches—rotate foot clockwise in complete circles—now counter-clockwise. Switch to other foot.
3. Cross right ankle over left—reverse, moving the toes of both feet.

Toes

Goal: To improve/maintain range of motion.
Active exercises: (Do each exercise 10 times.)

1. Curl your toes down—straighten your toes out—pull toes up. Repeat.
2. Tap your toes. Start slowly, then speed up.

20

Ageism and Disabilityism: Double Jeopardy

Phyllis Rubenfeld

To set the theme for my presentation, I would life to quote Saul Alinsky: "What follows," he said, "is for those who want to change the world from what it is to what *we believe it should be.*"

In order to understand why we who are disabled or aged are received either with mixed emotions or with outright prejudice, we must be aware of our roots. Historically, we people with disabilities have been viewed in a wide variety of ways. For one example, society at large saw us as people possessed by evil spirits—objects to be ostracized, feared, devalued, or (at best) ignored. Sometimes we have been seen as religious objects, symbols of suffering, chosen because of our inherent goodness to bear the sufferings of the world. These early, primitive beliefs have been institutionalized into the present-day repressive system.

First, society translated the notion of possession into the notion that the disabled must be institutionalized for life. The motivations underlying this change were not humane, and the same motivations, still offered today in defense of institutionalization, are no more so. This is documented by numerous references in the literature and by current stories of mental and physical abuse.

Similarly, the object of religious veneration was translated into the passive, infinitely patient, and understanding cripple—a term that deprived us of our humanness by defining us in terms of our condition rather than in terms of who we are. Any opposition to this cruel system leads to charges that we are hostile, maladjusted individuals with chips on our shoulders. Vash (1981) summarizes it well. She writes that, "as a group, we have been and continue to be oppressed, hidden, stripped of power, and often made to feel ashamed of the nature of our being."

Ageism discriminates against the old with inaccurate and misleading stereotypes, just as racism and sexism discriminate against skin color and gender, and just as disabilityism discriminates on the basis of physique. Old people are seen as senile, rigid in thought and manner, garrulous, and old-fashioned. Ageism encourages the younger generation to see itself as a thing apart from anything that has gone before. Subtly, it leads the young to see their elders as not fully human. Unlike racists and sexists, who will never be forced to change places with those whom they despise, ageists are at least dimly aware that if they live long enough, they too will end up being old (Butler, 1977).

Similarly, disability is a state that will probably come to us all sooner or later. We all want to survive into the golden years. Many of us look forward to being able to enjoy leisure time, and to do all those things we were not able to do during our child-rearing years or while we pursued careers. And we all seem to want to stay in the same physical shape we enjoy today. But we, the disabled, are different in many ways. Yet we, too, try to deny reality to some extent by telling ourselves that the only thing that is different about us is that we are disabled.

Where does ageism come from? There are many cultural influences, ranging from social pressures to produce commodities to a thinly disguised attempt to avoid the realities of aging and death (Butler, 1977). Aging, as Butler reminds us, begins with conception. The classic dividing line between middle-age and old-age—the sixty-fifth birthday—is completely arbitrary. It dates only from Bismarck's social order, which was established in the 1880s.

In the United States, there are now more than 27 million people over 65. There are 36 million people with disabilities. Among the old, 10 million are over 73 and 2 million are 85 or older. By the year 2000 there will be more than 100,000 centenarians. Amazingly, the 75-plus age group is the fastest growing demographic category in the country. The old constitute 10% of the population, and progress in medical care and public health will only make their ranks swell with every passing year. Pageis (1980) estimates that in 50 years, when the post-World War II baby boomers enter old age, the old will make up 17% to 20% of the population. The disabled, too, are living longer and occupying a larger place in the general population as a result of medical advances (Butler, 1977).

As the numbers grow, it becomes more important that we concern ourselves with the quality of life that the old and the aging disabled can expect to enjoy. Guaranteed resources must accompany the advances of medical technology. And we must begin to face the fact that if we make it possible for people to live longer and longer, we must also find something for the old to do with their lives. In 1978, Congress raised the mandatory retirement age from 65 to 70, but 70 may be just as arbitrary and unfair—consider the age of our president, for example. Governor Lamm of Colorado believes that the old owe it to their juniors to wither away, quickly and quietly. I suggest to you, however, that we as a society may be doing ourselves a grave disservice by insisting that the old are of no further use, that the experiences and knowledge that they have gained over the years are of no value.

Unlike the great cultures of the East, which see human life and death as a complete, circular whole, we in the West see death as something apart from life, something completely outside everything we think of as belonging to ourselves. To be a person, we think, means to be alive, first of all. It also means to be in control and aware of what is happening to us. The Western emphasis on control makes death a violation, an insult, rather than the natural and inevitable end of life.

The disabled elderly get the worst of both worlds. It is estimated that about one-quarter of the elderly are alone, that another quarter of them live at or below the poverty line, and that more than one-third of them experience conditions that limit their activities (Pageis, 1980). Because most of us want to grow old in dignity and in reasonable comfort, it is hard to see why more people don't grasp that we all share a common need to make these things possible for everyone. At the very least, you would think that the advocacy groups most concerned would be able to organize together in this field. Yet neither the aging groups nor the disability groups seem to feel any particular responsibility for the disabled elderly. Who, for example, services the disabled old person who is newly blind? Where are such people sent for help? The disabled elderly suffer from all the prejudice and cruel stereotyping that afflict all disabled people—inaccessibility, segregated facilities, the belief that the disabled are not equal to nondisabled—while they have many problems all their own. They must deal with professionals who have accepted without question the use of terms like "frail"—usages that strip the old of all of their strength and dignity. I am told by professionals that the term *frail elderly* has come to denote those over the age of 75 who have chronic conditions or are multiply disabled. What a term! I had polio at the age of 7, but no matter how good my general health is, when I turn 75, I will be considered "frail" because polio is a chronic condition! What does this kind of language really say to the old? How insulting it must be!

Let us look for a moment at the connections between chronicity or disability and illness. One may be disabled without being ill. There is no cause-and-effect relationship, necessarily, between disability and illness. The two are not synonymous. I beseech you to understand the difference and to incorporate it into your professional thinking, and, especially, to take it into account in all your dealings with the elderly disabled.

Much of the difficulty is attitudinal, and it involves both the elderly and the professionals who work with them. Take the euphemisms—"I'm not blind, I just have trouble seeing," or "I'm not deaf, I'm just a little hard of hearing," or "It's not that I can't walk, I just tire easily and need to use a wheelchair." These euphemisms spring from negative feelings towards disability that abound throughout society, even among the disabled themselves.

Loss of economic independence for the newly disabled is a devastating experience. Income from SSI does not cover decent health care, hospital coverage, accessible housing, or travel by cab, van, or ambulette to visit friends, go to the theatre or to the park, or go on vacation. Are we to accept the idea that these things are luxuries that the disabled elderly are no longer entitled to? Many people in the rehabilitation field seem to believe that as long as Medicare, Medicaid, public assistance, and local public health services are available, then everything is taken care of. But what about the isolation and the severe restrictions on simple pleasures that the rest of us take for granted? We must not let these get lost in the shuffle.

And what about housing? What about home health care and attendant care? It is crucial to keep people in their own homes as long as possible. Yet Independent Living Centers specialize in people between the ages of 16 and 40. Why are they not welcoming the disabled elderly with open arms? After all, 10% of the monies available under the Rehabilitation Act goes to the elderly.

Housing brings us to the issue of institutional versus noninstitutional care for the elderly. The older members of the American Coalition of Citizens with Disabilities tend to be strongly opposed to the idea of institutional care because many of them were institutionalized when they were first disabled. Of course, they recognize that institutional care sometimes becomes necessary, but they prefer home care for as long as possible, and they want to be the ones to decide when to enter an institution. Many elderly disabled people go into institutions only because they or their families believe that that is the best or only solution. They often believe this because some professional told them so. All too often, professionals have no real idea how it feels to be institutionalized, and they are unable or unwilling to explore other possibilities.

Of course, staying at home is not easy. It means "exchanging the safety of custodial care for the risk, stress, and effort involved in making the innumerable large and small decisions that shape one's life" (Crewe & Zola, 1983). It means dealing with a world that does not provide access for the disabled. It means finding transportation, attendants, and anything else that may be needed. And it means facing the ignorant assumptions of most of our society that it is easier to pay the high cost of institutional care than to face the thousands of problems, large and small, that the disabled will face on the outside (Crewe & Zola, 1983). This is a difficult problem, both for the disabled and for professionals who may not be very interested in dealing with situations where they cannot have speedy and gratifying results, as they often can with younger client populations.

Many older disabled people have little choice but to become passive and dependent. Their lives are dominated by the necessity of seeming grateful for any and all services, no matter how grudgingly rendered. This problem confronts all disabled people. I think that the first words disabled children learn are "please," "thank you," and "you're welcome." But the disabled elderly *must* feel that they are in control of their lives, just like everybody else. Clients and workers should jointly develop contracts or independent living plans (ILP) that will enable the disabled person to function as independently as possible in his/her daily life. This should happen without our having to organize a separate-but-equal division of the Gray Panthers!

The disabled elderly have years of valuable experience to share with the aging disabled. And those of us who are younger can help our older brothers and sisters to gain access to the system. We can be their advocates. We can help them gain services. We can join them to form one of the strongest political power bases ever seen in this country. And we can be there to understand the difficulties and heartaches they suffer.

The stigma of disability is ingrained in all of us. So is the fear of death. But professionals and advocates in the fields of disability and aging must come together and start talking about making old age respected, productive, and enjoyable again. Too often, we think of aging as something that can only be handled by the medical profession. But you aren't sick just because you're old, and there are many things about productive independent living that professionals in the aging field could learn from their colleages in disability. The bulk of American medical practice has historically been based on an "acute illness, curative model," and this is clearly inappropriate for the care of many disabled old people (Dobrof, 1984). Disability is not the end of the world. It is another phase of life, with new, different, and often highly complex problems. But knowing that there is a working network in one's neighborhood can make life significantly easier and more enjoyable.

I propose an alliance between the aging groups and the American Coalition of Citizens with Disabilities (ACCD). The ACCD is a nonprofit, tax-exempt 501 (c) (3) national advocacy organization that represents the needs of disabled people throughout the country. It is composed of over 180 national, state, and local organizations and associations of and for disabled people. It has thousands of individual members. All told, it represents 8 million people. ACCD's work includes promoting the human and civil rights of disabled citizens, improving their image in the media, and encouraging consumer involvement in the public and private sectors. Much of this work is accomplished through coalition-building, sharing resources with member organizations, and through training, research, information, and referral.

The goals of ACCD are to be an advocate for people with disabilities; to promote involvement in policy-making at state, local, and national levels; to work to assure that citizens with disabilities have the full exercise of their rights; to provide accurate information and appropriate referrals; to coordinate leadership for the disability rights movement; and to establish an effective networking system for disabled citizens throughout the nation.

As a result of my being invited to speak here, ACCD has formed a Committee on Aging. We believe that the time has come for us all to draw together. Cutbacks in Social Security, SSI, and programs for the disabled may affect us all. We all experience prejudice and discrimination. We desperately need to build a coalition.

We all have much to learn, but we also have much to offer. We can learn from each other, while coming together on issues of common concern. Let's work together to make senior centers accessible to the disabled aging. Let's make sure that institutional care is imposed only when absolutely necessary and allows the recipient his/her full measure of dignity and autonomy. Let's make sure that people don't lose control of their lives, even in little ways. Let's have motorized wheelchairs, even though it may be easier for staff to push people around. Let's make sure professionals watch their language and stop throwing around words like "frail."

Above all, let's forget about territorial jealousies and the need to be recognized as individual authorities in our own separate fields. We *can* work together. We *should* work together. And, things being what they are, we *must* work together.

REFERENCES

Butler, R. N., & Lewis, M. I. (1977). *Aging and mental health: Positive psychosocial approach*. St. Louis: C. V. Mosby.

Crewe, N. M., & Zola, I. K. (1983). *Independent living for physically disabled people*. San Francisco: Jossey-Bass.

Dobrof, R. (1984). *Gerontological social work in home health care*. New York: Haworth Press.

Pageis, D. C. (1980). *Health care and the elderly*. Rockville, Maryland: Aspen Publications.

Vash, C. L. (1981). *The psychology of disability*. New York: Springer.

21

Employment of the Older Disabled Person: Current Environment, Outlook, and Research Needs

Neal J. Baumann, James C. Anderson, and
Malcolm H. Morrison

OVERVIEW

The economic and social problems of our elderly and disabled population are enormous, especially in terms of the size of this population, the social cost, and quality of life issues. The next 20 years will see a doubling of the number of elderly and disabled and exponential growth in the cost to the nation for their support.

Presently in the U.S., 36 million people are functionally disabled (Pati, Adkins, & Morrison, 1981); and 42 million are either disabled and/or elderly (age 65 or over). This group comprises the largest minority in the United States. It is estimated that persons age 45 and over who are disabled, account for 1.5 to 2.1 million of total U.S. unemployment.

A U.S. Commission on Civil Rights Report to the President (1977), indicated that 50% to 60% of the disabled population is age 50 or over. Little needs to be said on the "Aging of America." Census data (1980) indicate that the number of people age 65 and over will double in number to 51 million by 2030. By the year 2000, there likely will be one physically disabled, chronically ill, or over-65 person for every nondisabled under-65 United States citizen; and one-half of our population will be over the age of 50 (Bowe, 1981).

With these projections and data in mind, it is clear that the problem is large, growing, and must be addressed on a national basis. The problem of disability is frequently a problem for the older person.

Perhaps the most critical factor is the rapid increase in life expectancy. A person who reached age 65 in 1980 will, on average, live to be 81. This increase is dramatic and will continue, as a result of medical, nutritional and fitness advances. Disabled persons, whether disabled in early, middle, or late life, will continue to live longer and require ongoing rehabilitation and employment services.

There is today a growing recognition that the problems of disability are, with increasing frequency, combined with age. In the foreseeable future, chronic health problems among the aging will continue to increase; as a consequence, rates of disability will rise. Under conditions where public disability benefit payments under Social Security have reached $17 billion per year, and with increasing private insurance payments, disability is now a major fiscal problem. In addition, and especially for the matured disabled, permanent loss of employment reduces productive capacity and tax revenues and increases dependency on public and private benefit programs. Some have, in fact, asserted that disability is now used as a form of early retirement that increases the number of persons being supported by public benefit payments.

Almost since the inception of the Social Security disability program, the prevailing view has been that the older disabled are unemployable and must remain dependent on public or private income benefits indefinitely. The very limited numbers of older disabled leaving the SSDI or SSI Programs for employment has, of course, supported this view. And there is no doubt that older disabled persons have lowered propensities for return to work and less success in achieving this goal. But, economic incentives to remain dependent, combined with limited or no motivational intervention, have resulted in "benign neglect" of the older disabled.

Under circumstances where their numbers and costs are increasing and where medical treatment has been able to improve functional capacity for many, continuing to disregard the employment potential of the largest number of disabled is neither rational nor practical. It is hardly sensible to continue to view all older disabled as incapable of vocational rehabilitation and productivity. There is already enough evidence to refute this approach. The issue is to develop effective strategies to improve re-employment rates for the older disabled.

ONSET OF DISABILITY

The age of onset or occurrence of disability is of major concern when deal-ing with issues of adjustment, training, and employment potential. A clear process of adjustment to disability has been demonstrated by numerous authors (English, 1977; Kerr, 1977; Shontz, 1975; Wright, 1977). The issue of adjustment is most important in the prevocational portion of the rehabilitation process. Age of onset of disability has a number of effects.

Early-life onset:
   Older disabled clients are more likely to have adjusted to their dis-abling condition.
   If employed, they may have skills and experience appropriate to their limitation.
   They are more likely to have a realistic outlook and job goal.

Mid- to later-life onset:
   Client is more likely to experience continued problems of adjustment to disability.
   Client may have more needs in the areas of evaluation, vocational counseling, and training.
   Client may be more unrealistic in his/her approach to employment.

The identification of these factors is an important requirement of the vocational rehabilitation intake assessment process. Once they are iden-tified, rehabilitation counselors must assist the client in this adjustment process prior to employment.

An important issue for all rehabilitation clients is avoidance of "fixation" of a handicap that results in reduced motivation and negative attitudes toward rehabilitation. Most of today's early identification and intervention programs for the disabled are designed to reduce or eliminate fixation. These types of programs seem to be effective irrespective of age of onset. However, more serious motivational problems often occur for older dis-abled persons who have been away from their jobs for long periods of time and who *do not expect* to return to work. For those clients, who comprise large proportions of both public and private disability case loads, different intervention strategies are needed to reduce the expectation of lifelong dependency and lack of productivity. Development of such approaches has lagged behind that of early intervention strategies.

However, there is now some evidence that re-employment counseling combined with actual job opportunities and economic incentives (wages and benefits) can produce positive employment outcomes for the long-term disabled. Re-employment of these types of clients was formerly considered to be virtually unattainable. But reduction of long-term disability case loads is an important objective in terms of cost containment and productivity.

As with all disabled persons, the motivation and self-respect that accompany productive activity are additional advantages for older disabled persons who return to work. It is difficult to establish level of effort criteria regarding the distribution of resources for rehabilitation of the long-term disabled. But given the distribution of the case load and lengthened expectation of life, the present limitations of resources for rehabilitating the long-term disabled must be reexamined. In practical terms, resources must be focused on persons with the greater likelihood of successful rehabilitation. We know that age of client is often an inappropriate criterion on which to base intervention. Thus, in order to justify increased resources for longer term older disabled clients, new valid criteria must be developed which can be used to evaluate rehabilitation potential.

CURRENT SERVICES—STATE OF THE ART

Older disabled Americans currently can receive employment services from a wide variety of sources. The critical fact, however, is that many receive no services at all.

The most likely source of help for an older disabled job seeker is one of the many excellent older worker employment programs throughout the country. Programs such as Skills Available in Cleveland, Ohio, and Senior Employment Services of Wichita, Kansas, are two examples of outstanding programs of this kind. They are staffed with paid and volunteer professionals who provide job-seeking skills, training, and job placement services to older (usually age 55 and over) persons. Significant numbers of older disabled persons are placed by these programs. Their major strength is their close interaction with employers and older job seekers and the use of volunteer staff.

Older disabled persons are also served by the traditional vocational rehabilitation network of state and private vocational rehabilitation organizations. However, the older person is underrepresented and ineffectively served by this network. Meyers (1983) noted that persons age 45 and over represented, on average, only 23% of state vocational rehabilitation (VR) case loads throughout the United States. This compares with their 50% to 60% representation in the total population of disabled. These data are a dramatic indication of the lack of service provided to this group.

In an unpublished survey, Aging in America, Inc. (1981) identified an

80% job placement rate for Projects with Industry (PWI) programs funded by the U.S. Department of Education (N=65). This placement rate fell to 29% for clients age 50 and over. PWI programs have an outstanding 15-year track record of successfully placing thousands of disabled persons of all ages in competitive employment. This is done in close partnership with business, industry, and organized labor. Beside having limited success with older disabled persons, managers of these PWI programs indicated lack of awareness of aging issues and the "aging" network and requested technical assistance to serve this population more effectively.

Older disabled clients are also served by other private and public employment programs such as the Job Service, departments of labor, departments on aging, and Mature Temps.

The picture of an underserved group becomes clear. In response to this need, the U.S. Dept. of Education, Rehabilitation Services Administration has funded Aging in America, Inc., through its PWI program, to provide technical assistance to PWI, State VR and older worker programs throughout the United States. This successful program has helped develop highly effective networks at 16 locations throughout the country. In addition, a model statewide program has been established with the cooperation and support of the New York State Office of Vocational Rehabilitation.

These networks have successfully changed two important conditions: (a) the lack of awareness of older disabled people, and (b) the lack of networking and cross-referral between aging, vocational rehabilitation, and employment organizations.

VR programs, such as PWI and state VR agencies, are best equipped to provide employment services to older disabled persons. They are staffed with trained rehabilitation personnel who have extensive experience in placing disabled persons. However, it is the team or "networking" approach between VR and "aging" programs that will best serve these clients.

PROFESSIONALS' SENSITIVITY TO WORK POTENTIAL

Not every older disabled person has a desire to work. Many desire recreation, hobbies, volunteerism, and other activities. However, a disabled person, no matter what age, must be considered potentially employable. Although the decision is ultimately the client's, all health and rehabilitation professionals must be open to and suggest the possibility of competitive employment.

The physician, who very often is the first contact point, must be aware of employment potential. This potential should be an integral part of the rehabilitation process. Other professionals such as nurses, social workers, occupational therapists, and physical therapists also must be sensitive to this potential outcome. One of the critical patient/client goals should be VR. Obviously, the patient or client must make this choice. But they should be encouraged to consider employment as a life option. Certified rehabilitation counselors can serve as the coordinators in this process. Trained in counseling and rehabilitation of disabled workers, they are skilled to manage the client through this process.

The question is one of independence and choice. All of us believe in independence for older disabled persons, but potential employment must be suggested and explored with each client. Far too often we, as professionals, allow age to be a factor in determining employability. Rehabilitation counselors, medical professionals, and employers, all tend to let ageism, as a value judgment, affect the direction and advice provided to older persons. These persons must control their own destiny and have a right to unbiased advice and assistance from all of us.

There is, of course, the belief that "integrated" medical, psychological, social and vocational services are usually provided to disabled clients. In practice, however, research has shown that the degree of integration is often limited and effects on clients highly variable. When case management results in clients being served by too many service providers who do not interact closely, service integration is severely reduced. Unfortunately, our disability income benefit programs are not closely enough linked to rehabilitation service provision. This initial problem often results in slow referral and weakened intake procedures. Subsequent to intake, however, older persons often face almost insurmountable problems in receiving properly integrated services.

Once referral occurs, older clients frequently face counselors who are unfamiliar with the characteristics of older persons, and who have limited experience with this population. This leads to limitation of services and to lessened VR efforts. Of course, counselors are aware of biases against older disabled persons in the employer environment. Rather than seeking to work around these, counselors often simply give cases less scrutiny and attention.

In an environment where numerous VR services are available, counselors often do not have access to a "service team" consisting of medical, psychological, social, *and* vocational specialists. For all clients, a team approach has many advantages. But particularly for older persons, such an approach can result in services more carefully designed around the individual's capacities and potentials. Furthermore, the approach can permit the rehabilitation counselor to focus more directly on employment while appropriate professionals perform needed medical, psychological, and social rehabilitation services.

EMPLOYMENT AND HIRING DECISIONS
IN AN ENVIRONMENT OF WORK SCARCITY

In a perfect world, this is all well and good. However, this country faces many employment challenges over the next 30 to 35 years. In our opinion, there simply will not be enough jobs for everyone. Consequently, two questions must be answered: "Who gets the jobs?" and "Why hire an older disabled worker?'

In an environment of work scarcity, legislation prohibiting discrimination in hiring practices cannot protect against unemployment falling unevenly across the population. As a result, the burden of unemployment will continue to be most heavily allocated to the poor, the elderly, and the disabled.

Although the utilization of the mature disabled person might not seem urgent, this does not make the plight or the interests of these people any less important. But from a management point of view, the impact is not yet being felt. The major demographic fact in the United States is the baby boom, and the baby boomers will not reach retirement age for another 30 years. The real impact will hit in about the year 2010. Today, there is plenty of talent available in the 28 to 35 age range.

General attitudes toward mandatory retirement were explored in a survey conducted by William M. Mercer, Inc. The majority of corporate executives favored mandatory retirement and saw no reason to alter retirement policies, despite their agreement that such a policy "deprives society of the experience and value of older people." The consensus was that a mandatory retirement age was necessary to ensure job openings and promotion opportunites for younger employees.

In spite of the laws dealing with the employment practices of the mature and disabled person, perceived discrimination against this group of people is widespread. In the report, "Age Discrimination in Employment: A Growing Problem in America (Anderson, 1984)," the following is stated:

- In 1981, 9,479 age discrimination charges were filed with the Federal EEOC, representing a 76% increase over the number of charges filed in 1979. (This number had grown to 13,373 in 1982, 16,100 in 1983, making ADEA EEOC's fastest growing enforcement jurisdiction.)
- Eight of ten Americans believe most employers discriminate against older workers. Nine of ten oppose discrimination and their opposition has grown stronger in recent years.
- Six of ten employers believe older workers today are discriminated against in the marketplace. Eight of ten predict a significant increase in the number of age discrimination lawsuits in the future.

Because the willingness to make use of legislative provisions will be conditioned by the probability of success, the number of Equal Employment Opportunities Commission (EEOC) charges is probably significantly understated. In the United States in an average year, only about half the total charges filed with EEOC are recommended for investigation. Further, of the much smaller number of completed conciliations, more are unsuccessful than successful for the employee in a majority of years.

Two other factors may contribute to the low utilization rate of the legislation: lack of knowledge concerning the rights of individuals and awareness of a depressed labor market and fear of retaliation by the employer.

The disabled are more likely than the nondisabled to be older, black, less well educated, less skilled, and have an erratic work experience—characteristics that, most unfortunately, in and of themselves are obstacles to employment.

The more important question is why perceived discrimination in employment practices still exists after a decade or more of specific laws prohibiting such acts. The answer probably lies more in the number of jobs than in personal bias. For when work is scarce, who is to say it is more or less discriminatory for an employer to hire a woman rather than a man, a black over a Hispanic, or a younger person over an older one? It would be naive to suggest that personal bias does not exist. It does. And not only does it exist in business, it exists throughout our society. What allows it to exist in the labor market would seem to be a lack of jobs. The point is, it is difficult to discriminate against someone if he/she is needed.

Looking to the future, there is reason to doubt that the disadvantaged, particularly the mature disabled person, will enjoy plentiful employment opportunity. Business is investing heavily in cost reduction methods, not in capacity expansion (although recent data shows some reversal in this trend). As an example, it is estimated that for every robot installed, one job will be created in the "robotics industry" while three will be lost in other manufacturing sectors.

It is wrong to ignore the fact that the effects of technology depend on what happens to employment in the whole economy, not just the industry immediately affected. For example, if labor cost savings inputs are reflected in the consumer prices of products, these savings result in the release of purchasing power which, in turn, will result in demand and, hence, employment elsewhere in the economy. The relevant employment-related question is not how many jobs are lost in just the firm or industry experiencing productivity increase, but whether the resulting released purchasing power creates fewer or more jobs than those lost and whether the new jobs created are better or worse than those lost.

But one cannot overlook the concentration of effects in a relatively narrow sectoral, occupational, and regional setting. In particular, robotization, along with other and frequently related developments, could diminish employment opportunities for semiskilled operatives and unskilled laborers in durable goods industries especially in the metalworking sector. These considerations imply that the displacement will be of sufficient groups of workers to be a cause for concern.

It is well to keep in mind, however, that robots do not buy products or services and neither can people who are not working. For this reason companies must face the fact that they have a commitment to provide jobs if for no other reason than to maintain their own health. The intent of raising these arguments is not to suggest that we use our industries as a basis for a national employment policy. The British experience serves as ample warning against pursuing that path. However, unless as a society we can agree on how to alter the direction of our treatment of the nation's disabled persons and our older citizens, the future of America may literally be unaffordable.

Nationwide spending today for the disabled on the federal, state, and private levels, is approximately $200 billion annually, or greater than 9% of the GNP. Similar factors apply to the nation's elderly population, in that 25% of the entire federal budget is allocated for services to the elderly (Bowe, 1981). With a continuation of current growth rates of these expenditures, by the year 2030 programs designed for senior citizens could comprise as much as 65% of the federal budget.

Shortly after World War II, the ratio of people receiving Social Security benefits to those employed was 1 to 16. Today, it is roughly 1 to 3, and by the year 2025, it will have fallen to 1 to 2. Early in the next century, the eligibility age for Social Security likely will be pushed up before the number of senior citizens begins to swell as members of the baby boom generation reach age 65. However, raising the mandatory retirement age to 70, or the Social Security benefit age to 68, will solve little unless we can find ways to use the abilities of our older workers.

A 1981 Harris poll revealed that 73% of persons over age 65 would prefer to work for remuneration, at least part-time, rather than to be on full retirement—most for economic reasons, some for a sense of self-worth and general well-being.

ECONOMIC NEED

Only 30% of the men and 13% of the women receiving Social Security benefits are also receiving income from a private pension. In addition, only 50% of nongovernment workers are covered by pensions. Further, pension plans protect the upper income jobs far more than lower-paying ones, those more likely to have been held by today's mature disabled persons.

Assuming a 5% annual rate of inflation, a person living on a nonindexed pension plan (97% of private pension plans are not indexed) will lose 23% of his/her purchasing power at the end of 5 years; at the end of 10 years, a 40% loss; and by the fifteenth year, a 54% reduction. A point to be noted, as stated previously, is that individuals who reach the age of 65 will live to be 81 on the average. Without an indexed pension plan or other income most, it appears, will need to continue to work.

There is a general agreement that a 60% to 80% replacement rate measured against gross preretirement income is necessary in order to maintain a constant standard of living. It is estimated that the vast majority of workers with 30 years of service are enrolled in private pension programs that provide insufficient Social Security and pension benefits to meet this range.

HIRING DECISIONS

In the situation where there are not enough jobs, on what basis should an employer hire? There are today various pieces of legislation protecting people against discrimination in employment practices:

Age Discrimination in Employment Act
Rehabilitation Act
Title VII of the Civil Rights Act
Vietnam Era Veterans Readjustment Assistance Act

However, these laws do not require an employer to hire from any particular group. They only prohibit discrimination in employment practices. Equal opportunity policies do not advocate special treatment to members of protected groups. Therefore, companies will continue to emphasize the hiring of the best qualified candidate.

By one means or another, we must decide how work will be allocated in our society: between men and women, old and young, black and white, skilled and unskilled, educated and uneducated, able and disabled. When work is scarce, for whatever complex reasons, we have to choose policies that do the most for corporate effectiveness and also for the quality of life in the society as a whole.

Lacking an explicit national consensus, our choice has been to allocate unemployment most heavily to selected disadvantaged groups: particularly the poor, the elderly, and the disabled—those who have fallen off the train. The pattern of unemployment during periods of economic problems clearly reveals our implicit choice of work allocation. The 16 to 24-

year-old group is three times as likely as adults to be unemployed; females 40% more likely than males; blacks twice as likely as whites; and Hispanics 75% more likely than whites. Anywhere from 50% to 75% of the handicapped are likely to be unemployed, as are 20% of people age 45 or older. One-half of all discouraged workers are 45 or older; and to lose one's job, particularly if you are older and disabled, almost invariably forces a person to the end of the hiring queue and to the bottom of the skills ladder when seeking another position (Anderson, 1984).

None of us is a villain. We all want the same thing—economic security. And, if necessary, at someone else's expense. When public opinion polls ask about desired job characteristics, economic security shows up in many ways. Older workers want seniority hiring and firing so that worries about layoffs can be confined to someone else—new workers. Restrictive work rules are designed to provide job security.

With income security during retirement depending on private pensions, job security while working becomes directly tied to income security during one's old age. Industrial sons and daughters are not expected to take care of industrial mothers and fathers in their old age. Instead, they depend on pensions that are attached to jobs.

Our society is not likely to alter radically its attitude toward the allocation of jobs in an environment of work scarcity. Change comes slowly and under pressure and sometimes not at all. Therefore, it is not certain, even with an improving economy, that the mature disabled person in the next 10 to 20 years will enjoy abundant opportunities for employment. As long as jobs remain scarce, the priority of hiring will tend to place this group of people at the end of the queue. But one thing is certain, this group is too large to be ignored. Change will come either by way of more legislation or through society's and business's self-interest. Given the number of people that the nation is already supporting outside of the labor force, and the ever-increasing expenditures to do so, a change in our nation's policy is inescapable. The directions of this change have not yet been determined but must involve greater use of the productive capacities of older and disabled persons. The pace of change may depend on the economy and on fiscal and monetary policy. But unless the nation is willing to endure a substantially higher tax burden, a change in employment policy will be forthcoming.

CRITICAL STRATEGIES

Although the problem is immense, the solutions are relatively simple in conceptualization. Older disabled persons must control their own future.

The first step toward achieving this is an open-minded attitude by *health care professionals*. They must consider employment as an alternative and present this option to the patient.

Second, trained rehabilitation professionals, such as the certified rehabilitation counselor must be involved early.

Third, both state and private VR agencies must view the older client with an open mind. Acceptance for services should not be affected by age.

Fourth, the helping network must coordinate efforts and work together. Health services, VR, older worker employment programs, and state/federal agencies must network and function as a team. Many older disabled persons live in the community with no knowledge of their employment potential. These people must be reached and given a choice. In addition, all of these health and employment professionals must be trained in serving the vocational needs of the older disabled person and must be made aware of the VR network. This communication is essential.

Fifth, PWI programs, a network of more than 100 business–rehabilitation partnerships, must be utilized to provide employment services to these clients. The PWI program at Aging in America currently provides technical assistance to PWI programs throughout the United States to improve employment services to this population.

Sixth, business, industry, and organized labor must be involved in the VR process. They, along with the client, are the customers of the VR services that we provide. We must listen to them and work with them in providing effective services.

Finally, business must take this opportunity to avoid being "broadsided" with an older pool of job seekers in the next 30 years. With the rapid aging of the baby boom generation, this country will have large numbers of older and older disabled persons in the workforce. With continued work scarcity, the most likely change will come in the form of legislation. Government intervention in the employment process is inefficient at best. Government and business have an opportunity to set national policy now and have the time to test this policy before the problem becomes an emergency.

RESEARCH NEEDS

From all of this, a number of distinct areas for research can be identified. This research should be explored by the National Institute of Handicapped Research (NIHR) and other appropriate agencies. They are:

Attitudinal barriers by physicians, VR gatekeepers, and employers. We must understand the dynamics of these attitudes, how they develop, and their effects, and design effective strategies for change.

Standardization of evaluation and measurement systems for an older population. Appropriately standardized evaluation systems and instruments must be identified and developed to guide older disabled persons in the VR process.

Effects of advancing age on permanent disability. With advances in medical treatment, severely physically disabled persons are surviving and advancing to ages once viewed as impossible. We must understand the combined effect of advanced age and severe disability on a person's physical, emotional, and vocational status. What are the implications for employment stability?

Alternative and creative approaches to Social Security Disability Insurance (SSDI) and other disincentives. Removing an older disabled person from the SSDI rolls is a difficult task. We must explore the feasibility of alternatives such as significant tax credits for those who leave SSDI for competitive employment. This will require a creative and cooperative approach by NIHR, SSA, the Congress, and the administration.

Utilization of existing technology. Older disabled persons, for the most part, fear the new advances of technology in the work place. Funding should be provided for research and training that promotes the utilization of technology, such as personal computers, in the home and the work place.

SUMMARY

In conclusion, we must remember that the problem of disability is very often a problem of the older person in the United States. Effective employment of these older disabled persons requires a coordinated, effective approach by health care, employment, and VR services. Patients or clients must be encouraged to make a free choice in the direction of their lives. To make this choice possible, we must help them to consider employment and stand for equality of all ages in the VR process.

Through business and rehabilitation partnerships, such as the Aging in America PWI program, we can provide the needed employment services. With research support from NIHR and other sources, we can explore and reduce the employment barriers that older disabled persons must face.

We are in the fortunate situation of having the time to experiment and develop effective intervention approaches which will permit many more older disabled persons to remain employed or re-enter employment. Let us join together to set a national strategy to achieve this goal.

REFERENCES

Aging In America, Inc. (1982). *Survey of national PWI network.* New York: Author.

Anderson, J. C. (1984). *Hiring decisions in an environment of work scarcity.* Unpublished paper, Aging in America, Inc. Bronx, NY.

Bowe, F. (1981). Disabled and elderly people: What role for the corporation. *New Jersey Bell Journal,* 4(3).

English, R. W. (1977). The application of personality theory to explain psychological reactions to physical disability. In J. Stubbins (Ed.), *Social and psychological aspects of disbility.* Baltimore: University Park Press.

Kerr, N. (1977). Understanding the process of adjustment to disability. In J. Stubbins (Ed.), *Social and psychological aspect of disability.* Baltimore: University Park Press.

Meyers, J. E. (1983). *Rehabilitation of older workers.* (Rehab Brief, VI(8)) ISSN: 0732-2623.) Washington, DC: U.S. DOE, NIHR.

Pati, G., Adkins, J., Morrison, G. (1981). *Managing and employing the handicapped: The untapped potential.* Lake Forest, IL: The Human Resource Press.

Shontz, F. C. (1975). *The psychological aspects of physical illness and disability.* New York: Macmillan.

U.S. Commission of Civil Rights. (1977). *Discrimination in federally funded programs—A report to the President of the United States.* Author.

Wright, B. A. (1977). Spread in adjustment to disability. In J. Stubbins (Ed.), *Social and psychological aspects of disability.* Baltimore: University Park Press.

Part VI

Conclusions

22

Can You See What I See? A Summary

Don A. Olson

There is an old saying, "Duncan Hines and Daniel Boone saw different things along the same trail." Our past education, experiences, attitudes, and outlooks frequently lead us to seeing different things on the same path. If, however, we are to truly understand the needs of aging and the aged disabled, we must train ourselves to see the same things. We must train ourselves to see the real needs of the aged and the aged disabled and, more specifically, how to implement plans and programs for them. This conference, "Aging and Rehabilitation: A National Conference on the State of the Art," has been a unique experience for us. We are indebted to the National Institute of Mental Health, the National Institute on Aging, the National Institute of Handicapped Research, and the University of Pennsylvania, Research and Training Center on Aging, for coordinating the more than 20 federal agencies who have worked to pull this program together. We have had the privilege of hearing an outstanding faculty representing a variety of disciplines and groups interested in the aged and disabled. We now have considerable knowledge on the aged and the aged disabled. We have a common basis on which to build programs. We have some similarities in background that should make it possible for us to see the needs and unique factors that exist in this very special population.

Newspapers report of "anguish of aging" due to the continued lack of programs for the aged disabled, lack of understanding of this population, and lack of agreement among professional groups as to the training, education, and curriculum needed to meet the needs of this special population.

The 1980's have been termed "the decade of the aged." Changes in growth of the aged population have brought warnings of new and unmet challenges to our health care system. Longer life for our citizens means increased numbers of disabilities within the aged group. Unique programs are needed for this group. Are we prepared, ready, and truly interested in responding to the needs of this growing population? Or do we plan to use the same approaches within the confines of our separate professional interest groups?

Rehabilitation as a discipline has been viewed by many as presenting the medical and psychosocial model that can best meet the needs of the aged disabled. The comprehensive and holistic approach of rehabilitation provides the type of patient management that could well serve as the basic model for programming management and meeting the health care needs of the aged disabled.

Model programs within the rehabilitation field have provided a format for care of the aged disabled individual. The spinal cord injury care systems have been especially effective, and their comprehensive model can be easily applied to the aged population and provide a comprehensive health care program. By bringing together aspects of prevention, cooperative community hospital and acute care approaches, integrated rehabilitation programs, vocational and avocational needs, special community programs, approaches to housing, medical, and transportation needs, the spinal cord model has been a cost-effective model providing increased quality of life to the spinal cord injured.

In addition to learning from successful model programs, rehabilitation and the spinal cord care system programs point up the need to relate to other fields and to integrate other fields successfully in meeting the needs of the aged and disabled. It is simply not enough any longer to be aware of existing fields and to know what they can bring to a certain population. It is important to go the next step and integrate that knowledge into actual usage for the aged and the disabled. A philosophy is effective only if it can be applied to a specific population and information taken and integrated into the management of that patient or client population.

Rehabilitation itself is an excellent field and shows models of patient care to be duplicated or imitated. The field itself is not an original field; rehabilitation is made up of other medical, allied health, and nursing specialities, and has many of the problems of those specialty areas. Although it is a comprehensive and holistic approach to patient care, in large measures it lacks supporting clinical research. Rehabilitation is a growing field, just beginning to attract medical interest and professional support. Its lack of acceptance, however, is still very evident in that approximately 50%

of the medical schools do not have a department of rehabilitation medicine. On the other hand, the field of rehabilitation of the disabled is obtaining more acceptance throughout communities. Improvement in community attitudes toward the disabled is resulting in growth of needed programs and integration of the disabled into the community.

Consequently, shortages continue to exist in the needed professionals to work in the specialty area of rehabilitation. Most important, rehabilitation has been built on a cost-effective basis, and the basis is one that programs for the disabled aged need. The aged person needs a comprehensive program; the aged person needs strong medical, professional allied health, and nursing interests. For programs to develop and survive within the health care system, attitudes have to be broken down regarding the aged and programs developed that are cost-effective.

This conference has brought together a large variety of information. It demonstrates, however, that our various fields have proceeded independently. We have all attempted to achieve a professional level, seek out our own territory, and manage specific types of patient populations. The conference points out a strong need, as described by Elaine Brody in her presentation, for integrating and consolidating our information and, more important, increasing collaboration between all interested groups. We have a wealth of knowledge, but the wealth of knowledge is not being used or applied to the patient population at this time. We must take that next step, that is, communicating, consolidating, collaborating, and moving in the direction of applying knowledge to the aged patient.

Dr. Rubenfeld, in her excellent presentation on "Ageism and Disabilityism: Double Jeopardy," vividly described one of our major problems, professionally and within our communities. The major problems are of attitudes toward the aged and our lack of advocacy for the aged. Historically, professionals have not been leaders in developing programs for their disability groups. Parent groups and consumer groups have had to take the lead because of their increased motivation, and professionals have followed in the development of needed programs. This reflects a problem in professional attitudes toward specific groups and one that must be dealt with very openly. We must take a greater role in being active advocates of the patient populations. The aged population is one that needs a strong advocate group among all of the professionals interested in working with them.

This conference firmly established the need for more accurate dissemination of materials regarding the aged and rehabilitation. The myths, described by Dr. Williams in his opening presentation, are still very much a part of the reality of most professional and lay groups. Dissemination cannot be limited to professional journals but must be more a part of continuing education, innovation publications, displays, special programming, and whatever means it takes to reach an audience, at consumer, community, and professional levels, that is needed to make changes in management and programming for the aged disabled.

This conference has brought up the need for *relevant* therapeutic intervention with the aged disabled. Information that is not used correctly is frequently antitherapeutic to the aged patient. Unfortunately, some of the "known facts of aging" and means of maximizing aging are not integrated into existing programs for the aging. For example, structured stimulation is felt to be a highly important aspect of good management of the aged individual. Most settings for the aged lack appropriate stimulation, and activities are void of meaningful psychosocial and interpersonal pursuits. Mobility is a major problem for the aged individual, and yet there is a dearth of innovative programming to aid the mobility of the patient as far as transportation is concerned and, even worse, as far as consistent exercises for ambulation are concerned. Meaningful activities of daily living, such as feeding and dressing, are not appropriately addressed in the majority of facilities. Likewise, innovative means of approaching the cognitive problems of the aged, more effective use of leisure time, concerns over safety, alternate living arrangements, and nutrition have not been addressed in a relevant fashion. Obviously there is need to understand better how the aged learn or relearn, and then help them meet some of the preceding primary needs.

In all, as professionals, we attempt to create a therapeutic community, a community, in which the aged can maximize their potential and enjoy their quality of life. This conference has brought together a mass of knowledge regarding the aged, and it is now up to us professionals to integrate this knowledge and apply it in a meaningful manner to the persons with whom we have chosen to work. Aging can be an anguish if needs are not met. Aging can be a sad time of life when programs are misunderstood. And aging can be a disaster if a comprehensive approach is not implemented.

To enjoy life is a goal we all desire. We can help the aged to enjoy life with the skills we possess as professionals in this challenging area.

23

Aging and Rehabilitation:
The Birth of a Social Movement

Robert H. Binstock

One way to perceive this conference would be as the birth of a social movement. Administrators, researchers, clinicians, and practitioners from a wide variety of professions—some primarily oriented toward rehabilitation and some primarily oriented toward geriatrics and gerontology—have come together, perhaps for the first time, to share a large common ground of experiences, issues, and aspirations.

A general mood of therapeutic optimism, the keynote theme sounded by Dr. Fenderson, has pervaded these discussions. To be sure, there have been some areas of disagreement. The presentation by Drs. Fulton and Katz emphasized that the goals of therapy ought to be maintenance of existing functional capacities, and compensation for lost capacities. Others have argued that restoration of lost functional capacities is an important goal. A great many issues for further research have been identified, as well as a variety of challenges that can be usefully met through: (a) education and training to change professional attitudes, (b) dissemination of new and advanced clinical techniques, and (c) proposals for coalitions, multidisciplinary cooperation, organizational change, outreach, and coordination. And of symbolic importance, we have been told several times—always with a note of incredulity—that 20 federal agencies communicated with each other, perhaps even cooperated to some extent, in the process of putting this meeting together.

ISSUES CONFRONTING THE MOVEMENT

If this conference is indeed the birth of a social movement, what can be said of it? How timely is the movement? What will it move toward? What are its ultimate goals? How far can it move? How fast?

Certainly, the birth of the movement is *not* a *premature* birth. As someone who has been involved in the field of aging for some 20 years, it is amazing to me that this meeting is a milestone in that it emphasizes *rehabilitation* as well as *care*. According to my imaginary count, there have probably been 273 conferences on aging and long-term care over the past 5 years but none on aging, long-term care, *and* rehabilitation.

An occasional advanced-thinking leader has previously raised the issue of rehabilitation for functionally disabled older persons. Frank Williams, for example, has stressed over and over again the theme of a comprehensive philosophy of rehabilitation. But the main thrust of discussions to date has been *care* for residual human entities as their functional capacities gradually erode or precipitously decline before death. If nothing else, let this conference mark that start of an era in which any meeting dealing with aging and functional disabilities will be structured to include an emphasis on *both* long-term care and rehabilitation. This conference has successfully framed a broad and extremely important set of challenges. How widely these challenges will be recognized and how well they can be met are the difficult issues that we will confront in the months and years ahead.

Stanley (Steve) Brody's paper clearly conveyed that the existing framework of relevant public policies is meagerly funded, highly fragmented, and heavily emphasizes the medical model of treatment and care and an employment/productivity goal in rehabilitation. Neal Baumann has given us a bleak picture of the labor force outlook for vocationally rehabilitated disabled persons of all ages, but especially older persons. Elaine Brody made it evident that we are foolish to persist in the notion that "the family" is a vast reservoir of untapped support to provide for long-term care, let alone for rehabilitation. Indeed, she has strikingly indicated that family supports might be stretched to their limits already and may soon be pushed past the breaking point, in the context of changing family structures and increasing family economic needs.

At the same time, Carl Granger, Frank Williams, and speakers at the many different topic groups have underlined, conceptually and practically, a number of ways in which rehabilitation efforts—*if properly focused upon and adequately funded*—would have an optimistic future. But how can we achieve such a rehabilitation focus, and from where can adequate funding come?

The funds needed to achieve the laudable objectives delineated at this conference would be enormous. And to our credit, we have not entirely ignored the issues of how to obtain more funds. In some of our discussions it has been suggested that a persuasive case can be made of greater public financing of rehabilitation on the grounds of cost effectiveness. In principle it might be argued that it is far less expensive to society in the long run to invest in the effective rehabilitation of older persons than to support the costs of long-term care and maintenance of the nonrehabilitated. Although such an argument is appealing on its face, it is unlikely to be effective, either evidentially or politically. Proponents of community-based long-term care for older persons have been trying to make a similar case for some years, arguing that such care would (a) be less costly than comparable care in a nursing home, and also (b) save money in the long run by preventing or delaying institutionalization. But the arguments have not held up under the close scrutiny of responsible research.

It has also been suggested at this conference that substantially greater mileage could be achieved through existing funds if we would design and implement more comprehensive and coordinated service systems. But this too is highly unlikely. Many characteristics endemic to the American political system virtually preclude the adoption and implementation of comprehensive and coordinated policies. Among the most notable of these is a fragmentation of power within the public sector, as well as between the public and private sectors.

If one conceives of modern democratic systems arrayed on a continuum ranging from centralized to fragmented or dispersed power, the American system is among those characterized by extreme dispersion. Public power in our country is fragmented among 80,000 governments, semiautonomous structures within those governments, and tens of thousands of quasi-public entities. In addition, power is dispersed among innumerable private entities—economic, social, professional, and religious elites; commerical, industrial, and trade organizations; political parties, political action groups, and organized citizen constituencies—that not only have influence in nongovernmental spheres of activity but also have influence on governmental structures and decisions. In such a context we should accept the fact that an effectively comprehensive and coordinated policy and service system for any purpose would be a political aberration, especially on a nationwide basis.

POLITICAL STRATEGIES

Phyllis Rubenfeld, however, has raised the possibility that the disabled and elderly could join forces in a coalition that might be powerful enough to influence greater funding and policy responsiveness to the issues of rehabilitation for persons of all ages. She suggested that a coalition of the two groupings could "form one of the strongest political power bases seen in this country." With due respect to Dr. Rubenfeld, I do not think this is a promising suggestion, either in terms of political efficacy or in terms of philosophical values.

The Myth of Single-Issue Voting Blocs

The suggestion that a combination of the disabled and elderly would provide a very strong political power base presumably rests on the assumption that tens of millions of disabled and elderly citizens would express themselves as a cohesive force through voting and other forms of political behavior. But this assumption is probably unwarranted, because evidence repeatedly demonstrates that persons who are 65 years of age and older do not behave in a politically cohesive fashion. Older persons are heterogeneous in their political attitudes, attachments, and interests and display this diversity in their political activity. Election exit polls have shown over and over again, for example, that the votes of older persons distribute among candidates in about the same proportions as the votes of middle-aged and younger persons. In short, the political differences within any age grouping are far greater than those between age groups.

Our tendencies toward ageism, disabilityism, and sexism apparently cloud our perceptions of political life even as they distort our views of other social arenas. Certainly the media and single-issue interest groups rule our tendencies by purveying homogenized images of large, artificially categorized constituencies of citizens; in turn, we use our predilections toward stereotypes by accepting these characterizations of groupings as if they were single-issue, cohesive voting blocs. Admittedly, I am not familiar with any data on the voting behavior of disabled persons. But it is certainly clear from ample data that relatively few older persons and relatively few women cast their votes solely on the basis of age-related or sex-related issues. Moreover, to the extent that older persons and/or women are responsive to such specific issues, the responses are highly differentiated within these artificially constructed constituencies. This is precisely what one might expect of large, heterogeneous groupings that are highly representative of the diverse American citizenry.

Limitations of Interest Group Politics

But what about the power of interest group organizations and coalitions of interest groups? After all, self-styled advocates of the aged, the disabled, and other interests that have been portrayed in single-issue terms were successful in 1960s and 1970s in establishing a variety of public programs to further their interests. That is why, in some respects, we are here at a con-

ference undergirded by the cooperative auspices of some 20 federal agencies.

The social interest-group successes of that era, however, were extremely limited successes. They did gain some degree of societywide recognition for a variety of social problems, along with limited funding bases for launching the development of programs to deal with those problems. Yet these programs have largely been evaluated as ineffective or of minor import by a large body of scholarly literature that has measured them either in terms of stated programmatic goals or in broader terms of their effectiveness as measures for solving social problems. Perhaps more important, in my view, they were "humanistic failures" in that they were constructed in a fashion that implicitly framed conflicts between one type of social problem and another, pitting one form of human misery against another. For those reasons, particularly in the context of the contemporary economic and political environment, I do not believe that traditional interest group politics—a coalition of the disabled and elderly—is a promising or desirable strategy for providing impetus to the movement that has been born at this conference.

To underscore this point, let me step back for a moment to consider what has happened over the last several decades. In the 1960s and 1970s—a period that has been termed the era of "interest-group liberalism"—public resources were perceived as plentiful, and there were few debates over the wisdom and propriety of public initiatives to solve social problems. The presumption was that if a social problem could be identified (the number of issues that could be articulated and subsequently legitimated as social problems was limited by little more than the reformer's imagination) it required a governmental response. In effect, there was an overload of demand on Congress for social programs.

To cope with this overload Congress developed what might be termed a "circuit-breaker" formula through which it could symbolically appear to be responsive to each interest and avoid becoming embroiled in the conflicts between interest groups. The central ingredients in this formula were (a) the enactment of a meagerly funded program with a title that satisfactorily conveyed evidence of responsiveness to the social problem; (b) a legislated formula for distributing the small amount of funds among state and local entities; and (c) only general rules about what should be done with the thinly distributed resources.

This formula was a political triumph for Congress, if not an effective approach to social intervention. Political conflicts were shipped out of Washington to be fought out in state and local arenas by interest groups seeking to direct meager allotments of funds toward their respective priorities. A by-product, of course, was a proliferation of federal social programs, or what David Stockman has termed "the social pork barrel."

Although the Older Americans Act is an excellent example of the use of this formula, the Developmental Disabilities Act of 1970 is a classic illustration of how Congress papered over political conflicts and passed them along to be fought out in states and localities. In the late 1960s the National Association of Retarded Children sought federal legislation to provide funds to the states to develop services and facilities for the mentally retarded. Concurrently, advocates for the epileptic and the cerebral palsied were besieging Congress for competing legislative initiatives to further their respective interests. Congressional staff responded to these three specific and competing interests by packaging them together in one small grant-in-aid program, symbolically harmonized through the use of broad language: "developmental disabilities." But the conflicts among these single-issue interest groups hardly dissolved. They proceeded to fight each other for years, at the state and local levels, over the program authority and meager funds made available through the federal legislation.

In the 1980s, as we know, public resources for social programs, for any programs, are perceived as scarce. Keynesian economics is out of fashion and "balancing the budget" is the overriding imperative of domestic politics. Containing health care costs is one of the most popular issues of the day. And in the field of social welfare programs, the watchword is that we must "target scarce resources" more effectively.

The problem, of course, is that there is no magical technology for targeting scarce resources that evades political conflicts between competing interests, needs, and values. Congress may have evaded those conflicts in the 1960s and 1970s by passing them along to state and local arenas. But it is unlikely that the circuit-breaker formula will be used to accommodate traditional demands from social issue interest groups in this decade. Rather, it is likely that the conflicts among competing sectors—defense, economic development, health, and social welfare—and the more specific interests within sectors, will be resolved with some clear winners and clear losers. Already, for example, we are seeing public issues framed for discussion in a fashion that trades off the presumed needs and interests of older persons versus children.

VALUES UNDERGIRDING THE MOVEMENT

Here is where the fundamental issue of this conference lies. What values and implicit value conflicts will undergird the nascent movement focused on Aging and Rehabilitation? I would not like to see the movement to which this conference has given birth go forward on the basis of a power conflict framed in terms of the elderly and disabled *against* other social groupings. Our society is already in grave danger of adding breadth and depth to the quiet and informal ways that we have accepted practices through which the value of one human life is traded off against another.

The great contemporary fervor to contain health care costs, for example, may lead us into confronting more widespread and severe practices of rationing acute health care—on the basis of demographic and socio-economic characteristics—than we have ever known, even in the decades before the establishment of Medicaid and Medicare. Likely targets of such expanded rationing are those elderly persons who are primarily dependent on public insurance to pay for their health care bills. Do advocates for the elderly want to engage in developing arguments that compare the cost-benefit ratios of sustaining older persons versus the cost–benefit ratios of sustaining severely disabled premature infants from the time of birth? Plausible cost–benefit arguments can be made either way, depending on one's underlying premises. I fervently hope that such arguments will not be developed. I do not think that we want to add to the agenda of tradeoffs in the value of one human life against another.

Although it may seem incredibly idealistic to say so, I believe that the primary challenge is to formulate a politics in which we confront and transcend our customary practices of trading-off human beings. We have heard a great deal at this conference about the demographics of population aging, the emergence of an "aging society." But the implications of these demographics cannot be derived by simply "plugging in" larger numbers and greater proportions of older persons into policies, patterns of social relationships, institutions, and issues with which we are already well acquainted. The implications of population aging may be qualitative, not simply quantitative.

We must begin to think about an aging society as, possibly, a very different kind of society, even as agricultural societies, mercantile societies, and industrial societies have been sharply different in their natures. Elaine Brody's paper provides a magnificent perspective for helping us to begin undertaking this challenge. She has indicated, persuasively, that it will soon be normal for the vast majority of middle-aged and older adults to have very old, disabled relatives dependent on them for financial, social, psychological, and physical care and rehabilitation. If such a phenomenon becomes pervasive in our society, we may see a variety of policies, institutions, and practices that are sharp departures from those that are familiar today.

In the context that she has outlined, it is highly plausible to imagine a thriving private sector market in which middle-income adult children purchase a wide variety of long-term care and rehabilitative services; group insurance plans in the workplace that incorporate benefits for care and rehabilitation of one's parents as compulsory portions of the plan, just as maternity benefits are compulsory today even for those who do not and cannot have children; compulsory national long-term care and rehabilitation insurance, perhaps replacing today's Old Age and Survivors Insurance; large-scale state and local long-term care and rehabilitation services, financed through state and local public revenues, even as police, fire, and public health services are financed as "essential services" today. In short, the predominant values in an aging society, and the practical ways in which they are manifested, may be very different from those to which we are accustomed. The generations, the problems, the various burdens that we experience may be bound together for all of us, inseparably.

I suggest to you that if this Birth of a Movement that has taken place here in the last 2 days is not to become, in retrospect, a "stillbirth," then we will need to transcend our traditional modes of interest-group liberalism by meeting a challenge. The challenge will be to start framing the issues with which we are concerned in terms of new value bases that can undergird a fundamentally different type of society in which we are going to live. Certainly I hope that these will be values that do not trade us off, one human being against the other. How we here at this conference, and those who join us, respond to that challenge will have much to say about the quality of life and the nature of justice in an aging society.

24

Aging and Rehabilitation: Summary of Meeting

Carl Eisdorfer

At the risk of being simplistic, one can divide the world into a number of kinds of people. There are those who say "no, no, no," and there's the group that says "yes, yes, yes." And then there's the group that says "yes, but." I guess you are going to hear three in a row of the "yes, but" types.

At the outset, let me give my evaluation of the meeting. This meeting has been a success. I believe it has been a smashing success not just because of the attendance but in the coming together. In the process and the joining of the issues and all of us saying "yes, but," it should be remembered that we recognize that success.

For this summary I will focus on four issues reflecting on the problem of clinical care. The first issue is the problem; the second is what I consider the growth of everyone participating in this conference; the third is an outgrowth of a concept we're all familiar with, i.e., acute care, chronic care, short-term long-term care, long-term long-term care, and terminal care. In honor of Elaine Brody, I have coined a new phrase "interminable care." That is the third issue. And finally, as the fourth, a philosophy of clinical service.

THE PROBLEMS

I believe that in essence we heard what most of us already knew: that we have problems in numbers, in money, in belief, in definition, in separation, in counting, in law, in modes of practice, and in personal, family, social, and physical environment—probably no surprise. We know there are many more aged. But more to the point for the immediate situation, we're no longer talking about the graying of America, we are now experiencing the whitening of America.

We are dealing with an increasing number of aged with chronic impairments and must learn to redefine phrases like impairments, disabilities, and handicap. We know that money is a major problem. Indeed, for some it has become the major problem. If we track the history of health care over a century, we started out with caring, then we got into curing, then we got into counting and now we're into the costing business. My concern is that we don't get into a convulsion as a result of accounting.

Clearly, we have a problem in the financing of health and human services. Among the points on which I have to agree with Bob Binstock is the confusion as to why 10% of the GNP spent on health is such a toxic proportion. Perhaps the figure 10% is a problem. When we had 10% of the population in the country over 65, we recognized an aging problem. At 10% of the GNP, we have a health problem. I don't know why there's a health problem and what is magic about 10%; but we are so magically oriented that the words connote special symbolic meanings. Perhaps as a psychologist, psychiatrist, formerly a social worker, and for a long while a teacher, I have become oversensitized to symbols and people's own fantasies about them, but I doubt it. I do feel that we ought to understand our own beliefs and feelings because they affect what we do and other contingent beliefs. We retire workers as a matter of economic or political expediency, then believe that they are retired because they are no longer qualified to work. What's magic about 65, what's magic about 10%? More magic in a little bit.

The capping of the cost of caring has clearly become a misapplied replacement for quality, in that we no longer use the latter term; nor do we have a policy of quality of care, substituting the strategy of capping of cost, as if that were the principal end we should aim to achieve in health services. The magic there is impressive. The belief system itself is the problem. There are other belief systems we all know: The belief system of curing versus caring. The belief system that work is all that life is about and that rehabilitation is defined as work-related while caring is defined as something soft and only life-related. Now we face the coming together of these principles that have to be fit together for reasons discussed here at this conference.

We have other examples of the magic of words. We all know what we mean by a diagnosis, but when we say diagnosis as opposed to functional diagnosis or functional evaluation, it connotes a particular and wholly different concept. Most of us in this room don't believe in the unalloyed value of diagnosis unless it says functional in front of that term, because the two terms imply entirely different sets of clinical approaches, consequences, and often of actors.

We identified other kinds of separations. We have rehabilitation versus aging, which this conference targeted and began to address. We identified physical versus psychological problems. Sadly, we couldn't agree on the data describing the prevalance of mentally ill or psychiatrically impaired patients or dementia patients in the nursing home. One would think we would certainly have those data. That this isn't true about this country's burden of the mentally and emotionally impaired should say something to all of us.

Our problems are ensconced in law. We heard a spectacular dissertation with many numbers that didn't translate immediately. This was specifically noted by Stanley Brody addressing the nature of our bureaucratic organization and the basis and nuances of entitlements of our reimbursement system with Titles such as XIX, XX, etc., ad nauseam, each title relfecting a different focus and separating care, when, in fact, care needs to be integrated.

Modes of practice are a very specific problem and they are associated with their own magic—M.D., R.N., O.T., P.T., R.T., E.S.P.—each one, of course, reflecting ownership of a piece of the problem and the patient. We often get to the theme of ownership of the problem which may be the most important thing we've been fighting about. Unfortunately, it is the ownership of the problem which is the focus for much activity, not the solution to the problem. In a time of diminishing resources, perhaps we will realize that we don't need to own the problem any longer and that we're ready to come together. Perhaps in this way we can extract something good out of the current difficult situation.

Now, on the issue of growth. We recognize the imperative of a coming together. Growth is, after all, a process of differentiation and integration. We have come from a recognition and concern that something must be done to a differentiation of orientations played out by a variety of specialists. Conferences such as this have as a primary purpose, that of bringing together these differentiated elements. And that is a major phase of growth, the integration of our system of care through the integration of one's conceptual system of the world.

We heard a plea for an alliance of the aged and the disabled. Unlike Bob Binstock, I don't think it's a bad idea. It could be bad if it's couched in terms of the aging and disabled against all the rest. Indeed, any concept like that is a bad idea. But the building of coalitions can hardly be bad. Binstock has been proposing a coalition of the aging and the poor for many years. And so, perhaps, a meeting of aging and the disabled is not an unreasonable coalition to be joined by the poor, the young, the Republicans, and the Democrats. I think that ultimately we need a coalition of the whole. I don't reject this. Quite to the contrary, I accept categorically the idea of coming together because I think that's what growth is about. I would even add that we ought to throw geriatrics and gerontology in along with everything else and have a coalition in support of human kind.

Sometimes definition helps. It was valuable to redefine handicap more in social terms, and I appreciate the separation of terms such as impaired, disabled, and handicapped since it gives us insights into our way of doing things.

There is a problem that has not been resolved here, however. The problem of work-oriented rehab versus caring-oriented rehab and a general belief that the focus on work is the more legitimate and principal reason for a rehab orientation.

Clearly, though, it's important to recognize that with this coming together and growing we must learn to say implicitly and explicitly: "Okay, isn't it about time we forgot our territorial and professional jealousies and begin to focus on a philosophy?" What we're really talking about in rehab and in aging is a philosophic approach. And I think what aging does is to say the individual, the human being, is worth caring for. Forget the productive capacity for the moment. They have an enormous productive capacity, but that's almost irrelevant.

And now the rehab group is saying we have the philosophy. It's a philosophy of rehabilitation. It transcends medicine. It transcends the professions. It's an orientation toward the completion of the individual and helping the individual achieve a higher potential.

On the issue of kinds of care, what I'm identifying at this moment is interminable care. The subtitle of this is the lament of the wife or oldest daughter: "How long, oh Lord, how long?" After that superb presentation by Elaine Brody, we do not, I would contend, talk enough about the impact on the broader society of the millions of individuals who are being cared for by members of the family. I'm not just talking about the emerging data that caring for an Alzheimer's patient increases the potential for stress-related psychiatric disability. I'm talking about the toll on the family who are getting no resources and are still being blamed for "dumping" patients. This is despite the fact that Elaine Brody pointed out that for more than 20 years the data have been clear that families are really heroes or heroines and certainly need to be painted as such in heroic proportions and helped. And we need to explore the role of that professional group—the professional group of the family helping members.

I probably know about as much about managing Alzheimer's disease as any physician I've ever met. Certainly not more than some, but as much as any. I have been working with that disease for about 19 years. Virtually everything I've learned about caring for an Alzheimer's patient I learned from family members. The textbooks haven't meant a thing. My professors, as brilliant and magnificent as they were, taught me very little except an examination of pathology and histopathology of the brain and something about the prognosis. And much of what they taught me about prognosis, by the way, was wrong.

The families have totally restructured what we know about the course of the disease, and it's interesting that they've become so involved that they're now trying to reteach society, or teach society for the first time. The physician—whether psychiatrist, neurologist, or primary care doctor—and nonphysician health professionals are running after the family trying to catch up to that bandwagon. And I think that's a very powerful example. I've used it only because it demonstrates that the families are not merely a collection of poor, helpless, hopeless individuals but they are persons of talent, ability, and effectiveness who transcend our professional accomplishments. Which brings me to the other focus—the patient, the client, or the victim. Always we have to worry about painting the picture of disability when we're really talking about how we maximize ability. In a sense, by the very nature of what we do, we're the helpers and they are the helpless. Between being a helper and a helpee, I would much rather be a helper, and I wonder why.

Caring is tougher than curing, and I think that professionals in the rehabilitation, gerontology, geriatrics, aging business all recognize that. It is tougher than curing for a variety of reasons. It takes more time. You don't have the obvious appearance of success because you have to restructure what you mean in a very limited way. You don't get the acclaim of society; it's not what you were taught; it doesn't meet your fantasies of making miracles happen because you have to redefine miracles in terms of daily change. A step becomes a miracle. The legs don't grow back. The nerves do not restructure. Wouldn't it be nice to sew a new head onto somebody? Wouldn't it be nice to sew new heads onto a lot of people? And wouldn't that be much more dramatic than what we have to do?

Now, the implications of what I am saying are various. In fact, everyone is going to walk away from this meeting, or ride away, or fly away, or however you leave this place, with different insights. Hopefully, meetings like this force us to reconceptualize and redefine what we do, and I think that's precisely what is needed. We need to redefine the processes in which we're engaged in terms of new information. That's really what education is all about.

I have decried repeatedly the idea that in psychiatry we are head shrinkers or brain washers. We are brain expanders. We are educators. In that sense I consider all of us in this room to be educators of one kind or another. But the first thing we need to do is to redefine what we mean by caring for the aged or by rehabilitation. If rehabilitation stops when somebody is retired at 65, that needs to be redefined. If long-term caring means nothing but custodial care, that must be redefined. In both instances it's that redefinition that needs the bringing together of groups like this and may be a cause of more bringing together. You have to think of function in a very different way. Just as we have to think about handicap and its reciprocal capacity in differing ways. Clearly, we need research—basic and clinical research. We heard about a public health model of research, but we need more than that. We need a restructuring of the educational system. Everyone in health who has given any thought to our problems knows this.

Some of you already are oriented toward rehabilitation. But two of the primary health care disciplines, medicine and nursing, simply are not. And it's to them I'd like to talk for a moment. I'll talk specifically about medicine, mainly because in a broad sense I'm responsible for some of our training and I have to accept the *mea culpa*. I think the way we train physicians is clearly all wrong for the process that we want to undertake. In all candor, it's not that much better with nursing, but that's a different issue and somebody else should comment on that point.

Our attitude is wrong, our technology has clearly not been addressing a rehabilitation orientation, and we heard that repeatedly. The problems that excite us in medicine, the exciting people on the faculty who stimulate us may be wrong types of individuals, particularly in terms of the numbers and the aging of society and the proportion and absolute number of persons who have and will have chronic disease. The very structure of teaching in medicine and nursing schools virtually precludes working with patients for long periods of time. If you have 1-week sessions in a clinic or, at most, 1 month on a service where you have to see ongoing patients and focus on the workup of admitting patients, the only thing you really see is the diagnosis and very short-term cure, if you even see that. Most of what you see is diagnosis.

The medical student frequently doesn't know how to interview or manage a patient. The completed medical student knows very little about that process because it involves the process of caring. We've trained physicians particularly, but we've trained all health professionals to be autonomous when, in fact, what we really need are coalitions. Coalitions are tougher to form than being a solo boss. And by solo boss, now, I am absolutely not restricting myself to any one profession.

All of us are trained to be autonomous and yet reminded repeatedly in our work that we must collaborate. There is the autonomous nurse, the autonomous O.T., the autonomous P.T., the autonomous R.T., and each is as toxic as the autonomous physician. The only difference is that the physician can write a prescription, whereas for most of the rest the prescription doesn't get filled by the pharmacist.

The piecemeal disease problem is a difficult issue. We don't teach anything about interpersonal skills and, except in rare instances, we don't have systems by which we teach and evaluate interpersonal skills. Social work, psychiatry, and clinical psychology often try. But many of us don't learn that. We certainly don't learn the role of the patient and the family in the caring process.

The Chinese have a very interesting system. You have to work for a couple of years and then the community decides whether you can "become a physician." And now if you use the characterization of the medical school in Beersheva, there is a week-long process where the interpersonal studies are much more important because anybody who's ever gotten an *A* in anything can get into that medical school. Here, you have to have an *A* in everything and have spoken to nobody for years.

What is the legitimate role of the patient and of the family? Who is really responsible for care? We are just beginning to wake up to those decisions. Clearly, we can do something about the mechanisms of funding. We did see a coming together around the modest issue called Social Security. When it was positioned in such a way that there was a degree of enlightened self-interest, I think we saw a clear coming together. One could argue the politics of it, but there wasn't any question in my mind when President Reagan said, "Once and for all I'm telling you I'm not going to touch Social Security," that he spoke as a political being rather than from his earlier perspective. I think that message clearly got across.

I think the role of the medical center as a teaching entity has been totally unexplored. I think, last time I counted, that there are 23 different residency programs at Montefiore. There is very little cross-fertilization except that the doctors refer back and forth to each other.

Since we're not learning a lot of the things we need to learn in medical school, what's the role of the medical center? Do we have a teaching role? Do we need to force those coalitions? Perhaps, yes. And maybe we have to examine that. Even in the light of the fact that we may be turning out too many physicians, maybe what's more important is that we focus on the different kind of team player. And if you don't learn how to be a team player by reading the signal books, you'll learn on the playing field. And you learn if from a different kind of coach and often from opposing players. I think maybe that's what's happening to us in health care today.

Clearly, what we still have in this country is something I characterized as a joke over a decade ago. On the crown of every soda pop was the phrase that I thought characterized the attitude toward the aged: "no deposit, no return." It is a phrase I give you for the coalition movement. No deposit, no return. I think it's very apt for rehab.

The issue, however, is that in rehab the investment was characterized for appropriate political reasons as an investment in returning to work. And that doesn't sit well with the elderly for two reasons. First they don't work, and second we're told that over the next 15 years they may not be able to get jobs, along with many of our young people. But still the issue remains.

No deposit, no return. And that's a very powerful message for a coalition.

We're also learning that in the new society information is a product. You can even produce information in your home. You can sit with your own computer and now we'll no longer die with our boots on, we'll now terminate at the terminal. A different work ethic may emerge.

I absolutely support Binstock's contention that we are facing a very different kind of society. If we continue to structure society the way its been structured, we can anticipate an unqualified disaster. It cannot be. You don't have to look hard. Look at the projections from Stanley Brody. Within 70 years we are talking about 5.5 million nursing beds, 8.7 million patients with dementia, 600,000 hip fractures. We can't continue to provide care along the ways we've been providing it, so in a sense, the beginning of the movement that we're talking about is a different kind of coalition. It's a coalition in perception. It's a coalition that's going to have to look at the value of work and the value of life itself and the role of the living in protecting everybody else.

It's been my contention that the reason we have to keep mentally retarded kids alive is because if we decided in society to eliminate them, whom do we eliminate next? And we haven't determined if work is the only ethic. Isn't life an ethic unto itself? Can we afford not to be responsive to it? At the same time, once we've accepted that responsibility, by what model of degradation can we walk away from the existing problem?

That's really what I think the conference has unleashed. Anybody who thought this was going to be a mild conference, bringing together two disparate groups who should have been working together for 20 years, suffers, I think, from the possibility of a mistake. What we're really talking about is a synthesis. We're talking about a belief system that says that people are worth an investment. And it is to that good that I think we have the beginning of an important work.

Index